'Eric Shiraev's third edition of *Russian Government and Politics* remain[...]
length for teaching schedules as it brings existing material on governmen[...]
to date. It retains effective features from previous editions, including th[...]
prompt student discussion. Welcome additions include an expanded section on Russian foreign policy –
vital to understanding Russia in today's world politics.'

                                  – Pamela A. Zeiser, *University of North Florida, USA*

'This is an essential guide for grasping the nature of Russian government and politics. The text is highly
comprehensive – stretching from the time of early Russian state formation to the Constitutional amendments in 2020 – and yet doesn't lose sight of the complexity (and paradoxes) of the material covered. It
offers an admirable overview of the institutional machinery of Russian government, and surveys with
critical precision recent politics and policies in key domains such as the economy, social issues and foreign
relations. Students as well as teachers will be grateful for such a well-organized work of synthesis, based on
thorough knowledge and written with insight.'

                             – Peter Vermeersch, *Katholieke Universiteit Leuven, Belgium*

'*Russian Government and Politics* is a comprehensive, up-to-date and accessible guide to the contemporary
politics of Russia which will help students develop a deeper and more rounded understanding of this vital
field of study.'

                             – Eleanor Bindman, *Manchester Metropolitan University, UK*

RUSSIAN GOVERNMENT AND POLITICS

Third Edition

Eric Shiraev

This edition published 2021 by
RED GLOBE PRESS

Previous editions published under the imprint PALGRAVE

Red Globe Press in the UK is an imprint of Macmillan Education Limited, registered in England, company number 01755588, of 4 Crinan Street, London, N1 9XW.

Red Globe Press® is a registered trademark in the United States, the United Kingdom, Europe and other countries.

ISBN 978-1-352-01103-6 hardback
ISBN 978-1-352-00778-7 paperback

This book is printed on paper suitable for recycling and made from fully managed and sustained forest sources. Logging, pulping and manufacturing processes are expected to conform to the environmental regulations of the country of origin.

A catalogue record for this book is available from the British Library.

A catalog record for this book is available from the Library of Congress.

*To Lee Sigelman and the enticing elegance
of his research into politics*

Contents

List of Illustrative Material

Preface

Countries change with time. It has been a promising, yet painful and dramatic period of change for Russia over the past 35 years. Russia has transformed as a nation. It has transformed its entire political, social, and economic system. After the end of the Soviet Union in 1991—Russia was one of its 15 constituent republics—the country moved to redefine its role as a global player and an efficient member of international institutions. These three-and-a-half decades saw a difficult process of reinventing, rebuilding, and restructuring. Almost nothing went smoothly. Russia, in many ways, is still changing today. For those who study Russia, grasping these developments and interpreting them remains an exciting challenge.

Why is this task challenging? Almost everything in Russia these days is a "work in progress" marked by sudden accelerations, slowdowns, turnarounds, and paradoxes. For example:

- Russia is a federation (a union of partially self-governed entities), but its political structure, as defined by the 1993 Constitution, allows the central government to exercise almost unlimited power over those entities.
- Russia is a democratic society. Yet the government increasingly avoids transparency and limits the scope of political competition.
- The Russian government controls television and regulates political speech in many areas of life. However, the Internet—uncensored and basically free of government control—was thriving for years. Now the government has moved to heavily regulate it too.
- The Russian government controls key profitable industries; yet it continues to encourage private investments in all spheres of the nation's economy.
- The Russian government supports free enterprise. At the same time, it maintains the system of crony capitalism, in which winners and losers are too often picked by the government.
- Russia has one of the lowest incomes and capital gains taxes in the world, but simultaneously maintains one of the worst bureaucratic systems, suffocating free enterprise.
- Russian people are suspicious of the West and its policies, but at the same time many of them—if not most of them—tend to admire the culture, economic prosperity, and political systems of the West.

Mikhail Zhvanetsky, Russia's most celebrated stand-up comedian and writer, once said that Russia's freedom is like a traffic light with all three lights flashing at the same time. When you study Russia, you constantly encounter inconsistencies and contradictions. This book reflects on these changes, challenges, and paradoxes.

A distinct feature of the book is its structure, the way it presents the materials. After the introductory chapter and two chapters covering history, every chapter focuses first on basic facts, or key developments. These are crucial, formative events that have played an important role in the social and political life of Russia. These events and facts should help us to better understand the current processes, their roots, underlying causes, and future possibilities. Chapters often refer to the last days of the Soviet Union in the 1980s or the very early years of the new Russia.

Some examples are drawn from Russia's more distant history. This background is necessary before we turn to the current state of events. Then the chapter considers major government institutions, laws, and principal decision makers. Next, each chapter discusses various critical interpretations of these key developments, facts, events, and policies. Presenting the material in a sequence of facts and their interpretations should provide an opportunity to compare various points of view on the same subjects and critically evaluate different assessments and forecasts.

The book incorporates a critical thinking approach. The emphasis on critical thinking should encourage the reader to be an informed skeptic and distinguish facts from points of view. The book also brings together various facts and theories from the fields of political science, international relations, history, sociology, and political psychology. In a nutshell, the structure of each chapter may be presented like this:

The book incorporates several pedagogical devices designed for classroom use and homework assignments. Each chapter contains a brief prologue and ends with a conclusion. In every chapter you will find several boxed features including diagrams, tables, "Key figure" boxes and "Case in point" boxes related to specific examples or individual personalities. A set of multiple choice questions and lecture slides are available for teachers on the book's companion website at www.macmillanihe.com/companion/Shiraev-RGP-3e.

The website also contains the most recent updates, factual data, interviews, editorials, and opinion polls related to current developments in Russia. And it features specially selected links for readers who are either studying or already proficient in the Russian language. In addition, practice examination questions for students are posted on the website. Words and phrases that are **emboldened** in this book are defined more fully on the website.

THE STRUCTURE OF THE BOOK

The book is structured in four parts. Part I is introductory. The opening chapter deals with the subject of Russian studies, methods of studying Russia, and introduces various theories explaining Russian society and politics. The main focus of the other two chapters is a historical background of today's Russia, from early Slavic states to the final days of the Soviet Union.

Part II of the book deals with the three major branches of government and Russia's key government institutions. Special attention is given to the executive, the most powerful branch of the Russian government. The chapter about the legislative branch describes both the history and the contemporary dynamics of Russia's parliamentary system. The chapter on the judiciary also pays attention to Russia's law enforcement and administration of justice.

Part III contains three chapters dealing with various aspects of political behavior, participation, and communication. These three chapters are dedicated specifically to political parties, elections, and the mass media in contemporary Russia.

Part IV of the book deals with Russia's policies. The five chapters deal with foreign policy, defense and security, economic and business policies, and social policies. The two chapters on Russia's foreign policy deal with the country's major strategies as well as specific regional policies. The book ends with a short conclusion.

WHAT IS NEW TO THE THIRD EDITION?

This new edition has undergone a number of important changes. In particular:

1. The coverage of Russian foreign policy is expanded and is now covered in two chapters. New material focuses on Moscow's increasingly assertive role in global affairs.
2. The critical discussion of the Russian political and social system, often referred to as "managed capitalism" in Russia, is expanded in every chapter.
3. Every chapter also incorporates more discussions of social and cultural issues and their interaction with politics; new materials underline the role of individual personalities and informal political and business networks in Russia.
4. The new edition contains new research, current statistics, opinion polls, and other facts and opinions relevant to Russian government and politics.

This new edition is updated with references to 120 new sources. In addition, there are new data on presidential elections, political protests, and participation, voting behavior, constitutional amendments, foreign policy, civil rights, political parties, political mobilization, social and health policies, pension reform, and economic policies.

Many things in Russia can change today, exactly when you are reading these pages. We will try to address them quickly on the book website and also on Facebook (Russian Government and Politics Textbook). Russia will remain for some time a fascinating work in progress.

Eric Shiraev

Acknowledgments

This book could not have been realized without the vital contributions and support of many individuals. It has benefited from the insightful feedback and advice of colleagues and reviewers, from the diligent efforts of research assistants, and from the patience and understanding of my family members and friends. In particular, I wish to acknowledge Marlene Laruelle, Henry Hale, Renée Lerner, and Henry Nau (George Washington University); Phil Tetlock (University of Pennsylvania); James Sidanius (Harvard University); David Sears (UCLA); Dimitri Simes (Center for the National Interest); Alan Whittaker (National Defense University); Jennifer Keohane (University of Baltimore); Sergei Samoilenko, Mark Rozell, Mark Katz, Eric McGlinchey, Peter Mandaville, Fred Bemak, Nelson Lund, Craig Lerner, and Robert Dudley (George Mason University), Irina Van Dusen and Rafael Saakov (Voice of America); Yury Zhigalkin (Radio Free Europe/Radio Liberty); Martijn Icks (University of Amsterdam); Ursula Jakubowska (Polish Academy of Sciences); and Holger Molder (Tallinn Institute of Technology). My special thanks to Ariel Cohen, Paul Saunders, Jason Smart, Vitaly Kozyrev, Sergei Tsytsarev, David Levy, Emma Neris, Dmitry Shiraev, Dennis Shiraev, Alex Shiraev, Sophie Shiraev, and Nicole Shiraev.

I received tremendous help from my colleagues and friends in Russia including Konstantin Khudoley, Natalia Tsvetkova, Dmitry Lanko, Stanislav Eremeev, Stanislav Tkachenko, Olga Deineka, Leonid Ivanov, Olga Makhovskaya, Vladimir Gritskov, and Anton Galitsky. Sergei Pavlov provided photographs for this book. A special word of gratitude goes to my parents Boris and Nina: I could never thank them enough.

I would also like to thank the book's reviewers for their insightful comments.

A special word of appreciation is due to the administrations, faculty, staff, and students at George Mason University, George Washington University, and other academic institutions where I have consistently been provided with incredible research opportunities. I also would like to take this opportunity to acknowledge the tremendous support I received at every stage of this project's development from the team at Red Globe Press, in particular Peter Atkinson and Amy Brownbridge. Additional thanks go to the management and staff at SPi Global and especially Rathika Ramkumar and Peter Atkinson.

Last, on a more personal note, I wish to express my feelings of thankfulness to Vlad Zubok (London School of Economics), my colleague and friend, for his continuous inspiration and support.

The journey continues.

Eric Shiraev

Part I
Russia: Continuity and Change

Why do we study Russia? What makes this country important, and in some ways distinct, in a global world today? Who are Russians as a people, and how has Russia developed as a state? In Part I of the book we will describe Russia as a country, briefly review its government and policies, and then turn to its rich history. We will first review the development of the Russian state from its foundations to the end of the Russian Empire in 1917. Then we will learn about the Soviet Union, the first sovereign state in the world that was built on the communist ideology. After that, we will study the reasons why the Soviet Union imploded and how this affected the process of difficult social, political, and economic transitions that followed.

1 Studying Russian Government and Politics

Russia, officially known as the Russian Federation, is a major global power with vast natural resources, a strong military, a large nuclear arsenal, an educated population, and significant economic capacity. A country with a rich history and traditions, Russia is now defining its role and status in the 21st-century world. Its journey to this point, to the country's potential prosperity and stability, has so far been difficult and contradictory.

WHY WE STUDY RUSSIA

Today, Russia no longer has food shortages, but the country's economic inequality is staggering. The roads are paved in big cities where supermarkets are plenty, but the countryside is struggling. Russia seeks international peace and global stability, yet its government constantly perpetuates in its people a belief in growing foreign threats against it. Russian people enjoy some political freedom, but in many areas, their civil liberties are seriously limited. Russia embraces democracy in some areas of life yet has increasingly turned to authoritarianism in others.

Russia today is a constant newsmaker. Many strategic decisions taken by its leaders domestically and internationally may appear perplexing to an average observer. However—and this is one of many reasons why we study Russia—behind Russia's policies, there is a complex strategy based on a comprehensive yet contradictory vision of today's world. Russia's actions during the first two decades of the 21st century have caused serious concerns in many countries, especially in the West. What are Russia's strategic long-term goals? What does Russia want as an international player? Is Russia a partner or a foe to the West? Do people—in the United States, Canada, the United Kingdom, Japan, Germany, and elsewhere—have to embrace Russia and its policies? Is cooperation with Russia a better alternative than confrontation? These questions need serious and informed answers.

Russian leaders can immediately change some elements of their country's complex strategy, but the most essential ones are likely to remain the same for some time. For any person who studies politics and international relations, for a future diplomat, journalist, entrepreneur, educator, officer, analyst, or policymaker, it is essential to learn about, understand, and correctly interpret Russia's strategies and specific policies based on the country's previous actions. Therefore, we need to better learn about Russia's rich history, better assess its current potentials and weaknesses, and better analyze the motivations of its leaders.

Today and for the past three decades, Russia has presented itself as a fascinating case of democratic transition and seemingly difficult and unsuccessful experiments with liberal values and transparent governance. The country's ineffective embracing of democracy serves as a teachable moment in history. It poses many questions, including the difficult ones, such as,

"Are some countries like Russia simply not ready for democracy? Or, are we maybe too quick to judge Russia's experiences?" Russia's historic experiences and today's practices are also very important in our studies of federalism and its opportunities and limitations in a multi-ethnic state. The country's federal model is vital for our understanding of national identity and nationalism, especially in today's world when more governments are turning to populism to set their domestic and foreign policies. Russia's experiments with the free market and capitalism can help us to learn more about the nature of the sources of countries' economic growth and the role of natural resources, as well as about inequality and injustice.

In the light of the many problems that have surfaced in the past 20 years in the relations between Russia and the West, several important tasks for foreign policy, defense, and security decision makers in the West will likely remain. Among them will be monitoring Russia's international actions; assessing Russia's economic capabilities and its global energy policies; assessing Russia's military capabilities; and checking Russia's ambitions and actions in various regions. It will also be important to seek means of productive cooperation in several key areas, including conflict resolution, nuclear security, and counterterrorism.

Our understanding of the political, social, and economic developments in Russia and our study of Russian domestic and foreign policies should help in developing effective bilateral relations between Russia and other countries, including, but not limited to, the United States, Canada, the United Kingdom, China, South Korea, Brazil, and India, and with the European Union. Knowing more about better forecasting Russian policies should also facilitate the effectiveness of many international organizations and nongovernment groups. This should help, hopefully, in preserving and building a more secure, stable, and prosperous world (Box 1.1) (Map 1.1).

Box 1.1 The importance of definitions

In the English language, the word "Russian" refers to something or somebody associated with Russia. However, if you translate this word into the Russian language, you have to be careful, because there are two different meanings for this term. One refers to "Russian" as an ethnic category ("*Roos-ski*"). The other ("*Rossiy-ski*") refers to something or somebody belonging to or associated with the Russian Federation as a sovereign state; this is a civic not ethnic category. Both these adjectives are translated into English as "Russian," which may create confusion. Some people from various ethnic groups living in Russia may be sensitive to the way you apply the term "Russian" to them. They might have been born and raised in Russia and retain Russian citizenship, but not be ethnically Russians (Sakwa, 1993: 116). If you speak Russian, you can avoid this confusion by using the right adjective. In English, you have to provide additional explanations of the word "Russian" as referring to either an ethnic group or citizenship.

What makes this country important, and in some ways distinct, in today's global world? What can we expect from Russia in the immediate as well as the distant future? This book should provide some answers to these and many other questions. For starters, as a preview of Russia as a country, consider a few facts and opinions.

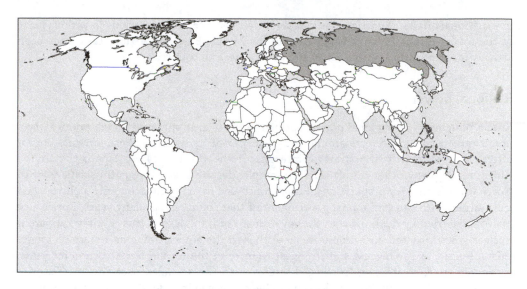

Map 1.1   Russia in the world

RUSSIA AS A COUNTRY

Location, size, and geopolitics

The Russian Federation stretches over 6.5 million square miles, which is more than 17 million square kilometers (Russia, like most countries in the world, uses the metric system). It is almost twice the size of the United States, Canada, or China. Russian territories stretch from Central Europe to the Sea of Japan. Russia covers ten time zones extending across Eurasia. When you arrive at midday in Kaliningrad, Russia's most western seaport in Europe, it is 1 p.m. in Moscow, Russia's capital, and already 10 p.m. in Petropavlovsk, a city on the Kamchatka Peninsula in Russia's Far East. Russia borders the Baltic Sea in the west, the Black and the Caspian Seas in the south, the Arctic Ocean in the north, and the Pacific Ocean in the east. Russia shares borders with five NATO countries (Norway, Estonia, Latvia, Lithuania, and Poland), faces a sixth (Turkey) across the Black Sea, and is separated only by the 53-mile-wide Bering Strait from the United States. Overall, Russia borders 16 internationally recognized member states of the United Nations. Russia is among the top ten most populous countries in the world. Its 143 million citizens live on one eighth of the planet's inhabitable area.

Any country's location and size are important factors determining its politics and position in the world. For centuries, sovereign states used **geopolitics**—the theory and practice of using geography and territorial gains to achieve political power or seek security. Geographical position gave some countries clear benefits in security matters, while others remained vulnerable. The facts of Russia's size and location are important geopolitical factors affecting its domestic and foreign policy: anything that happens adjacent to Russia Eurasian territories can appear critical to Russia and cause it to react. Whether or not Russia can be considered to be a global power is debatable. Meanwhile, Russia is actively engaged in international affairs. It participates in several UN peacekeeping operations in various parts of the world. Russia remains very active in the Middle East and Africa. Russia has been actively reaching out to several Asian and Latin American countries.

Regional power

Russia remains a key regional power. Located in Eurasia, it pursues its own political, economic, and security interests around the perimeter of its borders. These pursuits do not often correspond with the strategic interests of the United States, Japan, the United Kingdom, or many other countries. For example, despite Russia's unenthusiastic view of North Korea's military preparations, Russia continued to maintain economic, political, and cultural ties with the communist government of that country. For many years, Russia also maintained friendly relations with the government of Iran, despite this country's apparent nuclear ambitions and anti-Americanism. Although the Soviet Union as a state no longer exists, Russia, as the biggest and strongest country of the former Soviet Union for years, continued to claim its own "privileged interests" in the so-called post-Soviet territories (Medvedev, 2009; Putin, 2012b). Russia has been engaged in at least two military conflicts with its sovereign neighbors (Georgia in 2008 and Ukraine in 2014) and annexed a territory of Ukraine. All these and other facts point to Russia's essential regional role.

Military power

Russia remains a very strong military state with immense nuclear capabilities. Having strong military capacities has always been the highest priority of Russian leaders in the past (Pipes, 1984). Russia began to produce nuclear weapons in 1949 and had reached nuclear parity with the United States by the 1970s. In the first decade of the 21st century, Russia maintained a nuclear arsenal and delivery systems generally comparable to the arsenal of the United States (Legvold, 2009). In the past ten years or so, Russia has taken important steps to modernize its military capabilities. Russia constantly develops new conventional and nuclear weapons and military technologies including strategic bombers and ballistic and supersonic missiles. Russia's military expenditure grew between 2011 and 2015 but remained relatively unchanged in the following years. Although Russia remains behind the United States and China in terms of its military budget, it has already surpassed countries such as France and the United Kingdom (Chatham House, 2018).

Economic and energy power

Russia is an economically developed country. The country's gross domestic product (GDP, or the value of all goods and services produced over a specific period), is one of the world's twenty largest. Russia's economy, relative to its size, lags behind those of the United States, China, the European Union, Canada, and India, among a few others. It is ahead of South Korea, Mexico, and Spain. Russia has a functional economy with both private and state control of major industries (IMF, 2020) (see Figure 1.1). Russia entered the 1990s as a decayed, centralized, yet disorganized economy, which was transformed within ten years (Shleifer and Treisman, 2004). Russian exports (mostly oil and gas) and fiscal austerity generated

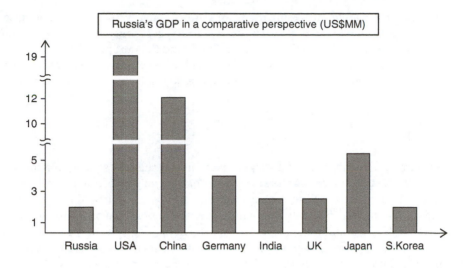

Russia	USA	China	Germany	India	UK	Japan	S.Korea
21.4	1.6	14.1	3.8	2.9	2.7	5.1	1.6

Figure 1.1 Russia's GDP in a comparative perspective
Source: IMF (2020).

steady economic growth in the early 2000s (McFaul and Stoner-Weiss, 2008). Russia's management of its economy, based on free-market principles coupled with government regulation of key industries, worked well during the period of very high prices for energy resources, as Russian leaders have acknowledged themselves (Putin, 2012d). In addition, capital gains and personal income taxes remained low in order to attract foreign investments. By the early 2010s, Russia had achieved financial stability and a budget surplus. Inflation remained modest, and the Russian economy grew at a steady pace of around 6 to 7 percent annually. Wages, on average, went up 350 percent, compared with the late 1990s (Strategy, 2020). For most Russians, living standards in the second decade of this century have been higher than at any time in Russian history (Chatham House, 2018). However, a series of global developments (Chapter 10) and falling oil prices, as well as mistakes in economic policies (Chapter 13) contributed to Russia's slower economic growth and economic stagnation in the late 2010s. Many foreign investors pulled out of the country's markets.

Russia has nearly 22 percent of the total forested land in the world, a zone larger than the entire continental USA (Greenpeace, 2012). In the 21st century, Russia also became one of the biggest world energy suppliers. It has vast reserves of natural gas and oil on its territory, which could be available for exploration and extraction in 10 or 15 years (if this becomes necessary). In addition, Russia is near to Arctic gas and oil reserves, a large, unexplored source of hydrocarbons. Moscow claims that these energy resources must belong to Russia. Other countries disagree. This could cause serious legal disputes and even tensions in the future, especially if hyperhydrates remain a major source of energy in the future. Because of its size and economic infrastructure, Russia is one of the biggest contributors to greenhouse gases, and stands behind only the United States, China, and the European Union as a global polluter. Russia is generally aware of these facts as well as its role as an important decision maker in global environmental policies. Yet oil and gas remain essential to Russia's economic and energy policies.

Cultural hub

Natural resources, technologies, and deadly weapons are not the only sources of a sovereign country's power. Countries also possess **soft power**, or their ability to influence other countries as well as international politics by means of example, persuasion, and reputation. The liberal tradition of international relations emphasizes the importance of economic and cultural factors (such as economic aid, fashion, or sports) in making a country's foreign policy effective. Russia's soft power—to some degree—is rooted in its rich culture. Russia remains an important cultural center of both the European and Eurasian civilizations. Despite the country's exceptional geographic location in both Europe and Asia, Russians tend to consider their culture as part of Western civilization. Russia has given the world many celebrated composers, such as Tchaikovsky, Glinka, and Rachmaninov. Russian writers including Tolstoy, Dostoevsky, Nabokov, and Chekhov (not the character in *Star Trek*!) became known worldwide. Russian ballet, with its unique choreography and performance, is among the best in the world. Several Russian cities, St Petersburg in particular, were designed by top European architects, including great French and Italian masters. The art collections in Russian museums such as the Hermitage are priceless.

Today, Russian youth listen to Western rock and hip-hop, follow British and American celebrities on Twitter and Instagram, dress very much like their peers in London or Boston, and watch live broadcasts of European soccer tournaments and NBA games. Yet, despite Russia's warm, seemingly pro-Western cultural orientation, the country overall maintains a very ambiguous love–hate relationship with the West, with its liberal democracy and civil liberties, and with its politics. Nationalism in its intolerant, even violent, forms has been on the rise in Russia for years. Many forms of nationalism have penetrated Russian politics. Understanding Russian history, cultural values, interests, identities, modern realities, and their inconsistencies as well as their impact on policy is a challenging yet a very important task (see Box 1.2)

A multiethnic state

About 80 percent of Russia's citizens identify as ethnic Russians. As a group, Russians share common Slavic ancestral roots (including cultural and linguistic) with many peoples of Eastern and Central Europe such as Belarusians, Ukrainians, Slovaks, Czechs, Serbs, Poles, Bulgarians, and Montenegrins. There are also about 30 million people in Russia who are not ethnic Russians and identify with about 70 different ethnic groups. They are called "nationalities" in Russia, which is a rather unusual label. Nationality—in legal terms—refers to a person's formal identification with a group of a people who share a common geographical origin, history, and language and are unified as a political entity—an independent or sovereign state recognized by other countries. In Russia, however, "nationality" refers mostly to

---

Box 1.2 True or false? A brief trivia about Russia

Which of these assumptions are true and which are false?

During World War II, the United States and the United Kingdom fought against Nazi Germany and communist Russia.
Answer: False. The Soviet Union, the United Kingdom, and the United States were allies. Together they fought against Germany and Japan from 1941 to 1945. The Soviet Union lost almost 26 million people in that war.

The Soviet Union and Russia are just different names for the same state.
Answer: False. Before 1992, Russia was just one part of the Soviet Union (or Union of Soviet Socialist Republics, USSR), a federative republic that included 14 other, smaller republics (such as Georgia and Azerbaijan). Russia was then called the Russian Soviet Federative Socialist Republic. The Soviet Union was dissolved at the end of 1991, and since then we talk of Russia as an independent state.

The Soviet Union was the first country to launch a nonpiloted satellite and then a piloted space ship into orbit.
Answer: True. The Soviet Union completed these launches in 1956 and 1961. The first person in space was Yuri Gagarin, a national hero. He died in 1968 in an accident.

Russia continues to have food shortages.
Answer: False. There were some food shortages in the early 1990s. These days, however, Russia's stores are filled with products. A typical Russian food store resembles a typical Western store or supermarket in many ways. The economic sanctions against Russia imposed after 2014 and the country's countersanctions against the West made a difference on Russian supermarkets' shelves: most food products are produced in Russia or imported from non-Western countries.

Most Russian people are critical of their government and believe that Russia is on the wrong path.
Answer: False. Antigovernment political demonstrations may catch the attention of the media, but they do not necessarily paint a picture of Russians' complex attitudes. According to polls, most Russians, reluctantly or not, support their government in Moscow (Levada, 2019a; Slatinov, 2012; CSR, 2012). Of course, opinion polls might show a different picture by the time you read these pages.

---

an ethnic, cultural, or even religious group. Some of these cultural groups, or nationalities, are concentrated within 26 separate administrative units, but there are no official restrictions on where any Russian citizen may live in Russia. Among the largest ethnic minorities are Tatars, Ukrainians, Belarusians, Chuvash, Bashkir, Armenians, Chechens, and Moldovans. The overwhelming majority of people in these ethnic groups speak fluent Russian (which is the only official language in the country), and in most interethnic marriages Russian is the first language (Rosstat, 2017, 2019). Tens of thousands of Russian citizens identify with German or Jewish origin (these are also called "nationalities"), but their numbers have declined over the past 30 years as a result of massive emigration of people from these groups to Israel or Germany and other Western countries.

It is estimated that Russia has approximately 7 million legal migrants who have obtained short-term status as temporary workers. In addition (there are no exact numbers), there are approximately 3 to 4 million undocumented migrants. According to the government's reports, about 800,000 undocumented migrants were deported from Russia in 2019 alone (Ministry of Internal Affairs, 2020). This number of migrants can increase or decrease due the conditions of Russia's economy, the exchange rates of the ruble (the official Russian currency), the implementation of various residency laws, ongoing regional conflicts, the severity of anti-immigrant sentiment within Russia, and, of course, a few other reasons.

Russia officially recognizes four major (or "traditional," as they are referred to in official documents) religions: Russian Orthodox Christian, Muslim, Jewish, and Buddhist. More than 70 percent of people in Russia identify in opinion polls as Orthodox Christians. Approximately 10 percent of Russians identify as Muslims (mostly Turkic groups living across the country). These estimates do not include temporary migrants, most of whom are laborers from the post-Soviet states who tend to identify as Muslims. There are between 1 and 2 million Protestants, about 700,000 Buddhists, and about 200,000 Jews (these estimates vary). Despite considering themselves believers, most Russians do not practice religion or maintain firm religious beliefs. For example, only 30 percent of Russians stated, according to polls, that religion played either a "very important" or an "important" role in their lives. For various personal or political reasons (Levada, 2015), many people, including Muslims and Christians, do not openly acknowledge their religious identity.

As a strong economic and military power, as well as a rich energy supplier, Russia is searching for its own role as an international player in the 21st century. How does it build its relations with the world?

Russia and the world

As we shall learn in Chapters 2 and 10, Russia has historically maintained robust relations with its neighbors and other foreign countries. There have been conflicts and wars as well as long periods of stability and cooperation. In the early 21st century, Russia developed stable and even friendly relations with many countries, including China, Iran, and India. However, the relations between Russia and the West (including the United States and the United Kingdom) have deteriorated.

From Russia's perspective, its strategic interests do not generally correspond with the strategic interests of the United States, Japan, the United Kingdom, and their allies. As a result, Russia tends to conduct policies that challenge most Western countries. For example, despite Russia's unenthusiastic view of North Korea's military posturing, especially in recent years, Moscow has for decades maintained its economic and political ties with the government of that country. By contrast, the West has mostly cut its relations with the government in North Korea. Russia has also maintained friendly relations with the government of Iran, despite this country's nuclear ambitions and support of international terrorism (based on Washington's point of view). We will discuss, of course, Russia's international actions and the causes and consequences of Russia's foreign policy in Chapters 10 and 11.

HOW WE STUDY RUSSIA

Information about Russia is easily available. Opinions about Russia's policies are abundant. Policymakers and international security analysts, investors, business advisers, diplomats, researchers, and travelers have to rely on dependable and accurate information about Russia. Yet which information about Russia—and which sources—are most reliable?

Official reports

Government and private organizations in Russia issue official statements and other publications related to economy, foreign policy and defense, welfare policy, tourism, employment, and law enforcement—to name but a few. Political parties upload official statements and publish their leaders' interviews and press conferences. How reliable are such reports?

When working with foreign sources, always keep in mind that their accuracy is typically related to the professional prestige of the institutions, quality of previous reports, or competition from other sources of information. On some occasions, governments deliberately distort data. In the communist Soviet Union, for example, before the 1980s, many government organizations knowingly falsified their published statements to cover up existing problems or create a false impression of success. Most of the published official statistics about crime in the former Soviet Union provided deliberately lowered numbers. Thus, it was next to impossible for a scholar to know the actual number of violent crimes or prison inmates in the Soviet Union.

These days every government office on the federal and regional level has its own website containing regular updates, media commentaries, policy statements, and statistical information. In this book and on the book's website, you will find links to official sources of information provided by government and nongovernment institutions. Many of these government sites have English versions.

Most of the published, official government reports in Russia are reliable. There are unlikely to be deliberate government interventions that distort statistical information, especially if it does not affect the personal interests of Russia's top leaders. For example, it is next to impossible to obtain official data about the real income of top government officials. True, there are official tax documents available to the public. These forms show the officials' modest salaries and incomes. At the same time, investigative journalists in Russia keep posting their independent reports about luxury mansions, private jets, businesses, and other expensive assets that belong to top government officials.

Documents, letters, and communiqués

Official statements and other documents usually explain how government agencies interact with one another, and how the state communicates with other states and international institutions. A communiqué, which is an official report, provides information about the intentions, expectations, or actions of political leaders, government agencies, or negotiating sides. Correspondence between state leaders is an important source of information. For example, official letters exchanged between US President Franklin D. Roosevelt and Soviet leader Joseph Stalin during the World War II revealed important historic information about both countries' strategies. Many government documents related to defense and foreign policy remain classified for years.

Today, Russian public officials, including the president and prime minister, frequently use televised interviews, press conferences, and live Internet chats to convey the government's or their personal vision of policies and events. Of course, official lines of communication can be used to distort the facts or mislead the public, as has happened in the past (Pearson, 1987). As we will see in Chapter 9, most independent experts tend to see most Russian media sources as controlled by the government, which makes it difficult to receive candid information about Russian politics. However, there are a few independent media organizations in Russia. With the spread of the Internet and social networks, the number of independent reporters has also grown, which makes distortions and cover-ups more difficult. An example of a popular source of information is a blog and a YouTube channel by Alexei Navalny, a lawyer and activist, who gained international recognition for his criticism of corruption in Russia (see, for example: https://navalny.com).

Always keep in mind, though, that not all web-based sources are reliable. They may be important for the study of opinions, but their facts and even their references must be independently verified. Disinformation via trolling is a method used by authoritarian governments to promote their policies and discredit their political opponents.

Intelligence reports

In a general sense, **intelligence** is information about the interests, intentions, capabilities, and actions of foreign countries, including government officials, political parties, the functioning of their economies, activities of nongovernmental organizations, and the behavior of private individuals. Today, most intelligence information about foreign countries comes from open sources such as official reports, press releases, opinion polls, and interviews with government officials. Specially trained intelligence professionals gather and interpret "open source" information.

State leaders can use intelligence information effectively, but they can also manipulate and misuse it. It is customary for many political leaders to "push" their intelligence agencies to produce information that corroborates their own views of foreign policy. In 1982, the head of the Soviet security forces (the KGB) and soon-to-be top Soviet leader, Yuri Andropov, pushed intelligence professionals to generate evidence of US preparations to launch a surprise attack against Russia (Zubok, 2007). In the United States, there were periodic scares produced by the military and intelligence establishment that the Soviet Union was getting ahead in the nuclear arms race. Although the Soviets were not necessarily getting ahead, the US Congress, on the basis of such reports, periodically voted for huge military appropriations to retain American strategic superiority.

Memoirs and eyewitness sources

An **eyewitness account** is a description of an event or other developments provided by an individual who observed them directly. In some cases, eyewitness accounts are the only available source of facts that are not necessarily supplied by the official media. Ambassadors publish their own accounts of important events, as former US ambassadors Jack Matlock (2005) and Michael McFaul (2019) did in their informative books. Personal translators to

Case in point: historical fabrications

Government officials may spread deliberate lies about past events. They may fabricate documents, manufacture facts, or produce witnesses of events that never happened. By fabricating sources or creating "fake" facts, officials try to manipulate public opinion, and gather sympathy and support in the hope of justifying their policies or actions. Consider an example.

In 1940 Soviet authorities ordered the execution of thousands of Polish officers captured during the Soviet annexation of a large portion of Polish territory. The event, which became known as the Katyn massacre (after the place where it occurred), was later referred to by both German and Soviet officials for political purposes. After Germany occupied Poland in 1941 and the mass graves of the Polish officers were discovered, Nazi propagandists cited it as an example of Russian barbarism, to sow discontent between the Soviet Union and its allies, primarily the United Kingdom and the United States. Soviet officials resorted to denial. They accused Germany of having committed the murders. The Western allies of the Soviet Union, who were anxious to retain their strategic good relations with Moscow, accepted the Soviet government's version and rejected the reports of an international medical commission suggesting that the murders had in fact been committed by the Soviet secret police. For decades, Soviet history books contained this distorted account of the massacre. Only in the 1990s did the Russian government acknowledge these killings, although they played down the tragedy by claiming it not as a political decision generated in Moscow but as a "military crime."

Source: Sanford (2009).

political leaders, such as Pavel Palazhchenko (1997), and family members of top diplomats, such as Naomi Collins (2007), provide valuable observations on official documents. Biographical studies of Russian leaders can be helpful too. Biographical research often provides a comprehensive picture of how a leader's policies were formed. For instance, *The Man Without a Face* (Gessen, 2012) and *The Strongman* (Roxburgh, 2012a) provide factual information about President Putin's ascendance to power and analyze the motivation behind his policies. Still, we need to understand that the personal views of these and other authors writing biographies may affect their discussion of facts, especially in relation to politics.

Many Russian officials, usually those who have retired from active politics, now write memoirs and provide valuable information about their past decisions (Gorbachev, 1996; Yeltsin, 1994; Yakunin, 2018). Political memoirs often include details previously unavailable even to experts. Beware though: most leaders do not write memoirs to describe their mistakes. They want to show off their achievements. Even when witnesses try to describe facts truthfully, they almost inevitably put their own spin on them.

Investigative journalism today has brought a new dimension to eyewitness accounts. In many countries, this type of journalism was especially effective in dealing with government corruption or political censorship. Unfortunately, investigative journalism frequently meets with resistance from Russian authorities (though they routinely deny this), and many such investigators deal with threats against them because they provide truthful information about large-scale corruption, abuse of power, and government cover-ups.

One useful research technique, used for the quantitative examination of reports, is **content analysis**. This systematically organizes and summarizes both the manifest (what was actually said or written) and latent (the meaning of what was said and written) content of information. Researchers today increasingly use content analysis and methods of computational linguistics (an interdisciplinary field concerned with the statistical or rule-based modeling of natural language from a computational perspective) to detect certain measurable trends in political reports, interviews, and speeches (Oates, 2017). A researcher, for example, can analyze transcripts of speeches. As an illustration, former President Medvedev, in his first annual address to the Federal Assembly (parliament) in 2008, mentioned the United States ten times, but only twice in the three subsequent years of his presidency. President Putin, after 2012, mentioned America in his speeches significantly more often (Green, 2015). Does this suggest anything important about Russia's priorities in foreign policy? Perhaps yes. Most official statements of Russian leaders as well as government documents published between 2006 and 2020 suggested Russia's reorientation in its foreign policy toward a more confrontational approach toward the West.

Media reports

When Russia was part of the Soviet Union (we will discuss Russia's history in Chapters 2 and 3), the government controlled the press, and any truthful information about the real state of affairs in the country was difficult to gather. Experts studying the Soviet Union exchanged anecdotes about the "tricks" they used to unravel facts from the accounts and photographs in Soviet newspapers, such as examining the type and size of top officials' hats, or studying the order of names of senior party leaders attending public funerals to determine who had moved up or down the bureaucratic hierarchy. Today researchers on Russia use the Web and other open sources to find information about a wide range of events. There are thousands of professionals around the globe who translate and analyze television reports, websites, blogs, and newspaper articles related to Russia. These professionals work for investment companies, businesses, defense and intelligence institutions, environmental agencies, and human rights groups, as well as many other government and nongovernment organizations. Government agencies, research institutions, investment firms, nonprofits, and marketing firms hire seasoned professionals as well as college graduates for this job. It is important to know that, as the diversity of media sources increases, so do the chances that the information will become inaccurate. It is worth repeating that you must learn more about the Internet sources you are using, their owners, political affiliations, and sources of their information. This book's website provides a sample of relatively reliable sites that deal with Russia, its policies, and people (in English or Russian).

Surveys

Polls or **surveys** are investigative methods in which large groups of people answer questions on a certain topic. Today's Russian polling companies are highly reputable professional organizations. Many Russian researchers studied the art and science of polling in Western Europe or North America. They use advanced techniques of information gathering and publish their results immediately after taking a poll. In general, surveys are difficult to design and expensive to administer. Therefore, most organizations that conduct surveys these days are relatively big commercial enterprises.

Table 1.1 Percentage of Russian people believing their country is moving in the right direction compared with people believing that their country is moving in the wrong direction

1995	1999	2003	2005	2007	2011	2013	2015	2017	2019
14/66	10/75	35/51	37/51	49/34	44/39	40/40	60/23	56/28	49/40

Source: Levada (2019a).

Opinion polls can give an instant assessment of people's perception of specific events or government policies (see Table 1.1). For example, in 2019, 49 percent of Russians believed that the country was moving in the right direction, compared with 40 percent who disagreed (Levada, 2019a). This simple fact alone makes it clear that in Russia, as in many other countries, people are not necessarily united in their perception of the country and its government's actions. Surveys also can show changes in people's attitudes about policies. Asked the same question in 2008, more Russians (59 percent) believed that their country was on the right path while only 27 percent disagreed (Levada, 2009a). In 1999, only 14 percent of people were satisfied with the country's direction. Based on an analysis of these and other surveys, an expert can try to suggest why people's perceptions have changed. Surveys are not always conducted on national samples. Many researchers use small-scale, personalized surveys to study tendencies in people's opinions on a variety of topics related to their daily lives (Carnaghan, 2008).

Surveys also can be used to predict the results of local and national elections. Over the last 15 years, most professional polling organizations in Russia have correctly predicted the general outcomes of presidential and parliamentary elections. The 2011 parliamentary elections were the rare exception, to which we will return in Chapter 8.

Other survey-type assessment methods are less expensive than full national surveys. **Focus group** methodology is used, for example, in foreign policy planning, conflict resolution analysis, and commercial or academic research. The typical focus group contains between seven and ten participants who discuss a particular situation or problem and express their opinions to the focus group moderator. In the past, the United States Information Agency (engaged in international public diplomacy and public affairs) used this methodology to study people's attitudes in various countries, including Russia, where public opinion studies were impossible or difficult to conduct (Dobson, 1996). Many scholars used this valuable information for their research and assessments. Leading research centers have long used focus group methods (CSR, 2012). The principal advantage of this method is the opportunity to analyze specific policy issues in an informal atmosphere where people can speak freely and are not necessarily constrained by the presence of authorities.

An **expert survey** is another popular method of research, where the respondents are experts in the subject rather than a cross-section of the wider population. Such surveys can reflect reliable professional opinions about Russia's domestic and international actions. For example, Freedom House in Washington, DC, an internationally recognized organization, publishes annual reports on the degree of democratic freedoms in most countries. Based on experts' evaluations, the *Freedom in the World* survey provides an annual rating of a country's treatment of its citizens' most basic liberties. These ratings determine whether a country is labeled *free, partly free,* or *not free.* Russia was, over many years, rated as "not free." Many commentators in Russia have been displeased with such assessments and called them wrong because of the experts' alleged bias against Russia. Undoubtedly, such critical evaluations affected Russia's image in a negative way: tourism, international business, and educational exchanges were likely to be affected as a result.

Transparency International (TI) is another well-known nongovernmental organization (NGO) which uses survey methods to create the internationally recognized Corruption Perception Index. It asks international entrepreneurs and business analysts how corrupt they perceive various countries to be, then ranks the countries accordingly. Russia has consistently ranked very low on this list (meaning that corruption is perceived as a major problem): in 2019 it was in 137th place out of 180 countries examined (the United Kingdom was 12th and the United States was 23rd). You can easily check the latest TI numbers online. Senior Russian government officials in the past have openly considered corruption to be one of the most serious domestic problems (Bastrykin, 2008; Medvedev, 2009; Putin, 2012a, 2012d).

Web

You can check these and Russia's other contemporary global rankings according to expert surveys by visiting the companion website for this book.
Freedom House: www.freedomhouse.org
Transparency International: http://www.transparency.org/

International experts' opinions about the lack of freedom and corruption in Russia are frequently disputed in Russian sources. Many critics in Russia have criticized Freedom House and Transparency International for ignoring "positive" facts about Russia (Dubin, 2008a; Levada, 2012a). Such discrepancies in evaluations between international and domestic experts are common in cases of authoritarian countries: most professional commentators in such countries have to remain loyal to their governments. However, Russian political commentators themselves regularly disagree about facts, policies, and other developments in their country. Foreign specialists often do not find common ground either (Shlapentokh, Shiraev, and Carroll, 2008). Therefore, our next step will be to briefly review the most common views of Russia and its government and politics.

VIEWS OF RUSSIA AND ITS POLITICS

Is there a best way to understand Russia and its politics? Some may state the obvious: just accumulate the facts and learn from them. However, facts, even the most comprehensive and accurate ones, have to be summarized and explained.

On facts and theory in studying Russia

Historians often refer to facts from the past in the hope that they can provide important lessons for us today. For example, the lessons from the Cold War, the 40-year-long period of confrontation between Russia and the West, appear extremely valuable (Zubok, 2007). Yet two historians may look at similar facts from the Cold War and draw two different conclusions from them. Political psychologists guide us through the map of personal motivations of Russian leaders to better understand their individual strengths and insecurities, and, hopefully, predict their actions (Tetlock, 1989). But how accurate are these psychological evaluations and predictions? Like historians who often disagree about the past, political psychologists disagree about their observations and forecasts. Political scientists may say that a better way to understand Russia is to understand its interests (Shleifer and Treisman, 2011). Yet these analysts often disagree over what those interests are and why Russia chooses some interests over others.

Knowledge of Russia takes more than observation and fact accumulation. *Analysis* is the breaking of something complex into smaller parts to understand their essential features and relations. This is difficult enough, but even more is needed. If policy analysts and diplomats only did analysis, they would remain hopelessly confused by the weight of facts. Which facts are more important than others? Which deserve immediate action—and what kind? To answer these and other questions, decision makers have to look at the facts in the light of broader ideas about how Russia lives and works. They need theory. Theory is a powerful tool in the studies of any country and its behavior. Theory allows analysts and decision makers to transform a formless heap of numbers and files into a logical construction. Theories can then be applied to evaluate specific issues. Theorizing about Russia and its policies requires both strong empirical knowledge and creative imagination.

Theories explaining Russia and its policies have always been diverse and frequently contradictory, and they still are today. Specialists in London or Washington, DC, just for the sake of example, who see Russia as an authoritarian power and an international bully, conclude that Western democratic countries should maintain a tough, uncompromising approach in their relations with Russia and treat it from a position of strength. They argue that an aggressor cannot be appeased, only resisted by means of isolation, and economic and political sanctions.

Others disagree. They are likely to recommend a business-like approach. They argue that sanctions rarely change other countries' policies. Instead, a form of cooperation should be offered to Russia to guarantee Russia's role as a reliable partner but only in limited areas, such as international security, environmental protection, or energy policies. Yet others see Russia as a sovereign and proud country in transition and in need of respect, assistance, and engagement. For that reason, Russia, from their position, has to be treated as an equal partner and not like a foe. Both patience and goodwill should make a difference.

Which of these assessments appears closer to your own? If you have one, see if it has changed when you finish reading the last chapter of this book. Now consider other views in some detail.

Domestic politics and views of Russia

Historically, the domestic economic and political situation had a serious impact on views of Russia. Its recent history can be divided into three periods. During the Soviet period (until the late 1980s), there were severe restrictions on Russians' ability to scrutinize and criticize their government and society. Typically, people could grumble about small problems of daily life (such as a long wait to see a doctor or buy tomatoes), but were not allowed to criticize the ruling Communist Party and its top officials, as we will examine in Chapters 2, 3, and 9. Soviet society and its history had to be interpreted in only one, positive way, approved by the government.

During the second period in the 1980s and 1990s, in the final years of the Soviet Union and the early years of sovereign Russia, many alternative and critical views of Russia appeared. Russian historians, political and social scientists, economists, and journalists developed and expressed diverse views and theories of their country, its history, and its political institutions (Shiraev and Bastrykin, 1988).

The political situation began to change in the late 1990s, when President Putin came to power in Moscow. During the third period, the government, aided by loyal political forces, began to apply substantial political and institutional pressure on various commentators to portray Russia from a uniform point of view (Shlapentokh, 2009). This point of view is based on several assumptions, which many in Russia see as undisputable truths (Isaev and Baranov, 2009).

First, Russia has always been and remains a great, strong, and independent power that must be reckoned with and respected. Russia has its own unique path of development, different from various "foreign" models.

Second, during its long history, Russia has had two types of leaders: those who weakened the country often by looking to the West and those who strengthened Russian statehood by all appropriate means.

Third, Russia has been (and continues to be) surrounded by unfriendly foreign powers attempting to undermine Moscow's authority and sovereignty.

The idea of Russia as a unique civilization, constantly surrounded by enemies, yet often rescued and then guided by strong patriotic leaders (like President Putin, for example) found support among many Russians. To develop and preserve a certain vision of history, in 2009 the Russian government established a special commission under the Russian president to resist attempts in the country and abroad to interpret history to the detriment of Russia's interests. In 2020, President Putin made several statements regarding his presumably "correct" version of the causes of World War II, accusing other governments of collaborating with Nazi Germany, and justifying Russia's own actions.

Other views of Russia and its politics and history grew stronger, especially in the second decade of this century. Its critics underline the nationalism and chauvinism that have emerged in homegrown, official approaches to explaining Russia. They believe that there should not be one, uniform view of a country's past and present. People change as well as their ideas. The critics also argue that the aging political establishment is clinging to the ideas that support their grip on power. A stronger middle class as well as a younger electorate in Russia would be less interested in strengthening the government's power but rather in consolidation of individual rights and democracy (Dmitriev, 2012).

In the West, domestic political and ideological factors also play a major role in the way Russia as a country and its policies are perceived (Shlapentokh et al., 2008). Despite their different ideological backgrounds and theoretical approaches toward Russia, most European and North American specialists saw a growing consensus among them that began to emerge in the second decade of the 21st century.

Many specialists studying Russia have emphasized its foreign policy as a threat to the territorial integrity of other countries, and to international stability and security. These experts and politicians tend to support a tough approach toward Russia and believe that any attempts to bargain with or "please and appease" Moscow will be ineffective or even counterproductive. For years, from the 1990s until the end of the past decade, such a critical and tough approach toward Russia—held primarily by politically conservative commentators and decision makers in the West—received little support among their liberal counterparts in policy centers and governments. From their point of view, Russian foreign policy was a reflection of Russia's insecurity. It was also rooted in a weak democracy. When Russian democracy strengthened, it should positively affect its foreign policy. It was believed that it would be a mistake to maintain confrontational attitudes toward Russia. Foreign governments should engage with Russia and use cooperation rather than confrontation in solving bilateral and global problems.

Global realities, as well as experience with Russian domestic and international behavior, have influenced these views of Russian government and politics (Sestanovich, 2020). A consensus among scholars grew that Russia had become an authoritarian state with a vast bureaucratic machine to support the power of the few. Using a wide repertoire of methods—ranging from populism, demagoguery, and disinformation to electoral fraud and violence against political opposition—the rulers in Moscow doomed themselves to years of international isolation, economic and political sanctions, and even confrontation. Yet even under these conditions, some authoritative specialists suggest that a "pragmatic approach" toward Russia would be wiser than a direct conflict (Graham, 2019). As you can imagine, these views can evolve slowly or change rapidly with the changing international and domestic situation in Russia.

CRITICAL THINKING IN STUDYING RUSSIA

Critical thinking is not all about criticism and rejection. It is an active and systematic intellectual strategy that helps us to examine, evaluate, and understand facts on the basis of reasoning and valid evidence (Levy, 1997). It is a skill (or set of skills) that can be successfully taught, learned, and mastered. It is a process of inquiry that is sometimes skeptical and cautious. The use of the critical thinking method requires the observer to display three important virtues: curiosity, doubt, and intellectual honesty. Here we look at several important ways in which critical thinking is used in this book to evaluate factual information.

Emotions and judgments

Emotions frequently affect our judgments. Our personal interests and preferences may bias our thinking: often we equate our description of what "is" happening in the world with our perception of what "should be" from our emotional point of view. For example, a supporter of democracy may be displeased that the process of democratic transition in Russia is taking such a long time. This person will consider the Russian political system to be fraudulent and might easily miss many positive developments taking place in the country. On the other hand, an enthusiastic supporter of Russia's policies could tend to overlook many obvious examples of electoral fraud, corruption, and censorship. We also have to be critically careful about published reports containing predictions of the inevitable "collapse," "fall," or "failure" of Russia. Such doomsday predictions were common in the past (Shakhnazarov, 1997: 19). They sure make headlines, but frequently lack scientific validity because they are based largely on emotional assessments. In studying comparative politics and international relations, we need to reduce the impact of emotions on judgment.

Differences in perception

Similar facts may give rise to different options, often because of the observers' perceptions. As we discussed earlier, there are different ways to explain the relations between Russia and the West. Most experts maintain that any difficulties were primarily caused by Russia's own policies. Others, especially in Russia, disagree and maintain that most Western powers have overlooked Russia's success and placed too much emphasis on its setbacks and mistakes (Simes, 2007). Therefore, in dealing with Russia, other countries have to pay attention to mutual possibilities rather than disagreements. Reconciliation between Russia and the leading world democracies is possible, but it will require substantial effort from both sides (Graham, 2019). Analyzing policies, we will try to look at different points of view and compare their strengths and weaknesses.

Multiple causes of events

As a critical thinker studying Russia (or indeed any other country), you need to consider a wide range of factors affecting an event, decision, or policy. For example, some people might think it is easy to explain the collapse of communism in the Soviet Union: it was the result of US President Ronald Reagan's policies of military and political pressure. However, that is a simplistic view and not a fully critical one. The end of the Soviet Union was probably caused by several intertwining factors, including the Russian people's disillusionment with communist ideology, a growing economic crisis in the country, and the hurried reforming policies of the Soviet leader Mikhail Gorbachev. An increasing amount of archival evidence suggests that the military pressure from the United States played only a marginal role in the remarkable ending of the Cold War and the Soviet Union (Zubok, 2007).

Political pressure

We tend to believe that scholars should be ideologically and politically neutral: they identify facts and build their seemingly unbiased theories based on their findings. This is not always the case. Political climate and political pressure sometimes have a role in determining which theories scholars develop. Lessons from history teach us that governments may "suggest" to scholars how they should interpret the facts. For example, different presidential administrations in the United States have required specific interpretations of information about Russia to substantiate their policies. President Nixon's advisers needed data to support his policies of detente (peaceful cooperation with the Soviet Union) in the early 1970s. In the 1980s, President Reagan liked and relied on advisers whose theories supported a tough approach in dealing with Moscow. Similarly, in the early 1990s, President Clinton's advisers welcomed research suggesting that Russia had lost its competitive edge to justify a period of general inaction in US foreign policy toward Moscow. Studying various views of Russia, we should try to identify, whenever possible, what has motivated an expert to present a particular point of view.

Overall, in studying Russia, it is very important to realize that each theory describes only a fraction of reality, and this description is taken from a particular, and almost certainly biased, viewpoint. This viewpoint is just one light on, or one reflection of reality. A critical thinker ought to look for many reflections to form a more complete picture of that reality.

CONCLUSION

After the Soviet Union as a sovereign country disappeared from the map in 1991, Russia, formerly a part of the Soviet Union, both weakened and isolated, was becoming a less popular area of study than it had been before the 1990s. Some believed that Russia was "finished" as a leading world power. At least two scenarios were expected. First, and this was the best-case scenario, Russia would become an automatic ally of the free world. In the worst-case scenario, Russia would remain adversarial yet irrelevant as an economic and political power. Unfortunately, in the 1990s, many Russian studies programs in European and North American universities began to downsize. The justification for this downsizing was seemingly compelling: why should research centers have to invest their efforts and resources to study a country that is neither a threat nor a promising opportunity?

Today, Russia is "back" as a major power, an international player, a subject of study, and a source of new concerns. Those who argued that Russia was "irrelevant" now realize their error of judgment. Russia is a formidable military, economic, and political player. It has vast energy resources. Its people are educated. Russia actively pursues its interests near its borders and around the world. It frequently challenges Western countries' policies. However, Russia is unlikely to be seen as "destined" to remain an adversary of the Western democratic world. Russia considers itself closer to the West, culturally and historically, than to any other region. Yet it also remains a Eurasian power with interests and aspirations that have to be recognized and acknowledged. Russia's national symbol is a double-headed eagle looking both east and west. It will be a challenge to engage Russia in a mutually productive and reliable cooperation, but this challenge is worth pursuing.

It is difficult to understand a country and its contemporary politics without learning about its history. In the next two chapters we will learn about the most important past events, and individuals who have played significant roles in the development of the Russian state and its people. Very often, the seemingly chaotic and incomprehensible developments of contemporary politics as well as clear strategic trends have grown from the roots of earlier political battles, reforms, wins, and failures. That is where history often comes in to help us critically understand what we are seeing today.

2 The Roots: The Russian Empire and the Soviet Union

History is often a wise, unobtrusive teacher because it allows its students to learn their lessons themselves. History is also, often an underappreciated teacher: its lessons are not always evident, and its students tend to have a very short memory span and often ignore what they have learned. In the history of Russia, we can identify many events that have had an obvious and long-lasting influence on today's state of affairs. However, this influence is not necessarily direct; different events have had different impacts, and the lessons were too often not learned. Of course, Russia cannot be explained by the events that took place centuries, decades, or even years ago. Yet, if we apply our knowledge judiciously and critically, history should help us to navigate through the events of today. There are at least two types of facts to deal with.

The first type refers to material, substantive, tangible developments that create a legacy or material heritage for future generations. For example, territories conquered and lost, wealth plundered and wasted, or roads and bridges created or destroyed—all these developments of the past should matter for future generations. The second type refers to mostly nonmaterial, subjective factors that make up the political culture, or predominant institutions, ideas, and customs, that have played their roles in politics and social developments. These are political traditions and values directing the behavior of political leaders, elites, and the masses. We will look at both of these types.

What do we have to know about Russian history when we study Russian government and politics today? What sorts of events in the past have had the most significant impact on today's developments in Russia? Let us answer these questions by reviewing Russia's history.

EARLY RUSSIAN STATES

Russia today is a multiethnic state. The majority of Russian citizens—80 percent, as you remember from Chapter 1—are ethnic Russians. Historians have a compelling body of evidence suggesting that the Russian people have their roots in eastern Slavic tribes who practiced agriculture and populated a vast territory in Europe roughly between the Baltic and the Black Sea.

The early consolidation of these eastern Slavic tribes, and the forming of an early Russian state, were key developments which took place probably in the 9th century. Whether the Viking rulers from Scandinavia took a major part in the creation of the Russian state, or whether this founding story is a myth, is still being debated. First Novgorod, then Kiev became political and economic centers of the Russian lands. The term *Kiev Rus* refers to the time of a centralized Russian state headed by Kiev, a large city and trade center with several thousand inhabitants. Russian rulers called *knyazes* (translated as princes or dukes), despite unremitting internal disputes, continued to expand their lands and possessions through the 11th century. Dukes and other large-property owners began to retain servants, or serfs— people legally attached to the land where they lived. However, there were also plenty of free peasants living in various communes across Russian lands.

The Slavic people were pagans: they believed in multiple gods. In 988, Duke Vladimir accepted Christianity. Later Russians chose Orthodox Christianity, which was predominant in the Byzantine Empire, as the official state religion, which Russia maintains today. The acceptance of Christianity is commemorated today as a very important spiritual and cultural event. Most Russians these days are Orthodox Christians. Many of their beliefs and practices may be similar to, while some—such as their religious calendar—may be different from beliefs and practices of Catholics and Protestants. By the time Vladimir had "baptized" Russia, the Russian alphabet (rooted in the Greek alphabet, but still evolving) was already in use. Kiev Russia also had its own legal code based on practiced customs and previous legal rulings.

The consolidation period had ended by the 12th century, and the process of dissolution of the unified Kiev state began (although some researchers maintain that the Kiev Rus was never consolidated to begin with). It was succeeded by a number of smaller states, which grew from 15 in the middle of the 12th century to almost 250 two centuries later (Orlov et al., 2008: 35). This separatist tendency went hand in hand with strengthening of the **boyars**, the emerging regional elites who possessed the most military, economic (as land-owners), and political power. New cities grew rapidly. One of them was Moscow, first mentioned in records in 1147. Princes consolidated their power, sharing it commonly with the boyars, and also, in states such as Novgorod, accepted governing councils and plebiscites— referendums to make important collective decisions and elect religious authorities. Some historians say that the city of Novgorod was a prototype of an early democratic state (Yanin and Aleshkovsky, 1971: 56).

Mongol rule

In the 13th century, Russian states lost their political independence to the khans—the rulers of the *khanates*, vast Eurasian territories east of Russian lands and spreading through Central Asia and China. These territories are frequently identified as the Mongol World Empire. The western Muslim khanate called the Golden Horde began to control Russia after a series of devastating invasions in the 1230s and 1240s. The Russian states fell under the political, economic, and military power of the Golden Horde. Politically, Russian princes retained their titles and most territorial possessions, yet they had to receive licenses or permissions from the khan to rule. The Golden Horde forced Russian city dwellers and peasants to pay various tributes. Russia was allowed to retain its Christianity, and Orthodox priests did not pay tribute to the khans. Russian princes had to send warriors to participate in the khans' military operations. Some Russian princes also fought against western conquerors, especially against the Teutonic knights—warriors of a Catholic religious and political order. Russians today commemorate Alexander Nevsky (1220–63), grand prince of the cities of Novgorod and Vladimir, who defeated the Teutonic knights in 1242. The Russian Church canonized Alexander Nevsky as a saint. Many city streets and landmarks in Russia are named after him.

From the 14th through the 15th centuries, the influence of Mongol-Tartars (the most common Russian name for the rulers of the Golden Horde) deteriorated. From the 1480s, Russian rulers began to annex the lands of several khanates located east of Russia. A consolidation of Russian lands continued (Skrynnikov, 2006a).

The strengthening of Moscow

The consolidation of Russian lands took place during a period of strengthening for Moscow's rulers. Moscow enjoyed economic, military, and political dominance after the end of the Golden Horde's rule. After refusing to reach a deal with the Catholic Church in Rome and after the Ottoman capture of Constantinople, the heart of the former Byzantine Empire, in 1453, Moscow unilaterally assumed the role of the center of Orthodox Christianity.

During the reign of Ivan III (1440–1505), independence from the khans was completed. Assuming the title of Great Prince, Ivan III expanded Moscow's possessions. He contained the Crimean khan and fought against Lithuania. Most Russian princes received the status of boyars, which placed them under direct control of the Great Prince, or as he is also known, the great duke. The most powerful of them joined the **Boyar Duma**, an advisory council serving the great prince.

Ivan III introduced a new symbol of his power: a double-headed eagle, which would later become the official state emblem of Russia. Ivan's comprehensive legal code established property rights and a legal foundation for slavery (thus legalizing the possession of people by other people) and **serfdom**, a system of legal dependency for individuals who worked on leased lands belonging to landowners. Serfdom, lasting until 1861, would become a key legal and economic foundation of Russian society and a source of social and political tensions (Skrynnikov, 2006b).

Under Ivan IV (1530–84), the Russian state grew in size. Commonly known as Ivan the Terrible, he was the first Russian to take the title of czar. What is the symbolic significance of this decision? In acquiring this title, Ivan IV stressed the importance of the Russian throne, whose occupants were no longer "dukes" but sovereigns who claimed to be equal to European kings. The czar demonstrated his growing power by conquering new territories. Among his most significant acquisitions were large areas of the Astrakhan and Kazan khanates, which expanded Moscow's possessions to the Volga River. Russian military detachments penetrated deep into the territories of the Ural Mountains and western Siberia. Several strategic fortresses appeared there. Less successful were Moscow's attempts to expand its territories westward. Russia faced tough resistance from the rulers of Poland, Sweden, and Denmark.

Ivan IV increased authoritarian methods of government. He had unmatched individual power as a ruler fighting against various rival boyar families. One of his most noteworthy moves was the establishment of **Oprichnina**, the declaration of his own rule over vast areas of Russia, and a significant expansion of political prosecution and terror against his political opponents and the civilian population. The supporters of this policy maintained that it was necessary to preserve the unified state. However, in the Russian language the term Oprichnina, used metaphorically, means coercion and injustice. Critics of authoritarianism often use this label to describe today's Russia.

Up to the early 17th century, Russia experienced a difficult period of political and social instability and was devastated by foreign invasions. Historians call this period the Time of

Troubles to indicate the gloomy state of affairs in the country, including starvation, violence, and substantial territorial losses to Lithuania, Sweden, and Poland. This period lasted for almost two decades, until the installment of Czar Mikhail (1596–1645) on the Russian throne in 1613 by an Assembly of the Land, which was a prototype of a parliament representing nobility, clergy, merchants, and townspeople. Mikhail was the first representative of the Romanov family, which remained in power until 1917.

In Russian history, the Time of Troubles is also associated with the popular revolt led by Kuzma Minin and Dmitry Pozharsky, who headed a large army of volunteers to fight the ongoing Polish occupation of Moscow, which lasted until 1612. Russian patriotic and nationalist forces continued to use this popular revolt as an example of Russia's victorious struggle for independence. Some commentators have used this episode of Russian history to scorn Poland (Brazhnikov, 2008). These commentators, however, are few.

New land acquisitions took place under Czar Alexis I (1629–76). Russia gained control of lands west of Moscow stretching to the Baltic Sea and continued its colonization of Siberia. Among several major events was a treaty of unification with Ukraine in 1654. Planned by Ukraine as a strategic union against Poland, the treaty resulted in the effective Russian annexation of Ukraine. This event, as you can imagine, receives different interpretations in Ukraine and Russia. Experts in both countries use the 1654 treaty to draw different conclusions: while many Ukrainians claim that their country never volunteered to lose its independence to Russia, many Russians argue that the treaty established Ukraine as a legitimate and natural part of Russia.

A new legal code strengthened Russian peasants' dependence on their landlords and restricted the migration of free peasants as well as residents of cities and towns. The Church reform of the 17th century standardized the liturgy, religious scriptures, and rituals across Russia. The size of the central government in Moscow grew. Small local administrative units were assembled into larger entities governed by officials appointed in Moscow. This was the beginning of Russia's transition toward absolutism—a type of unrestrained monarchical power (Platonov, 1937/2009).

RUSSIA AS AN EMPIRE

The transition toward absolutism is associated with Czar Peter, who was Alexis' son. Peter remains one of the greatest figures in Russian history. During his reign, Russia grew in size and became a major power in European affairs. Peter was also responsible for a radical transformation of Russia's government and the radical "Europeanization" of Russia's upper-class culture.

Reforms of Peter the Great

Czar Peter I (1672–1725) is frequently referred to as Peter the Great to emphasize the grand scale of his polices and significance of his reforms. He dismissed the Boyar Duma and established the Senate, an appointed collective institution, which played a supervisory and partly legislative role, as well as being responsible for taxation. Peter established a Prosecutor's Office to supervise the activities of the expanding government's institutions. He wanted to reform the Russian government based on the best examples of governance in Europe and

Western patterns of statehood. For example, following the Swedish model, he founded 12 government departments (called collegia, prototypes of ministries). Each department was responsible for a particular statewide activity, including foreign affairs, military affairs, and naval affairs. In 1721, a new institution in charge of religious affairs, called the **Synod**, was added to the collegia. Thus, Peter eliminated the institution of patriarchs as heads of the Church, essentially eliminating the autonomy of the Russian Orthodox Church. Now the government was in charge of religious affairs. He often followed his own designs. Peter moved the new Russian capital from Moscow to St Petersburg, a brand-new city on the eastern coast of the Baltic Sea, which had been founded in 1703. (In 1918 the capital was moved back to Moscow by the communists.)

At this time, Russia adopted a uniform system of administrative protocol, document circulation, and other bureaucratic procedures borrowed from Europe. A Table of Ranks provided a novel hierarchical system of formal ranks and official responsibilities for state employees and the military. A new administrative system was set up, establishing eight large provinces (each headed by a governor), with local units below them. The rights of the Russian nobility or landlords were formalized. By the early 18th century, a vast bureaucratic system had been created. Many components of this system are still in place today.

Peter reformed the armed forces and built a brand-new, formidable navy. He replaced the old military force with one recruited under a new system according to which, from every 20 peasant households, one young male was chosen for military service. Military regulations established the responsibilities of officers, soldiers, and sailors. All male members of the nobility also had to serve in the armed forces. Peter hired thousands of foreign experts to teach engineering, mining, and other disciplines to local specialists. Russians began to study in Europe, and Europeans began to discover Russia. Peter promoted a culture of patriotism and militarism amidst Russia's engagement in many military conflicts at that time.

During his reign, Russia fought several wars. Defeating Sweden after a 12-year conflict, by 1721 Russia had acquired the lands of contemporary Latvia and Estonia, and a portion of the northwestern territories of the Baltic coast. In the south, Russia fought to gain access to the Caspian Sea, with mixed results. In the east, Russia was building new fortresses in Omsk deep in Siberia and Semipalatinsk in the eastern part of today's Kazakhstan (see the maps on the website). The Nordic War (1700–21) against Sweden was the first conflict in which Russia participated in a coalition with several European countries. Peter strengthened his absolute power and, after the victorious war against Sweden, assumed the title of emperor. European monarchies gradually recognized this title. This symbolic recognition indicated that Russia was indeed becoming an empire—a vast, increasingly multiethnic, and centralized state. It was emerging as a legitimate and powerful player in European and Asian affairs.

In the social sphere, Peter mandated compulsory education for the nobility, and established new European-style fashions for the aristocracy, including dresses, pantaloons, shoes, and wigs. He ordered all upper-class males to shave their beards off. Only peasants and clergy were allowed to grow beards, along with other individuals who were willing to pay a "beard tax." Previously prohibited, tobacco smoking was legalized. Formal receptions and balls for dancing and socializing became a custom. Peter simplified the Russian alphabet and changed the traditional Russian calendar to a European version. He founded the Academy of Sciences and the university in St Petersburg. Russia began to employ European artists, architects, musicians, and scientists. The architectural style of major Russian cities began to change. When he died, Peter left a country quite different from the one he had inherited (Hughes, 2004).

Becoming a major power

In the 18th and 19th centuries, Russia continued its territorial expansions and became a vast multiethnic state stretching to the Pacific Ocean. It contained about 30 million people by the end of Peter's reign in 1725 and grew to 125 million, according to the first Russian census of 1897. By that time, Russia had acquired the territories of today's Baltic states (Lithuania, Latvia, and Estonia), Poland, and western parts of Ukraine. It also added to its possessions Finland, the Crimean Peninsula, the Caucasus states (Armenia, Georgia, and Azerbaijan), and Central Asian states (Kazakhstan, Turkmenistan, Tajikistan, Uzbekistan, and Kyrgyzstan). In the east, Russia possessed Siberia and vast areas of the Eurasian continent north of China, spreading to the Bering Strait, which separates Russia from North America (see Map 2.1 and the map on the book's website).

The Romanov dynasty remained in power. Despite plots and assassinations, the dynastic foundations of the monarchy were preserved. Two empresses, Elizabeth (1709–61) and then Catherine II (1729–96), together spent 54 years on the Russian throne. By the end of the 18th century, Church lands had become the property of the state. The majority of Russian peasants were dependent on either local landlords or the central government. In

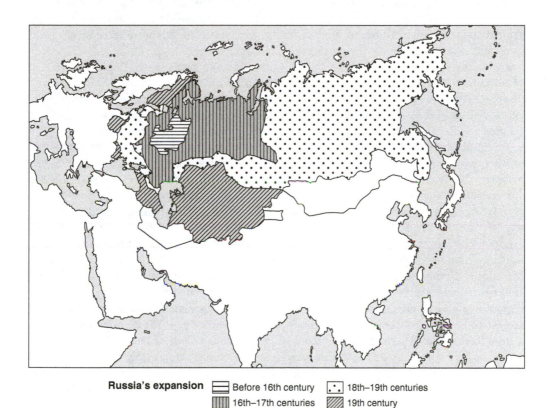

Russia's expansion
- Before 16th century
- 16th–17th centuries
- 18th–19th centuries
- 19th century

Map 2.1 The expansion of the Russian state, 1613–1914

the ethnic provinces (those with a majority non-Russian population), however, local governments applied their own rules related to the peasantry (Orlov et al., 2008).

Russia began to take an active part in European and Eurasian affairs. The country participated in three consecutive partitions of Poland late in the 18th century and later incorporated a substantial part of Poland into the Russian Empire. The Russian Emperor Pavel I (1754–1801) joined coalitions with Austria and Great Britain to contain the French Revolution, which was perceived as a threat to European monarchies. Thus, Russia turned to military actions in Europe far away from its own borders. During the American War of Independence, Russia proclaimed neutrality, but in practice its politics were supportive of the American revolutionaries. In 1809, Russia and the United States established diplomatic relations, but Washington at that time stayed out of European wars.

Russia's active engagements in international affairs continued under Emperor Alexander I (1777–1825). The French army invaded Russia in 1812 and captured Moscow. However, Napoleon and his troops had to retreat from Moscow and eventually the whole of Russia, suffering significant casualties in the process. This departure and final defeat in 1814 is viewed in Russia as the biggest Russian military and political triumph of the time. Pursuing stability and order in Europe, Alexander I and the sovereigns of Prussia and Austria signed a treaty in 1815 founding the so-called Holy Alliance, a military and political pact to preserve the existing dynastic principles of government and prevent democratic revolutions in Europe. Russia supported antidemocratic forces across Europe. St Petersburg sent troops against the uprising in Hungary. Russia's foreign policies in Europe were increasingly seen as reactionary and aiming at the preservation of monarchies.

Inside Russia, the executive branch of the government strengthened. During the tenure of Alexander I, a system of ministries appeared and their number increased. The Emperor's Chancellery assumed several important executive functions. The Senate began to play legislative and judicial functions including discussion on and initiation of new laws. The State Council appointed by the emperor became an advisory board to the monarch.

Emperor Nicholas I (1796–1855) expanded the bureaucratic system developed by his brother, who had died in 1825. During his reign, Russia also gained multiethnic territories between the Caspian and the Black Seas, and fought a difficult and costly war there. The annexation of the region would remain in the collective memory of many ethnic groups populating the northern Caucasus. These developments also stirred tensions and a constant tug of war not only with local rulers but also with the Persian and the Ottoman Empires. Russia turned to its soft power (see Chapter 1) by pledging its defense of Christians living in the Holy Land (today's Israel and Palestine) and in other places such as Greece, Bulgaria, Macedonia, Serbia, Montenegro, and so on, which were controlled by the Ottoman Empire. These territorial expansions and geopolitical claims threatened the power balance in the region. Diplomatic miscalculations intensified tensions between Russia, on the one hand, and Great Britain, France, and the Ottoman Empire, on the other. These countries declared war on Russia, which suffered a painful defeat in the Crimean War of 1853–56. This war was a historic lesson given to Russia by European powers that were not willing to accept Russia's territorial expansion and growing political influence. One of the consequences of the war was the selling of Alaska to the United States in 1867 and the evacuation of all Russian colonies from the Americas.

Meanwhile, in Asia, Russia continued its strategic rivalry with Great Britain for new possessions and supremacy in Central and South Asia—the process that historians call the **Great Game**. While St Petersburg expanded its influence in Asia, London considered Russia's action as a serious threat to British interests in Afghanistan and India (Hopkirk, 1992).

Nicholas I strengthened the executive branch, consolidated the law under the code system, and introduced and developed the Emperor's Chancellery, including the **Gendarmerie**, the highest law-enforcement and investigation agency. Despite these reforms, Russia retained serfdom, a legal, economic, and political system allowing a small group of landlords and the government to keep control over more than 23 million peasants, almost 30 percent of the Russian population. Serfs who occupied a plot of land and worked for the owner of that land could be sold or traded. Although many people understood the immoral nature of this virtual half-slavery, others had reasons to support serfdom. One reason was economic: the landlords needed peasants to work the land to produce income. The other reason was military: the Russian state used serfdom as an effective mechanism for military conscription (Moon, 2002). In addition, the government could not find an acceptable political and economic model to replace serfdom. By 1861, Emperor Alexander II (1818–81) had seemingly found a solution.

Case in point: the Decembrists

The revolt of December 14, 1825 remains one of the most remarkable events in Russian history. Several young officers and civilians (informally known as the Decembrists) attempted an armed revolt in St Petersburg after the death of Emperor Alexander I. Russia had witnessed many palace coups in the past. This time, the plot was different because of its magnitude and visibility. The plotters wanted to arrest the new emperor or force him to abdicate, and replace him with a provisional government. The second goal was to proclaim a constitution to guarantee basic political freedoms, end serfdom (thus liberating the peasants), and establish mandatory military service for all men regardless of their social status. The constitution would also guarantee jury trials and free elections. The plotters gathered their troops on the Senate Square, just a few blocks away from the official emperor's residency. After unsuccessful negotiations, the revolt was put down by artillery fire. It was followed by an investigation and trial, and five leaders of the revolt were sentenced to death by hanging.

Debates about the Decembrists and their role in history have continued (Solonevich, 2005). Antimonarchist forces have always considered the plotters as revolutionary heroes, as representatives of an early wave of the Russian liberation movement. In Soviet textbooks, the revolt was romanticized as a heroic and patriotic attempt against autocracy and serfdom. The revolt was also used by official communist propaganda as a case to demonstrate that a plot not supported by the masses is doomed to fail (in contrast to the success of the later Marxist revolutionary movement which enjoyed the support of many). Contemporary commentators in Russia emphasize the fact that the Decembrists had taken up arms against the legitimate state authority. Russian monarchists, expectedly, condemned the revolt.

What military plots and armed revolts in other countries have produced a mixed historic assessment of their role and impact?

The reforms of the 1860s–70s

Emperor Alexander II decreed the General Statute about Peasants Released from Serfdom. According to the 1861 law, all peasants would gradually become free. They could leave their homes and keep their personal belongings. However, if they wanted to take ownership of the land they farmed, they had to first lease it from their former landlords for nine years. Only then could they claim possession. Peasants could also purchase land outright, without leasing it, if they could afford to pay for it.

Alexander II's second set of reforms modified the structure and functioning of local governments in Russia. More power was given to elected bodies called **Zemstvos** in local areas, including running elementary schools, managing medical care, sanitation, and street planning. Each Zemstvo could institute local taxes. According to the 1864 law, any land or other property owner received the right to help elect representatives to a local Zemstvo for a three-year period. These local representatives could then elect their own representatives to regional bodies.

The third set of reforms eliminated the old military recruiting system, established universal mandatory service for all men, and set up a military reserve. In addition, there was judicial reform which mandated transparency for court hearings. It established new procedures including an appellate system, trial by jury, and legal defense.

The members of a small radical organization of young revolutionary socialists called People's Will assassinated Alexander II in St Petersburg in 1881. His son, Alexander III (1845–94), rolled back some of his father's reforms. He strengthened the power of aristocrats by increasing their presence on local councils (the Zemstvos) and in courts. Universities gave up their autonomy, some literary journals were closed, and elementary schools returned to the control of the church authorities (Highest Manifesto, 1881: see Kukushkin, 1996). Alexander III's official social policies were authoritarian and nationalistic: their goal was to unify the country and promote everything Russian (Odelburg, 1949/1991). Many Russian commentators speak of informal parallels between the authoritarian policies of Alexander III more than a century ago and President Putin's policies 130 years later.

THE REVOLUTIONS

Russian history books call the events of the early 20th century "the three revolutions." This refers to the events and political changes of 1905–07 (the first revolution) and fundamental political transformations in February and October 1917 (the second and third revolutions). These events marked the end of the monarchy and the creation of a communist state.

Of the more than 125 million people who lived in Russia during the reign of Nicholas II (1868–1918), about 65 percent were native Russian speakers. Still behind most European countries in terms of living standards, Russia was becoming a major economic power. The global economic slowdown of the early 1900s soon turned into a massive economic recovery. Russia was building new factories, bridges, and roads. The total length of railroads was second only to America's vast network. On the global scale, Russia was second in oil production, fourth in machinery building, and fifth in coal extraction. Russia was among the top five nations in steel manufacturing, and first in production of wheat—the main ingredient of bread (Orlov et al., 2008).

The government pushed forward with new labor laws, mandating health and accident insurance for workers in large factories. Factories began to pay pensions to retired workers. A massive agrarian reform conducted by Prime Minister Pyotr Stolypin (1862–1911) allowed and then forced peasants to leave their traditional residential communes, to which they had been legally attached. They could now receive their share of land for free. The reforms also created a supply of new laborers for industries. Many of the new workers, however, were unable to compete in a free market and ended up in poverty. Stolypin's role remains controversial in Russian history. His supporters mention his deep-seated patriotism. His opponents associate his name with deepening economic inequality and the brutal suppression of political opposition. Why did this suppression take place?

The revolution of 1905–07

In 1905 Russia suffered a painful defeat in the Russo–Japanese war. Both countries were competing for territories, resources, and influence in the Eurasian Far East, and both chose military conflict to resolve their differences. Russia lost that war. Not only did it cede significant territories to Japan, but it also sustained almost 50,000 casualties and accumulated a huge financial debt. Several European countries, especially France, later became Russia's key sponsors (MacMillan, 2013). Taxes went up to pay for the war, and the prestige of the monarchy in Russia reached its lowest ebb.

Russian society was officially divided into social castes (such as nobility, clergy, and peasants). The peasants, who represented more than 75 percent of the population, and the growing working class had very few social and economic rights. Most of them remained in poverty. Unlike the people of most countries in Europe, Russian people could not form political parties or labor unions. They could speak critically about neither the government nor the Orthodox Church. People of all social classes believed that reforms were necessary.

Antiestablishment social movements and parties (still illegal) appeared. In 1898, the Russian Social Democratic Workers' Party was secretly formed in Minsk. The group dedicated its activities to the liberation of the working class and was an early prototype of the future ruling Communist Party. The Socialist Revolutionaries (SR) Party appeared in 1902 and claimed the right to defend the interests of the poor peasantry. Many Russians had joined various proreform movements by 1905. On the other hand, supporters of the monarchy gathered strength too. Various nationalist, anti-Jewish, antisocialist groups appeared, claiming their need to defend Russia's heritage, social order, and religion.

In 1905, massive strikes and demonstrations paralyzed many industrial regions of the country, including St Petersburg, the Russian capital. Political pressure on the czar continued. Trying to ease tensions, Nicholas II introduced a law establishing a new legislative body, the Duma. On October 17, he released a manifesto proclaiming basic political liberties including freedom of speech, assembly, and conscience (Manifesto, 1905; see also Chistyakov, 1994). The manifesto, in general terms, called for universal voting rights and promised the Duma broad legislative rights. The first national elections were called in 1906. New laws eliminated political censorship. Political prisoners obtained their freedom.

Despite these significant political concessions from the government, social tensions in Russia continued. Using all available legal means including the Duma floor, the growing antimonarchy opposition began its relentless attacks against the government. Political extremism also grew and became rampant. Anarchists, socialists, nationalists, and other groups clashed openly with the government and among themselves, causing social instability.

These developments brought a harsh response from St Petersburg in June 1907. New decrees ordered the suspension of certain freedoms and prohibited several political parties, most liberal newspapers, and student organizations. The emperor gained powers to nominate, promote, and elect loyal Duma deputies. Remarkably, more than 100 years later, Russia's leaders from the executive branch de facto exercise their control of the elected representatives. We will study this in Chapters 4, 5, and 7.

The revolutions of 1917

The continuing inner political struggle determined the course and outcome of the historic events of 1917. Several developments contributed to this struggle. Among them were the devastation caused by World War I, the enduring ineptness of the government, the complacency of the ruling class, and the growing economic and social polarization of society.

Early in the 20th century, Russia remained a major international player. Russia was also building major international coalitions to address its own security concerns. Alarmed by the rapid economic and military developments in Germany, it joined Great Britain and France to form a military bloc. Germany, in response, gathered its own allies and wanted to diminish the growing power of the rival states. World War I started in 1914 and brought unprecedented and devastating consequences to many nations.

Many people in Russia initially supported the war out of patriotism. An anti-German mood swept the country. As an illustration, St Petersburg, capital of Russia, was officially renamed Petrograd (to sound more Russian). However, the wave of nationalistic feelings soon diminished. The Russian army began to lose battles, suffering heavy casualties. The country mobilized more that 15 million people over the four years of the war. Official statistics of Russian losses were not gathered. However, modern researchers consider that nearly 2 million were killed and about 4 million were wounded (Krivosheev, 2001). Socioeconomic conditions had worsened dramatically by 1917. Many believed that, to reverse the developments, a new, efficient, and popular government was necessary.

The czar and his close supporters meanwhile showed ineptness in handling both military and civil affairs. The reputation of Nicholas II also suffered because of his alleged connection to Grigory Rasputin (1869–1916), a flamboyant religious healer with a questionable reputation. Rasputin, a priest and alleged practitioner of black magic, was accused of having too much influence over the czarina (the czar's wife) and the royal family. Although historians are uncertain about the extent of his influence, the public's perception of this bizarre connection was very unflattering to the czar. Rasputin was killed in December 1916 in a plot. To this day, many Russians perceive him as a mysterious, almost legendary villain.

The events of February 1917

By the end of February 1917, the central government could not control the situation in the capital. Severe food shortages, the continuing war, disunity among government forces, and strengthening of the political opposition all contributed to instability. Bread disappeared from stores in St Petersburg, and the city was shaken by riots. On February 28, the Duma formed a provisional committee, which announced that it was taking power in the country. In March 1917, Czar Nicholas abdicated the throne.

From March to October, Russia was a state with dual power, a situation in which a country is run by two institutions both exercising executive and legislative functions. On the one hand, there was the Provisional Government formed by the Duma. The main task of the Provisional Government was to run the country's affairs before the Constituent Assembly was elected. It was intended that this assembly, a national representative body, would decide on future governments. On the other hand, there was a growing network of so-called **soviets**, or elected councils. They represented factory workers, soldiers, and peasants. In addition, in St Petersburg, political parties opposed to the Provisional Government assembled to form the Soviet of Workers' and Peasants' Deputies. Which side would prevail? It was a turning point in Russian history.

Political forces supporting the Provisional Government, including three major political parties, stood for liberal reforms and a new social-democratic government. They differed in many details, but all wanted to secure a legitimate transition from the monarchy to the Constituent Assembly. Among the most powerful opponents of the Provisional Government was the left wing of the Russian Social Democratic Labor Party. Members of this wing were frequently called Bolsheviks. This name later became associated with the Communist Party of the Soviet Union. The Bolsheviks wanted to usurp all power through the soviets. Unlike most of their political opponents, including parties on the left, Bolsheviks wanted to end the war, nationalize land, and hand over factories to workers. Using these ideas as political slogans, they generated support across the country and received majorities in the Moscow and Petrograd soviets. Yet, by all accounts, this support was not substantial enough to win a majority in national elections.

The Bolshevik leader, Vladimir Lenin (1870–1924), chose a strategy to usurp political power in Russia rapidly, without a national election. It was a favorite communist tactic, applied later in many revolts throughout the 20th century: win political power by any means, conduct radical reforms quickly, and let history judge later (Brown, 2009).

The events of October and November 1917

The opportunity for revolt came to Lenin on November 7 (in most sources the revolt is called the October Revolution because it took place on October 25 according to the old Russian calendar system). The Bolsheviks were in control of an armed workers' militia and therefore could enforce their decisions. They also formed a Revolutionary Committee in St Petersburg and began to rapidly take over key government centers, post offices, bridges, and train stations. The Provisional Government was arrested. The Bolsheviks wanted to seize as much political power as possible before the opening of the All-Russian Congress of the Soviets.

The Congress approved the removal of the Provisional Government and issued three decrees of historic significance. The Decree on Peace called on all the nations at war to start peace negotiations. The Decree on Land confiscated all private land and nationalized all natural resources in Russia. Finally, the Declaration of the Rights of the Peoples of Russia announced the end of ethnic discrimination and gave minority groups the right to secede from Russia. The Congress also established the Council of People's Commissars, the highest executive body, with legislative functions. The first chairman of the Council was Lenin. Officially, these were provisional measures until the Constituent Assembly was elected.

Table 2.1 Major decrees of the new Russian Government, 1917–18

Issue	Policies and measures
Private land	All private lands were confiscated, and the country's natural resources nationalized.
Banks	Nationalization of all private banks in Russia. Annulment of the state's debt obligations. Private accounts were confiscated.
Factories	First, workers were mandated to manage factories; then all the factories were nationalized. Fixed wages appeared along with an eight-hour workday.
Private property	All private real estate in cities and towns, and Church property and assets were nationalized.
Foreign debt	All foreign debts were annulled and repudiated.
Political power	Criminalization of any claims on political power of any group other than a soviet.
Courts	A new system of elected judges began to function along with special revolutionary tribunals.
Family	Civil unions were established. All forms of inheritance related to private property and assets were abolished.
Military	The control of all military policies and operations was seized by the new government. All military ranks were abolished. All commanders had to be elected by popular vote.

However, the Bolsheviks and allied parties did not want the Assembly. They boycotted the newly elected Assembly in 1918, then they simply dissolved it. Right after the revolution, the new government issued decrees to change the political, social, and economic foundations of the Russian state (see Table 2.1).

The core ideology of the government and the Bolsheviks, as the ruling party, was Marxism, a set of theoretical principles formulated by the German philosopher and economist Karl Marx (1818–83). Applied to politics, Marxism claimed that capitalism was a fundamentally unjust form of production reinforced by an oppressive political regime. Working people are the main producers of value. Therefore, they should become the true owners of resources, capture political power, and establish a new political and social system of universal equality called communism (Lenin, 1917). In the 20th century and later, Marxism became a major ideological foundation for many communist, socialist, and social-democratic movements around the world.

Vladimir Lenin, the leader of the Bolshevik party, a lawyer by education, and head of the new Russian state, was a Marxist. He believed in the inevitable and rapid collapse of capitalism on the global scale (Lenin, 1916/1969). By liberating the oppressed, he wrote, the world's working class, called the proletariat, would eliminate private property once and for all, thus simultaneously destroying the roots of injustice and war. A new world could be established through revolutionary violence against oppressive social classes. Lenin justified dictatorship of one party as a tool to overcome domestic resistance and build a new society.

The Bolshevik Party claimed to be a representative of the working class and peasantry. The party adopted a hammer and sickle as its motif on the red flag and coat of arms of the new state. All symbols of the old regime, including the Russian traditional tricolor flag established early in the 18th century, were abolished. (The tricolor was restored as the national flag in the 1990s.) By July 1918, the Bolshevik government issued the first Russian constitution, legitimizing the dictatorship of the "city and rural proletariat and poor peasantry" with the goal of eliminating capitalism in the country. Thus, the ruling party established an early legal precedent for its own almost unlimited power, which lasted for more than 70 years.

THE DEVELOPMENT OF THE SOVIET STATE

The first three decades of the development of the Soviet state can be divided into several periods. The first was associated with the Russian civil war. The second was a 20-year stretch of reconstruction and rebuilding that ended with the World War II. In the third, postwar period, the invention of the atomic bomb and changes in foreign policy made the country one of the two most important players in global affairs. In just 28 years after the end of the civil war, Russia would become a global superpower.

The civil war

The 1917 revolution was a traumatic event for the entire country. Millions of people supported the change; others had no choice but to reluctantly accept it. Others chose passive resistance. It has been estimated that 2 million people emigrated from Russia during that period (Sabennikova, 2002). Many others took arms against the new regime. A devastating civil war started in 1918 and lasted until 1923.

The war had several interconnected causes. Millions of people lost their property, legal possessions, and monetary savings in 1917. The government established a rampant confiscatory policy. Peasants had to surrender large portions of their harvests and stock to specially appointed representatives of the government. Attempting to consolidate power, the new government launched a policy that became known as the *red terror*, establishing revolutionary tribunals and conducting executions. All these and other reasons caused people to resist, and this resistance rapidly grew into violent confrontation. Most of the nation became divided into two large camps. **The Reds** supported the communist government and the general course of its reforms. **The Whites** opposed it and were unified by the desire to end Bolshevik power. Russia had lived through many internal conflicts before, but this one was particularly monumental.

At the end of the civil war, the new Russian state emerged without the territories of Finland, Estonia, Latvia, Lithuania, and Poland, which became independent states. Neighboring countries occupied portions of Ukraine, Belarus, Moldova, Armenia, and some territories in the Far East. Production levels had plummeted by 80 percent; agricultural output had dropped 40 percent compared with the pre-World War I period. Scores of people became unemployed. Inflation was rampant, and food shortages constant (Erlichman, 2004). This was the sad legacy of World War I and the civil war. Nevertheless, the country had a functional centralized government which had finally established control over the vast territory. Under these conditions, the state of the Soviet Union was officially formed on December 30, 1922.

Key figure: Vladimir Lenin (1870–1924)

Vladimir Ilyich Lenin (his original last name was Ulyanov; Lenin was a pseudonym; Ilyich was his middle name derived from his father's first name, according to the Russian custom) was the first leader of the new Russian state and the Soviet Union. His government tenure was short. He suffered a series of strokes in 1922, withdrew from government work, and died in 1924 at the age of 53. During his period in power, from 1917, he won practically unlimited power within the ruling party and government. How did he become a leader of such magnitude?

Lenin was born into an educated family from the provincial city of Simbirsk, located on the Volga River in the heart of Russia. His older brother, Alexander, was convicted and executed for his participation in an antigovernment plot. In his student days and after obtaining a law degree, Lenin too participated in illegal political activities, for which he was arrested and sentenced. In 1900, he left Russia for Europe (although he returned briefly to Russia in 1905–07). There he worked on theoretical publications and began assembling a new political party. After the February Revolution in 1917, he returned to Russia permanently. In a remarkably short period, he and his associates managed to gather a large and efficient political network protected by armed units, which played a crucial role in the October Revolution of 1917. Lenin was personally involved in the creation of a new communist state. He supported extremely violent methods to implement his radical policies.

For almost 60 years after his death, the Soviet Union's official propaganda promoted an image of Lenin as a benevolent, intelligent, and caring individual with saint-like personal qualities. He became a symbol of the Soviet state. He was admired by millions of people in the Soviet Union and globally. Cities, factories, ships, and schools carried his name. Every Soviet city and town had a major street or square named after Lenin.

Lenin's opponents portrayed a different picture. To them, he was a brutal, shifty, shallow, and selfish individual driven by jealousy and vengeance (Solzhenitsyn, 1976; Avtorkhanov, 1990). Today, the Communist Party of the Russian Federation continues to glorify his name and his deeds, considering him one of the greatest political leaders of Russia, the founding father of the Soviet Union. Opinion polls show a generally positive yet somewhat mixed picture of support and rejection. In 2017, 56 percent viewed Lenin's role in history positively compared with 22 percent of his critics and 22 percent undecided (Levada, 2017a).

In 1922 (see Map 2.2), the Russian (1), Ukrainian (2), Belorussian (3), and Caucasus republics (4) formed a new Soviet state. Notice that republics such as Georgia, Armenia, and Azerbaijan did not have that status until 1936. Asian republics (5) received their status in the 1920s and 1930s. Estonia, Latvia, and Lithuania (6) became Soviet republics in 1940 as the result of Soviet occupation. Moldova (7) became a republic in 1940 after Romania surrendered a portion of its territory to the Soviet Union.

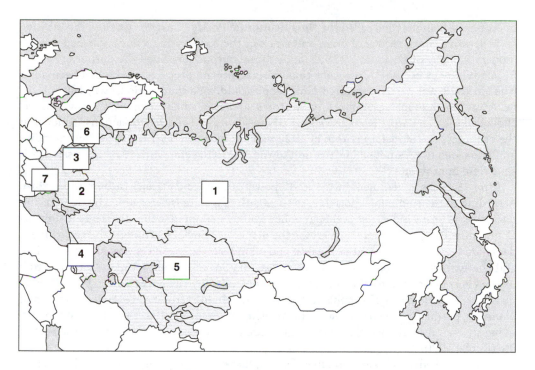

Map 2.2 The Soviet Union, showing its 15 republics

Industrialization

In 1922, the new Soviet State had only 4 republics. Their number grew to 15. Many smaller autonomous republics (with limited rights) were also created within the Soviet Union. In 1923, most of the central institutions of executive power were set up. They were called commissariats (but were later renamed ministries). The new constitution of 1924 declared the Union of Soviet Socialist Republics (USSR) a federation of states. On paper, each state had the right to leave the federation. Each member state also had the right to apply its own educational, welfare, and labor policies. In reality, Moscow controlled all local policies. The supreme legislative power belonged to the All-Union Congress of Soviets, with a Central Executive Committee remaining in charge between sessions of the Congress. The Council of People's Commissars possessed the executive power. The Constitution underlined the superior political rights of the working class, and denied voting rights to some categories of former private property owners as well as the clergy. The constitution officially proclaimed Moscow as the capital of the Soviet Union. The headquarters of Soviet leaders and many other government institutions was a large fortified complex at the heart of Moscow called the Kremlin, and the term "the Kremlin" usually refers to the national (federal) government from this period onwards.

An urgent task was to restore the economy, stimulate trade, and improve the worsening living standards of the population. As a start, in 1921 the government introduced a policy of economic liberalization called the **New Economic Policy**. This policy halted the massive and excessive confiscations of grain and stock in the countryside and established a more moderate policy of taxation. By 1925, agricultural output surpassed the output of czarist Russia (Orlov et al., 2008). The right to own small private property, which had been abolished in 1918, was partially restored. Now people could, for a short period, own, sell, or lease bakeries, repair shops, restaurants, retail stores, and even small factories. The government abolished the mandatory labor service for city residents and allowed foreign investments in the economy. The monetary reform of 1922 reduced inflation. By 1926 the government no longer needed to ration food in cities and towns. The living standards of most Russian citizens were improving.

After 1925 the government introduced a policy of rapid and massive **industrialization**. According to the communist doctrine, the strength of a state is determined by the size and quality of its heavy industries (a similar policy would be adopted in the 1950s by the Chinese Communist Party). Therefore, to increase the manufacturing of machinery, the government demanded rapid development of the coal and oil industries, metallurgy, road construction, and the extraction of other natural resources. The Soviet economy began to switch to a highly centralized system of administration. Controlled by the government, factories and plants became elements of a sophisticated network administered by a centralized system of planning, production, distribution, and management. From the 1920s until the late 1980s, in big cities and small towns, a huge bureaucratic machine was in charge of every aspect of life (Ruble, 1990).

It was believed, as a basic communist dogma, that economic planning was the key to economic success. The Soviet Union in 1929 introduced a new system of national economic management based on five-year plans. These plans were prepared in Moscow and contained detailed targets for production. Managers on all levels became responsible for the realization of the plans. Although the very ambitious targets of the first five-year plans were not fulfilled, over a very short period the Soviet Union developed an advanced industrial sector capable of competing with leading economic powers including the United Kingdom, Germany, and the United States.

Agricultural policies

In 1927, the 15th Congress of the Communist Party proclaimed a new policy, by which peasants were to be organized on a massive scale into **collective farms** whose members shared property and land. Local committees of the party received instructions about the necessity of this massive reorganization. In 1930, Moscow established quotas for each region, with the purpose of achieving total collectivization by 1932. The official policy was to "liquidate" (the exact term) wealthy peasants as a social class. Although, officially, membership of collective farms was voluntary, in reality the process of collectivization turned violent and deadly. Most peasants who did not want to join were forced to do so. Economically successful individuals suffered the most. Based on new laws, the government imprisoned or forcibly relocated millions of well-to-do peasants and their families. Hundreds of thousands perished. Their property was confiscated and given to the collective farms. By controlling the media, the Kremlin suppressed all negative information about collectivization. There were cases of mass starvation in the 1930s in Ukraine, the Northern Caucasus, and some other regions caused by collectivization (Shlapentokh et al., 2008: 58), but practically no reports of them emerged in Soviet newspapers.

The government introduced mandatory quotas for harvests and established extremely low prices for agricultural products, and this significantly reduced the peasants' incentive to produce (Conquest, 1986). The process also enabled the government to establish almost total political control over the peasantry. Most tragically, the collectivization process was an act of genocide according to contemporary definitions: it involved the purposeful extermination of people based on their social status and identity. Some Russian historians, while accepting the fact that many peasants died, argue that the deaths were "collateral damage" and an unfortunate consequence of the transformative policy. Many dictators in the past have used a similar argument of "collateral damage" to justify violence against their own people.

By the end of the 1930s, more than 90 percent of Soviet peasants lived and worked on collective farms (in which land and property were leased by the farm collective, which had obligations to the government) or soviet farms (in which land and property belonged to the government and the farm members were state employees). The forceful collectivization campaign had a profoundly negative impact on Soviet agriculture for many years to come. Its negative consequences are still felt today in Russian villages.

Government bureaucracy

The Communist Party played a major role in all areas of economic and political life in the Soviet Union. The highest power in the party belonged to the Party Congresses, which were called regularly, usually once every few years. Between these meetings, an elected Central Committee was in charge. The Central Committee controlled numerous departments, each in control of a particular sector of the economy, area of social life, or policy. A few of the most powerful people composed the managing body of the party, which was called by different names at different times. The most recent was the Politburo (political bureau). In the regions, the party established regional committees (or republican committees in ethnic republics) for managing the party organizations in factories, schools, offices, and the armed forces.

The party established an official internal policy called **democratic centralism**. It was based on three key principles which were laid down early on in the Communist Party Regulations. The first was mandatory elections in every party organization at all levels. The second was mandatory compliance to the majority in every organization, and the third principle underlined mandatory acceptance of the decisions of higher party organizations by its lower structures. For the sake of unity, the party regulations prohibited any factions or internal opposition within the Communist Party. This prohibition was crucial in maintaining a relatively effective control within the party.

Gradually, the Communist Party installed its members in practically all important government positions and at all levels. The party assumed control of the media, including radio and newspapers. There was no area of social, political, and economic life free of party control.

Foreign policy

Although a detailed discussion of Russian foreign policy will follow in Chapters 10 and 11, here a few highlights are worth mentioning. In the late 1920s, the Soviet Union pursued an active role in international relations. Moscow initially supported Germany in its attempts to revise the Versailles Treaty, signed in 1919, which seemed an unfair burden on the German people. Gradually, the Kremlin's policies became more assertive. Moscow sent military personnel and volunteers to fight on the side of the left-wing government in Spain during the Spanish Civil War (1936–39) and in China (1927–36). Moscow was involved in several military confrontations with Japan in 1938–39. While negotiating with France and Great Britain, Stalin secretly consulted with Nazi Germany and in 1939 reached a political agreement known as the Molotov–Ribbentrop Pact (named after the names of the countries' foreign ministers). In the wake of this treaty, Soviet troops attacked Finland in 1939 and seized some of its southern territories. For this action, the Soviet Union was expelled from the League of Nations. Moscow soon moved its troops to Estonia, Lithuania, Latvia, and portions of western Belarus and Ukraine, which were Polish territories.

Political repression

To increase its grip on power, the government established a vast system of domestic security based on internal spying. In the late 1920s and especially in the 1930s, the government launched a massive campaign against "enemies of the state" (the official label used in propaganda). The party itself underwent several "cleansing campaigns." As a result, many prominent party leaders, factory managers, military commanders, and thousands of regular members were expelled from the party, imprisoned, or executed (Barnes, 2011).

The cleansing campaigns did not spare nonparty members. Scores of people were arrested, taken for interrogation, and never returned to their homes and families. Local officials were often given quotas, i.e., told how many people they should arrest. Faced with threats against their families, many of the arrested signed forced "confessions" to crimes they had never committed (such as "deliberately promoting antisocialist views"). Many innocent people were found guilty on the basis of fabricated allegations. Some were executed, and many others were sent to labor camps (that is, prisons, usually in remote areas, where they were forced to undertake hard labor). The government continued to maintain that these were necessary defensive measures against the growing number of internal enemies of the Soviet Union. The state-controlled newspapers did not report most criminal prosecutions, imprisonments, mass deportations, and confiscations. Although historians both inside and outside Russia differ in their estimates of how many people were persecuted in the Soviet Union during this period, most believe that millions became victims (Shlapentokh et al., 2008).

What was the logic behind this policy of repression against Soviets themselves? Josef Stalin, who succeeded Lenin in the 1920s as the national leader, seems to have had several reasons. He used violence as a political tool, to rid the party of noncompliant members and unify its ranks. The terror policy was also a means of eliminating political opponents, both real and imagined. It is also quite possible that Stalin's individual personality—he was prone to unfounded jealousy, suspicion, and even paranoid ideas—played a part in his political decisions.

Political mobilization

To boost its support among ordinary people, the government sponsored many mass organizations to back the Communist Party and the Soviet government. Young people had to join several youth leagues, the largest of which was called the Komsomol (translated as the

Communist Union of the Young). There were several defense-oriented organizations, and party-controlled labor unions. Many people joined them enthusiastically, while others simply had no other choice. Public schools and mass organizations began to serve as active promoters of communism. In fact, many Soviet people supported the system wholeheartedly. They refused to see any deficiencies in their country and believed that it was immoral to criticize the regime. Many authoritarian regimes in the past and today heavily invest in such attitudes.

Atheism was an official policy of the Communist Party. The Soviet government declared war on organized religion. Church property was confiscated, and priests were harassed, imprisoned, or executed. The government criminalized the production and distribution of religious literature. Under orders from Moscow, authorities across Russia demolished churches and temples or converted them into warehouses or swimming pools. Only much later, in the 1940s, did the government permit some churches to reopen. Stalin's war efforts needed the support of what remained of the Orthodox Church, provided it was loyal to his government.

In 1936, a new constitution declared the creation of a socialist society in the Soviet Union. According to this document, the country had completed its transition from capitalism to socialism. A union between the working class and the peasantry became the social foundation of the state (Constitution, 1936). Such constitutional declarations strengthened the legitimacy of the Communist Party. They also strengthened the authority of its leader.

Josef Stalin (1878–1953)

Lenin did not leave an official heir, but Josef Vissarionovich Stalin, who had become general secretary of the Communist Party in 1922, gradually consolidated his position as the new leader of the Soviet Union. Although Lenin had been skeptical about Stalin's ability to head the party and the state, Stalin managed to sustain and strengthen his position, which he kept until 1953. What was his role in history?

As with Lenin, the name "Stalin" was a pseudonym. Josif Jugashvili (his real name) was born in the town of Gori in Georgia. Ethnically Georgian, Stalin spoke Russian fluently but with a heavy accent. He began his political activities early in life. In 1905, he met Lenin and they began to collaborate. Stalin became a member of the Central Committee of the Russian Social Democratic Labor Party in 1912. At the same time, he began contributing to *Pravda*, the newly created party newspaper. Between his initial appointment in 1917 and his inheritance of the party leadership in 1927, Stalin occupied many posts in the party. His power remained unchallenged from the late 1920s until his death in 1953.

Stalin initiated the policies of industrialization and collectivization. He also directed the massive and coordinated policy of intimidation and terror against his own people. During the war against Germany (1941–45), Stalin strategically revived Russian nationalism and directed the effort to defend the Russian homeland against the invading enemy. Like Lenin, by leading the country through times of great peril and hardship, he solidified his position in the Russian collective consciousness as "father of the nation." Supporters of Stalin's repressive actions often suggest that political violence was necessary to overcome the difficulties of the transitional period. Opponents of Stalin's policies strongly disagree. They portray him as a classic tyrant: that is, someone who rules without law, whose power is virtually unrestrained, and whose ambitions are unchecked (Haslam and Reicher, 2007).

Table 2.2 The views of Russians on Stalin

Percentage agreeing that Stalin's role in history of their country was:

	2003	2011	2019
Certainly positive	18	8	18
Rather positive	35	37	52
Rather negative	21	25	14
Certainly negative	12	10	5
Difficult to say	14	20	11

Source: Levada, 2019b.

In 2019, 70 percent of Russians viewed Stalin's role in history positively compared with 19 percent who saw him negatively and 11 percent undecided (Levada, 2019b).

Overall, as you can see from Table 2.2, Russians have over the years tended to express diverse yet increasingly positive views about Stalin's role in the history of their country (see Table 2.2).

World War II

Unfortunately, the Soviet Union came to the major military confrontation of its history unprepared. In the 1930s, the strength of the Red Army was built up and there was an expansion of the military bureaucracy. However, Stalin removed and persecuted many top military commanders in 1937. This seemingly inexplicable political move seriously disrupted the country's defense policies and the process of modernization of the military. Although Stalin thought that a confrontation with Germany was inevitable, he did not believe that it would start in the summer of 1941, when the army was still not prepared to fight a war of this magnitude.

On June 22, 1941, Germany attacked the Soviet Union. The German plan was for the Soviet Union to be destroyed militarily, occupied, broken into pieces, and converted into several vassal states. But the Soviet Union resisted fiercely. This led to the most devastating war in the history of Russia.

By the end of 1941, the Soviet Union had mobilized more than 14 million people between the ages of 18 and 61. Despite the mobilization of all available Soviet resources to resist the aggression, German troops reached Moscow and St Petersburg (which had been renamed Leningrad in 1924, though it resumed its original name in the final year of the Soviet Union) in the fall of 1941. The situation was critical, and the central government prepared for evacuation. Although the Soviet troops pushed the German armies back, by that winter Leningrad had been encircled by them and was under siege.

The siege of the city lasted for more than two years and cost 1 million Russian lives, more than the combined total of British and US losses during World War II. In 1942, German troops pushed back into the southern part of Russia, captured several strategic regions in the Caucasus region, and reached the major city of Stalingrad (it was renamed Volgograd in 1961). The Soviet Army defended the city in a historic battle, then began a full-scale counteroffensive in 1943, winning a decisive battle near the city of Kursk. In 1944 the army, aided by the British and American troops of the Second Front in Western Europe, began a decisive push. They ended the war in Europe in May 1945 by capturing Berlin.

For the Soviets, the victory in what Russians call to this day the Great Patriotic War was bittersweet. The whole European region of the Soviet Union was ruined, and the country's resources exhausted. The country had lost about 26 million people, including about 11 million military casualties (Krivosheev, 2001). The victory is considered today as one of the most glorious events in Russian history. The many battles they fought, including those for Moscow, St Petersburg, Stalingrad, and Kursk, are glorified in their mass culture. In 2015 and 2020, massive celebrations commemorated the seventieth and seventy-fifth victory anniversaries (the latter was delayed due to the global pandemic). Opinions vary today, however, about the role of Stalin in the victory against Germany. His decisive role is as undisputable as it is controversial. He is credited as the supreme commander but is criticized for making fatal mistakes, not just in the preparations (including the execution of military commanders) but also in the conduct of the war.

Most Soviet people felt that the victory over Germany was a triumph of the Soviet system. They accept the official view that their country acted as the defender of humankind against aggressors. The Soviet Union, in their view, also unified its many ethnic groups, who all fought shoulder to shoulder against the enemy. Nationalistic feelings grew: the war awakened Russian national self-identity (Grossman, 1970). Russians to this day are very sensitive about any evaluations of World War II that seemingly downplay the role of the Soviet Union in ending the Nazi regime in Germany. They tend to give less weight to Stalin's mistakes and the aggressive nature of the Soviet Union's foreign policy after 1945. In a national poll in 2009, 77 percent of Russians considered the actions of the Soviet Army in occupying Central Europe by the end of the war as "liberation" and only 11 percent saw the actions as "establishment of communist regimes" there (WCIOM, 2009c).

THE SOVIET UNION DURING THE COLD WAR

After 1945, the Soviet Union emerged as a substantially weakened yet victorious nation, unified around its ruler. Although the leaders in Moscow, Washington, and London had established very productive relations during the war, in 1945 they failed to create the conditions for lasting good relations. The period from the end of the war to the late 1980s is known as the **Cold War**. This describes the global state of tension (though not outright warfare) between the Soviet Union and its closest allies on the one hand, and the United States with its allies, on the other.

There were several causes of this bitter division. The United States and the Soviet Union were examples of different types of political system, and both claimed that the other's system was inhumane and dangerous. The Soviet ideology maintained a belief in the inevitability of a conflict between communism and imperialism. Anticommunism was an official policy in Washington. By August 1949, the Soviet Union had become the second nuclear power after the United States. The emerging nuclear competition brought fear and distrust to both countries. Personal factors also contributed to the tension. Stalin, for example, became increasingly fearful about a nuclear conflict with the West, and even believed that it was inevitable (Zubok, 2007).

For almost the entire second half of the 20th century, both countries engaged in an endless global competition. The Warsaw Treaty Organization, the Moscow-dominated security bloc of Eastern and Central European communist states, emerged in 1955 in response to the Washington-dominated NATO. Russia became a major international player and tried to counter any real or perceived advance of the United States and its allies, in almost every part of the world. The Soviet Union joined China and North Korea in their fight against troops from the United States and the United Nations in South Korea in 1950–53. In a similar way, Moscow sent instructors, military aircraft, weapons, food, and money to the Vietnamese forces fighting against the United States during the Vietnam War in the 1960s and early 1970s. The Soviet government sponsored communist parties in their attempts to win or retain power in countries in Central Europe. Moscow crushed anticommunist revolts in Hungary in 1956 and in Czechoslovakia in 1968. The Soviets openly supported Fidel Castro in Cuba, and placed nuclear missiles there in 1962, causing one of the most significant nuclear crises in history. In 1979, the Soviet military entered Afghanistan to support a friendly communist government there and remained in the country for the next eight years. Moscow provided supplies and either openly or secretly participated in violent conflicts in Guatemala, Palestine, Angola, Mozambique, Ethiopia, and many other countries.

The postwar reconstruction

Back in the 1940s, the Soviet Union needed to recover from the postwar economic crisis. Most attention was given to heavy industries, many of which had been transferred temporarily during the war to eastern parts of Russia. The authorities continued to use semimilitary policies. In some places, people who skipped work or underperformed were treated as criminals. The Kremlin continued to publish reports about alleged domestic enemies, saboteurs, and foreign agents. In the countryside, most small collective farms were reorganized and incorporated into larger collective or state farms. The number of these farms fell to 94,000, three times fewer than before the war (Orlov et al., 2008).

The economic situation began to improve in the late 1940s. The food rationing that had been introduced during the war was gradually eased, then abandoned. Monetary reform took place in 1947. State-controlled retail prices were lowered. Local governments began to restore ruined cities and towns, build new apartments, and distribute them for free among the neediest. However, there remained a housing shortage, and the lack of good quality, affordable housing has been a problem for decades.

The thaw

Stalin's death in 1953 was an agonizing event for the entire nation. He had been the country's supreme leader for more than 25 years. His name in the minds of millions of people was associated with his country's most spectacular achievements, including the victory in the war and the postwar reconstruction. However, a new political leader, Nikita Khrushchev (1894–1971), who came to power in the Kremlin, challenged these perceptions. A down-to-earth, energetic, accessible, and outspoken person, he was a direct contrast to Stalin, who had seldom appeared in public and remained in many ways a mysterious figure. But personality was not the only difference between Khrushchev and Stalin: Khrushchev was a pragmatic and populist leader. He sincerely believed in communist ideas, but he also believed that the country needed to change its direction.

One of Khrushchev's major decisions was a daring attempt to demolish the "personality cult" that had grown up around his predecessor. At the 20th Congress of the Communist Party in 1956, Khrushchev delivered a classified speech focusing on the mass repressions and human rights violations that had taken place in the Stalin era. Khrushchev stopped short of calling Stalin's behavior criminal, but the signal was clear. Soon Stalin's statues began to disappear from offices and city squares. Stalin's embalmed body was removed from the mausoleum near the Kremlin where it had been placed next to Lenin's body (which is still on show there today) and buried in a grave by the Kremlin wall. Khrushchev's new policies called for openness and collegiality in decisions. At the same time, Khrushchev attempted to dismantle the powerful myth about a person who for two decades had been admired and feared by millions. To many, Stalin remained a symbol of stability and pride (Levada, 2011a).

By the end of the 1950s, the quality of life had improved substantially for most citizens. By the early 1960s, television had become affordable for many Soviet families. Technology also brought opportunities to listen to foreign radio (although this was not formally encouraged). The government began to allow some trusted people to travel abroad (which had been forbidden formerly) and opened up limited opportunities to participate in foreign student and professional exchanges, especially with socialist countries. All these developments helped people acquire a more realistic image of their life and society. So Khrushchev's ascension to power and the implementation of new policies created an atmosphere of hopeful anticipation of change. Foreign policy was changing too. Khrushchev proclaimed in 1956 that global war was preventable, and that Soviet foreign policy would focus on the process of peaceful coexistence between the two antagonistic systems: communism and imperialism (Zubok, 2009).

The stagnation period

However, many senior communist leaders were unhappy with Khrushchev's hectic leadership style and reckless decisions, and they voted him out of power in 1964. Under the next three leaders, Leonid Brezhnev (1906–82), who was in power until 1982, then Yuri Andropov (1914–84) until 1984, and Konstantin Chernenko (1911–85) until 1985 (who all remained in power till their death), the country's economic development slowed down and liberal political reforms did not take place.

Overall, the Soviet Union remained a socialist country with a complicated system of internal control (Simanov, 2009). According to the Soviet governing doctrine, all economic decisions were made in Moscow by government planning and managing organs. Production targets were determined for each enterprise. Factory managers and regional party bosses were under tremendous pressure to fulfill these targets (Stephen, 1991: 36).

The governments of the 1970s and 1980s suppressed and marginalized most intellectual opposition. Censorship was strengthened and remained effective. Most people had only limited access to Western countries (through infrequent tourism) and almost no access to the Western media. There were only rare instances of mass local resistance to the regime. Public acceptance of the system and private unhappiness with it were the norm. Most Soviet people recognized the profound corruption and duplicity of government bureaucrats. Yet they showed formal support for the government and its leadership, no matter who occupied the highest offices in the Kremlin. However, the 1970s was also a time when the prestige of official ideology and labor ethics was in decline. Mass cynicism (a mixture of skepticism and fake enthusiasm) spread. The period from the late 1970s to the middle of the 1980s was a time of pervasive political apathy in the Soviet Union. Not surprisingly, this period is frequently called "the stagnation." The events of 1985 and the political ascendance of Mikhail Gorbachev (discussed in Chapter 3) brought this phase to a close and changed the country forever.

CRITICAL THINKING ABOUT RUSSIA'S HISTORY

To begin, search Google Images for "Red Square." This is the center of Moscow, the area outside the Kremlin. Which pictures appear? On some you will see a beautiful yet eclectic architectural assembly. Others will show red flags and marching soldiers. Yet on others there will be individuals happily strolling across the square. For some people, the very name "Red Square" automatically conjures up associations with a brutal political regime of the past. To many others, this place is associated with stability, inspiration, and hope. All of these perceptions illuminate only a certain part of reality. Theories interpreting Russian history essentially do the same.

The imperial–moralistic tradition

According to this view, which is popular in Russia, Russia's might, influence, and success have always been associated with a strong, authoritarian power that was capable of consolidating the country. In contrast, all decisions and policies that caused disunity in Russia were harmful to the country and caused significant problems to its population. The early periods of disunity among Russian dukes were the cause of major economic and military weakness and the ultimate inability to resist the Mongol invaders. The great dukes of Moscow later overcame their disunity. They expelled foreign rulers and built the foundations for the rapid economic and social development of their lands.

To supporters of the **imperial–moralistic view**, the main lessons of Russia's history are clear. Continuously over hundreds of years, hostile neighbors surrounded Russia. The only way for Russia to survive as a nation and a state was to consolidate its resources in the hands of a strong central authority. This authority needs to preserve unity and ensure the state's survival. A unified Russian state (and by extension, Russian Empire) is an example of strength and stability. People taking this viewpoint accept that none of the authoritarian rulers of Russia have been perfect, but they believe that, in spite of their alleged (and real) violations of human rights, these rulers pursued the policies that were necessary to keep the country unified and strong (Fillipov, 2009).

Several key arguments can summarize this view, explain its contemporary status, and prescribe actions for the future.

First, as Russia's history proves, Russia must remain united territorially and politically. Unity is the only way for it to survive and prosper.

Second, because of its size and diversity, Russia is not necessarily "ready" for democracy along liberal, West European, or North American lines (Putin, 2019a). History shows that only a strong power in the Kremlin is capable of keeping Russia unified and "working."

Third, although there have been antidemocratic policies and abuses of power, critics tend to judge these too harshly. These policies were necessary because they helped Russia reach a higher goal of national unity.

Fourth, as long as Russia remains strong and unified, powerful enemies will never rest. In fact, in the late 1980s only 13 percent of Russians believed that Russia had enemies. Twenty years later, the number had gone up to 70 percent in some polls (Gudkov, 2008b). In 2017, the number was 66 percent, a slight decline from 80 percent in 2015 (Levada, 2018a). Many people came to accept the government's belief that the Kremlin has no option but to resist (Dmitriev, 2012).

Overall, this view emphasizes mistrust in other countries and exaggerates the necessity of hawkish policies for Russia. International institutions, diplomacy, and global international agreements are frequently and mistakenly seen as threatening Russia's interests. Nevertheless, Russian leaders apparently endorsed the imperial–moralistic view as the most appropriate interpretation of their country's history and a useful way to draw lessons from it (Putin, 2020a).

The critical–liberal tradition

Supporters of the **critical–liberal** outlook reject these major assumptions of the imperial–moralistic tradition. They argue that enemies have not necessarily always surrounded Russia during its history. Authoritarianism was not the only efficient way to govern in Russia. In fact, history suggests that a democratic path of development provides better conditions for a country, its people, and its relations with other states. Concentrating power and resources in one location within a "feudal" system of governance was harmful to the country's economic and political development (Shlapentokh and Woods, 2007). For example, Russia's victory in World War II is not a demonstration of the efficiency of the authoritarian system. It was the effort of millions of people who, in fact, won the war despite Stalin's serious miscalculations at the onset of the war (Karatsuba, Kurukin, and Sokolov, 2006; Sokolov, 2008). The critical–liberal view highlights the lessons about the historical significance of liberal reforms in the country, and the necessity of Russia's openness and cooperation with other countries, especially democratic ones. This view finds substantial support in the West but only modest support in Russia.

The "unique experience" models

Unlike the supporters and opponents of the imperial–moralistic tradition, who focus on what should happen in Russia today on the basis of its "good" and "bad" historical experiences, supporters of other models emphasize one particular aspect of Russia's past and try to explain its history from that point of view.

For example, supporters of the **Eurasian model** of Russia's development set forth two main propositions. First, Russian history is unique and its experience cannot be assessed by models applicable to other countries. Second, Russia's true destiny lies in preserving its natural Eurasian roots and avoiding the temptation to imitate Western European and American models of government and culture (Gumilev, 2004). The "Eurasians" tend to dismiss the positive impact of Western experiences on Russia and claim that Russia is capable of creating its own statehood without foreign, especially Western, influence (Orlov et al., 2008).

Others argue that certain Russian policies can be explained not by ideologies but by the circumstances surrounding Russia. These circumstances were unique. For example, Russia grew in size and expanded because it could: there were few natural barriers preventing its Eurasian expansion. Although Russia could be viewed as an aggressive and imperialist state, its policies were determined by Russia's unique geographic position, under which the policy of expansionism was a natural one (Åslund and Kuchins, 2009). The United States' history of westward expansion may resemble Russia's.

The old and new Sovietologists

Sovietologists (the name used for foreign specialists studying the Soviet Union) have developed at least two major schools of thought regarding the Soviet Union. The first is the totalitarian school, which has emphasized the abusive and extreme authoritarian nature of the Soviet system that was responsible for every aspect of life (Levinson, 2008a). Many scholars, including Hannah Arendt (1951) and Zbigniew Brzezinski (1966), have supported this stance of understanding the Soviet Union as a totalitarian society. Prominent totalitarianists have portrayed the Soviet Union as a complex system rooted in prerevolutionary Russian authoritative traditions. The totalitarian theorists, as a rule, overestimated the Soviet regime's strength, stability, and foreign threats. They also ignored the Soviet people's disaffection with the communist regime.

The other is the revisionist school, which has largely presented the Soviet Union as a "normal" society, one among many with similar features. Revisionists, while understanding the weaknesses of the Soviet regime, were sometimes too eager (for ideological or political reasons) to portray the Soviet Union as a society not much different from any other country (Fitzpatrick, 1986). They often overlooked political repressions, censorship, interventionist foreign policy, and periods of violence as inseparable elements of communist policies. Some, like Walt Rostow (1967), believed that the Soviet Union was just one of many modern industrial societies. Others suggested that the Soviet experience could become a model for developing countries in Africa or Asia, especially those that had freed themselves from colonialism. Some scholars emphasized the welfare nature of the Russian state. They underlined, for example, that in the Soviet Union, women were given paid leave before and after childbirth, and the government had established a nationwide system of daycare centers and kindergartens for preschoolers. While theorists of the totalitarian school condemned the Soviet regime, the revisionists (although they dislike this label) yesterday and today tend to treat Russia in a rather accepting way (Shlapentokh et al., 2008; Graham, 2019).

Prominent historians such as Richard Pipes (1984) have argued that socialist ideas did not in fact play an important role in Soviet history, seeing them only as a thin cover for Russo-centric authoritarianism and paternalism. Pipes also disregarded the socialist nature of the 1917 October "coup" and a number of political developments that followed, and downgraded the significance of Marxist ideology in the belief systems of the original Russian revolutionaries. Socialist ideology, in his view, was only a convenient rationalization for power-thirsty Bolsheviks to grab control of the country. Another prominent author, Robert Tucker (1961), saw the regime that emerged under Lenin and Stalin as a type of neo-czarist order that labeled itself socialist. He considered the developments that took place in the 1930s as a setback in the direction of the Russian imperial order and saw the later Soviet policies as attempts to overcome the country's historical backwardness (Tucker, 1990).

CONCLUSION

A history of any country sometimes looks like a parade of names. Russians are proud of their heroes. With only a few exceptions, they praise Duke Vladimir for "baptizing" Russia and Alexander Nevsky for defending the land from the Teutonic knights. They recognize Peter the Great for building a strong empire, and Field Marshal Kutuzov (1745–1813) for defeating Napoleon of France. They glorify Marshall Zhukov (1896–1974) for his leadership during the Great Patriotic War in 1945 and are proud of Yuri Gagarin (1934–68) for being the first person in space in 1961.

In other cases, people are well known but their impact is largely controversial. Was Ivan the Terrible a great statesman conducting brutal policies or a mentally unstable villain? Lenin, seen for many years as a saint-like figure for three generations in the Soviet Union, appears these days in many sources as a vengeful dictator. The events of the fall of 1917 are called by different names by those who saw it as positive and those who saw it as negative and illegitimate: one person's Great October Socialist Revolution is another's October Revolt. Should Stalin be praised for building a powerful nuclear state, or should he be condemned because of the millions of innocent people who died because of his policies? Did Khrushchev strengthen the country by revealing Stalin's abuses of power, or did he weaken the economy and plant the seeds of doubt in the minds of many Russian people? Debates continue.

As you may see, all these questions approach historical facts from different angles. History teaches different lessons to different people. Russian politicians often interpret and use these lessons in a pragmatic way: to justify their policies today, as we will see in the following chapters.

3 The Soviet Transformation, 1985–91

"Who lives well in Russia?" A celebrated Russian poet and critic, Nikolai Nekrasov (1821–78), posed this question, which is memorable to many Russians in his unfinished poem, studied in every school of the Soviet Union. Not only did the school curriculum require all Russian literature teachers to analyze Nekrasov's beautiful rhyme and metaphor, but also to remind eighth graders about the injustices of tsarist Russia, where almost everybody had to endure an unjust and dismal life. Socialism was supposed to be different, better. According to official textbooks, speeches, and media publications, life in the Soviet Union was stable and prosperous. Most people, however, were ultimately unhappy with the direction their country was heading.

THE BEGINNING OF THE TRANSFORMATION

Socialism, according to the official Soviet doctrine, was supposed to be a social and economic system more advanced than capitalism. Yet by the early 1980s, the whole of Soviet society had seemingly reached a point of economic and moral inertia and stagnation (Hosking, 1992). Most people were ultimately unhappy with Soviet socialism and increasingly critical of their government and its domestic and foreign policies. There were several major sources of their dissatisfaction.

Mounting problems

The country was experiencing serious *economic problems*. The Soviet economy was struggling. The growth rate of GDP declined steadily through the years when Brezhnev was in power (1963–82), from 4.7 percent per year in the middle of the 1960s to 2.0 percent in the early 1980s. Major slowdowns continued in industrial production, agricultural output, labor productivity, capital formation, investment, and per-capita income (Hewett, 1988: 52). Gigantic state subsidies to industries and agriculture and growing military spending put a tightening noose on the country's financial system. The government in Moscow could not address most of the basic socioeconomic needs of the population (Gaidar, 2007). Key consumer products were chronically absent from retail stores, while many others were in very short supply: in big cities, for example, people could buy only three kinds of cheese and one kind of butter. In most provinces, good quality beef, pork, and lamb were all but absent from local stores. Instant coffee was a rarity; so was toilet paper. It was next to impossible to find disposable diapers and many kinds of medications. The waiting lists to buy a Soviet-made car were a minimum of five years. All in all, the country was far behind the West in average living standards (Shiraev and Zubok, 2000).

Second, consumer problems and the increasing economic failure went hand in hand with massive *social problems.* Bureaucracy and corruption at all levels exemplified the enormous organizational inefficiency. Bribery became an everyday norm: people paid money illegally to policemen to avoid a traffic ticket, to store managers to obtain a pair of stylish German shoes, or to government-employed plumbers to fix a leaking faucet (as you should remember, private businesses were illegal in the Soviet Union). Soviet society was an undeclared caste system. On the one hand, there was a small but powerful circle of people with status, perks, and limited privileges. These were party bureaucrats, government officials, and people with direct access to the state-run and corrupt distribution of goods and services such as retail stores, theaters, or hospitals. On the other side, there was the majority: people with jobs but little or no assets and insignificant cash savings.

Third, *social apathy* was widespread and growing. In the absence of real political competition within a one-party system, voting was a mockery staged by the governments and silently accepted by most people (Bahry and Silver, 1990: 837–8). People in two successive generations recognized that, in reality, American, Swedish, and West German living standards were much higher, and that the gap between the Soviet Union and most Western countries was widening. Most people, at that time, believed that the wealth disparity between the Soviet Union and the West was caused by the inefficiency of the socialist system, which was repairable if only the right people—honest, enthusiastic, and educated—were to take charge of it (Gorbachev and Mlynar, 1994).

Overall, in the 1980s, the Soviet Union lived in a state of suspended belief in possible change. Very few people, however, including many silent critics of the regime—for open criticism of it was outlawed—believed that the change would come as rapidly as it did.

The rise of Mikhail Gorbachev

Within a short period, two top party leaders died of natural causes: first Yuri Andropov in 1984, then Konstantin Chernenko in 1985. In March 1985, the new General Secretary of the Communist Party, 54-year-old Mikhail Gorbachev, made a brief televised address to the people. Despite his relatively young age, Gorbachev was not a novice in the Soviet system. He had spent nearly 30 years in the ranks of the party bureaucracy, gradually moving to the highest position. His arrival there meant the beginning of a new and final stage of the Soviet Union (Kort, 2006).

When Gorbachev took power in March 1985, he immediately initiated changes. But how far should they reach? Very few people, including Gorbachev himself, knew how difficult and unpredictable the changes would be (Gorbachev, 1985). However, he believed in socialism and thought it could be reformed from within. Most people in the Soviet Union shared this point of view (Shlapentokh et al., 2008).

Attempts to revive the old system

Once in power, Gorbachev made it clear that he was a dedicated Marxist. He compared his proposed changes in 1985 to Lenin's revolution, started 70 years ago. He regularly mentioned Lenin's New Economic Policy of the 1920s (see Chapter 2) as an informal blueprint

Key figure: Mikhail Gorbachev (1931–)

Mikhail Gorbachev was born in 1931 near Stavropol, in a southern region of Russia. His town was under German occupation for several months in 1942. After finishing high school with honors, he studied at the prestigious Moscow State University, from which he graduated in 1955. He earned a law degree there (in the Soviet Union this required five years of undergraduate studies). Almost immediately after graduation, he received a political appointment to work for a regional Youth Communist League in Stavropol. Later he occupied a number of different party posts, gradually climbing up to the position of First Secretary of the Stavropol Region Party Committee in 1970. It was a prestigious appointment: he was in charge of one of the largest agricultural regions of the Soviet Union. Many top party leaders from Moscow would spend their vacations in exclusive resorts on the Black Sea, in the same region. His official position and frequent contacts with Soviet leadership put him on the shortlist of candidates for appointment to the highest ranks of the party. In 1978, he was elected Secretary of the Central Committee of the Communist Party in charge of agriculture. After 1984, as a Politburo member, he was in charge of the party ideology (the responsibility involved control of the media, publishing, creative arts, youth and social organizations, sports, and so on). This appointment also brought him an informal second position within the hierarchy. After Chernenko's death in 1985, Gorbachev became General Secretary, and he kept this position until 1991. He was also elected chairman of the Supreme Soviet (parliament) in 1989, and then President of the Soviet Union (elected in 1990 by the members of parliament, according to the Constitution). After his resignation in 1991, he continued for many years as a commentator, writer, speaker, and public figure known for his generous charitable work.

for his own economic plans. Gorbachev's picture appeared frequently on official posters with Lenin's profile in the background. Comparative politics teaches that it is common for government leaders conducting reforms based on an ideology to claim that their new policy is "in line" with the established ideological doctrine (as in China) or religious tradition (as in Iran).

Gorbachev initially won broad support among the elites and ordinary people alike. Party officials, factory managers, and military commanders saw Gorbachev as a leader who could revive the declining economy and hopefully consolidate more power in the institutions of the rejuvenated Communist Party. Most ordinary people saw him as an energetic leader who could fire bureaucrats, introduce long-awaited reforms, and quickly make the entire country work efficiently. And finally, most critics of the communist regime hoped that Gorbachev would push for radical political and economic changes within the country.

As early as 1985, Gorbachev publicly suggested several major changes. He wanted to make factory management more efficient by introducing incentives in the workplace so that people could make more money by working harder and being innovative. He hoped that socialism would be preserved and that the state would still control all the elements of the Soviet economy. Yet a limited and regulated market economy with a flexible price system was a possibility. But what was a market economy? According to the recollections of Anatoly Sobchak (1937–2000), a university professor, mayor of St Petersburg, and boss of future President Putin, the term "market" was confusing to people who had never experienced it (Sobchak, 1992). Gorbachev wanted to make serious changes within the socialist system. But was that possible without destroying its foundations?

A new term, "socialist entrepreneurship," appeared frequently in newspaper editorials. For the Kremlin, this meant an ideologically correct blend of socialism with elements of the free market (the government of China uses the term "market socialism" to label the economic reforms in their country). Factory managers were told to embrace a new kind of socialist entrepreneurship and produce more of everything, of greater variety and quality. However, these instructions contained little substance except for ambiguous proposals for more incentives and, at the same time, more government control. The entire bureaucratic system of the country resisted innovation.

Some reforms led to unfortunate blunders. In May 1985, the Kremlin launched a new anti-alcohol reform. Excessive drinking was (and remains today) a serious social problem. Tens of millions of workdays were missed every year as a result of heavy drinking. The number of alcohol-related traumas and deaths had grown, overcrowded rehabilitation facilities could not provide decent treatment, and millions of families suffered. The new anti-alcohol campaign limited the production of hard liquor, beer, and wine. Cities and towns established shorter hours of operation for state-run liquor stores. The government prohibited drinking alcohol in the workplace. Unfortunately, the reform backfired. Long lines to buy alcohol appeared on the streets of every city. Many families began to hoard and stockpile wine and vodka as assets for barter. Day laborers customarily accepted vodka as payment for their work. Facing limited production and rationing, some people turned to "moonshine" (illegally produced alcoholic drinks) and surrogates. The reform was a flop, poorly planned and badly executed.

Mistakes in other areas were abundant. Although Gorbachev promised honesty and transparency in all areas of Soviet life, he and his advisers did not always follow what they preached. One of the worst examples of such inconsistency was the reaction of Moscow's officials to the nuclear power plant incident at Chernobyl in 1986. Although the accident had caused substantial loss of life and threatened the lives and health of millions of people in the areas adjacent to Chernobyl, Gorbachev was slow to allow the state-owned news organizations to disclose this information for days.

Gorbachev was aware of these and other mistakes. Before long, he realized that a few superficial measures could not revive the sluggish economy or weaken party bureaucracy. The country needed a massive reform in all areas of its political, social, and economic life. The deep and sweeping changes initiated by Gorbachev and his close supporters received the famous labels **perestroika** and **glasnost**.

PERESTROIKA AND GLASNOST

In the Russian language *perestroika* means "restructuring" and *glasnost* means "openness." These two key words relate to the process of massive reforms undertaken in the second half of the 1980s and commonly associated with Mikhail Gorbachev, their initiator. What were the key elements of the reforms? We will look at domestic changes first and then examine Soviet foreign policy.

Opening up

Perestroika and glasnost were the names given to policies of massive restructuring in political and economic areas. These policies greatly changed people's access to information. Perhaps the earliest real change that most people felt after 1985 was the rapid weakening and virtual disappearance of political censorship.

In a series of dramatic moves, many previously prohibited books and movies were allowed to be printed, copied, or sold. In December 1986, Gorbachev personally ordered the release of Andrei Sakharov (1921–89), a renowned physicist, Nobel Prize winner, and critic of the communist regime, from his internal exile in the city of Gorky. In October 1987, Gorbachev became the first Soviet leader to publicly denounce Stalin (as was mentioned in Chapter 2, Khrushchev had done so 30 years earlier but only through classified party channels). Gorbachev called Stalin's crimes "enormous and unforgivable" (Doder and Branson, 1990: 183). He appointed a commission to review the purge trials of the 1930s, when numerous innocent citizens were falsely accused and executed. Gorbachev called these trials a "gross violation of socialist legality" (Taubman, 1987: 1).

The middle of the 1980s was a time of rapid political enlightenment among ordinary Soviets. With most restrictions against grassroots movements and social organizations lifted, scores of people joined new social and professional groups. For the first time people tested their personal freedom. Increasingly often, officials allowed massive public gatherings, public debates, rock concerts, and street rallies.

Daily newspapers and weekly magazines played a crucial role in the reforms. Weakening political censorship did not mean that all publications immediately changed their content and tone. As often happens in history, it took a few brave individuals—producers, editors, and journalists—to accept responsibility and take the initiative (Korotich, 2000). At first, most articles and interviews critical of socialism were relatively "soft." However, by 1988, most printed media were involved in a relentless campaign of attacking socialism as a system. Their daily and weekly editions were quickly sold out in street kiosks.

Television was changing too. In the mid-1980s the Soviet Union had basically one, government-controlled network called Central Television. It was responsible for programming and broadcasting all across the country. (An interesting detail: Soviet television was commercial-free, as the government underwrote all broadcasts.) In addition to the programs generated in the capital and distributed through the network, people had access to one or two local networks. With the loosening of party control over programming, television professionals were allowed to produce almost anything they wanted. It was, in some ways, the "golden age" of Soviet television. The late 1980s was the time of a genuine outburst of investigative journalism revealing corruption, nepotism, and fraud. New entertainment programs, concerts, and game shows appeared. Most popular were late-evening live talk shows. Their hosts discussed hot topics of the day and answered phone calls live—which was entirely new to the viewing audience. People liked these unrehearsed and innovative programs for their spontaneity and honesty.

Reforming the Communist Party

Gorbachev hoped to prompt discussions within the party about how to reform it. The Communist Party Regulations, a sacred rulebook for several generations of Soviet communists, specifically prohibited any factions or disagreements within the party (see Chapter 2). In 1988, Gorbachev said yes to dissent, which was a clear break from the communist dogma. As Gorbachev noted at a Politburo meeting on December 27, 1988, he had hoped that openness would revitalize the Communist Party (Politburo Meeting transcript, 1988). However, many party members were unhappy and believed that the party was taking a wrong turn toward self-destruction.

Meanwhile, Gorbachev was making the party more transparent and democratic. He wanted to increase the power of local elected officials at the expense of the party committees who had traditionally held all the power (Gorbachev, 1996). It took almost two years to set up multicandidate competitive elections for party officials, factory management, and local government bodies (Taubman, 1987). Gorbachev also weakened party control over economic issues. The Central Committee Secretariat, which was essentially in charge of Soviet industries, had to turn to internal, party-related problems.

In March 1990, Gorbachev assumed the newly established office of president, which enabled him to become free of direct party control. He intended to hold the presidency for a five-year term and then run again in multicandidate presidential elections (Imse, 1990: 1). That same month, the Communist Party reluctantly agreed to revoke Article 6 of the Soviet Constitution, which had enshrined the Communist Party as the "leading and guiding force" in Soviet life (Gorbachev, 1995: 317). It was a formal yet historic political change. Most party hardliners—although they were in the minority—were against this amendment. Their disagreement with the change was understandable. From that moment, the party lost its legal right to control elected bodies and other branches of government across the entire Soviet Union.

You should not assume that the Communist Party was an assembly of reactionary forces—mostly old and uneducated people—who were blindly opposing the reforms. Many party members were educated, open to experience, and critically inclined people. They wanted to see the Soviet Union as a strong, efficient, friendly, and respected country. The problem was that they did not *agree* regarding how far and deep the reforms should go. As comparative politics teaches, almost every country has politicians who demand fast and sweeping reforms as well as those who believe only in gradual and carefully planned changes. The Soviet Union was no exception.

There is a temptation in every reformist movement to move quickly and make radical changes in as many areas of life as possible. However, as history often shows, such rapid and massive political and social reforms can easily backfire and have undesirable consequences.

Further political changes

In December 1988, a new law, On Elections of People's Deputies of the USSR, outlined a new type of parliamentary elections free from the party's control. The first elections of a newly created national parliament were held in March 1989.

In May 1989, the First Congress of People's Deputies gathered in Moscow. Although the selection of the delegates was not entirely uniform (some delegates were selected by official organizations such as labor unions, the Academy of Sciences, and the Communist Party), the process was quite open and free. Honest, frequently raucous debates took place during the Congress's opening sessions, which were broadcast live. By June 1989, the delegates of the Congress had elected a new Soviet parliament. The next year, people voted for regional and local soviets. The elections removed from office many conservative communists who had actively opposed the reforms. Now, proreform deputies constituted a majority of newly elected councils in Moscow, Leningrad, and many large cities.

After the crucial Article 6 of the Constitution, guaranteeing the monopoly of the Communist Party on power, was amended in March 1990, nascent political parties sprang up almost overnight. Within six months, some 250 parties had registered in Moscow; the relatively small Republic of Georgia registered more than 160 parties. Poorly organized, with sketchy ideological platforms, and having virtually no prominent leaders, these parties had little political influence (Glad and Shiraev, 1999).

The policies of glasnost had accelerated the development of political freedoms. Political reforms produced free elections. Yet in the economic sphere, the reforms were for the most part slow and inefficient. What was the essence of such problems?

Economic reforms

As you should remember, the entire economic system in the Soviet Union was based on central planning. The State also controlled natural resources, manufacturing facilities, machinery, banks, stores, and commercial institutions (Kenez, 2006). A few small-scale economic measures were introduced during the first two years of perestroika. They involved easing the strict system of centralized management. On the local level, the government allowed limited forms of free entrepreneurship. Buying wholesale and selling retail to make a profit became legal. Many small-scale enterprises such as repair and tailor's shops appeared in every city. Within days, scores of new businesses began to sell counterfeit Levi's jeans (nobody knew or cared how to obtain licenses to avoid trademark violations), Lacoste shirts, and many other locally produced products. Enterprises could now legally use cash instead of carrying out the traditional financial transactions on paper. As you probably know, cash transactions, without legal paperwork attached, are among the easiest avenues for corruption and fraud.

One of the most important legal changes took place on May 26, 1988. A new law allowed private enterprises to be set up. It let people incorporate small private partnerships with collective property. The newly established economic cooperatives (as they were legally called) could keep their profits, both domestic and foreign. The federal monopoly on foreign trade was lifted on December 22, 1988 (by Decision 1526 of the Council of Ministers). It gave businesses a chance to bypass the federal government in international business deals. The law signaled a radical change. It was almost revolutionary. For years, citizens of the Soviet Union had been forbidden to own foreign currency and make deals with foreign citizens. In 1988, private possession of dollars and other world currencies was finally lawful. Almost immediately, many people using interpersonal contacts began to exchange their rubles (although, in insignificant amounts) for US dollars or other foreign currencies. It was a form of investment and protection from inflation that was already getting out of control.

In publications and official documents, these and other economic changes received the label "**radical economic reform.**" The word "radical" meant that the government had repealed many existing Soviet regulations related to economy and trade. Companies could buy directly from one another without Moscow's approval. In Gorbachev's optimistic plans, the State itself was to be a customer, although a preferred one (Doder and Branson, 1990: 239–40). Unfortunately, the ongoing rapid economic and political changes brought the economy into deepening chaos. On the one hand, the State was the principal owner of factories, plants, natural resources, and agricultural land. The vast majority of people remained state employees. On the other hand, the Kremlin allowed and encouraged people to embrace the principles of the free market. People could own private property now.

A new challenge emerged from the republics of the Soviet Union: their governments now wanted even more reforms; they hoped to establish their own independent economic policies (Brumberg, 1991: 53–4).

Weakening the federal system

In a federal republic, which the Soviet Union claimed to be, there must be a division of powers between the federal government, and the governments of the subdivisions. At least two factors contributed to the weakening of the Soviet federal system during perestroika. The first one was the Kremlin's federal policies and the ongoing economic and political decentralization. The second one was that the weakening of political censorship strengthened many local oppositional groups demanding more freedom and even independence.

The rapid growth of powerful nationalist movements went through three stages of development. First, many such groups, such as the Sajudis in Lithuania, appeared as student, professional, or cultural organizations. Their initial goal was to assist with the ongoing political and socioeconomic reforms on a local level. In 1988 and later, they began to demand more autonomy for their republics. Finally, several such movements grew into strong political parties fighting for total independence. By 1990, the Kremlin had no effective political or administrative resources to suppress demands for national sovereignty (Brown, 1996).

From the very beginning of the reforms, Gorbachev and his followers had not planned to dismantle the Soviet Union as a sovereign state. A majority of Soviet people, especially in Russia, did not want the Soviet Union to disappear. The country held a national referendum in March 1991. The question on the ballot was, "Do you consider necessary the preservation of the Union of Soviet Socialist Republics as a renewed federation of equal sovereign republics in which the rights and freedom of an individual of any nationality will be fully guaranteed?" Of those who voted, 76 percent answered yes. Nevertheless, in a little less than nine months, the Soviet Union had disappeared as a country from the political map (Sakwa, 1999).

Changes in foreign policy

Gorbachev, according to his close confidantes, wanted to make a big impact in international relations. He wanted to champion ideas of common sense, moderation, and mutual interests (Chernyaev, 2000). Gorbachev called his initiatives in foreign policy **new thinking**. Indeed, it was new. He questioned most of the basic assumptions of international relations in the midst of the Cold War. In particular, Gorbachev raised three important points.

First, he argued that the ongoing confrontation between the superpowers should stop immediately and without preconditions. Second, all nuclear countries, particularly the Soviet Union and the United States, should reduce their deadly arsenals to the minimum needed to guarantee mutual security and international stability. Third, the new world of the end of the 20th century should stop ideological competition and turn to what were described as the *universal values* of peace and cooperation in international relations (Gorbachev, 1985: 1). He was convinced that the world should and could function according to mutually agreed basic values of peace and mutual accommodation (Sheehy, 1990: 220).

The "new thinking" foreign policy led to progress in arms limitation talks with the United States. Top-level meetings between Gorbachev and US President Ronald Reagan in Geneva (1985), Reykjavik (1986), Washington (1987), and Moscow (1988), resulted in the signing of the Intermediate Nuclear Forces (INF) treaty. Reagan and Gorbachev established open and informal personal communications, which helped to develop mutual trust (Chernyaev, 2000). Both leaders soon began to talk about burying the Cold War for good. The dismantling of the confrontation between the superpowers proceeded apace, in 1989, and later, under the George H. W. Bush administration (1989–92).

Gorbachev took unilateral steps to implement his vision of a new world. By 1989, the Soviet Union withdrew its troops from Afghanistan, ending the deadly war that had resulted in almost 15,000 deaths and more than 50,000 serious injuries on the Soviet side. Moscow stopped supporting pro-communist insurgencies around the world. By 1990, the Warsaw Pact, the Soviet-led military and political coalition in central Europe, was dissolved while the Soviet troops remained in their barracks. East and West Germany were on the way toward unification.

Case in point: GRIT versus insecurity

During the Cold War, some experts believed that an effective solution to international tensions might be found if one of the competing sides would initiate a series of small goodwill steps toward its opponents (Shiraev and Zubok, 2020). Such steps would not undermine security; seen as sincere intentions supported by policies, they might pave a way out of the spiral of insecurity. Small, incremental, and conciliatory steps represent the core concept of the model called graduated reciprocation in tension reduction (GRIT). This model was often criticized as a romantic dream of idealists until Soviet leader Mikhail Gorbachev implemented it in his foreign policy in 1987–9, and by doing so transformed the entire security doctrine of the Soviet Union. The ultimate result of GRIT was the end of the Cold War.

In today's world, politicians and the media frequently discuss the strengths and weaknesses of this approach to bilateral and international relations. What do you think: for example, should governments negotiate with governments that are perceived as hostile (for example, North Korea or Iran)? Should your governments maintain relationships with dictators? The GRIT case shows that, under particular circumstances, engagement in diplomacy can be more beneficial for international security than economic and political sanctions and open confrontation. But what circumstances should exist to lift political and economic sanctions against Iran or Russia, for example?

Changes in the military

The Kremlin initiated several important changes in the Soviet military organization. In December 1988, Gorbachev announced his plans for a unilateral reduction of 500,000 in the number of Soviet military personnel. Generals who disagreed were removed from their posts or had to retire (Bunich, 1992: 260–2; Odom, 1990: 58). The Kremlin no longer felt that it should deceive the West about the size of its military budget, and in May 1989 it revealed its "real" size. It was about four times larger than had previously been acknowledged (*The State*, 1989: 11).

Despite the continuing changes and some encouraging poll numbers, Gorbachev was facing growing criticism. Although most people believed that reforms were necessary, opinion differed about the scope and direction of the changes. Many people believed that the liberal reforms did not go far enough. The opposition demanded that the reforms slow down. The main argument of the opposition was that the changes had resulted in social instability and were harmful to the country's economy and national security.

UNINTENDED CONSEQUENCES

In 1990, five years after Gorbachev had introduced the reforms, the Politburo published an assessment of the situation in the country: "People are upset with lack of stability in the society. Crisis continues in the economy. There is a hard financial situation. [We see] the overall decline of discipline and order. Crime is flourishing" (*Materialy Politburo*, 1990). The country was indeed in crisis.

Growing problems

Perestroika did not bring about rapid economic revival. By 1989, the new private sector was unable to obtain enough goods and supplies, since most of these remained under central control. Price reform did not occur. Rapid inflation caused excessive buying and hoarding, which in turn contributed to the scarcity of consumer goods in retail stores (Medvedev, 1994: 39, 55). Wildcat strikes forced by economic hardships further undercut production. Close advisers told Gorbachev that people were turning against the erratic economic reforms (Chernyaev, 2000). In the 1970s, an average family spent about 50 percent of its income on food. By the 1990s, this number was close to 90 percent (Shiraev, 1999b: 114).

Bereft of direction from the Kremlin, many local party officials were confused. They constantly asked for advice and guidance, but the Kremlin's reply was that they should figure out everything themselves (Ligachev, 1996: 85). Glasnost, while it promoted freedom of speech, also produced many unintended consequences. The revelations in the media about Stalin's crimes and the relentless criticisms of socialism contributed to rampant pessimism about the country's future. Many people could not adapt to the growing uncertainties of perestroika.

Gorbachev soon became the target of popular frustrations. The results of a poll published in the best-selling weekly *Argumenty i Facty* in 1989 indicated that Gorbachev was not among the top ten most popular persons in the Supreme Soviet (Doder and Branson, 1990: 391). At the May Day ceremony (a major occasion in the Soviet Union, with large public gatherings and official rallies in all cities) in 1990, many people near the reviewing stand in Moscow jeered the government officials. They chanted and carried banners with the slogans, "Down with Gorbachev" and "72 Years to Nowhere" (referring to the years that had passed since the 1917 Revolution). By spring 1991, Gorbachev's approval ratings in the national polls had dropped to 14 percent (Brumberg, 1991: 54).

Criticisms of foreign policy

The growing conservative opposition was generally unhappy with Gorbachev's foreign policy. They accused him and his advisers of making several fatal blunders. These arguments are especially popular today among Russian political leaders. There have been three main points of criticism.

First, the critics maintained that Moscow had lost its strategic positions in Eastern Europe. They saw the disintegration of Soviet control of Eastern Europe—including Poland, Hungary, Czechoslovakia, East Germany, Bulgaria, and Romania, which overthrew their communist governments—as a defeat in the Cold War. Following the fall of the Berlin Wall in October 1989, East Germany was officially reunited with West Germany, creating a country firmly in the Western camp, and the Warsaw Pact was disbanded. Yet the US-led rival NATO alliance remained intact. This situation, as far as criticisms went, effectively put the Soviet Union in a very vulnerable strategic position.

Second, Gorbachev was accused of abandoning most of Moscow's long-term allies, such as Cuba, Nicaragua, Vietnam, Ethiopia, Iraq, and Angola. Such a policy weakened Soviet geopolitical positions because it was losing its partners across the globe (Katz, 1991). Critics also maintained that Gorbachev was setting a dangerous precedent, indicating to other countries that the Soviet Union did not fulfill its international obligations. Moscow's withdrawal pushed a few countries further away politically from the Soviet Union (Dobrynin, 1995: 622–32).

And finally, it appeared that the ongoing negotiations with the United States had really taken the form of unilateral concessions to the West. The Soviet Union was about to lose its superpower status. Critics underlined that, although the Cold War was ending, Moscow had had to pay an unfairly heavy price: the Soviets had lost their strategic allies around the world and accepted the global domination of the United States in the post–Cold War situation. Washington, on the other hand, the critics believed, offered almost nothing in return.

Calls for national self-determination became louder. In March 1990, the republics of Lithuania and Estonia declared formal independence. Soon Latvia and Moldova followed. On June 12, 1990, as a sign of distancing from the Soviet Union, the Supreme Soviet of the Russian Federation, influenced by a majority of reform-minded nationalist groups, issued an official declaration on Russia's sovereignty.

The strengthening of the opposition

The main source of the dissent to Gorbachev's reforms was national security apparatus, and among conservative Communist Party members. Although by 1991 two thirds of the important decision makers at all levels of the Communist Party and the entire membership of the Politburo had been replaced by people seemingly loyal to Gorbachev (Chernyaev, 1993: 63; Boldin, 1994: 293), a new opposition to the reforms strengthened. They used the free press to launch attacks against the reforms and against Gorbachev personally. The Orthodox Church pressured Gorbachev from a nationalist position.

In the light of this growing criticism, the Kremlin agreed to strengthen the powers of the military, police, and security forces. In April 1989, the military brutally cracked down (causing many casualties) on peaceful public protests in the Republic of Georgia. A presidential decree established a joint army–police patrol for enforcement of law and order on the streets of the Soviet Union. Another decree ordered security forces and the military to enter any establishment suspected of speculative activities and inspect their financial records. As a culmination of the growing crackdown, in early January 1991, federal troops in Vilnius and Riga used force to repress secessionist public demonstrations. Like in Georgia, there were human casualties among the protestors (Glad and Shiraev, 1999).

A strong opposition movement grew within the ranks of the reformers. It was informally called *democratic opposition*. A widely popular leader and future president, Boris Yeltsin, was its leader. Influenced by a personal power struggle between Gorbachev and Yeltsin, this movement found support among Russia's liberal intelligentsia, educated professionals, college students, and a substantial proportion of the working class. What did this very loose but massive group oppose and support?

The opposition believed that, in order to overcome the current crisis, the country should remove from power the most conservative, pro-communist political forces. The new opposition was in favor of the reforms in general. Their concern was with the slow pace and narrow scope of the changes. The democratic opposition was concerned that the reforms could be reversed as soon as Gorbachev was forcefully dismissed from power or—seeking a compromise—yielded under pressure.

Second, the "democrats" (a popular name attached to the democratic opposition) believed in a strategy rooted in a rapid acceleration of the political reforms and an unconditional break with the communist past. They supported Gorbachev's foreign policy and wanted, in general, to model their country's future on a Western example, the most suitable of which was the United States. This appeared to be a country resembling the Soviet Union in terms of its size, economic might, and multiethnic population.

Third, the democratic opposition supported national pro-independence parties in the republics. The "democrats" supported the idea that ethnic republics could eventually form independent states. They believed that Russia, as a sovereign country, would certainly defend and further develop liberal democracy, strengthen the free market, and pursue a robust but peaceful foreign policy.

Many women joined the movement and quickly become influential. Historically, the Soviet system had claimed to encourage women's participation in politics, but women appointed to political offices were expected to be (and were) loyal to the Communist Party. The democratic opposition gave women a real chance for political action. One of the brightest stars of the movement was Galina Starovoitova (1946–98), a sociologist from St Petersburg elected to the Soviet parliament in 1989. She was a dedicated supporter of liberal democracy and its institutions, national determination of the Soviet republics, and individual rights.

The democratic opposition's political platform won widespread public support. Yeltsin and his popular followers such as Starovoitova appeared as educated, trustworthy, and viable alternatives to Gorbachev. At the same time, Gorbachev's power and prestige were weakening. These two developments convinced the traditionalist forces within the party and government to act quickly, secure their positions of power, and avoid the looming demolition of the Soviet Union.

The August 1991 coup

In a private meeting with Gorbachev in late July, Boris Yeltsin, president of the Russian Federation, insisted that several senior officials in the government would have to be replaced after the signing of the Union Treaty—a recently proposed new legal foundation for the new and decentralized Soviet Union, keeping its 15 republics. This conversation, secretly taped by security agents, was made known to several high-ranking officials and convinced them to take action (Gorbachev, 1996: 643). In addition, Yeltsin vowed that the Russian government would execute its policy of taking direct control of all the natural resources in Russia as soon as the Union Treaty was signed and a new Soviet Union was formed. Those who continued to hope that the Soviet Union might be preserved as a state began to realize that its end could be nigh. They took a chance to save it.

In August 1991, a group of senior government officials, including Gennadii Yanaev (Soviet Vice President), Dmitry Yazov (Minister of Defense), Boris Pugo (Minister of the Interior), and Vladimir Kryuchkov (Head of the KGB, the federal security agency), made the decision to remove Gorbachev from power and declare a state of emergency in the entire Soviet Union. The plotters formed a State Emergency Committee in an attempt to legalize their actions. In fact, the Committee was a *junta*, a military or political group that rules a country after forcefully taking power. As in other courtiers after the dismissal of the legitimate government, the plotters planned the suspension of certain political freedoms and immediate political changes. In particular, the members of the State Emergency Committee wanted to stop the disintegration of the Soviet Union and discontinue the negotiations related to the Union Treaty.

Gorbachev was arrested at his summer residence in Crimea on August 19. His communications with Moscow were cut. The conspirators announced on national television, which they now controlled, that Gorbachev had resigned (in fact he had not) and that the State Emergency Committee was in charge. Within hours, local executive decrees in several regions suspended most civil freedoms such as the right to assembly.

However, public support for the coup across the country was weak. By the end of the second day of the putsch, only a few regional governments had supported it. In Moscow, Boris Yeltsin and the government of the Russian Federation defied the orders of the coup leaders. People went out on the streets to build barricades and protect local governments opposing the coup. Anti-coup demonstrations took place in the largest Russian cities, Leningrad and Moscow. Overall, the indecisiveness of the plot organizers, the strong resistance of Boris Yeltsin and his supporters, and public demonstrations caused the coup leaders to lose the support of the military. Most military commanders refused to use force against unarmed people. The conspirators surrendered. One of them committed suicide.

The failed August *coup d'état* accelerated the pace of political change and fragmentation in the country, and this led to its formal breakup four months later. The fragmentation of the Soviet Union did, however, leave most Russian government institutions intact. Boris Yeltsin occupied the Russian presidency. He had been elected in June 1991 in a popular ballot with 57.3 percent of the vote against five challengers. The Russian parliament—the Congress of

People's Deputies—had been elected earlier, in March 1990. Although the majority of deputies to the Congress represented the Communist Party, they were generally reform minded.

The word "romantic," which is often used in reference to this stage of the Soviet transition, reflects the widespread elation and high expectations with which many Russian citizens greeted the political, economic, and social realms following the August 1991 coup and the breakup of the Soviet Union later that year. The success of the popular resistance to the coup produced a sense of empowerment and optimism in many Russians, which lasted for some time (Gibson, 1996). Later polls revealed, however, ambiguous attitudes about Russia's policies immediately after the coup. In 2018, 38 percent of Russians believed that the 1991 coup was a tragic event in their country's history and 53 percent said that neither side was right in the conflict (Levada, 2018b).

In 1985, Gorbachev and other reformers wanted to make the economy more efficient and the political system less authoritarian. They did not envision (and were not ready for) the sweeping changes that led to the collapse of the powerful state in 1991 (see Figure 3.1). The Commonwealth of Independent States (CIS) appeared in place of the defunct USSR. Eleven out of the fifteen former republics of the Soviet Union have joined. (Estonia, Lithuania, and Latvia did not join, and Georgia left in 2008.) The CIS remains mostly a formal association without real political power.

At a highly secret meeting at a nature reserve in Belarus on December 8, 1991, Russian Federation President Boris Yeltsin, and the leaders of Ukraine and Belarus, agreed to dissolve the Soviet Union. A loose confederation called the Commonwealth of Independent States was created in its place.

This is a summative timeline of the reforms that led to the end of the Soviet Union. The arrows show the direction of the process and the interconnectedness of policies and their outcomes.

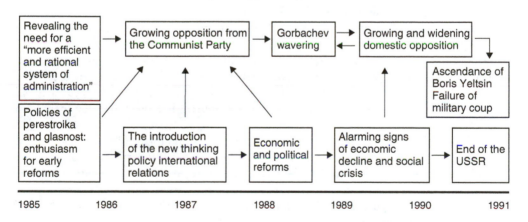

A summative timeline of the reforms that led to the end of the Soviet Union. The arrows show the direction of the process and interconnectedness of policies and their outcomes

Figure 3.1 The reforms of 1985–91: a summary

CRITICAL THINKING ABOUT THE SOVIET TRANSFORMATION

The peaceful ending of the Soviet Union and Cold War continues to present a considerable intellectual challenge to all experts working in the fields of political science, history, foreign policy, global affairs, and international security.

Back in the early 1980s, the most common assumption among professional analysts in the United States and Western Europe was that the US military buildup under Ronald Reagan and the continuing Soviet decline would generate a series of violent outbursts over the globe that could have triggered a global war. Yet in 1987–8, the feelings of fear and insecurity were melting like snow under the sun.

Why did the reforms take place? Why did they end with the collapse of an apparently solid state? Why did the Cold War end so rapidly? Various theories and assumptions attempt to explain the reasons for the reforms and their results (Strayer, 1998). We will distinguish theories that emphasize three groups of factors influencing the Soviet transformation between 1985 and 1991: international, domestic, and individual.

International factors: the Cold War pressures

A few experts, including government officials and academics, in the early 1990s were quick to claim that the stunning end of the Cold War was, in fact, a victory for the United States (Zubok, 2007). According to this view, called **triumphalist**, the Soviet Union lost the Cold War because of the policies of President Ronald Reagan and, in particular, his tough foreign policy course, aiming at the amplification of American strength and pressuring Moscow on all fronts. Several US and Western policies in the late 1980s further contributed to this outcome.

First, Washington refused to pursue a rapid disarmament and thus exhausted Soviet economic resources and finances, a substantial portion of which was given over to national defense. The announcement of the US Strategic Defense Initiative (SDI, also known as "Star Wars"), was the final straw that pushed the Soviets to seek ways to compromise with Washington.

Second, the United States had contributed to a military deadlock in Afghanistan by supporting the Islamic opposition (the mujahedeen) and other anti-Soviet forces there. The Soviet leaders understood that they could not win that highly unpopular war, yet they did not know how to end it quickly. As a result, Soviet resources had been draining there for a long time.

Third, by supporting Solidarity (an oppositional, anticommunist political movement in Poland) and other similar movements in Eastern Europe, the West further complicated the geopolitical status of the Soviet Union and contributed to the loss of its political prestige among its allies.

Fourth, by encouraging Saudi Arabia and other oil-exporting countries to reduce oil prices, the West reduced the Soviet Union's national oil revenue.

Finally, by waging a war of ideas, and by constant ideological pressure on Soviet leaders, the West undercut the Soviet ideological power bases, undermined the communists' confidence in themselves, and forced them into policies of retrieval and surrender. Soviet leaders had no choice but to throw in the political towel, ending their futile resistance.

Fear of the United States was a powerful motivational factor forcing the Soviet leadership to seek a solution to ease the strenuous arms race. However, most analysts believe that, although Western policies were important, they were not the most decisive factor in the Soviet collapse (Zubok, 2007). There were other factors that added to the outside pressure and eventually sealed the fate of the Soviet Union.

International factors: imperial overstretch

The pursuit for greater power might have brought the Soviet Union to a condition of acute economic and political exhaustion, a state known in comparative politics and international relations as imperial overstretch (Adomeit, 1998). From this point of view, like imperial Britain or France, the Soviet Union was doing too much and in too many places while using diminishing resources, and this caused its ultimate collapse.

The Soviet economy, exhausted by the enormous military expenditure it maintained during the Cold War, was both inefficient and extremely expensive to run (Gaidar, 2007). In addition, it was generally oriented toward military production and failed to overhaul itself to satisfy the growing consumerist appetites of Soviet society. Although the profits from oil exports temporarily offset the continuing Soviet decline during the 1980s, the Soviet Union finally overstretched its power and exhausted its resources (Zubok, 2007). Ultimately, it could not survive as a state despite its enormous military power, and considerable economic and technological resources.

Economic factors were no doubt important in the demise of the Soviet Union. However, there are so many other countries in history and today that have experienced greater economic hardship and yet survived as sovereign states. Economic reasons are necessary, but not sufficient on their own, to explain the implosion of the Soviet state.

Domestic economic and political factors

Several specific domestic factors contributed to the end of the Soviet Union. With its resources exhausted, the Soviet system needed efficient policies to survive. Unfortunately, the Soviet internal defects were more serious than foreign and domestic experts could understand (Gudkov, 2012). The foundations of this system were too fragile to support any rapid upgrading. As a result, the system imploded under its own weight in 1991 (Kotkin, 2008). Economists underline the fundamental domestic economic factors, including the planned economy that caused the country's inability to reform (Gaidar, 2007). Political scientists refer to the colossal organizational problems, including bureaucracy that plagued the Soviet Union and stalled the reforms. The country did not have social and political institutions that could have carried the weight and speed of the changes in the absence of an efficient central government (Bauman, 1994: 15). For ordinary Russian people, instability, inflation, and chronic shortages were among several reasons to turn against Gorbachev, whose approval ratings—to his surprise and disappointment—had rapidly shrunk by 1990 (Taubman, 2017).

The strength of the nationalist forces in the republics was also growing. By the late 1980s, facing major economic difficulties, Boris Yeltsin and the emerging new leadership in the republics switched to nationalistic rhetoric: they believed they would all be better off economically and politically without the vast bureaucracy of the Soviet Union. Boris Yeltsin and his supporters successfully challenged Gorbachev and won. Russia distanced itself from the Soviet Union. Gorbachev still garnered enormous international support for his new vision of international security and its foreign policy. Yet at the same time, his power platform at home weakened as a result of the unsuccessful domestic reforms. In the end, the state began to disintegrate under the pressure of ethnic separatist movements and strong democratic forces. However, in many countries, as history has shown, ethnic elites have been unable to form their own independent states within such a short period. Why did they succeed in the Soviet Union?

Domestic factors: the elites

Perestroika was also a practical result of an idealistic vision of a small group of party officials. The Soviet regime, although badly in need of reform, had sufficient resources to resist external pressures and maintain its self-sufficiency for a relatively long period. The crucial changes began not only because of economic problems, power struggles, and external pressures, but also because of the generational change in the Soviet leadership and its inability and unwillingness to preserve the system (Glad and Shiraev, 1999; Kotz, 1997). On the other hand, by deliberately weakening the party's ability to run the country, Gorbachev at the same time was ultimately undermining his own power (Taubman, 2017).

Gorbachev never realized, or admitted to himself, that the party could not be his instrument to carry through change. By the 1980s, the gigantic structure had become so rotten and demoralized that attempts to infuse it with democracy only hastened its death. As Taubman puts it, "by gutting the party's ability to run the country, he was undermining his own power." The Soviet Union itself was cracking up. Ukrainians were talking about independence; the Baltics—especially Lithuania—were openly defying central control; special forces had murdered 20 Georgian demonstrators in Tbilisi in April 1989. Most ominous of all, the Russian Republic—egged on by Boris Yeltsin—demanded and won its own Communist Party in June 1990. The media used their freedom under glasnost to attack Gorbachev on all fronts. For a silent but increasingly hate-filled majority in the party's guiding bodies, the familiar world was ending.

Gorbachev was also preoccupied with struggles among different groups of Soviet and Russian elites (Simanov, 2009). National elites in the republics (including Russia) finally prevailed and won the competition by the end of 1991. Other groups, witnessing the disintegration of the old planned economic system and the weakening of the old federal power, quickly found their own political roles in the process of reforms. In fact, the failed reforms of Gorbachev cleared the way for a massive privatization of property in the late 1980s and early 1990s, when the governing elites and a few powerful individuals gained access to the country's resources and promptly enriched themselves (Cohen, 2001).

Individual factors: the Gorbachev–Yeltsin struggle

The personal style of Mikhail Gorbachev, his management skills, personal limitations, and idiosyncrasies, significantly influenced the initiation, development, and eventual collapse of the reforms. His early collaboration and later rivalry with Boris Yeltsin made the most substantial impact on the eventual disintegration of the state. Yeltsin represented a somewhat more impatient and even intolerant wing of the reformers, who did not like to compromise.

In the process, he was confronting an increasingly inconsistent, hesitant, and frustrated Gorbachev. Their cooperation gradually evolved and later turned into rivalry. The early phase was Yeltsin's initiation into the elite party structures. For a short period, at the beginning of the transition, in 1985–87, Gorbachev needed Yeltsin to fight the most conservative elements of the party. As long as all the institutions in the Soviet Union—the Communist Party, the bureaucracy, the security apparatus, and the military—retained their monopoly on power, Yeltsin, who was widely seen as a reformer, needed Gorbachev for political protection, too.

At first, Yeltsin played the role of a populist challenging the Soviet bureaucracy. When he began to openly accuse Gorbachev of slowing the reforms down, he was dismissed from his powerful party positions. No wonder their relations deteriorated. Yeltsin remained in Moscow but occupied a relatively low-key ministerial position. During this period, Gorbachev practically ignored Yeltsin. Nevertheless, while Gorbachev's reputation was diminishing, Yeltsin's grew. As an articulate critic of communism and bureaucracy, Yeltsin gradually gained substantial popular support across the Soviet Union.

An open political rivalry and bitter confrontation between the two began after Yeltsin had returned to power by winning a popular election to the presidency of the Russian Republic in June of 1991. Yeltsin won a powerful popular mandate, which Gorbachev had never obtained because he never stood as a candidate in a free democratic election (something he later regretted).

The final period of political competition between Gorbachev and Yeltsin began after the August coup of 1991. Eventually, Gorbachev accepted a secondary political role as president of the increasingly weakened Soviet Union. On a personal level, according to his close confidants, Gorbachev was very ambivalent about, and sometimes bitter toward, Yeltsin. He would talk about his rival for hours, constantly scrutinizing his words and actions (Chernyaev, 1993: 218)

As you can see, the Soviet Union was probably brought down by a combination of factors including foreign pressures, overstretching, domestic economic and political problems, the unwillingness of the elites to preserve the union, and the unique nature of the Gorbachev–Yeltsin rivalry. Each of these factors alone was not sufficient enough to cause the transformation and the end of a powerful state. But appearing together they became a potent historic force, a "perfect storm" which practically every expert in the West in the early 1980s had failed to predict.

CONCLUSION

The 19th-century poem, *Who Lives Well in Russia?*, is still taught to tenth graders in Russian schools today in the 21st century. There is no formal pressure on teachers to persuade their students of the insurmountable difficulties of 19th-century Russia. Instead, the students are told to draw their own conclusions. What conclusions can they make? Will they compare their lives today with the conditions of the Soviet Union and tsarist Russia? Will they regret the dissolution of the USSR? The transformation of 1985–91 was full of contradictions, uncertainties, and disputed outcomes. Many contemporary Russian policies took root in the processes that began in the 1980s and which continued through the 1990s.

It is rarely appropriate to judge reforms as either absolutely successful or totally disastrous. A clear triumph in one area of reform may be accompanied by a prime failure in others. As critical thinkers, let us put the main and immediate outcomes of the Soviet transformation into two categories.

On the plus side, the people of the Soviet Union had obtained political freedom by the late 1980s. Censorship was gradually eliminated, and freedom of speech guaranteed. People could finally travel overseas with their own foreign currency and without going through a humiliating procedure of obtaining exit visas. The one-party political system was gone. Limited private property became legal, and small private businesses grew. The Cold War was over. Moscow and Washington agreed to destroy thousands of nuclear warheads and the means to deliver them. Russia and 14 former republics of the Soviet Union won their independence.

On the other hand, the reforms of the 1980s caused a profound crisis in all spheres of life. Sharp social inequality and polarization emerged. Inflation skyrocketed. Food shortages had become common by the end of 1989. Violent crime flourished. Corruption was rampant. In many regions violence sparked by nationalists broke out, taking thousands of lives and bringing destruction and despair to hundreds of thousands of people in the North Caucasus region, Chechnya, Ossetia, Armenia, Azerbaijan, Moldova, Abkhazia, Georgia, and several regions in Central Asia. The dissolution of the Soviet Union left several lingering territorial disputes or problems affecting Russia's relations with Lithuania (the Kaliningrad region), with Ukraine (the Crimea region), Kazakhstan (the Baikonur space center), and with Moldova (the Dniester region). Except in Latvia, Estonia, and Lithuania, democracy is still struggling in the former Soviet republics. Central Asian states turned to authoritarianism.

Any massive and rapid transformation of a country is a perilous enterprise. Although comparative studies show that in some countries speedy reforms can be effective, very few states have successfully undergone such a dramatic transformation, so rapidly and in all spheres of life, including the economic, political, ideological, and spiritual, as has the Soviet Union (Strayer, 1998). The Soviet Union did not have a powerful foreign sponsor and received no massive foreign aid, as did many European countries accepting Marshall Plan aid from the United States in the late 1940s. Moscow received relatively little help from the international community during the toughest transitional period. If such support had been given to Gorbachev and his government early, we might have seen a different course and outcome of reforms (Tetlock, Lebow, and Perker, 2006).

Gorbachev's motivation and personal qualities were crucial in the course of the transformation. Of the greatest importance was his belief that the Soviet system could be reformed and his rejection of the use of violence to achieve his ambitious political goals. Very few times in history (US President Woodrow Wilson can be mentioned here as an example) has the leader of a great power renounced the old rules of foreign policy in favor of a sweeping idealist agenda based on nonviolence, cooperation, and interdependence (Levesque, 1997). Without Gorbachev, the Soviet Union would likely still exist today. Most probably, the Cold War would have continued, and the world would have been a more dangerous place if the Soviet Union had had a different political leader in the 1980s.

Part II
Institutions and Players

Article 3 of the Constitution of the Russian Federation states that the only source of power in Russia is its people. The printed words are clear and simple: no person or group may usurp power in Russia. The Constitution also says that people exercise their power directly or through the federal and local government institutions. Yet how do people in Russia exercise their power in reality? What kind of government institutions does Russia have today, and how do they function? Who has most power in Russia, and who makes the most important decisions there today? Part II of the book will examine the three branches of government in Russia as well as key players—individuals as well as institutions—responsible for setting policies and making the most important decisions. A brief preview of key historical developments will open each of these chapters.

4 The Executive Branch

As discussed earlier in the book, St Petersburg was Russia's capital for more than 214 years. The name of the city has been changed three times: from the original, St Petersburg in 1703, to Petrograd in 1914, then to Leningrad in 1924, and back to St Petersburg in 1991. The seat of the capital in Russia has also been changed twice: from Moscow to St Petersburg in 1703, and back to Moscow in 1918. Did those name changes and geographic relocations affect the way the executive power in the Russian state functioned? Were they just symbolic measures or a reflection of great changes?

KEY DEVELOPMENTS

The executive branch of government in today's Russia is the paramount power. Although the judicial and legislative branches are constitutionally independent, the executive branch is in almost full control in most areas of life. To understand the nature of executive power in Russia, we have to examine briefly some key events of the 1990s and 2000s that have largely shaped the executive branch of the government today.

First, there was a peaceful transformation of executive power in Russia at the end of 1991, when the former Soviet Union disappeared from the map and the new Russian state emerged. Russia as a state preserved practically all the major government institutions left from the Soviet period.

The second key development was the constitutional crisis of the fall of 1993 and the adoption of a new Constitution later that year. The Constitution provided the legal foundation for the major principles of functioning of the Russian government. The adoption of the Constitution was instrumental in creating a very strong executive and relatively weak legislative and judiciary branches. The powerful office of president exercised its power during the 1996 presidential elections and kept President Yeltsin in office until 1999, when he resigned.

The third key development was the establishment of an uninterrupted transition of power from an incumbent to a handpicked successor (Shevtsova, 2005). Yeltsin chose Vladimir Putin, who later became Russia's second president. Putin further strengthened the executive branch during his two constitutional terms. The 2008 election of Putin's personally chosen successor, Dmitry Medvedev, reaffirmed this mechanism of power transition. Such precedents are common in history. What was almost unprecedented is that Medvedev, as president, recommended that Putin replace him after Medvedev's term was about to expire. Putin was again elected president in 2012 and 2018.

The adoption of the Constitution

Poland, Ukraine, and Slovakia, as well as some other countries that, like Russia, underwent democratic transition in the 1990s, produced strong parliamentary systems with relatively weak executive branches. Why did Russia produce a very strong executive branch?

One of the answers lies in the Constitution of the Russian Federation. The very way it was created was remarkable. Although the Constitution was adopted at the end of 1993, the preparations had begun almost four years earlier. The initial drafts appeared in 1990 when Russia was still a part of the Soviet Union. These drafts received only lukewarm support from the parliament, so work on the Constitution continued. The second draft was ready a year later, in 1991. Heated debates continued. By the spring of 1992, the Constitution still appeared unsatisfactory to the leadership of the Congress of People's Deputies. The tensions between the legislative branch and President Yeltsin grew: he wanted the Constitution to be adopted as soon as possible, while the majority in the legislature, including its leadership and its chair, Ruslan Khasbulatov (b. 1942), wanted to see a different version of the basic law. Besides Khasbulatov, the opposition included the Vice President Alexander Rutskoy (b. 1947) and many regional leaders.

Several factors contributed to these disagreements and tensions. The uncertainty of the political and economic situation in Russia and the absence of a dominant political party gave various political forces seemingly great opportunities. Many political groups competed for influence and a chance to draft a Constitution that would be favorable to them. This led to an open political struggle in Moscow, and especially within the Russian parliament. Moreover, the office of the president and his closest advisers did not have sufficient political skills to deal with different political groups or make valuable tactical concessions. Unlike today in Russia, the president in 1993 faced a generally unfriendly parliament. These developments caused serious delays in the process of the Constitution's adoption.

The conflict

The disagreement between Yeltsin and the parliament ended with violent conflict. The leaders of the parliament, who had been elected in the Soviet times, wanted to have a Constitution that would guarantee a strong parliamentary republic (Khasbulatov, 2008). Yeltsin, on the other hand, expected to build a strong presidential republic with a weak legislature. Next, Yeltsin wanted to develop a new economy based on the major principles of economic liberalism. His opponents opposed policies of economic liberalization in favor of government regulation and a welfare state (Filatov, 2008).

The hostility between supporters of the president on the one side and, on the other, supporters of the Supreme Soviet, intensified. Tensions in Moscow rapidly escalated. On October 3 and 4, 1993, deadly confrontations paralyzed the city. Moscow's police were paralyzed due to internal disagreements. Facing the magnitude of the situation, Yeltsin turned to the military. It was a historic decision. Several generals who were loyal to him rapidly gained control over the city. They launched a full-scale military assault, with tanks and machine guns, on the parliament building (CNN broadcast this event live). After a deadly battle, the members of the Supreme Soviet and their armed defenders were overwhelmed and arrested. They were all pardoned a few months later. The 1993 confrontation was a small-scale civil war with huge consequences. Fifteen years later, a survey found that almost 80 percent of the surveyed could not choose between the "right" or "guilty" side in this conflict (Levada, 2008d). In 2017, 71 percent of Russians maintained the same view (not supporting either side) of the conflict (Levada, 2017b).

On October 9, Yeltsin ordered the ending of the activities of all soviets (in other words, all kinds of elected parliaments) at all districts in Russia, and on November 10 a new draft of the Constitution was published. Yeltsin then proceeded hurriedly to hold a national referendum to approve the new Constitution. In December, the Constitution, with 58 percent of those voting in favor, was accepted. Yeltsin and his supporters had won a historic political victory. On the same day, people voted for the delegates to a new Russian parliament, a two-chamber institution including the Duma and the Federation Council (Yeltsin, 1994). This quick and decisive political development determined the future of the country for decades to come.

THE PRESIDENT OF THE RUSSIAN FEDERATION

The position of president was established in 1991 as the result of a referendum of the citizens of the Russian Federation, then a part of the Soviet Union. On June 12, 1991, Yeltsin was elected the first president of the Russian Soviet Federal Socialist Republic. The Constitution of the Russian Federation of 1993 drastically changed the functioning of the presidency.

As the head of state in Russia, the president has vast powers and responsibilities compared with those granted to presidents in many other countries with a similar political system rooted in democratic principles. According to the Constitution, the president is the guarantor and protector of the rights and liberties of Russian citizens. He (in the text of the Constitution, in the Russian language, the president is always referred to as "he," not "she") defines domestic and foreign policy. Initially the presidential term was four years. An amendment to the Constitution adopted in 2008 extended the term of the presidency to six years after 2012, with a maximum of two terms. About 60 percent of people surveyed supported this constitutional amendment at that time—which was a sign of their support of President Putin (Levada, 2008d). In 2020, in a new series of constitutional amendments, the terms of presidency were potentially extended for the incumbent president until 2036. The presidential elections are direct. Any citizen of Russia aged more than 35, who has lived in the country for more than ten years, has the right to run for the presidency. No one can occupy the office of president for more than two consecutive terms, according to the Constitution (due to legal and procedural maneuvering in 2020, the application of this rule has been reconsidered; see Chapter 6). However, former presidents may run again in the future. The president can be impeached if he has failed to adhere to the Constitution. There is a complicated procedure for impeachment by the legislative branch of the Russian Federation: first the State Duma petitions the Federation Council, then the Council carries out the impeachment hearings (this procedure resembles the United States' federal laws related to impeachment).

President's functions

As *head of state*, the president has to protect the Constitution as well as the sovereignty and territorial integrity of Russia. The president also coordinates the functioning of federal institutions and represents Russia internationally. The president is the *chief executive officer*

of the State. One of his major responsibilities is to outline both domestic and foreign policies. The president is the *commander in chief* of the armed forces of the Russian Federation.
In the event of actual or potential aggression against the country, the president may impose
martial law, a temporary system of administration of justice under the control of the military. This system may be established on the whole territory of Russia or only in one or
several areas. The president also appoints a prime minister (the accurate translation is
Chair of the Government of the Russian Federation). This must be done with the consent
of the State Duma (the lower chamber of the Russian parliament: see Chapter 5): the Duma
must vote and approve the candidacy. The president also appoints ministers, and has the
right to be present and serve as a chair during the Government of the Russian Federation's
meetings.

The president is the *chief legislator.* He introduces bills (drafts of laws) to the Duma. The
president also signs bills passed by the Duma into law. In addition, as a chief legislator, the
president can issue his own executive orders, which are mandatory within the territory of
the Russian Federation. Presidents have the right to grant political asylum to individuals
seeking it, and to issue a pardon or show clemency to (that is, reduce the sentence of) convicted criminals. The president has legal immunity: while he is in office, the law protects
him against prosecution or other legal claims. However, the immunity is not absolute.
Article 93 of the Constitution establishes the procedures necessary to impeach a sitting
president. Legally, the upper chamber of the legislature has the right to impeach, but it
must receive formal supporting decisions from the upper courts of the Russian Federation
(the Supreme Court and the Constitutional Court; see Chapter 6 for details).

In the event of the president's illness or incapability, the chair of the Government of the
Russian Federation (see later in this chapter) takes over and becomes a provisional president. In this case, the provisional president may not dissolve the legislature (the Duma), call
a national referendum, or amend the Constitution. According to the Constitution, as the
chief diplomat, the president appoints ambassadors, interacts with diplomats from other
states, and has the authority to sign international agreements on behalf of the Russian
Federation. This function is common in the constitutionally prescribed activities of presidents of many other countries.

As you can see, according to the Constitution, Russian presidents receive a superior position in the structure of the government. The president exercises significant executive and
legislative powers. Presidents can exercise judicial powers as well. For example, they can
make legal decisions such as issuing pardons or settling conflicts between the federal and
regional governments (Nikonov, 2003: 23).

Obviously, one person cannot perform all these executive and legislative functions alone.
As in other countries, Russian presidents as the highest executive officers rely on a vast
government bureaucracy. Among the most important institutions are the Government of
the Russian Federation (the Cabinet of Ministers), the Presidential Administration, and the
Security Council of the Russian Federation. There are other powerful agencies as well, which
we will examine later in every chapter.

Key figure: Vladimir Putin (1952–)

Vladimir Putin was born in 1952 in Leningrad and grew up in a working-class family with a modest income. His excellent grades in high school combined with his family's social background helped him gain admission to the prestigious Leningrad State University (in the Soviet Union, universities had to follow quotas to admit qualified students from working-class backgrounds) (Photo 4.1). He joined the Communist Party as a student. Membership was limited, yet highly desirable for anyone aspiring

Photo 4.1 St Petersburg State University, alma mater of President Vladimir Putin and former President Dmitry Medvedev

to a successful career in the Soviet Union. After obtaining a law degree (in Russia, this was a five year undergraduate degree), Putin received an offer to join the Committee for State Security (known as the KGB) in 1975. He ended up working there for 15 years. The KGB was a federal agency with a vast range of responsibilities including domestic spying and foreign intelligence. After 1985, Putin served as an intelligence officer in East Germany. There, he improved his German language skills and gained some experience in international affairs.

In the late 1980s, Putin had to consider new opportunities in the rapidly changing society. History shows (look at the French or American revolutions, for example) that some individuals can reach political stardom somewhat rapidly—all by having certain personality qualities and by being in the right place at the right time. Putin was one such individual. A former security officer, a university bureaucrat, he soon joined the office of the Mayor of St Petersburg. His new boss, Anatoly Sobchak (1937–2000) had once been Putin's professor. By the mid-1990s, Putin was working as a deputy mayor in St Petersburg. In 1997, after Sobchak lost in regional elections, Putin moved to Moscow (thanks to Putin's connections) as a Deputy Head of the Presidential Administration. After 1998, he took over the Federal Security Service (FSB).

Meanwhile, by the summer of 1999, Yeltsin was losing popularity across the country. The economic and financial situation was worsening. Illness and other personal factors, including alcohol-related problems, contributed to Yeltsin's notorious inefficiency as a leader. Under pressure, on August 9, Yeltsin sacked his entire government and named a new acting premier, Vladimir Putin. Yeltsin also named Putin as his choice to succeed him as president. Less than five months later, on December 31, Yeltsin, brushing away tears and pleading forgiveness, announced that he was resigning in favor of Putin, who became acting president (Sigelman and Shiraev, 2002). In essence, the outgoing president of Russia had handpicked the new one. Putin easily won presidential elections in 2000 and 2008. When President Putin's second presidential term was about to expire, he announced his support for Dmitry Medvedev (b. 1966), a lawyer by education and a long-time associate of Putin's, to run for the presidency. Putin agreed to serve as the chair of the government (prime minister) if Medvedev were elected in 2008. After Medvedev took office as president, he needed to deal with the common belief that Putin was still in total control of the country. Medvedev, commonly seen as Putin's handpicked successor, tried to dispel the assumption that his high position was a political maneuver to give Putin a chance to return to the presidency in 2012. Putin won the presidency again in 2018. In 2020, Putin proposed a constitutional amendment that would allow him to run in future elections and remain in power until 2036, when he will be 83.

THE TRANSFORMATION OF THE EXECUTIVE BRANCH

The early evolution of the system (1991–2000)

Back in 1991, the president of the Russian Federation established by executive order a new system according to which he, as president, would appoint the heads of the regional administrations and autonomous republics. The appointed heads of administrations were there to appoint the heads of city governments and other smaller administrative units (Presidential Decree, 1991). By 1992, most regions had established new administrations. In 1995, Yeltsin issued an executive order allowing regional leaders to be elected, not appointed from Moscow. By the end of 1996, elections had taken place in almost all regions of Russia. This was an important step toward democracy, a sign that the Kremlin was gradually giving political power away to the regions.

Critics, however, pointed out that Yeltsin's policies had weakened federal government and its ability to manage. One of the key arguments is that, in the mid-1990s, the regions received too much power (Isaev and Baranov, 2009). Many power-sharing treaties between the Kremlin and the regions that were signed around 1994 created confusion (Hughes, 1996: 40; Treisman, 1996a).

Strengthening the executive branch

In a remarkably short period, Putin transformed from an obscure functionary into the most powerful man in the country. He came from within the government system. He was part of it and promised to preserve it by consolidating power in the president's hands. Putin first relied mainly on Yeltsin's Kremlin insiders. In 2000, he began to build his own team of political players (Boxer and Hale, 2000: 2). He wanted to amend the Constitution by drawing attention to the many weaknesses of a decentralized system of management in a country of Russia's size. There were several specific reasons for strengthening the executive branch.

First, the president and his aides were increasingly dissatisfied with the Kremlin's inability to manage federal policies. Throughout the 1990s, the regions of Russia had received significant material and financial resources. About 60 percent of the federal budget was under the control of the regions (Gelman, 2006). Regional leaders, encouraged by local businesses and political groups, were constantly creating legal obstacles and barriers to increase their independence from Moscow.

The second reason was the complexity caused by the multiple bilateral agreements between regions and the federal government. Some of these agreements would give certain regions more power compared with others. Again, in many cases these agreements contradicted existing federal laws. The third reason was the rapid growth of local businesses and political, and ethnic elites, who were becoming increasingly powerful. Putin and his team saw this as a threat to the executive power of the Kremlin. Putin wanted to restore Moscow's authority.

From the spring of 2000 onwards, President Putin began to build and strengthen Russia's **"power vertical"** (or "vertical of power"—the term frequently used in Putin's speeches and in the media between 2000 and 2008). There is no really satisfactory English translation for this term, which stands for a strong hierarchy in the power system, a kind of line of subordination. In the eyes of Putin's supporters, this term meant an efficient system of management from top to bottom (Bourdeaux, 2012). Others saw the "power vertical" as an unprecedented strengthening and consolidation of Moscow's authority and the weakening of Russia's regions.

What is the structure of the executive branch today, and how does it function?

The Presidential Administration (the executive office)

The key functions of the Administration are mostly legislative, and oversight related. In terms of legislative functions, the Administration is responsible for the preparation of legislative initiatives for the Duma's consideration. The second function is to monitor the implementation of federal legislation and the president's directives. The third function is coordination and communication with government and nongovernment organizations within Russia and abroad. The president is formally in charge of the Administration. However, there is also a head of the Administration (chief of staff) who coordinates day-to-day work. The chief of staff has several deputies. The Administration employs around 2,000 people, and has about 20 major departments including legal, domestic politics, foreign policy, federal awards, constitutional rights, and others. The press secretary, head of protocol, aides and advisers to the president, the president's representatives in state offices, and the president's representative on the European Human Rights Commission also work for the Administration. The Office of Management takes care of financial and other technical issues.

The Presidential Administration is located in Moscow, and has offices in several buildings inside the Kremlin and in the vicinity of Staraya Square (whose name is sometimes used to refer to the executive office) and Ilyinka Street, which is associated with the former headquarters of the Central Committee of the Communist Party of the Soviet Union.

An important part of the Administration is the Security Council. Since Putin's return to presidency in 2012, the executive office has expanded significantly.

The Security Council of the Russian Federation

The Security Council advises and assists the president on questions related to the overall security of the country and the protection of Russian citizens' interests from internal and external threats. The Constitution includes the most fundamental provisions justifying the activities of the Security Council. There is also a 1992 law, "On Security," which details the responsibilities of this agency. The president is responsible for the appointment of permanent and provisional members of the Council according to the law. The Council has a secretary who is responsible for its daily operations. Among the permanent members of the Council are the most senior officials of the Russian government, including the prime minister, foreign and defense ministers, and the director of the Federal Security Service.

Among the official responsibilities of the Council are the identification of threats against Russia and Russian interests, the design and preparation of basic strategies related to national security, and the design of federal programs to implement these strategies. The Security Council develops a general strategy for Russia's national security determined by the president (Strategy, 2015; see Chapter 12 for a more detailed description). The Council also prepares recommendations to the president about specific security policies. It makes collective decisions about extraordinary situations that could have significant and catastrophic consequences on Russian territory. The Council makes recommendations to the president about whether or not he should declare a state of emergency in particular regions or, if necessary, in the country. It advises the president about the effectiveness of the existing federal institutions responsible for security and the necessity of creating new ones.

THE GOVERNMENT (CABINET OF MINISTERS) OF THE RUSSIAN FEDERATION

According to the Constitution, the government (Cabinet of Ministers) is a collective body exercising its power over the entire territory of Russia. The Cabinet consists of the chair of the government (prime minister), the deputies, and federal ministers. The president appoints the prime minister with the approval of the Duma. In theory, the Duma can refuse the nomination at least three times. After the third refusal, the president must dissolve the Duma and call new legislative elections. The government (the Cabinet) must resign as soon as a new president is elected. Russian prime ministers are granted substantial legal powers. In case of disagreements and tensions with the Duma, the prime minister can petition the president to dissolve the Duma and call for new elections. This has never happened to date, however. Vladimir Putin, after serving two terms as president, became prime minister in 2008. In 2012, former President Medvedev replaced Putin in this role, and in 2020 Mikhail Mishustin (b. 1966) replaced Medvedev.

Main responsibilities

Overall, the government of the Russian Federation is responsible for the planning of and control over the federal financial policy. One of its major tasks is preparing the federal budget. After the budget is approved by the lower house of the legislature (the Duma), the government is responsible for the budget execution. In addition, the Cabinet also manages the Russian Federation's federal property.

Besides planning and executing foreign and defense policies, the government has to prepare and carry out centralized federal policies in the fields of public education, healthcare, science, culture, social services, and environmental protection. It is also in charge of law enforcement, protection of the private property of Russian citizens, and the investigation and prevention of crime.

The executive branch of the Russian Federation functions on three levels. The first level comprises federal ministries. Their prime responsibility is to conduct federal policy in specific areas such as foreign policy, domestic security, defense, healthcare, education, finance, and agriculture. The second level comprises federal services. They exercise and control the implementation of specific policies. For example, there are institutions such as the Federal Anti-Monopoly Service, the Federal Customs Service, the Federal Service of Federal Statistics, the Labor and Employment Service, and the Patent and Trade Service. Federal agencies compose the third level. Their responsibility is to provide specific federal services. For example, there are federal agencies responsible for tourism, archives, forestry, railroads, and water resources.

After 2012, the top tier of the government of the Russian Federation had 33 executives including prime minister Medvedev, his 10 deputies, and 22 federal ministers (as in 2020).

Web

To learn more about the Administration and other branches of the government in Russia, see the companion website. Also visit www.kremlin.ru and click on the English version.

The president directs the work of several ministries, federal services, and agencies in accordance with the Constitution. Among them are the key Ministries of the Interior, Defense, Justice, and Foreign Affairs, and also the Ministry of Civil Defense and Emergency Services. The prime minister manages the activities of other ministries and a wide range of federal institutions. These include the Ministries of Agriculture, Finance, Transport, Energy, and Economic Development. Russia also has the Ministry of Education (responsible for children's education) and the Ministry of Science and Higher Education, which handles policies in support of scientific research across the country as well as college education. The Ministry of Culture carries out federal polices in support of the arts, including literature, visual and performing arts, museums, archives, libraries, and some other areas. The Ministry of Sports conducts policies in support of amateur sports, and a wide range of youth-related initiatives.

Table 4.1 Ministries of the Russian Federation

Ministries under the control of the president of the Russian Federation	Interior; Defense; Justice; Foreign Affairs; Civil Defense, Emergencies and Disaster Relief
Ministries under the control of the prime minister (chair of the government)	Health; Education; Science and Higher Education; Natural Resources and Environment; Culture; Industry and Trade; Labor and Social Protection; Ministry of Digital Development, Communications, and Mass Media; Agriculture; Transport; Finance; Energy; Sports; Economic Development; Construction, Housing, and Utilities; North Caucasus Affairs; Development of the Russian Far East and the Arctic

By the time you read these pages, some Russian ministries might have been dissolved and some new ones might have appeared (see Table 4.1).

The executive power of the government is based on the Constitution. We should not forget that the Constitution in Russia is a living document. It can be amended according to Articles 134 through 137. Several major developments that provided favorable conditions for the further consolidation and strengthening of the executive power in the country have taken place. We will turn to these later in this chapter and elsewhere in the book.

THE SUBJECTS OF THE RUSSIAN FEDERATION

According to the Constitution (Article 65), the Russian Federation consists of republics, regions (known as oblasts), special regions (known as *kraj*), two cities with special federal status (Moscow and St Petersburg), and autonomous regions. These are the subjects of the Russian Federation or specially recognized territorial units within the federal state. The definitions of these units are fairly complicated, and the exact number of the subjects has changed several times. Both republics and autonomous regions have this status because substantial proportions of their population are of non-Russian ethnic origin. In fact, these regions have limited ethnic autonomy within Russia. One autonomous region (the Jewish Autonomous Region) is based on the religious identity of its residents (although in Russia, Jews are formally defined as an ethnic group). With some exceptions, the borders of most oblasts of the federation are based on historical administrative divisions, dating from the time of the Soviet Union or even earlier. Each kraj must include at least one autonomous (that is, ethnic) region. There were a total of 85 subjects of the Russian Federation in 2020: including geographically defined regions, three cities with special federal status (Moscow, St Petersburg, and Sevastopol), 22 ethnically based republics, and four ethnic districts.

Federal districts

In 2000, Putin created a set of new federal districts, arguing that this new federal system would be more manageable. This was a significant change in the structure of the entire government. A comparison might be a US president announcing that he or she was setting up five major regions in the United States, combining the states into Atlantic, Pacific, Southern,

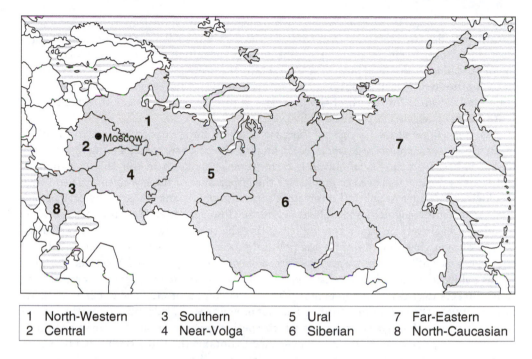

1 North-Western	3 Southern	5 Ural	7 Far-Eastern
2 Central	4 Near-Volga	6 Siberian	8 North-Caucasian

Map 4.1 Russia's federal districts

Midwestern, and Northern blocs and appointing governors there. In Russia there were initially seven of these new administrative units: Northwestern, Central, Southern, Near-Volga, Ural, Siberian, and Far-Eastern. In 2010, the eighth unit, the North Caucasian Federal District, was created (Map 4.1).

A representative of the president has to be appointed for each of the districts. The main task of the representative is to coordinate policies in the region so that they are in agreement with federal policies. As you might expect, the appointment of seven federal "tsars" to the regions almost immediately put them in competition with governors and other regional leaders. In a few years, the representatives, drawing on their direct support from the Kremlin, had gained significant power over governors, and even over some federal ministers and other agencies (Fedorets, 2018; Isaev and Baranov, 2009).

Russia as a federal state: some legal foundations

The Russian Federation is called a *federation* because it is a union of many self-governing subjects. The subjects' rights to make decisions are limited by the Constitution and applicable laws. For example, a subject of the Russian Federation may not send ambassadors to other states, issue its own currency, or form its own army, navy, or air force. However, the subjects may have their own constitutions provided they do not contradict the Constitution of the Russian Federation. In Chapter 5 we will examine in detail the two-chamber parliament called the Federal Assembly, which is the highest legislative body of the Russian

Federation. It consists of the Federation Council and the State Duma. The Federation Council includes two representatives from each subject of the federation. The State Duma is elected according to different principles. The Russian Federation is also a *republic* because its major federal institutions of power are electable by the people. There are term limits related to each office (with small exceptions concerning some legal offices, where some judges are appointed for life). The length of the presidential term is now six years; members of the State Duma are elected for a period of five years.

Russia is a **legal state**. Discussing Russia as a federal state, Russian leaders and scholars often use the term *pravovoye gosudarstvo*. In English, the best way of translating this is to say that it is based on the *rule of law*. This term gained popularity in the 1980s during the Gorbachev reforms. It is used to emphasize the importance of the law in comparison with ideological doctrines or political interests. People and politicians are equal before the law. Their rights are recognized and upheld in courts. However, there is a difference between defining a legal state on paper and implementing the rule of law in practice. A key consequence of overwhelming concentrating political power in the executive branch, as history shows, is a lack of transparency and the spread of corruption (Welu and Muchnik, 2009).

The subjects of the Federation have equal rights before the federal government. In addition, subjects may reach an agreement with the federal government about how to share power between them. The Constitution does not provide specific rules about how the regions should organize their governments or which specific governmental structures should be established. Typically, every regional government contains the three traditional branches: executive, judicial, and legislative. A common feature is that, in all subjects of the Russian Federation, the legislative organs must be reelected at least every four years. Another common feature in the recent past was that most senior executives in each subject were elected by local parliaments based on the recommendation of the president of Russia. This practice began to change in 2012, and more power has gradually been given to the regions.

Regional authorities exercise a wide range of responsibilities not determined by the federal government. In most cases, they do not need permission from Moscow to build roads or factories, hire and fire local officials, or allocate funds for various social projects. The interaction between federal and regional powers is frequently ambiguous. On the one hand, federal authorities have not yet put together a cohesive and uniform strategy to manage the regions. On the other hand, the Constitution itself gives federal authorities in Moscow a wide range of responsibilities on the regional level. This overcentralized nature of executive power in Russia unnecessarily reduces the capabilities of the regions. The lack of regional power also leads many regional leaders to seek special economic and political privileges. In other words, under contemporary conditions, those regional leaders with ties in Moscow are often able to bring more benefits to their regions compared with other leaders who do not have such connections.

Before 2000, governors and chairs of local legislatures automatically became members of the upper chamber of the Russian parliament. Putin discontinued this practice. He believed that the governors were gaining too much power as executive officers and legislators, often working their way into the institutions of power in Moscow. Putin annulled most individual treaties between the federal government and the regions. The president also accorded his office the right to dismiss governors and even local legislatures should they not follow some types of legal instruction from the courts. In this new system, there were also regional executive officials who were responsible for the implementation of federal laws and other decisions passed down from Moscow.

The most substantial reform took place in 2004, and it was a fundamental change in the way governors were selected. In the future, the president would suggest candidates for local governor and top executive officer posts, and the local legislatures would then have the opportunity to approve them. In reality, the reform meant in the eyes of many observers that the Kremlin simply appointed governors.

In an attempt to preserve some democratic principles of collegiality, a State Council (*Gosudarstvennyj Soviet*) was set up as a forum for the governors. This was broadly similar to a council established by Tsar Alexander I (1777–1825). As in the 19th century, the 21st-century Russian State Council does not have significant influence over important decisions made in the Kremlin. The Council is convened approximately four times a year. Between sessions, a temporary committee of seven governors is regularly cycled to avoid a concentration of power among a few individuals. To stimulate dialogue between federal authorities and ordinary people, a special institution, the Public Chamber, was set up in 2005. Prominent Russian individuals were appointed to this and given the role of conveying public opinion to the president, keeping him informed about ordinary people's views of his policies. The Chamber remains an institution with mostly symbolic powers.

Local government

Article 12 of the Constitution establishes local self-governance. The Constitution recognizes the ability of local authorities to manage a wide range of affairs in small villages and towns all across Russia. Local governments are not part of the system of federal government or of the governments of the subjects of the Federation. Individuals in charge of local government are either directly elected by local citizens or appointed under local institutions. Representative legislative institutions in larger towns are elected directly, not through party lists; there are none for towns and villages with a population under 5,000. In these cases, local authorities are required to call regular meetings so that people can ask questions, make requests, and discuss issues of their choosing. Federal and regional authorities can delegate certain powers to local governments, including decisions on property rights.

In reality, however, local governments have very little power. Local officers do not make decisions on most legal issues, which have to be decided at higher levels. For many years now, local governments have had to cope with power shifting to the regional centers. Local authorities also face chronic budgetary problems. In most cases, they have little capacity to collect taxes without seeking approval from the center. There were some attempts at recentralization of local power in the 1990s, but these were insufficient and unsuccessful (Lankina, 2004: 35). Corruption in Russia remains a serious problem (Freedom House, 2019).

THE RUSSIAN ESTABLISHMENT AND ITS EVOLUTION

In political science, an **elite** is a small group of people who control a disproportionate amount of wealth, political power, or both. In comparative politics this group is often called the establishment. It has significant power to influence most government policies in a country, directly and not. For decades, political scientists have studied elites and their political influence in different countries and Russia has been no exception. These studies, known as elite theory, have proposed that the establishment holds the most power and that the democratic process does not necessarily have a decisive impact on the elite's power. However, each country's elites evolve due to internal competition as well as many domestic and international factors (Bottomore, 1993).

Russia's new political elites were forming in the 1990s, after the collapse of the Soviet Union. Unlike in Poland (just to compare), where in the 1980s a formidable political opposition took shape and challenged the communist government, the Soviet Union faced a different political reality. The opposition to the Communist Party was diverse but disorganized. Gorbachev believed that he would be able to maintain control of many emerging political groups and movements, steer them in the right direction, and preserve his own power and, as a result, the establishment. He was mistaken and as a result lost his power. There have been at least three interconnected stages in the transformation of the Russian establishment since the implosion of the Soviet Union.

In the first stage, an eclectic group of decision makers emerged. They gained their positions in the federal government and other institutions because of their proximity to Boris Yeltsin or his most trusted political associates. Except for Yeltsin himself, they mostly had little previous political experience and almost no association with the highest echelons of the Communist Party. Yeltsin surrounded himself with mostly young academics and professionals such as economists, lawyers, social scientists, and others with scholarly degrees. The struggle between the Yeltsin camp and the opposition, as you will remember, resulted in the adoption of the 1993 Constitution (Khasbulatov, 2004, 2008).

In the second stage, from the mid-1990s to 2000, a relatively new type of establishment emerged and gained strength. The main feature of this group was their growing association with big business and the emerging political class in the Kremlin (Gatman-Golutvina, 2000). Using legal and—allegedly—illegal means, in a very short period, the most successful individuals became owners of these vast resources. In a few years a relatively small group of individuals acquired enormous wealth. They all supported the political system, but now they needed even more political power for themselves (Gatman-Golutvina, 2000). As new industrial, oil, and banking magnates, they sought government influence by providing generous financial support for federal programs, paying off federal debts, and even financing the presidential election campaign in 1996 (Barner-Barry, 1999). At the same time, Yeltsin—physically ailing and inefficient as a statesman—was becoming increasingly reliant on loyal security, military, and law enforcement officials (known as *siloviki* in Russia or, literally, "muscle people"). They provided a visible presence of solid support for him personally and for the groups supporting him (Roxburgh, 2012a; Gudkov, 2012). Still most important, Yeltsin himself made political decisions in Russia in the late 1990s. His most trusted family members (such as his daughter and his son-in-law) and a few members of his inner circle were also crucial in making the most important decisions.

In his memoirs, Yeltsin stated that he wanted to have a military man as his successor in the Kremlin; after considering several candidates, he chose an almost unknown colonel, Putin, who represented an elite group of *siloviki* that maintained generally conservative and nationalist views of Russia and its domestic and foreign policy. Like Putin, many members of the military and security elites retained their Soviet-era views of Russia, its people, and their country's role in global affairs (Yeltsin, 2000).

In the third stage, the 2000s, Putin increased federal control over increasingly vast areas of life in general and Russia's regions in particular (Gudkov, 2012; McFaul and Stoner-Weiss, 2008). Early during his tenure as president, the most important government positions in Moscow went to Putin's associates who had worked with him during his tenure in the office of mayor of St Petersburg in the 1990s. Many strategic government jobs later went to former security officials. This shift was noticeable, and its significance for Russian political life was obvious: Russia's establishment, its top echelons of power, were designed according to Putin's strategic concept of the "power vertical" (see the section "The transformation of the executive branch," earlier in this chapter). A viable political opposition in the top echelons of power had been drastically diminished (Greenberg, 2008).

Supporters of Putin's policies insisted that such a shift toward a tightening of Putin's power was inevitable and even desirable: after the decade of instability under Yeltsin, a "strong hand" in the government had finally emerged. Even during the four-year tenure of Medvedev as president after 2008, Putin still de facto controlled most important government decisions (Johnson and White, 2012; Fortescue, 2012). Critics thus maintained that, since the early 2000s, Russia was increasingly transforming into an authoritarian state (Shlapentokh, 2014; Sestanovich, 2020) with an increasingly narrow circle of people who ruled the country after 2012 (Zygar, 2017). A few outspoken insiders and supporters of the government in Russia believed that the system is the only right and effective one for Russia, considering its long history and contemporary context (Surkov, 2019).

CRITICAL THINKING ABOUT THE EXECUTIVE BRANCH

The strengthening of the federal power in today's Russia is a direct and logical outcome of domestic political struggles during the first decade after the disappearance of the Soviet Union. Will the process of centralization continue further? Will Moscow allow more power to other branches of the federal government? Will Russia soon see a wave of democratic reforms in the executive branch? As you can imagine, opinions vary. Many opinions discuss a very important question before addressing others: "How long will President Putin remain in power?"

Authoritarian power consolidation

It is apparent to many experts that Putin, from his early days as president, has been strengthening Russia's **authoritarian system** (Stoner-Weiss, 2006b), which already existed under Yeltsin. A political system is authoritarian if it is mostly nondemocratic and based on the arbitrary rule of a few individuals or groups, not necessarily and always the rule of law. This system has a strong executive branch. It often stages politically meaningless or even rigged elections in which winners and losers are decided in advance. Authoritarian systems typically suppress political opposition. The system also restricts some civil liberties and has a weak civil society (Brownlee, 2007). Based on these criteria, the Russian government had all the necessary features of an authoritarian system (White, 2008).

This system of power consolidation and distribution resembles authoritarian systems of the Middle Ages rooted in political, legal, and financial obligations between powerful "lords" and compliant "vassals" (Shlapentokh and Woods, 2007). Both sides often found these obligations mutually useful. In Russia, the Kremlin needs a vast centralized bureaucracy to manage a big country. The bureaucracy and *siloviki* need a strong center and a strongman such as Putin to cover the lack of political transparency and accountability. In exchange for loyalty, including electoral votes, the bureaucratic chain receives the freedom to use their power in any way they choose, including personal enrichment (Yaffa, 2012). Therefore, attempts to preserve the current power structure, clan-based interests, and personal top-level bureaucratic positions have been the Kremlin's political strategy (Gudkov, 2012). Garry Kasparov, former chess champion and an outspoken critic of Putin, wrote that the Russian president does not care much about ideology. His major concern is the manifestation of his personal power and the hunt for the most effective ways to transfer federal funds into his establishment's private hands (Kasparov, 2012). Similar assessments are common (Zygar, 2017; Myers, 2016).

Russia's authoritarianism is not necessarily unique. Comparative politics provides evidence that presidential systems of government in other countries going through political transition frequently produce authoritarian outcomes (Fish, 2005), especially if these countries do not develop a competitive political opposition (Åslund, 2007: 285). In other words, authoritarianism may be an inevitable by-product of growth or even a temporary answer to instability and chaos in places where self-governance has a very short history (Myers, 2016).

Only a few observers do not emphasize the significance of authoritarian trends in Russia or do not recognize them at all. These commentators come from a diverse field of experts and politicians, mostly living and working in Russia.

A unique Russian system?

Have Western experts and journalists misinterpreted the Russian developmental model and thus view it negatively? Many in Russia think so. They believe that their country has an essentially democratic system with unique Russian features (see Chapter 1). Many experts have referred to Russia as a transitional society, which has not yet chosen a particular way of political and economic development and thus has the right to make mistakes (Gaidar, 2002, 2007). Others have emphasized Russia's relatively wide range of political freedoms despite restrictions (Zaslayskaya, 2004) or similarities between Russian institutions of power and those in the West (Dubin, 2008a; Surkov, 2006). It is argued that, if people did not support the government, it would have been revealed in opinion polls. In fact, after 2000, people have consistently supported Putin in national surveys. The lowest level of trust was expressed in 2011, when only 45 percent trusted Putin. In other years, the number has been as high as 70 percent (CSR, 2012); has increased in 2014, and has since remained in the 60s (Levada, 2019a). It went down in 2000.

Russian experts acknowledge the superior power of the executive branch of their government. At least three arguments justified this superiority. First, a strong executive branch was necessary to correct the mistakes of the 1990s, when weak central power threatened the integrity of the state. Second, this system finds public support. Back in 2008, almost half of all Russians approved of the concentration of power in the hands of one person, whereas just 20 percent rejected this (Dubin, 2008a). Third, attempts to bring in foreign models of democratic governance and apply them in the Russian context have so far been ineffective. Western models rely on the ability of people to self-govern and regulate their relations without a powerful authority. Russian people cannot efficiently self-govern, at least not yet.

Russian leaders themselves have argued that the main accomplishment of Russia's political system has been economic security for its people (Putin, 2012a; Medvedev, 2009b). They argue that the government cannot guarantee immediate improvements in all areas of life.

Stability and predictability are what people want. They want trains that arrive on time, roads paved, and merchandise delivered. To many people, their economic security means more than their individual rights.

Even more daring arguments about Russian executive power have appeared from the statements and articles of Putin's close associates. According to this view, a new "Russian statehood" has emerged and Russia as a country has no choice but to embrace it because other alternatives would be impossible. Russians should reject the discussion of whether they have a democracy in their country and choose realism of history instead: i.e. they have to embrace the system that emerged under Putin (Surkov, 2019). The upper echelons of Russia's establishment and the ordinary people in Russia during its history have always had different lives, although the elites have engaged the masses in various activities, such as wars and political campaigns. But in this century, as far as the argument goes, Putin can finally relate to the masses and respond to their hopes like no other leader in history (Surkov, 2019). It is a unique system. It is also a more efficient political system compared with modern Western democracies. Because in Russia, as it is argued, unlike in the West, most people tend to trust the government.

It will be history's task to judge whether this statement about trust was true and the Russian system of government was more efficient compared with elsewhere. Yet how soon will such historical judgments be made?

The question of how many times

According to the Constitution, President Putin's presidential term would have expired in 2024. He would have been ineligible to run again (Article 81.3 of the Constitution). A new president would be inaugurated in May 2024. Prior to 2020, Putin stated that he would follow this basic law. His advisers confirmed these statements. Nevertheless, many foreign and domestic commentators doubted that Putin would leave. Indeed, in 2020 Putin suggested a series of amendments to the Constitution, mostly superficial, except one. Speaking before the Duma in March, he proposed an amendment that would allow him to run in future elections and remain in power until 2036.

To most, this development was expected. Earlier in his career, President Putin had already created a legal precedent when he temporarily occupied the office of Head of Government to run for and return to the presidency in 2012. Very few doubted that, using similar political and legal maneuvering, he would run again in 2024, and twice after that.

In Russia, based on the views of some Russian insiders described earlier, the law can be adjusted to follow the country's higher "interest"—however the establishment defines it. The Constitution can be amended in times of crises, military conflicts, or other extraordinary circumstances. The 2020 amendment, according to Putin supporters, including top Rossinian judges, was a difficult but necessary measure.

There is, of course, the assumption that Putin will not run in elections again. Will he choose his successor then? Most likely he would, and by doing so he could handpick the next president. This action appeared very likely early in 2020. Will the country wait to see the return of a 72-year-old man back to power in 2024?

CONCLUSION

Observers these days tend to see Russia as a system with strong authoritarian tendencies. To some, Russia has always been an authoritarian power, and changes to neither the name nor location of its capital city indicate anything but symbolic actions. Some, mostly in Russia, endorse the view that the current authoritarian system is the only appropriate one given Russia's economic and social conditions. Authoritarianism, in their view, will not necessarily last forever: most authoritarian tendencies can be reversed due to increasing prosperity or political pressure from the opposition. Other commentators predicted some years ago that it would not take too much effort to "rock the boat" and weaken the current executive branch in Russia (Dmitriev, 2012). History shows that authoritarian systems evolve over time. The examples in history of Spain, South Korea, Portugal, and Chile in the late 20th century should be considered (Remington, 2001). However, the troubling examples of democratic setbacks in Turkey, Iraq, Venezuela, and Egypt paint a different scenario for Russia. It will require an economic breakthrough, plus new talented people, goodwill, and patience, to stay committed to a true democratic change in Russia. Without doubt, Russians will need plenty of these qualities.

5 The Legislative Branch

Article 10 of the Constitution of the Russian Federation guarantees the **separation of powers**. The highest legislative body of the Russian Federation, according to the Constitution, is a parliament called the Federal Assembly. It consists of two chambers, the Federation Council and the State Duma. To understand better how the legislative system works, we will first examine several important developments in the relatively short history of the contemporary Russian legislative branch. Then we will take a look at the structure and functioning of the State Duma and the Federation Council.

It is important to keep in mind that there is a difference between what is written in formal legal documents and the actual reality of Russia. We could probably find such discrepancies, to a certain degree, in many countries. In Russia, this difference is substantial. In theory and on paper, the legislative branch of the government is powerful. In reality, the current legislature has little political power in relation to the executive.

KEY DEVELOPMENTS

Over a period of three decades, Russia has produced a relatively stable legislative system. However, it is different from the legislative systems in the United States, the United Kingdom, and many other democracies. The Russian legislature has become essentially a rubber stamp for the powerful executive branch. While earlier elections in 1993 and 1995 allowed for some strong parliamentary opposition, the following elections brought victory for the ruling pro-Kremlin party. Its victories were less decisive, though, in 2011 and 2016.

Although we discuss elections in Russia in Chapter 8, the following examples will help in understanding how the legislative system in Russia has been forming and evolving. Experts on and students of comparative politics and constitutional law should find them particularly fascinating.

The 1993 elections

The top legislative body in Russia between 1991 and 1993 was called the Supreme Soviet. It was the legislature elected in 1990 by the Congress of People's Deputies. The credentials of the Congress would have expired in 1995. The first chair of the Supreme Soviet was Boris Yeltsin (May 29, 1990 to July 10, 1991) until he was elected president. After the inauguration of the Russian Federation as an independent state, the highest legislative and executive institutions clashed continuously (see Chapter 4). An escalating war of words and legal resolutions grew into an open conflict (Khasbulatov, 2004). President Boris Yeltsin brought in tanks to shell the parliament building. The violent struggle between the executive and legislative branches resulted in the dismissal of the Supreme Soviet, rapid adoption of the Constitution on terms favorable to Yeltsin, and the parliamentary elections of December 1993.

These elections brought a somewhat unexpected success to political forces opposed to Yeltsin. In particular, the Liberal Democratic Party, led by the flamboyant and blunt Vladimir Zhirinovsky, gained 23 percent of the electoral votes, the best result of all the political parties participating that year.

The strong performance of Zhirinovsky and his party in 1993 provided at least three important lessons. First, not only in Russia but also in other countries, large portions of the electorate, very unhappy with the status quo, often have a tendency to vote for individuals or parties offering quick and simplistic solutions to social and economic problems. Second, unlike in some other countries, the victory of the opposition in the legislative elections did not change the policies of the executive branch: the new Russian Constitution had designed a relatively weak legislature (Zorkaya, 2004). Third, the elections of 1993 demonstrated that Russia, at that time, despite many authoritarian trends, was adopting several major features of the democratic political process, including the free competition of ideas, a multiparty system, and a relative transparency in electoral results (Bruter, 1999).

Key figure: Vladimir Zhirinovsky (1946–)

One of the oldest and most visible actors on the Russian political scene is Vladimir Zhirinovsky. Born in 1946 in Kazakhstan, a republic in the Soviet Union, he received college degrees in foreign languages and law. He also earned an advanced degree in philosophy (the topic of his dissertation was *The Past, Present, and Future of the Russian Nation*). Zhirinovsky is one of the founders of the Liberal Democratic Party and became its chair in 1990. This was one of the first political parties registered in the Soviet Union. He was elected to the State Duma consistently after 1993 and served as a faction leader and (by procedural rule) deputy chair of the Duma. He has been in constant but constructive opposition to the government. Zhirinovsky supports the parliamentary system but also praises authoritarian methods of government. His flamboyant rhetoric, verbal insults against his critics, populist proposals, sexist statements, and anti-Western declarations helped him maintain modest public support and eventually the votes necessary to win seats for his party. He is a frequent guest in the media. His critics portray him as a "clown" and an attention-seeking "agitator" (a section in Wikipedia in Russian contains a large separate section about Zhirinovsky's flamboyant acts and inflammatory statements). Supporters suggest he is a populist; they emphasize that his direct talk, uncompromising style, and lack of political correctness all make him stand out. For many years, the Kremlin tolerated his outbursts (Kolesnichenko, 2011). In 2016, he publicly made critical remarks about Hillary Clinton and openly supported candidate Donald Trump, who at that time was running for the presidency of the United States (Shiraev, 2019). Zhirinovsky is a convenient (for the Kremlin) oppositional leader who knows the rules of politics and, despite his aggressive demeanor, never crosses the line in criticizing Putin and his policies.

Changing the rules: elections between 1995 and 2003

According to the Constitution, elections to the Duma, one of the two chambers of the Federal Assembly, are carried out according to special federal laws. The Constitution does not specify the frequency of elections or other details; it simply establishes the number of delegates in the Federation Council (two from each subject of the Federation) and the exact number of deputies for the Duma: 450. The elections of 1995, in accordance with the law, were held two years after the first Duma elections. The law established a four-year period between parliamentary elections in the future.

The emerging electoral system was complicated. Half of the deputies were elected according to party lists: each political party received a number of seats in the Duma that was in proportion to the number of votes cast for it. The minimum threshold (below which the party would not receive any seats) was established at 5 percent. Such thresholds are common in other countries and serve primarily to prevent very small parties from getting seats. The other half of the Duma's deputies were elected in what are known as "one mandate" districts: several candidates run for each seat, and the one gaining the largest number of votes wins. The Federation Council was specified as consisting of the heads of the executive and legislative branches of each and every subject of the Federation, so there were no direct competitive elections for this second chamber of the Federal Assembly.

Because of the electoral thresholds, candidates aspiring to political offices realized how important it was to establish a strong and nationally recognizable political party in order to get more than 5 percent of the votes. They also realized that the chances of a party's succeeding in this would be improved if there were fewer competing parties. The number of parties participating in the elections kept decreasing. In 1999, there were 28, down from 43 four years earlier. In 2003, the number of competing parties was 23. In the process, many small parties were merging to form larger parties.

The elections also revealed that, when the electoral system is untested, elections may turn into a competition between groups taking advantage of the quirks in the legal rules. One successful tactic was for a group of people with significant financial support to form a political party a few months before the Duma elections. Its primary aim was to win seats for these group of people's associates (Bruter, 1999). Once this had been achieved, the party, as an organization, was no longer necessary until the next elections.

The reforms after 2005

A new law of May 18, 2005 called On Elections of the Deputies of the State Duma of the Federal Assembly of the Russian Federation significantly changed the electoral procedures. The law removed all one-mandate districts. All the parliamentary seats were now allocated to the parties in proportion to the number of votes they received. This was obviously a move by the Kremlin to diminish the electoral strength of political forces in the provinces. Now the power to elect candidates was given primarily to national parties and their Moscow headquarters. Forty-two percent of Russian people did not like this law, yet others agreed (Levada, 2009d).

Political parties now faced a more difficult organizational challenge. To nominate candidates for an election, a party had to meet a number of criteria. One of the most important requirements was that it must have at least 50,000 members. As a result, the Justice

Ministry responsible for implementing this regulation registered only 15 political parties, down from 23 during the 2003 Duma elections. Strong parties with a long history of political battles, such as the Communist Party and the Liberal Democratic Party, had no serious difficulty in meeting these new requirements. Many smaller and less organized parties, however, were virtually eliminated. Another important change was an increase in the electoral threshold for gaining seats from 5 to 7 percent. Forecasters quickly calculated that a party would need to get from 5 to 7 million votes to win representation in the Duma. It was a daunting task.

Other legal changes followed. The Central Electoral Commission significantly reduced the number of international observers for the Duma elections (Levchenko, 2007). Although official sources in Russia considered all the elections in the country fair and legitimate, critics disagreed: it now appeared that the new electoral system under centralized federal control had given pro-Kremlin parties (to be discussed in Chapter 7) a substantial advantage.

In the fall of 2008, President Medvedev, who had been elected earlier that year, proposed several amendments to the Constitution, and these were discussed and adopted in a remarkably short period, even by Russia's legal standards. As a result, the presidential term was increased to six years, and in the future, deputies of the State Duma were to be elected to a five-year term. Medvedev argued that the new terms were necessary for the country's stability.

In December 2011, new Duma elections took place. This time, based on new amendments to the law, parties receiving from 5 to 6 percent of the vote could get one seat. Two seats could be awarded to a party receiving from 6 to 7 percent of the vote. As a result, only four major parties kept their presence in the Duma. The opposition and ordinary Russians vigorously disputed the results of the elections and claimed massive electoral fraud. They used the results of exit polls and numerous reports of electoral law violations to argue their position. Moscow and other large cities witnessed mass demonstrations demanding a fair recount or even new elections. Public protests on this scale had not been seen since 1993. The Kremlin took notice.

Further changes took place in the following years. For the 2021 Duma elections, the new rule has been set to have half of the new members elected from one-mandate districts. The other half should be elected according to party lists.

THE STATE DUMA

Russia's first representative institution based on competitive elections was created only a little more than 100 years ago, in 1906. It was called the State Duma. This parliament lasted until 1917. The Russian word *duma* has two origins: it refers to both a council of people and a person's thinking process (close to a "thought" in English). Under Soviet rule, both the State and local legislatures, which were called soviets, were under total control of the Communist Party despite the formal existence of elections. Boris Yeltsin and his supporters returned to the original term "Duma" in the Constitution of 1993, partly as a symbolic gesture of respect for tradition.

Structure of the Duma

The State Duma of the Russian Federation consists of 450 delegates. The Duma elections are called by the president according to the law, usually at the end of the designated year. Since the constitutional amendments of 2008, members of the Duma have been elected for a five-year term. (The First Duma was elected for two years; subsequent ones before this change had a four-year term.) The official voting age in Russia is 18, and the age limit for candidates for the Duma is a little higher at 21. By comparison, in the United States citizens must be 25 to run for Congress and 30 to be eligible to run for the Senate.

The members of the Duma gather in Moscow for regular meetings called sessions. After each election, the new members elect a chair and deputy chairs. These individuals preside over the sessions and supervise the internal rules of the chamber during sessions. To organize and manage its work on a daily basis and in different areas, the Duma creates committees and commissions, exercises parliamentary supervision over many issues within its jurisdiction, and holds parliamentary hearings (see Figure 5.1).

The chair and the chair's deputies are elected by secret ballot. The legislature itself can decide on the number of deputies elected. Usually, party factions in the Duma nominate one candidate for the chairmanship. However, any elected deputy can also run for the chairmanship. The winner must receive more than half of the votes (that is, 226 or more). The chair has a wide range of responsibilities. He or she (there have only been men in this position so far) has to moderate the sessions of the Duma, schedule hearings, and coordinate the activities of the executive staff. The chair represents the Duma in the country and overseas, and coordinates its parliamentary activities with other branches of the Russian government. The chair can distribute certain responsibilities among the deputies according to the law. In theory, the Duma may override any internal order or decision of the chair by voting to veto it.

The chair also directs the activities of the Council of the State Duma. This institution comprises the chair and deputies, and conducts preliminary work on proposed legislation, and other organizational and procedural issues. Ranking members of the Duma have the right to attend its meetings and offer suggestions related to procedural questions (Organizational Procedures of the Duma, 1998).

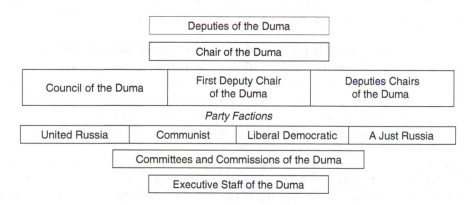

Figure 5.1 Structure of the State Duma elected in 2016

The deputies of the State Duma organize **party factions**, which are defined by the law as an association of the deputies elected according to their party list. In other words, speaking of the last elections, this is the group of elected representatives belonging to a party that received more than 7 percent of the votes and thus gained seats in the parliament. Each elected deputy can join only one party faction, and each one elects a head and deputies.

The Duma committees

According to the Constitution (Article 101), the State Duma forms parliamentary committees. Each committee works within a particular policy area. Committees have many functions, but mention of four will serve to illustrate their work:

- committees submit their proposals and comments for a forthcoming session of the Duma;
- they discuss drafts of legislation (in other words, bills) and propose changes, if they think it necessary;
- they work on various assignments given to them by the Duma;
- finally, they evaluate the implementation of the laws passed by the Duma.

There were 26 committees in the Duma in 2020, but the number is not fixed: it depends on the legislature's own decisions. Some new committees are assembled, and others dissolved. There are committees—fairly standard in most other countries—on labor and social policy, budget and taxes, energy, transportation, defense, foreign policy, science, education, culture, youth activities, sports, and so forth. The federal and local governments sponsor and supervise amateur sports in Russia, which is why the Duma has a special committee on recreational and competitive sports.

In the Duma, as in most legislatures in the world, deputies are appointed to committees largely on the basis of their experience. For example, specialists in agriculture tend to serve on agriculture-related committees, and former army officers are likely to join the defense committee. The committee membership also reflects each faction's proportional size in the Duma, so if one political party has a majority in the Duma, it will also have a majority on every committee. Individual deputies can serve on several committees, and the number of people on each committee varies, but it must be between 12 and 35, as the 2007 law required (Duma, 2007).

The Duma can also establish special **parliamentary commissions** to address more or less immediate questions related to the work of the legislature, a policy issue, or the implementation of previous decisions of the Duma. These commissions are typically set up on a temporary basis.

The Constitution sets out the conditions under which the Duma can be dissolved, and the procedures for doing this. It can be dissolved by the president of the Russian Federation, but only under special circumstances (see Chapter 4). The president may not dissolve it within one year of its election, and it also cannot be dissolved in the period between its bringing accusations against the president and a decision being taken on them by the Federation Council. It also cannot be dissolved during any period of a state of emergency or martial law throughout the territory of the Russian Federation, or within six months of the expiration of the president's term of office. So far, no president has attempted to dissolve the Duma.

Yeltsin's struggle with the legislature, as one should remember, took place weeks before the first Duma elections in 1993.

Functioning of the Duma

The Constitution establishes the jurisdiction of the State Duma. Jurisdiction means the practical authority or specific rights given to a government institution or branch of power. It sets specific limitations on how much power the Duma can exercise. It also, in theory, prevents future arguments or even conflicts with other government institutions about who makes decisions and under which circumstances. In particular, the State Duma:

- approves the president's nomination for chair of the Government of the Russian Federation (prime minister);
- makes decisions on confidence in the Government of the Russian Federation;
- appoints and can dismiss the chair of the Central Bank of the Russian Federation;
- appoints and can dismiss the chair of the Accounting Chamber and half of its staff of auditors;
- appoints and can dismiss the plenipotentiary for human rights acting in accordance with federal constitutional law;
- can grant amnesties (in criminal cases);
- can bring charges against the president of the Russian Federation for his impeachment.

All deputies of the Duma have the right of **legislative initiative**. This term commonly refers to the legal ability or capacity of an individual or institution to introduce proposals with a view to their becoming law. In Russia, the deputies can introduce draft laws (commonly called bills in the United States) for consideration. The State Duma also adopts resolutions on the issues within its jurisdiction. To be passed, these resolutions must be adopted by a majority of the votes of all deputies in the legislature. There are some exceptions related to special types of votes for which the Constitution sets special conditions. Once adopted by the State Duma, a draft does not immediately become law: it is then passed to the Federation Council for review within five days.

In some cases, the Duma and the executive branch must work together. For example, drafts on the introduction of new or the abolition of old taxes, financial exemptions, federal loans, changes in the financial obligations of the State, and other bills related to the federal budget may be introduced to the State Duma only with a corresponding resolution by the Government of the Russian Federation.

The legislative activities of the Duma are coordinated with the Kremlin's strategic plans. This should not be surprising when we recall how the legislative branch was built and developed. Here are just three examples of speedily passed laws. The first one sanctioned the blocking of websites featuring content inappropriate for children. Critics maintained that broad interpretations of the law would allow the government to shut down any website it chooses, including ones on LGBT issues or belonging to political opposition. The second law required nonprofit groups receiving funding from abroad to declare themselves *foreign agents*. This law would open the legal doors for financial audits and other inspections of these groups (Ponomareva, 2012, July 16). Similarly, critics saw this law as an attempt to control nongovernment organizations. The third law imposed harsh penalties (up to

$150,000) for public insult and slander. This legislative act was also widely criticized as directed against political opposition. From the start, the Kremlin showed its support of the proposed legislations, and after their passing by the Duma, they were quickly signed into law.

THE FEDERATION COUNCIL

Originally, the 1993 Constitution prescribed that every subject of the Russian Federation would send two representatives to the upper chamber of the Federal Assembly, the Council of the Federation. One representative was to be sent from its executive, and the other from its legislative branch. From 1995, the governors and speakers of regional legislatures joined the Council automatically. This practice was later discontinued, and a new one established. Although the Federation Council was supposed to represent Russia's diverse regional interests in the federal legislature, most of the changes in the way it is assembled have helped the Kremlin's consolidation of power, and in 2013, further electoral changes were introduced.

Structure of the Federation Council

At first glance, the structure of the Federation Council resembles the structure of the Duma, and indeed of many other legislative chambers in other countries. There is a chair, and also deputy chairs, heads of permanent committees, and executive staff. The members of the Federation Council elect the chair of the Federation Council and his or her deputies.

The chair and the deputies are responsible for organizational, strategic, and procedural questions relevant to the functioning of the chamber. One of their prime responsibilities is to draw up agendas for the Council sessions and submit proposed laws and other decisions to the members for discussion and voting. The chair presides over the sessions. He or she also coordinates the work of the committees. One of many ceremonial responsibilities is to administer an oath to newly appointed judges of the Constitutional Court and new prosecutors general.

The Council of the Chamber assists the chair. This is a collective organ designed to help in the preparation of documents for the sessions. It is a permanent institution which includes the chair, all the deputies, and the chairs of permanent committees of the Federation Council. Members of the Council make decisions collectively by majority vote. They are responsible for numerous procedural questions relating to the sessions, their duration, the list and order of presenters, the number of guests or experts invited to testify, and so forth.

Committees of the Federation Council

The Federation Council, like the State Duma, establishes committees and commissions, which are permanent and work along the lines of major government functions. Most committees of the Council resemble committees of the State Duma. Several of them reflect the differences in the functioning of these two chambers. For example, the Federation Council has a separate committee on order and organization of parliamentary work. There are also committees on regional politics and local self-management. All these committees are involved in parliamentary work related to discussion of new legislation, consideration of legislation (drafts of new laws) sent from the Duma, and supervision of the implementation of certain legislative decisions made in the past. Committees of the Federation Council may work closely with the Duma committees on drafts or legislative issues. There are also temporary commissions that can be assembled to address a specific legislative issue for a limited time.

Membership of the Federation Council

Although there is no official label "Senate" associated with the Federation Council, its members are commonly called "senators" in Russia. The Constitution (Article 95) states that the Federation Council must have two from each subject of the Russian Federation, one from the legislature and the other from the executive branch. A 2004 Federal Law (no. 160 FZ-3) details how the Council is assembled. The Council had 187 members in 2020 (the number may vary based on the number of subjects of the Federation and the fact that the president may personally appoint a few members). They can be either elected by regional legislatures or appointed by regional administrations.

The length of parliamentary service of the members of the Federal Council is not fixed, unlike that for the State Duma. Each senator continues to be a member for as long as is appropriate, depending on the rules for membership that have been established by his or her subject body. For example, if there is an election to the subject legislature, the credentials of this senator will expire at the time of the election. A newly elected legislature is supposed to decide on a new senator (or may keep the old one).

Critics maintain that there are no democratic elections to the Federal Council, because in practice, most decisions on the appointment of senators are made in the Kremlin, which suggests candidates to governors or local legislatures, who simply rubber-stamp them. Not surprisingly, senators disagree. They tend to argue that they have been elected by their local legislature in a democratic and fair manner.

Since Putin became President, almost twenty years ago, there have been only two Chairs of the Council: Sergei Mironov (b. 1953) and Valentina Matvienko (b. 1949), both close associates of Putin since their years together in St Petersburg.

While many people in Russia consider a seat on the Council as an "honorable retirement" for most of its members, many senators continue their active life in government and politics after they leave this legislative body. Thus Dmitry Mezentsev (b. 1959), who once served as First Deputy Chair of the Council, later continued as governor of the Irkutsk Region, head of an influential international organization, and then ambassador to Belarus.

In most (but not all) countries, heads of state may not appoint or dismiss members of parliament. One of the principles affecting this practice is separation of powers, a concept of constitutional law under which the three branches of government (executive, legislative, and judicial) are kept separate. In Russia, however, President Putin has the right to appoint new senators. After 2014, based on a Constitutional amendment, he may add (up to 17 so far) new members of the Council.

Functioning

The Federation Council exercises parliamentary supervision over issues within its jurisdiction and holds parliamentary hearings. The Council and its members have the right of legislative initiative. In other words, they can propose new laws or suggest amendments to existing ones.

The Federation Council must consider bills adopted by the Duma dealing with a number of specific issues and policies, including the federal budget, federal taxes and fees, and other financial and credit-related issues including printing money and issuing financial obligations. It is also required to consider laws that relate to the functioning of Russia as a state. This includes ratification and withdrawal from international treaties, issues about state borders and their protection, and war and peace issues.

The decrees of the Federation Council are adopted by a majority of all deputies to the Council. The sessions of the Federation Council are usually open to the public, but they can be closed in some cases. The Constitution defines the jurisdiction of the Federation Council. The jurisdiction is further explained in relevant laws. For example, the Council can make decisions about the use of the armed forces of the Russian Federation outside its territory. Senators should also approve changes of borders between the subjects of the Russian Federation. The Council also approves the president's decrees on the introduction of martial law (giving the military the right to administer justice for a limited period) and a state of emergency (suspending certain government functions and in some cases particular civil liberties). The Council calls the elections for the president of the Russian Federation and may impeach him. The Council is also responsible for the appointment of judges of the Constitutional Court of the Russian Federation and the Supreme Court of the Russian Federation. Its jurisdiction includes the appointment to office and the removal from office of the prosecutor-general of the Russian Federation.

To exercise control over the federal budget, the Federation Council and the State Duma together appoint an Accounting Chamber, the membership and rules of order of which are determined by federal law. If the Duma passes a bill but the Federation Council rejects it, both chambers may set up a conciliatory commission to try to resolve their differences. Once this has made recommendations, the bill is sent back to the Duma. If two thirds of the Duma members vote for the bill again, it is passed regardless of what the Federation Council decides.

Deputies may not work full-time for other agencies of the federal government or continue to receive a salary for any other activities except for teaching, research, and artistic work. Article 98 of the Constitution specifically acknowledges that the members of the Federal Assembly have legal immunity during their legislative tenure. They may not be arrested or searched, unless the law specifies otherwise, or it is essential to do this immediately for other people's safety. The attorney general can petition for, and a Chamber can approve, cases involving the termination of the legal immunity of certain deputies. For example, in 2019, member of the Council Rauf Arashukov (b. 1986) was arrested right in the conference chamber. He faced murder charges and other serious charges.

The Duma and the Federation Council: joint functions and procedures

The Federation Council and the State Duma normally meet separately, although the chambers may have joint sessions to listen to the addresses of the president of the Russian Federation, addresses of the Constitutional Court, or speeches of foreign leaders. A person may not serve in both chambers of the Federal Assembly simultaneously, and their members may not serve in local government at the same time.

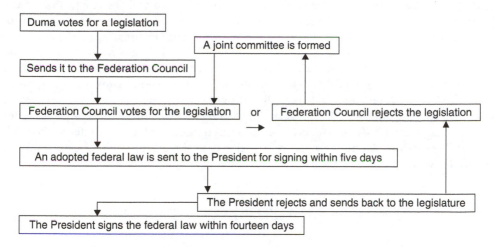

Figure 5.2 Passing a federal law in Russia

How do the Russian legislature and executive power interact to pass federal laws? The procedure is quite complicated (see Figure 5.2). Within five days of a federal law's being passed by the chambers, it is sent to the president of the Russian Federation for signing and publication. The president then has 14 days to sign it and make it available to the public via newspapers and/or the Internet. The president can, however, veto any submitted law. In these circumstances, the State Duma and the Federation Council reconsider it. If, during the second hearings, the federal law is approved in its earlier draft by a majority of not less than two thirds of the total number of deputies of the Federation Council and the State Duma, the president's veto is overridden, and he must sign it into law.

The legislative branch has the right to amend the Constitution, but the majorities required for this to be done are larger. Any amendment must be approved by at least 75 percent of the senators in the Federation Council, two thirds of the members of the Duma, and two thirds of local legislatures. The Constitution can also be dissolved by a decision of an all-state constitutional (constitutive) assembly, which can be called and elected by the people of the Russian Federation for that purpose. (This is much what happened in 1918 when the Bolshevik Party dissolved the first Constituent Assembly.)

Many critical questions about the nature of the political process in Russia arose after the remarkably quick adoption of the amendments to the Constitution in 2008 (extending the lengths of times in office) and particularly in 2020 (changing some procedural rules for the Federation Council and extending presidential terms in office). Critics within Russia and abroad expressed serious concerns about the legality of such actions. According to the law, for example, there is a mandatory one-year period for discussions of any proposed constitutional amendment before it can be adopted by regional legislatures. The Kremlin ignored these critical arguments.

Russia is a presidential republic. The president has significant executive and legislative powers. However, his powers are not unlimited. Not only does the Federal Council have the constitutional right to impeach a sitting president, according to Article 117 of the Constitution the State Duma, but it also has the right to demand the resignation of the government of the Russian Federation (the Cabinet of Ministers). A special normative procedure is set down for this too. If the Duma demands the government's resignation once, the president may or may not agree to satisfy the demand. If the Duma votes for resignation twice within three months, then the president must do one of two things: either dissolve the government or dissolve the Duma itself. In addition, the prime minister (head of government) can initiate a confidence vote regarding the government in the Duma. If the outcome of this is a vote of confidence, the president has the right to dissolve either the government or the Duma. In the 1990s, the Duma occasionally used these legal rules to influence Yeltsin's policies. Because of the strong pro-Kremlin majority in the Duma, such developments are very unlikely these days. Time will tell.

CRITICAL THINKING ABOUT THE LEGISLATIVE BRANCH

Although formally the three government branches are independent and equal in Russia, in reality they are not. As we saw in Chapter 4, Russia is a strong presidential republic with an exceptionally strong executive branch. As a consequence, the legislature in today's Russia is weak. It was designed to stay this way back in the 1990s, long before Putin became president.

Setting a weak legislative branch

Even at the outset, in 1993, the Constitution outlined a legislature that would not challenge the power of the executive branch. President Yeltsin wanted to have a political system in which the Kremlin would have a decisive voice and the final call on most important issues. Later in that decade however, the Duma began to gain strength and occasionally challenge the president: for example, it blocked the president's suggested candidate for prime minister in 1998. Yeltsin and his team continued efforts to weaken the legislature, and especially the power of the most dominant opposition in the 1990s—the Communist Party. They succeeded in this task. President Putin then weakened the legislature further by eliminating "one-mandate" districts and establishing party lists for the Duma elections. Several comparative studies have suggested that, in the past several years, the Russian Duma was among the world's weakest parliamentary assemblies, the decisions of which appear as just rubber-stamped actions under the control of the executive branch. Putin himself mockingly criticized West European parliamentary systems for their difficulties in forming functioning cabinets (Putin, 2020a). Nonetheless, Russia's business and political elites value membership in the Duma, and seats in this legislative body are sought after (Chaisty, 2012). Membership gives its holder an important social status attached to many formal and informal privileges and a network of useful connections.

The Kremlin needs a manageable legislature

Only large and powerful national parties can benefit from the current system of legislative elections. Under this system, as you will remember, even moderately strong parties that managed to overcome the difficult 7 percent barrier might get only a few seats in the parliament. New rules allowing one or two mandates for parties overcoming the 5 percent barrier do not make a significant difference. A one-mandate electoral system, as was used for legislative elections in Russia back in the 1990s, is used now (in combination with party lists) and is probably more democratic. Under this (one district–one member) system, two or more candidates run for a single seat in one geographical district, and the candidate who gets the most votes wins. Common sense suggests that a direct system is, to a greater extent, free from the bureaucracy and deal-making associated with internal party politics. However, it also has drawbacks, as the experience of other countries shows. The United Kingdom, for example, uses a "first-past-the-post" system in which each geographic constituency elects one member of parliament. (This is just one of several types of single-member constituency system, in which only one round of voting takes place and there is no redistribution of votes cast for losing candidates.) It tends to skew election results because small parties that gain significant numbers of votes across the country, but top the poll in only a few, if any, constituencies, get little or no representation, and this discourages their supporters from continuing to vote for them. One of the two largest parties almost always wins enough seats to form a government.

Nevertheless, there is an important difference between the Russian and British political systems. In the United Kingdom, one of the two large parties (plus smaller coalition parties) has been to the left and the other has been to the right of the political spectrum. Either one of these two coalitions is generally expected to win a majority of votes. In Russia, there are two large political parties, the Communist Party and the Liberal Democratic Party, that frequently stand in opposition to the ruling government. In a first-past-the-post system, between them, they might win a majority of the seats in the Duma, while under the present system they win only a sizeable minority. (United Russia, which is a pro-Kremlin party, won the majority of seats in the recent elections, as we will see later in Chapters 7 and 8.) With a majority, the opposition parties would have significantly more power, and this would change the dynamics of the political process. Nevertheless, one particular factor may spark further changes in the way the Duma elections are set. The factor is the diminishing popularity of the pro-Kremlin party and its legislators.

Yet why should authorities in Russia and Putin endorse the one-mandate principle and phase out, as was suggested, party lists? What if a new system produces a legislature that opposes the Kremlin? Although the Duma's power is no match for the power of the Kremlin, the president probably does not want to engage in constant disputes and clashes with the legislature, should the oppositional parties prevail in the future legislature.

One of several possible explanations is the diminishing popularity of pro-Kremlin political parties, the largest in Russia until now (Garmonenko, 2019). If future pro-Kremlin Duma candidates are carefully selected as independent candidates (again, because of the lowering prestige of the pro-Kremlin party), if their campaigns are properly financed, and if their local electoral offices are properly staffed, then the results of the future parliamentary elections should definitively be in favor of the Kremlin. In sum, the changes in the electoral rules in Russia should make sense these days mostly in the context of the interests of the executive branch.

CONCLUSION

Russia's legislature seems to have a solid legal foundation, but it is not fully built. It is relatively ineffective because of the overwhelming power of the executive branch. In theory, the Duma must represent the electoral will of the people. In reality, it represents the will of the executive branch and a political party affiliated with and managed by the Kremlin. It is true that, in other countries, there are political parties that are closely connected to the executive branch. However, citizens of those states have notably greater opportunities to affect the electoral process, vote one party out of power, and elect opposition candidates from other parties. In Russia, the system is different.

The second significant problem is that most outside observers see elections in Russia as not free and as lacking transparency. In particular, reputable foreign and domestic observers reported significant violations during the 2011 and 2016 Duma elections. The Kremlin rejected these accusations as deliberate provocations and fabrications. We will turn to these discussions in Chapter 8.

Historically, the Russian Duma was almost always in a vulnerable position: it was dependent on the will of the emperor of Russia early in the 20th century, and it has been shaped by the political calculations of the president in the 1990s and the 21st century. Several times during the short history of post-communist Russia, the electoral rules for the Federal Assembly have been changed, and there is no guarantee that they will not change again in the near future. Yet most probably, the future of the Russian state will depend on how much real power the legislature can obtain or preserve.

6 The Judicial Branch

The judicial branch has been affected by the same course of important events as the executive and legislative branches since the inception of the Russian Federation as an independent state, including several legislative elections, especially in 1993, and presidential elections. However, the judicial branch in Russia has not experienced dramatic changes or significant turnarounds over this period. Together with the system of justice administration, it has gone through a steady evolvement. Despite these gradual changes that have taken place in the judiciary since the 1990s, it has not achieved independence from the executive branch. The judicial branch—Russia's leaders and their critics talk about this openly—suffers from political interference, bureaucratic delays, and corruption.

KEY DEVELOPMENTS

Among the most noticeable developments have been the preservation and gradual modification of the federal court system and the trial system. The principal source of law in Russia is the Constitution. The Constitution states that only law courts administer justice in Russia. As in other countries, a **court of law** in Russia is supposed to establish the legality or otherwise of a certain action (which could be the behavior of an individual, a decision by an institution, or a government decree, for example), then pass a ruling. Judiciary power is exercised in four major areas: constitutional, civil, administrative, and criminal. The law courts in Russia, as is typical in other countries, constitute a hierarchy, with the higher courts having the right to overrule the decisions of lower courts. The creation of special or extraordinary courts that do not follow the procedures of the ordinary court system is prohibited.

The secondary source of law is the system of codes: in other words, a selection of written laws related to specific areas (Legal Acts of the Russian Federation, 2009). There were 21 such codes in 2020. Among them are the Criminal Code, which describes crimes and corresponding punishments, and the Civil Code, which regulates legal agreements, property rights, intellectual property rights, and so forth. There is also a Civil Procedural Code regulating court procedures in civil cases. Others include the Tax Code, regulating taxation, and the Land Code, which establishes the principles of land rights and regulations.

The federal court system

The Constitution identifies several federal legal bodies and outlines their basic responsibilities. Among them are the Constitutional Court of the Russian Federation, the Supreme Court of the Russian Federation, and various appellate and arbitration courts with established federal jurisdiction. These courts have the right of legislative initiative within their jurisdiction (see Figure 6.1).

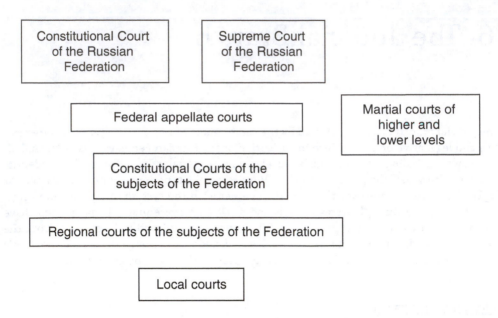

Figure 6.1 The court system of the Russian Federation

A federal judge in Russia must be a Russian citizen and a minimum of 25 years old, and hold a law degree. The Constitution adds another age restriction: an individual must spend at least five years in the legal profession before becoming a federal judge. Federal law may establish additional requirements for federal judges. Judges are prescribed to be independent in their decisions; they may not be suspended, replaced, or fired. They also possess immunity from criminal prosecution. However, federal laws also outline the conditions and grounds for exceptions to these rules. The president of the Russian Federation nominates judges to the Constitutional Court and the Supreme Court, who are then appointed by the Federation Council. Judges of appellate and arbitration federal courts are appointed according to federal law.

The trial system

The Constitution establishes that trials must be conducted on an adversarial and equal basis. According to Article 123 of the Constitution, all trials are open to the public. As in the United States and many other countries, criminal defendants in Russia have the right to appear in person at their trial (Benderskaya, 2008). Back in the Soviet Union, there were often court hearings *in absentia*, especially for the special tribunals and other courts assembled specifically to investigate political crimes at the request of senior Communist Party officials. Today the law in Russia lays down the limited circumstances in which there can be court hearings *in absentia*. For example, the Criminal Procedural Code allows a person accused of a crime (of low severity) to petition for the case to be considered without their being present.

Federal law (July 27, 2006) also allows courts to hear cases of severe crimes in the absence of the accused if they are outside the territory of Russia, or refuse to appear in court, and are not being tried elsewhere for the crime. For example, the North Caucasus district military court sentenced three military officers (who were absent during the trial) to lengthy prison sentences (11–14 years) for murders committed in Chechnya during the long-running military conflict in that area. In another high-profile trial on November 29, 2007, a court in Moscow tried entrepreneur and billionaire Boris Berezovsky (1946–2013) for embezzlement, over the 1996–97 alleged theft of more than $200 million from Aeroflot, a major Russian airline. The verdict was "guilty," and he was sentenced *in absentia* to six years in prison (Trofimova, 2008). In another trial in Russia in 2009, Berezovsky was convicted *in absentia* again in a different case and sentenced to 13 years. In both cases he denied the charges and insisted that politics had influenced these decisions. In 2013, Sergei Magnitsky (1972–2009), a Russian lawyer who died in prison under suspicious circumstances, was also tried *in absentia* (posthumously) and found guilty of tax evasion. This trial and the politics behind it prompted worldwide condemnation and contributed to massive international sanctions against Russia. We will return to this case in Chapter 10 on Russia's foreign policy.

The federal court trial system first began to use jurors years ago and since 2010, this system has been implemented across all Russia. Although there was a jury system in the Soviet Union, the jury members (usually two) directly served the court system and seldom challenged prosecutors and judges. The new system, the establishment of which was suggested but not mandated by the Constitution, was supposed to provide independence for the newly formed category of jurors (Federal Law of August 20, 2004). Further amendments to the law were made in 2016. Any Russian citizen over 25 years of age, without prior criminal convictions or serious psychological impairment, may become a juror. The size of the jury is from 6 to 8 people. However, jury trials have not become common in Russia. Jurors are supposed to be used only for a limited number of criminal cases, and government officials are not especially eager to install this new jury trial system. Critics insist that jury trials are too costly and slow down the adjudication of cases (Shamaev, 2018).

The Russian court system is complex and extremely busy. There are more than 23,000 judges working on federal and local levels. In a single year, the courts hear up to 10 million civil cases, more than 5 million administrative cases, and more than a million criminal cases (Lebedev, 2008; Judicial Department, 2019). How does the judicial system function, what problems does it face, and how does it interact with other branches of the government?

THE CONSTITUTIONAL COURT OF THE RUSSIAN FEDERATION

The Constitutional Court of the Russian Federation was first elected by the Supreme Soviet of the Russian Federation in 1991. The major role of the court is to consider the constitutional legality of laws, presidential decrees, or specific policies of the Russian Federation. During the constitutional crisis of 1993, the chair of the Supreme Court participated in negotiations between the office of the president and the parliament, in attempts to mediate and resolve their disputes. Twice in 1993, the Constitutional Court ruled against President Boris Yeltsin and found his actions—including dismissal of the parliament—to be unconstitutional. These rulings led to impeachment procedures. On September 21 of that year, Yeltsin dismissed the Constitutional Court and suspended its activities. Scholars will be debating the legality of this action of the Russian president for years. However, the court renewed its activities in February 1995. From that moment, its work has been based on the new Constitution and several amendments (Photo 6.1).

Photo 6.1 Two symbols of Russia's power: the building of Russia's Constitutional Court, with the silhouette of the statue of the Emperor Peter the Great on the left

The Court's functions

The Constitution describes the major principles and prerogatives of the Constitutional Court. Its main function is to resolve cases involving the compliance of certain legal decisions, rulings, or treaties with the Constitution of the Russian Federation. For example, a presidential decree, a federal law, an international treaty, or a treaty signed between two subjects of the Federation could be challenged in the Constitutional Court. The Constitutional Court can consider, for example, a hypothetical case in which one of the republics passed a law that might affect the jurisdiction of federal law enforcement within that republic. The court may also consider international treaties, but only if they have not come into force.

The Court has the right to interpret the Constitution. However, to initiate the procedures, a special request must come from the president, the Federal Assembly, the Government of the Russian Federation, or legislatures of subjects of the Russian Federation. Another essential function of the Constitutional Court is passing judgments to resolve disputes over jurisdiction. In other words, the court decides which federal or other government bodies have the legal right to make decisions, and under what circumstances. This is a typical function of most high courts in other countries. Another responsibility is reviewing the laws that might violate the constitutional rights and freedoms of citizens of Russia, on the basis of requests from other federal courts. The Court may also rule on the constitutionality of certain exceptional procedures in particular situations, such as when the president of the Russian Federation is charged with treason or other high crimes such as perjury of oath or refusal to obey a lawful order. (This has never happened so far.)

The Constitutional Court consists of 19 judges who are nominated by the president and then appointed by the Federation Council for 12 years. The court has its permanent residence and holds its meetings in St Petersburg. This is an unusual seat for a federal institution because virtually all other federal agencies are located in Moscow. However, this relocation was partly motivated by the desire of Russian leaders to keep the court away from possible political pressures in Moscow. The judges are divided into two chambers with equal legal powers, one containing ten, and the other nine judges. Some decisions can be made by just one of the chambers; others must be made by all 19 judges together. According to the 2010 Federal Law (#7), the chair of the Court should be nominated by the president and appointed by the Federation Council. The term of the appointment is six years and may be renewed.

Court rulings

During its establishment, the Court has issued thousands of rulings and judgments. Most of them have considered the constitutionality of specific laws and rulings, and, in approximately 15 percent of all cases, lower-court rulings have been overturned (Constitutional Court, 2019). For example, in 1995, the Constitutional Court upheld the decision of the federal government to use military force in the breakaway Province of Chechnya. In 1996, the Court struck down rulings restricting residency in several cities including Moscow. In 2005, the Court declared constitutional the decision of the president to appoint governors or chief executives for the subjects of the Russian Federation. In 2009, the Court ruled that the military might not detain a citizen—against his will—beyond the duration of mandatory military service. In 2019, the Court supported a claim from an individual regarding the comprehensive medical care and financial support he was entitled to due to a medical malpractice incident. There are decisions about customs duties, unemployment benefits, taxes, financial compensations, appeals related to criminal convictions, and many other issues that fall under the Court's jurisdiction. All rulings of the Court are published in Russian (Constitutional Court, 2019).

The Constitutional Court also reviews the constitutionality of certain enacted laws. In a 2012 case, the court considered the constitutionality of two federal laws related to government support to the families of law enforcement officers who had died or been injured in the line of duty (Constitutional Court Decision, March 27, 2012). Another case decided in 2009 was related to the federal law on mental healthcare. Based on an appeal from three Russian citizens, the Court decided that several articles of the Civil Procedural Code and the Federal Law on Psychiatric Help and Citizens' Rights Guarantees were unconstitutional. These provisions denied individuals the right to give testimony before a court that was supposed to determine their mental capabilities, including reasoning. The old law, as the Court found, also limited the right of plaintiffs with psychiatric problems to appeal lower courts' decisions. One substantial application of the Constitutional Court decision related to mental healthcare was that it is now illegal in Russia to commit a person to a mental institution without their consent, unless there is a special court decision (Constitutional Court Decision, February 27, 2009). This ruling was a substantial legal victory for millions of people with psychological dysfunctions and disabilities. The ruling also challenged an old legal and administrative tradition that allowed law enforcement, mental institutions, and relatives to make decisions about hospitalization and treatment on behalf of people with psychological problems, including substance addiction, severe mood disorders, or dementia.

Case in point: a controversial decision of 2020

Early in 2020, President Putin introduced a series of amendments to the Constitution of the Russia Federation. These amendments appeared insignificant, except the one that Putin proposed suddenly on March 10. He suggested a clause prohibiting a person from serving more than two terms (the current Constitution prohibited only two consecutive terms). However, and this was the main point of the amendment, Putin also proposed to "zero out" his own presidential term clocks by instituting that the new two-term limit would take effect only after the next presidential election. In other words, no one may serve more than two terms, but only after 2024. The clear meaning of this change was obvious: Putin was giving himself the right to run for office again, which the current Constitution prohibited. The amendment would eliminate this legal obstacle. Putin also suggested this amendment would stay if the Constitutional Court considered it "constitutional."

From the legal standpoint, this suggestion about the Court was puzzling. Russia's Constitution had been amended four times since 1993, and the Constitutional Court has never reviewed, those amendments for constitutionality. Furthermore, the Court has never been granted such reviewing authority. In previous cases, the Constitutional Court declined to review other constitutional amendments, claiming a lack of jurisdiction (the practical authority to administer justice within a defined field of responsibility).

However, in March 2020, Russia's highest court unanimously, after a hurried discussion behind closed doors, endorsed President Putin's proposed amendment, removing one of the final legal hurdles against his potentially remaining in power until 2036. A national vote was called in April to approve all the amendments including the "zero out" option for Putin. Due to the pandemic, the vote, was rescheduled to take place in June and July of 2020. As expected, Putin supporters claimed a legal victory. Most independent legal experts, however, believed this was a clear political maneuvering revealing how the executive branch was able to exercise its power over the other two branches of the Russian government, the judiciary in particular (RFE/RL, 2020).

THE SUPREME COURT

The Supreme Court of the Russian Federation is the highest judiciary body for civil, criminal, administrative, and other matters. The Supreme Court is different from the Constitutional Court and has jurisdiction over several designated areas. The Court has the right to challenge any decision of the Duma or the Federation Council, or a decree by the president or Cabinet of Ministers. The Court conducts legal reviews of legislative initiatives (requests) from the subjects of the Federation to amend specific federal laws. The Court interprets certain provisions of federal laws or legal codes. The Court also issues recommendations about the applicability of certain laws. It can legally terminate a national political party, a national religious or other social organization, or disagree with a decision of the Central Electoral Commission related to national elections. The Court has the right to designate any group as a terrorist organization (on the basis of the evidence presented to the Court, of course), and ban this group from Russia's territory. The court has jurisdiction over criminal cases filed against a federal judge or an elected member of the Federal Assembly.

This Court also reviews the decisions of lower courts and considers appeals against cases from lower courts. For example, an appeal related to a case decided in St Petersburg might reach the Supreme Court, and one of its judges would decide either to accept the case for consideration or to decline it. The Court may either affirm or reverse the decision of a lower court. If it is reversed, the Supreme Court can either render its own resolution or decide that the case should be reheard in a lower court.

The Supreme Court's structure

Judges of the Supreme Court are nominated by the president of Russia and appointed by the Federation Council. According to the federal law, there are 170 Supreme Court judges. In order to become a judge of the Supreme Court, a citizen of Russia must be 35 or over and have a legal qualification and at least ten years of service in the legal field. The Court consists of several boards or collective panels of judges. For example, the Civil Cases Board deals with civil, social, and labor-related cases. The Economic Cases Board works on business- or trade-related cases. The Criminal Cases Board considers criminal cases, and the Martial Board deals with legal issues related to the Armed Forces. Appeals on the decisions of these boards are brought to the Cassation Board. The Supreme Court studies lower courts' decisions and issues recommendations on how to apply certain laws.

To ensure its work is in touch with legal scholarship and practice, the Court has a special consultative body, the Academic Consultative Council. It consists of the Supreme Court judges, legal scholars, attorneys, and law enforcement professionals. The Presidium of the Supreme Court consists of 13 judges including the chair and deputy chairs (Federal Law, October 28, 1994), and performs coordinating functions, and reviews cases.

Court decisions

To obtain a better sense of how the Supreme Court functions, consider a few examples of verdicts or legal opinions rendered by the Court over the years. For example, in 2008, the Supreme Court stated that car insurance companies should pay out on damage and injury claims from their customers regardless of the person who had been driving the damaged car, provided this person had been driving the vehicle lawfully. Another decision stated that owners of pay parking lots are financially responsible for cars stolen from their property (Kulikov, 2008). There are rulings related to financial transactions. For example, in 2009, the Supreme Court clarified to lower courts some issues regarding monetary debts. Borrowers are responsible for paying back a loan that they take out from a bank, and should the borrower die before repaying the loan, the beneficiaries of their estate (their heirs) are responsible for paying back the debt (Kozlova, 2009). In January 2012, The Court challenged a federal regulation concerning the way inmates (in Russia, all prisons are federal) are transferred by train from one facility to another. The Court found that certain railcars used for transportation fell below legal standards and humanitarian norms related to the treatment of inmates. In 2019, the court ruled that residents of apartment complexes must let representatives of managing companies in to inspect any substantial renovations that residents have made in their apartments, even though they own them. Also in 2019, the Supreme

Court relaxed the rules according to which Russians are charged with possession of firearms and ammunition (they are illegal in Russia unless the owner has an official permit like those given to hunters or law enforcement officers). The Supreme Court's decisions are published in Russian.

Until 2014, Russia had the Supreme Arbitration Court to resolve economic disputes and other cases considered by lower arbitration courts. Citizens, companies, organizations, including foreign ones, could appeal to this Court to resolve their disagreements (Federal Law, April 25, 1995). This institution is now part of an expanded Russian Supreme Court, whose official seat is likely to be moved from Moscow to St Petersburg.

THE RUSSIAN CRIMINAL CODE

The Russian legal system is different from the US, French, and many other countries' legal systems in that it does not normally recognize judicial precedent as a major source of criminal law. The principal source of criminal law is the **Russian Criminal Code**. In general terms, a criminal code is a set of written laws related to criminal offenses and descriptions of a range of punishments that should be imposed on convicted offenders. The Russian Criminal Code specifies the minimum and maximum penalty for each crime it describes. This includes monetary penalties, jail terms, and suspended sentences. The 1997 Criminal Code remains the only legal definition of crimes and corresponding punishments on the territory of the Russian Federation. However, new federal laws can be sources of new amendments and additions.

The current Federal Code, which replaced a 35-year-old Soviet-era code, contains a very detailed and complete list of crimes and related penalties. Comparing the old and new criminal codes, legal experts in Russia maintain that the new one is distinctly oriented toward defending the rights and liberties of the individual, puts less emphasis on the interests of the state, and contains harsher penalties for severe crimes and lighter sentences for minor offenses (Krylova, 2000). Seventy new types of criminal offences were included in the Code along with the elimination of eighty Soviet-era types, such as homosexuality, spreading anti-Soviet propaganda, and possession of foreign currency.

It is important to realize that Russia's criminal law is almost exclusively in the hands of the federal government. Local authorities, such as governors or mayors, and subjects of the Russian Federation may not legislate on criminal law. For example, if the Criminal Code suggests a sentence of three years in prison for a particular type of violent assault, a local legislature may not pass a law or a judge may not extend the punishment to five or seven years or drop it below three. Similarly, any change in the criminal law must become an amendment to the Criminal Code of the Russian Federation.

Structure of the Criminal Code

The Code has two sections, known as a general and a special part. The general part of the Code describes broad principles of criminal law and their applicability. It defines concepts such as crime, the suspect, guilt, conspiracy to commit crime, punishment and its types, and release from criminal responsibility. The special part has 6 sections and 19 chapters describing various crimes and punishments. There is no crime recognized in Russia that is not indicated in the Criminal Code.

The Code classifies crimes into two categories. The first one is major offenses, such as rape, kidnapping, state treason, espionage, crimes against the justice system, and serious violent crimes such as murder. The second category consists of lesser offenses, such as offenses against property and disorderly conduct in a public place. This distinction has been used historically in Russia to determine the type of correctional institution (maximum or minimum security, for example) to which convicted criminals are sent (Nikiforov, 1995).

The Criminal Code is applicable on the entire territory of Russia within its state borders, and within the 12-mile zone of its territorial waters (Federal Law, July 31, 1998). Russia follows international standards and also applies the law within its airspace, for up to 100 kilometers above the surface. The law is also applicable on the continental shelf of Russia (Federal Law, November 30, 1995), and in special "zones of economic interest" within a 200-mile zone, established in international law (Federal Law, December 17, 1998). The law says that the government reserves the right to prohibit and prosecute activities in these areas such as creating foreign bases, unlawful drilling, or geological and other kinds of research (Komissarov, 2005).

The Criminal Code also applies to aircraft, piloted spaceships, and sea and navy vessels, under the flag of the Russian Federation, regardless of their location. However, the law allows some exceptions related to crimes involving drug trafficking, safety, terrorism, and other offenses. Under certain conditions, the Russian Criminal Code applies to Russian citizens living or serving abroad. Foreign citizens in Russia may also be prosecuted according to the Code if their actions are considered harmful to Russia's interests or the interests of its citizens (Bastrykin and Naumov, 2007).

There have been numerous amendments to the Criminal Code over the years. These amendments are related to legal interpretations and changing in sentencing for a wide range of offenses ranging from slander to kidnapping, from organized crime to deliberate damaging of official documents (Criminal Code, 2019).

THE PROSECUTOR'S OFFICE

The Constitution of Russia (Article 129) establishes the Office of the Prosecutor General of the Russian Federation. The purpose of the office is to act on behalf of the Russian Federation to supervise the observance of laws and the execution of judicial decisions according to the Constitution. The Office is independent from the executive, legislative, and judicial branches of government. This is a single, centralized system in which lower prosecutors are subordinated to higher prosecutors and the prosecutor general of the Russian Federation heads the hierarchy. The prosecutor general is appointed by the Federation Council, on the basis of a nomination by the president of the Russian Federation. Prosecutors of subjects of the Russian Federation are appointed by the prosecutor general after consultations with the subjects. Other prosecutors are also typically appointed by the prosecutor general.

Purpose of the Office

The major task of the Prosecutor's Office is to supervise compliance with the Constitution. A second task is to supervise the execution of laws within the territory of the Russian Federation. For example, the Office supervises the execution of any laws by federal executive authorities, legislative and executive bodies of the subjects of the Russian Federation, local governments, military administration bodies, and governing bodies of private organizations. It also supervises the observance of human rights and liberties in Russia.

The Office can investigate and prosecute any person but only within the scope of powers prescribed by the legislation of criminal procedure in the Russian Federation. It can challenge or appeal any court decisions, sentences, and rulings that are assumed to be contrary to the law. It also coordinates the crime-control activities of Russia's law enforcement agencies. The Prosecution Service of the Russian Federation can participate in law-making activities (Federal Law, January 17, 1992). The law acknowledges the Office's right to cooperate with governments of other states on legal matters and crime control, and it can participate in the drafting of international treaties related to the Russian Federation.

Structure

The Prosecutor General's Office is located in Moscow and coordinates the activities of numerous departments and institutions across the country. Overall, there are approximately 30 departments responsible for specific areas of supervision: for example, Supervision over Execution of Economic Legislation, Supervision over Observance of Human Rights and Freedoms, and Supervision over Execution of Transport, Customs, and Environmental Legislation. The Prosecutor General's Office is in charge of the prosecutorial work in the seven federal districts. Its organizational structure is outlined in Figure 6.2.

The Prosecutor General's Office supervises the work of the chief military prosecutor, who is responsible for supervising the execution of the law within the armed forces of the Russian Federation. It also supervises the Academy, a specialized research and educational institution within the Office. Specialized prosecutors' offices oversee the execution of the laws in special fields such as environmental protection, and in special institutions such as prisons, which are officially called "correctional institutions" in Russia. The attorney general is in charge of an Investigative Committee headed by the first deputy attorney general. Both the office and the position were created relatively recently.

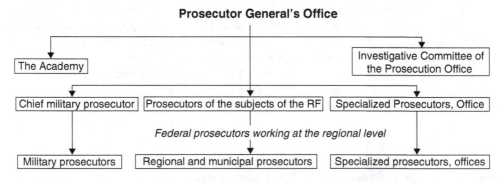

Figure 6.2 The organizational structure of the Prosecutor General's Office of the Russian Federation

The Investigative Committee of the Russian Federation

The Investigative Committee of the Russian Federation is a relatively new and very powerful institution having the ultimate federal investigating authority in Russia. It was created on the basis of the Investigative Committee of the Prosecutor of the Russian Federation, formed in 2007. The Investigative Committee has both investigative and supervisory responsibilities. Its central function and task is the investigation of the most serious crimes. One of the Committee's responsibilities is to use federal resources to carry out effective investigations of sophisticated crimes that require expensive means of surveillance and great coordination between local and federal offices, which cannot be achieved on the regional level (Bastrykin, 2008). In 2011, to strengthen the status and the role of the Investigative Committee, a new federal law designated it an independent federal institution, not a part of the federal structure. As the official site states, the Committee's power is a "continuation of presidential power" and an "element of restraints" in "the system of separation of powers" (http://www.sledcom.ru/history). Some of the most important fields of investigation include violent crime (especially against women, children, the elderly, and the poor); terrorism; corruption on all government levels; and embezzlement of federal funds. In recent times, the investigative functions of the Committee have expanded to include handling of public protests, such as those that took place in Moscow in July 2019, when thousands of people gathered to peacefully demand free and fair local elections. The Investigative Committee arrested and interrogated the organizers and more than 1000 protesters (Vasilchuk, Mineeva, and Torop, 2019).

THE MINISTRY OF JUSTICE

According to a 2004 presidential decree, the Russian Federation Ministry of Justice is responsible for the realization of federal policy in several designated areas. In particular these include the functioning of the courts, execution of criminal sentences, public defense services, and notary services, which perform a range of activities including registration of property, political parties, and religious organizations. The Ministry coordinates the activities of several departments and services, including the Federal Registry, Federal Service of Implementation of Sentencing, and Federal Service of Court Marshals. The Institution of Federal Marshals is generally responsible for the execution of the decisions issued by federal courts related to individuals, organizations, and their property. The Ministry also represents Russia in the European Court of Human Rights.

The Federal Service of Implementation of Sentencing

This federal service manages Russia's prison system. In 2020, Russia had more than 1,000 prisons and correctional facilities. Russia had approximately 544,000 prison inmates, down from 880,000 inmates 10 years earlier. There were more than 43,600 women among the inmates. Overall, the inmates made up less than 1 percent of Russia's entire adult population (people over 14 years old). Almost 25 percent of them had been convicted of murder (Russia does not have the death penalty). Eighteen percent had been convicted of theft, and 10 percent of armed robbery. About 56 percent of the convicted criminals were not in work or education prior to their conviction, and 66 percent were repeat offenders. On average, about 250,000 people receive jail sentences every year. About 55,000 of Russian inmates are HIV-positive. There are 13 special facilities in Russia to care for about 450 children of imprisoned women. To provide healthcare for the inmates, the government maintains more than 1,000 medical offices, larger clinics, specialized hospitals including drug rehabilitation facilities, and mental health clinics. The prison system has more than 300 high schools for inmates, about 300 vocational schools, and more than 500 religious offices that provide facilities and staff for services and prayer. The prison system has approximately 300,000 employees, so there is almost 1 federal employee for every 3 inmates. The Federal Service of Implementation of Sentencing runs a research center, seven colleges that train specialists in the fields of law enforcement within the prison system, and more than a dozen educational centers. It provides regular training and additional education for its employees (FSIN, 2020).

LAW ENFORCEMENT

The system of law enforcement in Russia is based on a hierarchical federal structure. The president is in charge of the Ministry for Internal Affairs. The minister is appointed by the president based on the recommendation of the chair of the government (the prime minister). The president also appoints the minister's deputies. Russian law enforcement units have the responsibility for protecting life, physical health, rights and liberties, property, and the interests of the state and society from criminal and other unlawful infringements. The Ministry exercises its activities in several major areas: criminal law enforcement, public security and safety, and migration of citizens. It is also responsible for criminal investigation of offenses, traffic control, control over weapons on the territory of Russia, and protection of state property (source: Ministry for Internal Affairs).

The Ministry is also in charge of a section of the armed forces called the Interior Ministry Troops. Major tasks of the Interior Ministry Troops include the protection of public order, the security of important federal facilities and shipments, the defense of Russia in the event of a war, assistance to the Federal Border Patrol in protection of the country's borders, and antiterrorist operations on the territory of Russia. During the escalation of the conflict in Chechnya from 1994 to 1996, the Interior Ministry Troops took part in major operations in that region. From 1999 throughout the first decade of the 21st century, the Troops have participated in antiterrorist operations across the entire North Caucasus region of Russia.

In 2011, a new federal law came into force to reform Russia's law enforcement. The reform started by abandoning the Soviet term *militsiya*, and adopting the more universal name *politsiya*, or police. However, the main goal of the reform was to further centralize the country's law enforcement, eliminate local financing of certain law enforcement units, reduce personnel, and increase the salaries of police officers. The new law also expanded the rights of individuals in police custody and limited the police's ability to arrest, interrogate, and detain. For example, Russian police may no longer detain people just to establish their identity, a common practice in the past.

In 2016, a new federal agency was established, with many of its functions related to law enforcement: the **Federal National Guard Troops Service of the Russian Federation** (*Rosgvardia* for short in Russian). This agency reports directly to the Russian president. The National Guard is separate from the Ministry for Internal Affairs and from the Russian

Armed Forces. Rosgvardia's key responsibilities include securing national borders, taking charge of gun control, combating terrorism and organized crime, protecting public order, and guarding important state facilities. The National Guard employs more than 300,000 people (Rosgvardia, 2020). We will discuss law enforcement in Russia further in the following chapters.

CRITICAL THINKING ABOUT RUSSIA'S JUDICIAL BRANCH

Most assessments of nearly 30 years of the Russian legal system's development are largely concerned with the course of the reforms and the relationships between the judiciary and the Kremlin, the executive branch, and Russian bureaucracy in general.

How independent is the system?

There are plenty of features of the legal system in Russia that indicate the system's lack of independence. Although the Constitution establishes a free judiciary, in reality it is not free, even by the assessment of many insiders. Some consider this an unsurprising development because the Constitution essentially gives the executive branch powers to limit the strength of the judiciary. However, although the office of the president has the most power in Russia, and other presidential republics have similar features, the judiciary, as critics admit, does not have to be dependent on the will of the Kremlin (Council of Europe, 2016).

Critics find examples of how the Kremlin and other federal offices have attempted to regulate the judiciary in the past and keep it under control through a well-managed system of promotions and appointments (Golz, 2009). This control allows Putin to secure legal support for his policies, as we have seen in the case of the 2020 amendments. Critics maintain that this is a perfect example of how the executive has increased its control over the judiciary.

Of course, it would be naïve to expect a Russian president to make an exception to his overall policy of power consolidation: why should Putin exclude the judiciary (and law enforcement generally, by the same token) from the Kremlin's control? Other examples demonstrate similar trends. The 2011 police reform was widely criticized for the absence of real changes in local law enforcement (CSR, 2012). However, the police reform has only increased federal control over law enforcement. A similar assessment can be made regarding the National Guard, which critics say is used to solidify the centralized control over ordinary citizens.

The Kremlin and its supporters dismiss these arguments. They point out that, in the United States, for example, the president has the power to nominate judges to the Supreme Court. Second, the system of judicial nominations is fair; in fact, the best and most qualified people receive nominations, and the elimination process is transparent. Supporters of government strategies also offer numerous examples of the judiciary challenging the government and suspending rulings of the executive branch. For example, the Communist Party was banned by the Kremlin two decades ago, but restored to functioning by the courts. Some decisions of the Constitutional Court challenge government policies (see earlier in this chapter). The decision to move this court from Moscow to St Petersburg, away from the Kremlin, is also an indicator—symbolic or not—of the increasing independence of the judiciary.

An unfinished work?

Both critics and supporters of the system generally agree that the judiciary and law enforcement in Russia are developing. They could not have evolved overnight from a Soviet-style legal system dominated by the Communist Party into one typical of a developed liberal democracy. The Russian legal system has made significant advances: for example, the 1996 Criminal Code legalized a number of activities that were seen as crimes in the Soviet period, such as homosexuality, handling anti-Soviet propaganda, financial speculation (buying and reselling with the intention of making a profit), and the possession of foreign currency. As in the countries of the European Union, there is currently no death penalty in Russia: President Boris Yeltsin ordered its suspension in 1996, although it has not as yet formally been abolished. The system of criminal prosecution is quite selective in the administration of sentences. Other facts are indicative of some ongoing changes in the Russian legal system, including an emphasis on individual rights in the ongoing police reform and related federal laws.

However, the lack of transparency is probably one of the biggest problems that the judiciary and law enforcement face today. Despite the federal authorities' positive assessments, most people see the current situation differently. They believe that the judges and executive authorities in Moscow and the regions are part of a unified system in which the judges serve for the most part the interests of the executive. They point to some (admittedly, selectively chosen yet numerous) high-profile cases which seem only to justify this critical evaluation.

CONCLUSION

The Russian legal system is an evolving project that displays many features typical of a dynamic, developing structure, traces of the old communist system, and authoritarian intervention and control. The Constitution establishes the independence of the judiciary. The existing reality is different from the written statute, however. The strength of the executive branch and the circumstances of post-Soviet developments have impacted the judiciary and the whole legal system. It still lacks transparency and remains very vulnerable to the relentless attempts of the executive branch to interfere. This is probably what the Kremlin needs these days: a cooperative judiciary and convenient law enforcement to go along with Moscow's policies, especially those related to the establishment's preservation of power. The government's supporters in Russia may say that it is essential to have an independent and transparent judiciary. However, they immediately assert that the problems it faces, such as the lack of transparency or being dependent from executive offices, are inevitable in any state that develops its institutions. The problem is that the authorities have not found or have not looked for efficient remedies for these problems. One day, many believe, Russia's legal system will be independent and transparent. But how soon?

Part III
Political Behavior, Participation, and Communication

Russian millennials are the first generation in Russian history to grow up with most political freedoms available to them. In centuries past, people in this country were not allowed to form political parties, vote in free elections, or express political dissent. What is the status of these freedoms in Russia today, and how do people exercise them? Part III deals with the functioning and dynamics of Russia's political system, its developments, and current state. Chapter 7 turns to political parties. The following chapter examines the electoral system. The last chapter in this section takes on political participation and mobilization.

7 Political Parties

Some things change. For more than 70 years, the Communist Party was the only legal party in the Soviet Union. Any person attempting to form another party or even publicly discussing the possibilities of a multiparty system in Russia could have faced criminal charges and a jail term. Russia has a multiparty system today. Yet it is different from those present in most democratic countries today. First, Russian parties play only a small role in Russia's political life. Second, the executive branch has created its own mass political party for unconditional support of the current government and its policies. Third, the Kremlin does everything possible to prevent the creation of an influential oppositional party.

This chapter first deals with the recent history of political parties in Russia, which should help in understanding the roots of Russia's party system today. Next, the chapter describes key political parties, their ideology, and main goals and activities. Finally, it provides a critical evaluation of Russia's multiparty system and the role of the executive power in partisan politics.

KEY DEVELOPMENTS

By the late 1980s, during the last years of the Soviet Union, the country already had an emerging multiparty system. After 1985, Russia's multiparty system grew rapidly out of the open political opposition to the government's establishment. Yet, many of the early "oppositionists" were part of the ruling elite, already within the top echelons of the Communist Party (see Chapter 3). The country appeared divided. There were considerable forces demanding radical reforms based on principles of liberal democracy and a free-market economy. Others supported change but hoped only for a gradual and cautious political and economic transformation (Glad and Shiraev, 1999).

Russia's multiparty system developed in an atypical way. Typically, according to what political science teaches us, political parties in developing democracies tend to embrace people with similar political beliefs and interests. In democracies, like-minded politicians join political parties to achieve their political goals (Hale, 2005a: 1). In other words, political parties emerge first and then they affect policies of the government. In Russia, it was government that was from the beginning affecting and altering political parties.

The Russian multiparty system has developed in several stages: a discovery stage, a growth period, a consolidation phase, and a centralization period. The first stage was short: it lasted from the late 1980s to the early 1990s. It was an exciting period of trial and error, when people suddenly realized that they could form political parties without facing criminal penalties. This was a fundamental change in the way people perceived and understood politics.

Discovery and growth

Commentators disagree on which new party was established first. Most probably, it was the Democratic Union, founded in 1988 by Valeria Novodvorskaya (1950–2014), a Soviet dissident, who became this party's chair. It stood for sweeping liberal democratic reforms, government transparency, and free-market policies. Another early party was the Democratic Party of Russia with Nikolai Travkin (b. 1946) as its chair. The party also promoted a broad range of democratic reforms. In 1989 the Union of Constitutional Democrats emerged, with a similar platform of political liberalism. The Christian Democratic Union of Russia emphasized the importance of democracy and Christian values. Russia's Peasants' Party, founded in 1990, represented the interests of Russia's rural regions. An important event was the creation in 1989 of the Liberal Democratic Party, with Vladimir Zhirinovsky as its leader. Because of Zhirinovsky's sparkling temperament and his loud statements, he quickly became popular nationwide (see Chapter 5). Almost all emerging political parties shared an anticommunist platform.

The second stage was during the new political climate of Russia, when the Communist Party essentially lost its monopoly on power and a new political system was emerging. In the early 1990s, overall three political orientations emerged among the political parties. First, parties of so-called democratic opposition (see Chapter 3) pursued mainly Western models of democratization and vast economic liberalization combined with social welfare policies (Isaev, 2008). Second, many small parties of the political center pursued balanced, pragmatic agendas. They supported the Kremlin's general policy of distancing from Soviet-style socialism but emphasized the importance of social protection. Third, parties pursuing radical, populist agendas also emerged. Nationalist groups were the largest, and the most vocal, but they were also extremely disorganized. By the end of 1992 about 40 large and small nationalist parties had emerged (Isaev and Baranov, 2009: 274). They demanded a radical change to Russia's policies in favor of nationalization of industries, social protection, guaranteed jobs, and even the restoration of the Soviet Union.

The third and fourth stages: consolidation and centralization

The third stage (roughly between 1995 and 2003) was the consolidation of smaller parties into large units, and the creation and management of national parties and electoral blocs from "above" specifically for the purpose of winning parliamentary elections (see Chapter 5). The fourth stage began approximately in 2003 and was related to the inception and development of a single and powerful party called United Russia. This party maintained a clear pro-government course, and quickly gained a commanding majority in the Federal Assembly and other branches of the government (Ivanov, 2009). The first real challenge to the ruling party took place during the 2011 Duma elections. More discussion about these stages follows below.

Case in point: the Communist Party on trial

Very seldom in history have major political parties had to defend their right to exist in court. In Russia, the Communist Party fought a very tough legal battle, which was one of the most remarkable developments related to the emerging Russian multiparty system. It was the legal case adjudicated by the Russian Constitutional Court during its early days. This case determined the fate of the Communist Party. The Court considered the constitutionality of Yeltsin's 1991 presidential decree that had suspended the activities of the party. Yeltsin's decree came out right after the unsuccessful August revolt of 1991, which was organized by several top communists in the government. Yeltsin then believed that it was the right time to strike against the Communist Party, which was accused of treason and other serious violations of the law. The hearings took place in Moscow and lasted for almost six months. The 1992 decision of the Court was in favor of the Communist Party and its right to exist. The Court ruled that the Constitution did not prohibit political activities, and that people had the right to form or join any political association. The Communist Party was officially back. This decision does not mean that, in today's Russia, any political party has the right to exist. The government can prohibit any group activities if they are found to be "extremist" according to the federal law. In 2020, more than 70 such groups have been identified (Minjust, 2020).

ON RUSSIAN POLITICAL TERMINOLOGY

Before we describe the development of Russia's party system, it is necessary to explain several political terms that are important for understanding Russia's partisan politics.

"Left" and "right" distinctions

Most of us have at least a general sense, gained early in life, of what is meant by the political "left" and "right": the left represents liberal, and the right conservative, beliefs and policies. However, comparative political scientists warn that these broad and imprecise terms can easily lead to misperceptions, because there are tremendous variations in the way they are interpreted in different countries.

In Russia, **the left** is typically associated with communist and socialist parties and groups promoting the nationalization of key industries and price control of most important products and services, including food, energy, and public transportation. The left supports the welfare state, with a vast range of social benefits and services mobilized for the least protected categories of the population. The Russian left today acknowledges the necessity of a multiparty system, and it supports basic political liberties. It also supports higher taxes on the rich, and big spending programs in the fields of education, housing, and healthcare. The left is a strong supporter of the Russian military. It views the 1991 dissolution of the Soviet Union as a negative, even tragic, event because a new era of capitalism, the system that it opposes, has emerged. In terms of international relations and foreign policy, the left:

- Is critical of capitalism, international corporations, and globalization in general.
- Considers the West, and especially the United States, as major adversaries of Russia.
- Criticizes Western liberal democracy, its sources, principles, and institutions.
- Believes that the relationships between Russia and the West benefit only the West. Russia, therefore, must show its strength when dealing with Western countries (Shiraev and Khudoley, 2019).

The right, for the most part, supports elements of the Russian welfare state but does not reject the free-market economy. The right supports social conservatism. The ideology of the Russian ultra-right embraces (among other views) monarchism, isolationism, populism, homophobia, and anti-Western attitudes. Some desire to restore Russia's armed forces to the meaningful levels of the Cold War. The right, in a general sense:

- represents a wide range of views focused primarily on regaining Russia's strength as a state and a global actor;
- scorns Western liberal democracy and social tolerance;
- supports nationalistic attitudes based on the glorification of certain developments in Russia's history, such as wars, associated with expansion and strengthening.

Some confusion can occur when one deals with concepts and labels containing the word "right." As in English, Russian translations of this word also mean—in addition to indicating the direction of the political spectrum (left–right)—the state of being "correct," "accurate," or "true." It is wise to pay attention in business and diplomatic communications, as well as in translations, to the context in which this term is used. The term "**center**" represents Russian "centrists" who generally support the Kremlin and its policies and often identify themselves as moderates by aligning with neither the right nor the left. The centrists in Russia tend to support a moderate nationalistic platform, which is less drastic than the views of the right or the left. In general, centrists also support a bigger and more assertive role for Russia in global affairs, but they reject xenophobic, anti-immigration views. Keep in mind that, for some people, however, centrism is a convenient label for a lack of particular political preferences or for a lack of general knowledge about politics (Shiraev and Khudoley, 2019).

The use of the terms "**liberal**" and "**conservative**" in today's Russia is also somewhat different from their use in the United States or the United Kingdom. It is probably inaccurate to equate Russian liberals with the left and conservatives with the right. In the classic textbook sense, *liberal* implies a range of views supporting basic political, economic, and personal freedoms. To be labeled a liberal in Russia today means that you support predominantly liberal democratic models of government, a free-market economy, a free press, a transparent government, and independent courts. A typical Russian liberal is easy to recognize because they vehemently oppose authoritarianism.

It is also, in most cases, inaccurate to equate Russian liberals with the left and conservatives with the right. Unlike most people on the left, Russian liberals tend to support friendly relations with the West. A conservative person in Russia generally stands for stability, order, and tradition. A conservative also supports the government's protection of social welfare, a mixed economy with a large portion of it being under government control, the image of Russia's greatness as a global power, and relative tolerance of authoritarianism. Russian conservatives tend to believe that the West undermines Russia (Nesterova, 2016). In a brief summary, liberal and conservative individuals in Russia significantly differ in their lenience toward authoritarianism, acceptance of free-market principles, views of the West and the United States, and views of Russia's role in the world.

Most communists support conservative views as well, except that the communists for the most part reject capitalism and back socialism instead. Pro-socialist attitudes are often identified in Russia as conservative, although communists tend to reject being called "conservatives."

Spectrum of attitudes

As mentioned above, traditional labels of the spectrum of political attitudes such as liberal, moderate, and conservative do not fit very well into the frame of Russian politics today. Russian conservative groups support the government's regulation of business, including the nationalization of large industries. They stand for substantial government support for the needy, higher income and capital gains taxes, and the urgent restoration of Russian military power (Nesterova, 2016). Most communists support these views as well, except that they, for the most part, reject capitalism. Russian liberal groups, on the other hand, tend to advocate free enterprise and less government intervention in the economy and business. Pro-socialist attitudes are more often identified in Russia as conservative. Many communists do not want to be called "conservatives" and support robust social-democratic reforms. In the past some observers suggested that the most effective way of describing the differences in political views in Russia was to put supporters of communism on one side and anti-communists on the other (Lebed, 1996). Other authors looked at the distinctions among liberal-democratic views, pro-communist views, patriotic ideas (nationalism, populism), and "the undetermined" (Bruter, 1999).

In the late 1990s, a new category of political attitude emerged: indifferent. People automatically supported any candidates so long as these individuals promised policies guaranteeing economic security and social order. Other factors, such as civil liberties or political rights, transparency, or accountability became less important if the politician promised economic benefits and social safety. In fact, the relative weakness of Russian political parties can be explained partially by these indifferent attitudes on the part of the population. Therefore, it is often useful to study specific attitudes toward specific issues instead of examining people's general political affiliations (see Table 7.1).

Table 7.1 A snapshot of Russian people's attitudes

Percent age of those who:
Are indifferent or do not like/do not care about politics: 54
Have never read the Russian Constitution: 42
Believe that Russia has its own "special" way of development: 48
Believe that Russia has enemies: 81
Believe that the current Russian political power is corrupt, criminal: 41
Identify themselves with the Orthodox Church: 80
Do not mind if their son(s) choose a career in the military: 63
Do not mind if their daughter(s) choose a career in the military: 30

Source: Pipiya, 2019; WCIOM, 2020.

MAJOR POLITICAL PARTIES

A 2001 federal law and several amendments (Federal Law, December 20, 2004) regulate political parties in Russia. According to the law, in order to be registered, a political party must have at least 500 members residing in Russia and regional offices throughout the subjects of the Russian Federation. This party's leaders must also reside in Russia. There could be ongoing changes in the way political parties are registered.

Which are the major political parties in Russia today? What are their political programs and aspirations? Which forecasts about their future role in Russian politics carry most weight?

United Russia

This has been the biggest Russian party during the first couple of decades of the 21st century. The early beginnings of the party can be traced to 2001, a year after Putin became president, when several parties and movements of the government-supporting political center unified their structures and programs and joined together as a single party. Boris Gryzlov, who later became the chair of the Duma, was elected the party leader in 2002. In 2003, the party took the name United Russia. Pro-government commentators maintained that United Russia was a natural product of the growth and consolidation of several parties sharing similar views of democracy, stability, and the free market (Ivanov, 2009). Critics are unanimous that United Russia was a convenient merger of several political groups that allowed Putin to maintain control of the government and neutralize potential opponents (White, 2007: 21–53). The party dominated the Duma for years. However, during the parliamentary elections in 2011, it lost a large number of seats and only barely maintained its majority, retaining 49 percent after the 2016 elections. About 47 percent said right after the 2012 presidential elections that they fully trusted the party (CSR, 2012). In 2018, 44 percent viewed the party negatively, compared with 47 percent who had a positive view (Levada, 2018c).

From the start, United Russia proclaimed that its purpose was to create a "presidential majority" and gain widespread popular support for presidential policies. By 2004, the party controlled the State Duma. The party endorsed Putin in its official documents and statements, calling him the "national leader." Putin became United Russia's chair in May 2008 and retained this post until 2012, after which Dmitry Medvedev assumed the chairmanship. Medvedev was reelected as chair in 2017.

The party's multiyear strategic policies included the development of "Russia as a unique civilization," the defense of a common "cultural space" and historical customs, an increase in Russia's global economic competitiveness, the provision of a "new quality of life" for Russia's citizens, and the support of "social initiatives." More specific goals included wage and pension increases, helping the needy with affordable housing, and increasing the country's defense capabilities (United Russia, 2007).

In the economic sphere, United Russia supports a mixed economy with private and state-run sectors. It supports antimonopoly measures, offers support for small businesses, and promises to reform the existing tax and tariff policies. The party endorses farm subsidies and supports the agrarian–industrial complex, the term commonly used in the Soviet Union to describe an economic infrastructure that coordinates industrial and agricultural production.

In the fields of defense and foreign policy, the party expects reciprocity in relations with foreign countries. United Russia considers the fight against international terrorism to be a priority and supports nuclear nonproliferation. The party underlines the importance of international cooperation on the environment and supports the idea of multipolarity.

In the social sphere, the party promises to stop the decrease in Russia's population and stimulate birth rates. The party also promises to establish transparency in all areas of "public life" and to conduct policies for the "moral development" of people in Russia.

The party promises policies to sponsor culture, the arts, and the performing arts. Special attention is paid to the promotion of the Russian language and literature. The party sees as a priority the formation of an "all-Russian civil identity" and of common values for all ethnic groups populating Russia (while respecting the minorities' unique cultural features). It supports youth movements and organizations promoting patriotism, education, and a healthy lifestyle.

The party had more than 2 million members in 2020 but has been gradually losing its popularity among the Russian people as well as its ability to effectively manage both national and local elections in favor of its candidates (Hale and Colton, 2017). In the 2019 local elections in Moscow, for example, many party members running for the city council preferred to file as independent candidates even though they retained their membership in the party: most of them did not want to be publicly associated with a party that was losing its popularity.

The Liberal Democratic Party

The Liberal Democratic Party of Russia (LDPR) was formed in 1989 as a social-democratic group and was officially registered as a political party in 1991. From its inception, the party has mainly been associated with Vladimir Zhirinovsky (for a brief biography, see Chapter 4) and his flamboyant style of behavior. Zhirinovsky received from 5 to 9 percent of popular support in three presidential elections and possesses a wide range of credentials within the party, which has almost 300,000 members.

The LDPR claims a commitment to general liberal values. Patriotism, according to the party's program, refers to the strengthening of the Russian people's power. "The Russian people should fortify the whole country," states the official party website. (The statement appears, of course, in Russian.) Liberalism is, according to the party, impossible without patriotism. A strong national state is a guarantor of liberal values and nonviolent solutions to political conflicts (LDPR, 2009). To better understand this party platform, let us look at the issues that the party opposes.

First, it opposes the communist ideology. Communism is a failed naïve utopia that promises equality and prosperity but never delivers them. No party can *make* people equal. Second, the party opposes liberal democratic ideology of the Western type. It claims that the West European and American liberal democratic models of a multiparty system (even though the party's name refers to liberal democracy) and a free press are not suitable for Russia. Russia should have its own model of government. Third, the LDPR is against one-party control over the institutions of power. It argues that the biggest problem in contemporary Russian party politics is that United Russia was created "from above" by the Kremlin and for the Kremlin.

What does the LDPR stand for? According to the party program, it supports strong presidential power, the three branches of government, and a one-chamber parliament (the Duma). At the same time, the party endorses the possibility of "a regime of personal power" during a transitional period (by which it probably means its leader, Zhirinovsky, taking power). The party also supports limiting the number of seats in the Duma that one party can have (to 40 percent). It wants the nationalistic principle, "what is good for the Russians should be good for the country," to be adopted. Russia should limit immigration and support all Russians living overseas.

In the fields of economic policies LDPR, like United Russia, supports a mixed economy. The state should control the industries related to defense, transport, oil and gas, communication, and the extraction of mineral resources. The party also supports the nationalization of the alcohol, tobacco, and sugar industries. Whenever necessary, the government should regulate prices, interest rates, foreign trade, and employment. Specifically, the government should keep energy costs low, create jobs, and pay for pensions, unemployment benefits, and healthcare. The party promises to overhaul domestic trade and establish caps on retail profits at 20 percent of the wholesale price. It also promises to establish price controls in the energy sector, and for agricultural and food products. The party also maintains that, when it is in power, it will allow a family with four children or more to build their own house for free (LDPR Program, 2020).

The party supports military service on a contractual basis (Russia currently has a military draft). It opposes the use of the Russian military overseas and thinks Russia should never give away foreign aid for free. The party believes that the United States and West European countries are Russia's adversaries, and it is against NATO expansion. However, it concedes that the United States could be Russia's partner in antiterrorist and disarmament policies.

The LDPR claims that Russia is the center of eastern Christian culture and civilization. The party states that "there will be the time when we will regain all our territories, and all Russians will live calmly, knowing that they have a Russian flag over their heads. But to achieve this, there is a need to have a Big Master—tough and predictable, strong and purpose-driven" (LDPR Program, 2020).

As you can see, the party program is filled with populist promises and declarations. Consider just a few of them. Women, by law, should work a shorter day than men. People who lost their savings during the economic turmoil of the 1990s should get them back. The government should provide free medication and pay for medical procedures for the retired. Mortgages with an interest rate of 2–3 percent should be granted for 30 to 50 years. The party promises, when in power, to cut the number of federal employees to a tenth of its existing level.

The party is vehemently against corruption and nepotism (an attractive position supported by many), defends the poor and the defenseless (another strong point), and picks on the government for any mistake or blunder it makes. LDPR frequently appears as a vocal critic of many government policies. It is an "anti-party" that always attracts a significant proportion of votes during parliamentary elections (Bruter, 1999). Nevertheless, in reality this party has never been a serious opposition to any government-backing legislative majority. In fact, LDPR has for years filled the convenient but largely symbolic role of an opposition party without real power (Dorell, 2018; Hale, 2005b).

The Communist Party

The Communist Party of the Russian Federation was formed in February 1993 and registered by the Ministry of Justice in March. Three important developments related to the party need to be considered.

First, President Yeltsin banned the Communist Party in 1991 after the August revolt. The Constitutional Court disagreed with the presidential decision, and the party was officially restored (see early in this chapter). Second, most members of the party previously belonged to the Communist Party of the Soviet Union (CPSU). Third, the CPSU itself went through a painful period of transition and inner struggle between 1989 and 1991. The main disagreement was between the liberal and conservative wings of the party: one side wanted to reform the party, while the other was willing to make small changes but insisted on keeping the basic ideology intact. In 1992, the new Communist Party brought several pro-communist groups together. Gennady Zyuganov became chair of the party's Executive Committee.

The party has more than 160,000 members (CPFR, 2019). In contrast, in the 1980s the CPSU had almost 19 million members. According to the party regulations in the Soviet Union, a communist had to be atheist. The rules and practices have changed. Almost 30 percent of the party members believe in God (Zyuganov, 2009).

Like the LDPR, the Communist Party opposes most of the Kremlin's economic policies. The party program calls these policies a "regression" which could cause a "national catastrophe" (CPRF Program, 2020). The party's platform also states that the core struggle between capitalism and socialism is not over, and the whole world eventually will move toward socialism. Two things must be accomplished: nationalization of economic production, and distribution of wealth according to each person's quantity and quality of labor. Three stages of reform are proposed: first, to reach stability; second, a transitional stage; and third, the establishment of true socialist principles of government and economy.

Specifically, the Communist Party does not want to nationalize small businesses. It supports the nationalization only of strategic industries including energy, resources, and communications. The government must establish price controls over essential products, and cap home utility bills (gas, water, and electricity) below 10 percent of family income. Being generally anti–big business, the party supports small and medium-sized private entrepreneurship.

In the social sphere, the party supports subsidies and discounts for the poor, and free services for the needy. It supports limited censorship of the media to limit "kitsch and cynicism," provide wider access for all political forces to the media, and stop the media besmirching Russian history. The party's motto is "Russia, labor, people's power, and socialism" (CPRF Program, 2020).

In foreign policy, the Communist Party sees the United States and other leading world capitalist powers as major threats to societal progress and peace. The party opposes almost every foreign policy decision of the United States and its allies. It considers Western policies to be imperialist, colonialist, and fundamentally unfair. Hoping to continue the old policy of the Soviet Union, the party supports parties and governments that conduct an anti-American or anti-Western foreign policy.

Opinion polls show that the Communist Party is commonly perceived as a strong and legitimate political institution, receiving support in parliamentary elections in the past two decades ranging from 9 to 20 percent (CECRF, 2020; CSR, 2012).

A just Russia

This party (another translation of the title is "Fair Russia") was formed in 2006 in a merger of three parties with center-left and left orientations. Several smaller parties with a similar orientation joined A Just Russia later. This is the third or fourth party in terms of representatives in the State Duma (having from 23 to 64 members of the Duma over the years), and its leader, Sergei Mironov, served until 2011 as chair of the Federation Council of the Federal Assembly. He justified the creation of the party as an exercise in democracy and claimed that the party was necessary to keep the government establishment in check (Mironov, 2009b). Critics maintain that this party is oppositional only in its name, and its activities are just a showcase to persuade the Russian people and world public opinion that the county has an efficient multiparty system.

The party's key concern is robust welfare policies. The party's official slogans call for the establishment of "democratic, efficient socialism" based on the principles of "justice, freedom, and solidarity." The party accepts private property but runs off a general anticapitalist platform. "We are not against the market economy; we are against the market society," says the party's program (Just Russia, 2016). Its goals are quite broad, including equal rights and liberties for all people, solidarity among generations, patriotism, responsibility, democracy, the well-being of the family, and social security (Just Russia, 2012).

The party also puts forth several specific goals. For example, it rejects Russia's flat tax at 13 percent and supports a new progressive tax policy with four income brackets. It supports the establishment of progressive luxury taxes on consumption. The party endorses three years' paid maternity leave for all employed women. It also promises a minimum retirement pension which should be at least 65 percent of a working person's salary. Married couples would receive interest-free mortgages. The party suggests an increase of cash payments to people who are 70 years of age. The party suggests a law to make corruption a form of treason, which would provide harsher penalties for those found guilty of this crime.

A Just Russia, similar to United Russia, accuses the West of unfriendly policies toward Russia and rejects liberalism in international economic and trade relations. Overall this party generally supports the domestic and foreign policy of the president. In 2018, for example, the party supported the candidacy of Putin in residential elections.

Other political parties

In addition to the four major parties described here, a few smaller parties function in Russia. One of the oldest is the Yabloko (Apple) Party, also known as the United Russian Democratic Party, which between 1993 and 2003 had its own small faction in the Duma. Until 2008, the party's leader was Grigory Yavlinsky (b. 1952), a charismatic economist of the perestroika period and a well-known political leader of the 1990s. He has remained a recognizable public figure over the past 20 years. Since 2008, the political role of this party has weakened. In the Duma elections, the party could secure from 1 to 4 percent of the votes. Since 2019 the party's chair has been Nikolay Rybakov (b. 1978), an economist and engineer by education.

The party under his leadership has always been in opposition to the government. It has maintained a center-left or libertarian position on most issues. According to its 2016 program, the party's domestic goal is to build a society based on major democratic and liberal values, in contrast to the authoritarian and antidemocratic trends that, from the party's view, are apparent in today's Russia. The party considers Russia's current leadership to be uninformed, complacent, and disinterested in global economic trends. The party also supports the rights of the LGBT community in Russia (Yabloko, 2016).

The Party of People's Freedom (abbreviated in Russian as PARNAS) was founded in 1990 and was able to elect its representatives to the Duma in the 1990s. The party embraces a center-right ideology and supports civil liberties, free enterprise, transparent elections, and an independent judiciary. The party, headed by former prime minister Mikhail Kasyanov (b. 1957), who served between 2000 and 2004, is critical of Russia's domestic and foreign policies and supports a series of amendments to the Constitution to strip future presidents of most executive functions and to transfer power to the prime minister (Parnas, 2017). Another group of oppositional parties appears under the label of The Other Russia, which as such began its activities in 2006. In 2011 it was refused registration as a political party. The main goal of the "movement" (a term preferred by its members) is to change the existing political regime in Russia by peaceful, legal means. The word "other" in the title indicates that this movement envisages a different government from the one existing in today's Russia. That, however, is where the common goals of the coalition's members end. The Other Russia coalition includes organizations quite dissimilar in their goals and ideologies, ranging from libertarian to radical left or even neo-Stalinist. For example, among noticeable people associated with The Other Russia was Garry Kasparov (b. 1963), former world chess champion, who is largely libertarian in his views and Eduard Limonov (1943–2020), a famous writer, known for his radical left and nationalist views.

As you can see, the development of political parties and the twists and turns of Russia's electoral procedures have proceeded side by side. One has affected and changed the other. The process is ongoing, and changes take place frequently. Yet although we need to recognize the dynamic nature of the Russian political system, we can also come to several preliminary conclusions.

CRITICAL THINKING ABOUT POLITICAL PARTIES

Russia's multiparty system is complex yet weak. The Kremlin makes sure the leading party is shielded from real political competition for the Federal Assembly. A serious problem is the lack of people's trust in major political parties, which makes the appearance of a new powerful party or strengthening of the existing parties especially difficult (CSR, 2012). Various views, as you should expect, reflect on the current state of political parties in Russia.

The developmental view

There is an old Russian proverb, "Moscow was not built at once," meaning that it takes time and sustainable efforts to create something meaningful. Commentators within Russia's political establishment accept that Russia's political dynamics are not without problems (Medvedev, 2009b; Putin, 2020a). In other words, any transformational process is bound to be fraught with difficulties. The current party system, as far as the argument goes, may be a natural reaction to the political instability and disarray of the 1990s, when too many groups competed for parliamentary seats and created meaningless parties for immediate electoral gains. Moreover, the worsening of the social and economic situation in the country in the 1990s gave rise to parties with radical left and ultra-right ideologies. Economic stability, on the other hand, was associated with popular support for the government and parties of the center, which evolve gradually (Isaev and Baranov, 2009).

Other political parties evolve too, like the Union of the Right Forces that for years represented the interests of the political opposition, endorsing individual freedoms, economic liberties, and the political openness typical of Western-style democracies. However, the party leaders increasingly often began to cooperate with the Kremlin, which prompted criticism from many rank-and-file members (this process prompted many commentators to assume that the government had begun to "buy out" the political opposition). Torn apart by internal disagreements, the party dissolved itself in 2008, which should be seen as a normal democratic process.

The process of political consolidation under a strong leading party is believed to be the sign of stability of the political system. Bringing representative government to a people accustomed to autocratic rule requires more than lifting the yoke of repression under which they have suffered. It is also necessary to build institutions to link the people to the government and develop respect for the rule of law. This building process does not happen overnight. With the right leadership, such as Putin, and the right vision, the developing system should remain stable and efficient (Surkov, 2019).

This view is promoted by government elites and finds substantial support in Russia. Its critics, however, point out that the authorities actually need this system to endure because it embraces weak political parties and thus strengthens the authoritarian system.

The authoritarian power view

The Russian party system functions within an authoritarian political structure. Authoritarianism, as was explained in Chapter 4, is a form of government with a highly centralized and often personalized power structure and a relatively weak civil society. Individual leaders, and not necessarily elected organs, hold much of the power, and political freedoms are often limited (Brownlee, 2007). In Russia, however—and this view remains popular in Moscow—under the existing conditions, authoritarian methods of government are the only viable option. As far as the argument goes, without an authoritarian core, the country would be significantly worse off regardless of the condition of political parties.

The main argument of supporters of this view is that, whatever political developments take place, their value should be judged by how well they serve Russia's core interests. The interests of Russia are defined vaguely: among the most commonly cited are Russia's territorial security, security of the borders of the former Soviet Union, absence of ethnic conflicts within its territory, and standing up to the West. It is argued that, for the sake of Russia's interests, the country needs a strong decision maker, not a handsome debater. A highly competitive party system, unfortunately, weakens the country. Russia still needs a multiparty system, but the parties must work in unison to ensure stability and steady development (Gudkov, 2008a).

Some Russian commentators have long maintained that the Russian people have been historically inclined to seek out strong leaders and be suspicious of uncertainties and choice. The experiences of the older generations under communism compounded these problems (Gozman and Etkind, 1992; Grunt et al., 1996). Individuals who are uncertain about the political future and disappointed with the present are apt to search for a strong guarantor of stability and order (Zorkaya, 2004; Mikulski, 1995). As far as this argument goes, Russia is probably incapable of functioning without a "big brother" carrying a "big stick," so they do not need a full-scale multiparty system.

The populist view

Russia's party system may be deeply rooted in populism—political strategies that pursue the goal of mass support of a person or party by appealing directly to most people's immediate needs. **Populism** is based on promises and corresponding actions designed to give people what they want. It is also associated with scare tactics and exaggerated threats, persuading people that their major values, assets, and way of life are in danger (Albertazzi and McDonnell, 2008). If people are anxious or uncertain about their future, they are likely to turn to politicians who offer simple solutions to problems. As the history of Russia and other countries shows, poverty and injustice frequently make ordinary people particularly susceptible to populism, and it has always been a policy of choice for both Soviet and Russian leaders. The lack of democratic principles of openness and accountability also helps populist politicians in winning sympathy and support. Because populism has been a common and convenient strategy for most political parties in Russia, it becomes difficult to distinguish among them and their electoral platforms.

With the coming of stability and prosperity, the need for populism should diminish. Meanwhile, because of all the uncertainties of the past 30 or so years, many people in Russia look for simple answers, and trusted politicians who could easily promise a better life in the short term. The Kremlin is using populist movements and parties for its own advantage (Van Herpen, 2018).

Elite politics

From this point of view, the problem with political parties lies in the nature of political power in Russia. For decades political scientists have studied elites and their political influence. These studies, known as elite theory, propose that the establishment holds the most power in every country and that the democratic process does not necessarily impact the elite's power (Bottomore, 1993). Elite theory also argues that policy does not result from people's demands but rather from elite inner agreement (Dye, 2001). Therefore, following this logic, any country's leaders will always create a party system to pursue two major goals. One is to satisfy their own political interests, and the other is to gratify the interests of their backers: financiers and industrialists. Systematically, as you remember, after 1991, various party substitutes emerged. Some were regional electoral groups supporting the aspirations of local elites, mostly governors or entrepreneurs. There were also national electoral political machines: "parties" specifically designed to win parliamentary elections. In effect, these "party substitutes" crowded genuine Russian political parties out of the electoral marketplace (Hale, 2005a). The government's reform of the electoral system during the rule of President Putin that began in 2000 was, in effect, an effort to strengthen a pro-government party, United Russia. Everything was done to consolidate more power in the hands of the Kremlin's incumbents and their circle (Manikhin, 2003; Trenin, 2006).

Some things change. Others remain the same. As discussed in this chapter, centralization and consolidation of political power by one party has been the signature feature of Russian politics for at least a couple of decades. Will this feature evolve and how soon? Change is a long process.

CONCLUSION

A multiparty system has emerged in Russia, but its evolution was significantly determined by the will and decisions of the executive officers. A strong executive branch was not the only basis of the current party system. The political transformations of the past 30 years were taking place within a specific political, cultural, and business environment. Business elites did not believe that strong political parties could help them to secure and improve their positions. Being unhappy with the difficulties of Yeltsin's era, a solid majority of the Russian people developed their support for the government that came after. Many people expect the Kremlin to guarantee stability, avoid devastating economic crises, and provide basic social benefits. In exchange, people agreed to accept the current political system.

Pessimists argue that studies in Russia as well as in China show that growth of the middle class does not necessarily strengthen people's attitudes in favor of economic and political liberalism. Optimists disagree. They assume that, as a response to authoritarianism, the demand for new, strong political parties should increase. This will mean that the political "market" in Russia is likely to produce them sooner or later. The fate of these parties will depend, however, on the government response and, hopefully, the strong will of Russia's people.

8 Presidential and Parliamentary Elections

Unlike their parents and grandparents back in the days of the communist state, the young in Russia can vote in presidential and parliamentary elections and use ballots with multiple names printed on them. How did this new system develop? How different is it from electoral systems in other countries? How transparent and free is the current system?

In this chapter we discuss these and many other questions related to elections in Russia. Because the chapter gives special attention to the transformation of the electoral system, the section on key developments only outlines several major themes, which are discussed later in the chapter. The chapter then pays attention to parliamentary and presidential elections and provides a critical evaluation of them.

KEY DEVELOPMENTS

Russia's electoral system has a relatively short but eventful history. To better understand how the system works today, several key developments from the past should be considered first.

Early democratic elections

Russia held its first national elections relatively late compared with the United States and most European countries. Only in 1905 did the emperor reluctantly agree to allow political freedoms in Russia. The reform established a parliament elected by popular vote through a multistage process—the State Duma. Political parties were legalized and began to compete for seats in the Duma. The 1906 Duma elections were the first democratic elections in Russia's history. Many categories of people received voting rights, including peasants and workers. In the following 12-year period, Russian people participated in several national ballots. Every time the electoral rules were different. Only once did the Duma serve its full term, because the emperor kept dissolving the legislature when it continually challenged the executive power. After the communists seized power in Russia at the end of 1917, national and local elections were no longer free.

Elections in the Soviet Union

The Soviet Constitution gave the ruling Communist Party exclusive political power. It was in charge of local and national elections. The local and regional party committees were responsible for selecting candidates for the soviets on the local and regional level and submitting their names for approval by superior committees. Most party leaders on all levels were among these candidates. Only one candidate's name appeared on the paper ballot given to a voter on election day. Officially, the ballot was secret and the voter could reject the candidate or write in any other name. However, because of the tight government control of elections, the real ballot count is unknown. According to publications in the party-controlled press, almost every candidate running for local and national parliamentary elections received 99 or even 99.9 percent of the votes.

It is a mistake to assume that Russians of older generations had no experience in democratic elections. Some elections in the Soviet Union were somewhat competitive and transparent. They usually took place on the local level or at the workplace, to elect managers in small working units, captains of sport teams, or even leaders of small party or youth organizations. Such elections allowed multiple candidates, open debates, and even public disagreements about whether a certain candidate had a good moral profile. Yet the core principles of the communist ideology were left out of the debates. Although the procedures of these local elections resembled a democratic process, their outcomes were insignificant because the elected individuals had very little political power in their hands. Besides, most elections were either organized or monitored by the Communist Party in such a way that only preselected and approved candidates were allowed to run and win.

The country moved gradually to free elections in the late 1980s. During perestroika, the Soviet people finally received an opportunity to nominate candidates more freely, participate in open electoral debates, and vote in multicandidate elections. One of the results of free elections in most Soviet republics was new and independent legislatures. They immediately started energetic and successful campaigns for their republics' independence.

The rapid formation and legalization of new parties and political organizations created a great deal of confusion among a significant portion of the electorate in the 1990s (see Chapter 3). Frequent national, regional, and local elections can cause "electoral fatigue" in the general population, a phenomenon quite common in some countries. Russia was not different. However, during a difficult transitional period, ordinary voters often tended to view the inefficiency of a multiparty system as a deficiency of democracy in general.

Now we briefly examine the evolution of the electoral system since the early 1990s and its lessons for today.

PARLIAMENTARY ELECTIONS

According to federal law, the **Central Electoral Commission** (**CEC**)—a 15-member institution appointed by the president and the Federal Assembly—is in charge of organizing elections on the federal level. It is appointed for four years and responsible for both presidential and parliamentary races (CICRF, 2019; Churov, 2009a).

The Kremlin's executive branch has played a crucial role in the way the electoral system developed. Elections in Russia during the past 20-plus years have transformed Russia's political environment and changed, both directly and indirectly, the structure and balance of political forces. The parliamentary elections of 1993, 1995, 1999, 2003, 2007, 2011, and 2016 have left a definite mark on Russia's political system and society in general.

Early Duma elections (1993 and 1995)

In 1993, Russian voters participated in their first free elections after the breakup of the Soviet Union. No political party was a clear favorite. No political group or candidate received an open endorsement from the Kremlin. The results of these elections have had a long-term impact on the entire electoral system. Its lessons have become historic.

After the elections, the parties of the pro-government center formed a slim majority over two parties of the left, including the Communist Party and the Agrarian Union (115 seats), and the nationalist–populist Liberal Democratic Party (LDPR) (64 seats). The biggest electoral winner, in fact, was the populist LDPR (23 percent of the popular vote), which directly appealed to voters disappointed with the worsening economic situation (Bruter, 1999; Ferguson, 1996: 44). The emerging multiparty system produced an eclectic parliament with no single party holding a decisive majority.

Two important lessons were learned after the 1993 Duma elections. The first was that it was becoming clear that a well-organized political party could attract a large number of voters and win seats during a time of instability and economic difficulty. Second, it also became apparent that, in order to win seats in the Duma, political candidates needed to pay very serious attention to setting up a political organization that would generate financial and logistical support.

By 1995, the time of the next election, approximately 50 national political parties had emerged in Russia. There were about 250 of these smaller organizations, representing a full spectrum of ideological and political orientations. As was mentioned in Chapter 7, these groups were largely party substitutes playing a clear role as legal organizational and financial structures assembled to win elections. Both the government and emerging business elites began to form parties to serve their strategic interests (Hale, 2005a). The competition began.

The Duma elections of 1995 demonstrated again that the composition of the new Russian legislature reflected the voters' disappointment with the course of the president's reforms. People were concerned about poor social protection, widespread crime, and rampant corruption. The results were favorable to the Communist Party. Parties of the left bloc, including the Communists, gained strength (211 seats in the 450-seat Duma), parties of the center gained 154 seats, and the LDPR received 51 seats (there were also 34 independent deputies). The Communist Party and political groups close to it became the largest voting bloc in the Duma. It was probably the most organized and unified political party in Russia at that time.

The 1995 elections also provided at least two major lessons, one procedural and the other political. From the procedural standpoint, the four parties that passed the required 5 percent barrier collected only 50.5 percent of the total ballots cast. Overall, 43 parties and electoral blocs competed, and 18 garnered at least 1 percent of the party list votes. This meant that almost half of Russia's votes in 1995 were "wasted" on small parties that were unable to reach the minimum percentage of votes required to win a seat (Ferguson, 1996: 44). The winning parties did not mind this outcome, but for those that lost out, it was an indication that the electoral system was deficient.

Second, just as in 1993, the elections demonstrated again that only well-organized and well-funded groups were capable of winning a substantial number of seats in parliamentary elections under the existing voting system. Russia's political and business elites continued to create such groups and finance them for purely electoral purposes. The Kremlin also learned an important lesson. Although the legislative branch was relatively weak, according to the Constitution, an oppositional Duma could have presented a problem to the Kremlin. Therefore, after the ascendance to power of Vladimir Putin, the federal government paid close attention to the parliamentary elections, to produce results favorable to the Kremlin.

Later Duma elections (1999–2007)

The main strategy for every party participating in the election in the fall of 1999 was to form or join a nationwide electoral coalition. Two major political groups emerged and began to form such powerful electoral coalitions—in official Russian terminology, "initiative groups." These groups started their campaign work just a few months before the elections.

The first was the Inter-Regional Movement Unity (nicknamed "Bear"), created in September 1999. The group backed Putin, then newly appointed as prime minister and heading toward his first presidency. This bloc won 23 percent of the votes. Later this movement grew into United Russia, the largest pro-government political party in the country. The second movement founded in 1999 (which also later contributed to and partially merged into United Russia) was called Fatherland-All Russia. Its major participants were Evgeny Primakov, former prime minister, Yuri Luzhkov, mayor of Moscow, and Vladimir Yakovlev, mayor of St Petersburg. Created in August, this bloc won 13 percent of the votes in the election four months later. The 1999 Duma elections significantly reduced the power of the LDPR to only 14 deputies. The parties of the left overall received just 127 seats, so they lost almost 40 percent of the seats they had held after the 1995 elections.

The elections of 1999 and 2003 were the beginning of a new period in the history of Russian elections and political parties. For the first time since the 1980s, Russia had a dominant political party. It was a legitimate political force supported by the governing establishment and the voters.

Chapter 5 already explained how a new party list proportional representation system was put in place for the 2007 elections. According to this system, political parties prepare lists of candidates for the upcoming election—naturally, with their leaders at the top of the list. Each party has to be operative right across the federation and meet tough membership requirements. Voters then cast their ballots not for an individual, but for a party. After the election, parliamentary seats are allocated to each party in proportion to the number of votes it receives. In addition, a political party might nominate unaffiliated candidates. This means that parties can put on their lists nonmembers of the party. This policy supposedly allows political parties to better appeal to unaffiliated voters.

Overall, these changes made it still more difficult for small parties to compete in the Duma elections. Many parties could not reach the 50,000-member requirement for registration. Furthermore, the bureaucratic system began to reject other parties for different reasons: for example, some of their required endorsement signatures were not accepted (this disqualified the Green Party and the People's Union, and a few others). Some parties were rejected (The Other Russia was an example) because the government categorized them as coalitions or movements rather than political parties.

Table 8.1 summarizes the number of political parties gaining seats in the Duma in elections from 1993 to 2016. Notice the decline after 1995. At the same time the "party of power" (United Russia) was going from strength to strength: in 2003 it won 223 of the 450 seats, and it increased its presence still further to 315 seats in 2007. It suffered some losses in 2011 but gained seats in the Duma again in 2016 (343 out of 450).

Table 8.1 The number of parties winning seats in Duma elections, 1993 to 2016

Year	1993	1995	1999	2003	2007	2011	2016
Parties	14	23	6	4	4	4	4

Duma elections of 2011 and 2016

In the summer of 2011, most commentators predicted that the dominant United Russia Party would manufacture a supermajority of seats in the parliamentary race. Furthermore, if Putin, who was prime minister at that time, decided to return to the presidency, he would have easy elections in the spring. The reality was that Putin was more vulnerable than often thought (Hale, 2011b). Indeed, the elections of 2011 took place in December after the incumbent President Medvedev had already announced his decision to step down and clear the way for prime minister Putin to run in the presidential elections in March 2012. Putin immediately became a presidential front runner, according to polls. Thus the Duma elections became a certain indicator of people's support for Putin and not only his party, United Russia.

For the first time in history, the candidates were elected for a five-year term in accordance with a 2008 Federal Law. Seven political parties were able to register. They introduced their candidates' lists. Political opposition was very critical of the fact that several parties were denied registration, thus losing their chance to run in the elections. During the electoral campaign starting on August 30, most criticism was directed at United Russia and federal and local authorities, who were often accused of unfair or illegal actions to promote the ruling party at the expense of the opposition. For this and other reasons, many political activists and organizations of dissimilar political views called for a boycott of the elections.

Despite criticism and calls to boycott the elections, the electoral turnout was 60 percent. Four parties were able to get enough votes and secure seats while overcoming a 7 percent electoral barrier. (Although as you remember, some seats could be allocated if a party received 5 or 6 percent of the votes cast. However, no party has done this.) United Russia received 49 percent of the votes and acquired 238 seats. The Communist Party came second and received 19 percent of the votes and 92 seats. The Just Russia Party earned 64 parliamentary mandates with 13 percent of the votes. And finally, the LDPR won 56 seats and 11 percent of the votes. For the first time since its inception, the ruling party lost a significant number of seats (77) compared with the previous elections. All other parties gained seats, each getting roughly 30 percent more than four years previously.

The elections, however, caused unprecedented criticism at home and abroad. The most noteworthy condemnation focused on the alleged unfair electoral practices favoring the ruling party, suppression of the voice of opposition, and the final vote count. The allegations and complaints of electoral fraud were serious and frequent. Most opinion polls in November placed United Russia significantly below the official count of 49 percent. Especially low numbers were predicted for the ruling party in large cities such as Moscow and St Petersburg (Gudkov et al., 2011).

Yet the official results were substantially different. Leaders of all major parties (except United Russia) doubted the legitimacy of the published results. The authorities vigorously brushed off the criticisms. Their key argument was that, although some irregularities had taken place here and there, they were not significant enough to call the elections off. President Medvedev called the elections "fair, just, and democratic," and his party, as he said, referring to the votes, "received exactly what it had" (Medvedev, 2012). However, the protests continued later, especially in Moscow, causing serious irritation in the Kremlin. In December, massive demonstrations—not seen for many years—took place in Moscow and other cities, demanding a recount and new transparent elections. Many people were arrested and charged with rioting. For the first time in many years, people openly condemned the ruling party and their leadership, calling them "crooks and thieves." This label, thanks to the Internet, quickly became a meme.

In the end, United Russia preserved its far-from-overwhelming majority in the Duma and was able to elect its representative, Sergey Naryshkin (b. 1954), former head of the Administration of the President, as its chairman (speaker).

The 2016 legislative elections took place in September with approximately 111 million voters eligible to participate. Compared with the previous Duma elections, this round was relatively uneventful, with no large public protests or arrests during or after the elections. The turnout was low, just below 50 percent. In Moscow and St Petersburg, the numbers were even lower: only over 30 percent of these two largest cities voted. For the first time after the 2014 annexation of Crimea, its voters could cast ballots in a Russian national election. Several countries, including the United States, the United Kingdom, France, and Ukraine did not recognize the legitimacy of the election in Crimea (which most countries consider a part of Ukraine).

Out of 450 seats, 225 are elected by proportional representation from party lists, the system you should remember from Chapter 5. The remaining 225 seats are elected in single-member constituencies where each candidate should win a majority of votes. Of the fourteen parties officially allowed to nominate their candidates, only four surpassed the 5 percent threshold and thus elected their candidates to the Duma. As a result, United Russia again won a strong majority of seats (343), which allowed the party to win legislative votes without forming a coalition with other parties. The new speaker of the Duma, Vyacheslav Volodin (b. 1964) like its previous one, came from the executive branch, where he served as first deputy prime minister.

PRESIDENTIAL ELECTIONS

Presidential elections in Russia have a relatively short history. The first election took place in 1996, as you should remember. Although Gorbachev and after him Yeltsin were called "presidents," the former's title was chairperson and the latter was elected in a republic that was still a part of the Soviet Union. As the first Russian presidential campaign got underway before the 1996 elections, the nascent Russian party system was extremely fragmented, polarized, and volatile, with virtually every conceivable ideological perspective and societal interest being represented, along with the personal followings of various leaders. Three out of every four Russians did not identify with any of the parties vying for their support (White, Rose, and McAllister, 1996: 135).

The election of 1996: anxiety and populism

With the presidential race starting just six months after the 1995 Duma elections, Yeltsin's prospects for reelection looked slim (Stavrakis, 1996: 14). In a nation in the throes of hyper-inflation and mired in an unpopular war in the breakaway republic of Chechnya, only 6 percent said they were planning to vote for Yeltsin (Treisman, 1996b), whose popularity had declined steadily since 1992 (White et al., 1996: 167–70). Sixty-five percent thought Russians' opinion of the government was worse than it had been in the former USSR (Grunt et al., 1996; Wyman, 1997: 125–7). The threat of the Communist Party taking over the Kremlin was very real. Some of Yeltsin's close supporters believed that the only way he could stay in office would be to cancel the election (Korzhakov, 1997). What happened next is indicative of Russia's politics over the past 30 years: to be in power means to use all the methods available to stay in power. It is also essential for the ruling establishment to never get caught red-handed in the process.

Yeltsin made a strong and astonishing comeback. In the first-round ballot on June 16 he received 35 percent of the vote. The early favorite Zyuganov, representing the Communist Party, made it into the runoff with 32 percent. The other candidates (including Zhirinovsky with 6 percent) were eliminated (Treisman, 1996c: 64; Mitofsky, 1996). Yeltsin won the runoff election with 54 percent of the vote; his opponent received 40 percent.

There were several reasons for Yeltsin's win, including bitter memories of communist rule, his aggressive campaign maneuvering, Zyuganov's poor strategy, the pro-Yeltsin media onslaught, and Yeltsin's relentless populist promises and pork-barrel programs for the regions (McFaul, 1997). The opposition to Yeltsin was disorganized during the 1990s (Abalkin, 1995: 30), and this became its major problem during the election year. Yeltsin's team ran a near-classic negative campaign, when a candidate wins not because people are enthusiastic about him, but because he portrays his opponent as a real threat to the country (Sigelman and Shiraev, 2002).

Moreover, Yeltsin and his electoral team believed they were justified in conducting a smear campaign against his opponent because it was so important to prevent a communist takeover. His opponents maintained that the Yeltsin team had used illegal methods including pressuring the media to smear Zyuganov's supporters and other communists, launching illegal financial operations, and even direct electoral fraud (Gallagher, 2017; Valenty and Shiraev, 2001). The leadership in the Kremlin ignored these allegations, but it must have brought it home to them how difficult it was to manage a successful presidential campaign without the organized infrastructure of a loyal, pro-government national party.

The presidential elections of 2000 and 2004: managing from the top

On December 31, 1999, Yeltsin announced that he was resigning in favor of Putin, who became acting president. Yeltsin's resignation and premature exit from the political scene had the effect of moving the presidential election, which had been scheduled for June, up to March 26, and of immediately establishing Putin as the unquestionable front runner.

The sudden resignation threw his opponents into near-total disarray, and brought Putin to office in an atmosphere of high hopes. In remarkably short order, Putin had been transformed from an obscure functionary into the most popular politician in the country. According to a nationwide survey conducted in January, Putin enjoyed a remarkable 79 percent approval rate for his early performance in office. This was widely regarded as a sure sign that he would be elected in March, and numerous poll results bore out that indication. In polls by national organizations after Putin succeeded Yeltsin in office, none of his potential or actual rivals ever came closer than 25 points behind him (Sigelman and Shiraev, 2002).

Many attributed Putin's victories to the dramatic turnaround in public support for the Chechen war. It was a very unpopular conflict, but Putin was able to present it to the public as Russia's ultimate struggle for survival against terrorists. He won widespread public approval for his strong stand. In the absence of an effective opposition, and aided by the three-month advancement of the election calendar occasioned by Yeltsin's resignation, Putin managed to elbow aside the other reformist and centrist candidates in the first round, and redefine the election as "a referendum on hopes about the future rather than on his own performance during the previous five years" (Treisman, 1996b: 3). It then effectively became a confrontation between dissatisfaction with the status quo and fear of the communists' return.

In 2004, Putin ran against five other candidates and easily won 71 percent of the votes. These were probably the least contested presidential elections in recent Russian history. Among the factors contributing to Putin's remarkable success were improving economic conditions and increasing prices for oil and gas, Russia's main sources of revenue (we will return to this issue in Chapter 10). The living standards of most Russian families at that time improved. Putin symbolized certainty in a country hungry for stability.

The 2008 elections: staying the course

As mentioned above, presidential elections are supervised by the CEC, which bases its decisions on federal law (in this case, a Federal Law of January 10, 2003). The Federation Council set the date for the next presidential elections (which had to be on a Sunday, between 90 and 100 days after the official announcement, which followed the date-setting) as March 2, 2008. This gave candidates about four months to campaign. In comparison, in the United States the earliest primaries and caucuses begin in January, about 10 months prior to the presidential elections.

According to the law, officially registered political parties can nominate presidential candidates in Russia, and individuals can also nominate themselves. About 30 people expressed their desire to run in 2008. However, only six people overcame the difficult, requirement-filled nomination process. This process appeared open and democratic. On the other hand, the system was heavily biased in favor of only one candidate. From the start, Medvedev was a clear front runner.

Medvedev had the support of the four major parties including United Russia. Most importantly, he had an official endorsement from the incumbent president. At one occasion, a spectacular televised show was designed to display both Putin and Medvedev walking together casually near the Kremlin wall and then Putin announcing before the cheering crowd his support for his young associate. Putin in turn received an offer from Medvedev to become prime minister in 2008 should Medvedev win the March elections. Putin agreed to accept the nomination (Lenta, 2007a). Opinion polls showed a lead for Medvedev as early as December, and his substantial support (60–70 percent) did not diminish during the winter. Medvedev refused to debate with any of his official opponents on television, a typical strategy of most clear front runners in presidential elections in other countries. His campaign involved travel into Russia's regions and staged televised meetings with local officials who certainly appeared supportive and loyal to him.

Should presidential candidates in Russia do fundraising? Sure, they are free to do so. Yet in Russia, it is the government that funds federal elections. Each candidate has the right to solicit and accept additional private funds. As expected, Medvedev drew more campaign donations than other candidates: he received 188 million rubles (about $7 million at that time), compared with Zhirinovsky's 160 million and Zyuganov's 53 million. However, unlike his opponents, who spent almost all their funds, Medvedev spent just 15 percent of his campaign fund (Raikov, 2008). He sure could afford to save the money mostly because of the positive media coverage of his candidacy. In the end, a very predictable campaign ended on March 2. According to the official results, Medvedev won with 70.3 percent of the votes cast. Zyuganov drew 17.7 percent of the vote, Zhirinovsky received 9.3 percent, and Andrei Bogdanov received 1.3 percent. Dmitry Medvedev duly became the third president of the Russian Federation.

In a 2009 poll, Russians were asked what they thought about Putin's future political career. More than 87 percent of respondents believed that Putin had preserved his influence on Russia's political life after leaving the presidency (Levada, 2009c). This was not a surprising result. Very few doubted that Putin as prime minister would lose his influence and would not run for the presidency again. And soon he was back.

The 2012 and 2018 presidential elections

According to the Federal Law, political parties represented in the Duma may propose a presidential candidate, who must be at least 35 years old. He or she must have permanently lived in Russia for at least ten years. Outside these restrictions, any person in theory may seek nomination. In this case, they should register, assemble a portfolio of documents, and collect 2 million signatures across Russia in support of their candidacy.

President Medvedev announced in September his decision not to run for the second term (although he had the legal right to do so) and suggested Putin as presidential candidate from United Russia. Medvedev also agreed to become prime minister if Putin were elected president in March 2012. Putin continued enjoying substantial electoral support across age, gender, and various social groups (Hale, 2011b).

Twelve candidates sought registration as presidential candidates in 2011. Only five were registered. The other seven were rejected for various reasons including missed deadlines, missing qualifying requirements, incomplete paperwork, or high percentages of fraudulent signatures from so-called supporters. Along with four representatives of major political parties, one candidate was new: Mikhail Prokhorov, an industrialist, investor, and multi-billionaire (he also at that time owned an NBA team) who came with a broad, centrist, and pro-business political program with the populist promises (such as giving away money to the needy) and targets (such as taxing some of the super-rich) that are almost obligatory for Russia. He declared Putin his major opponent (Prokhorov, 2012).

Most polls predicted Putin's victory in the first round, in which he had to secure more than 50 percent of the votes. In fact, Putin received 63 percent. Although it was less than he had won four years earlier, the victory was nevertheless decisive. His closest opponent, the communist Zyuganov, received 17 percent, almost 10 percent more than the billionaire Prokhorov, who finished third. Several mass demonstrations protested the results. The most significant was in Moscow, where riot police were bused in (Roxburgh, 2012b).

The 2018 Russian presidential election took place in March. Putin ran for the fourth time in his political career. Remember that, prior to becoming president for the first time in 2020, he had never been a political candidate in any major election. This lack of experience in an elected position is not unusual for politicians: consider Donald Trump in the United States, for example. What was unusual, though, was that Putin ran for the fourth term as president. Constitutional limits on executive power exist in all democracies, including Russia, yet in relatively few such countries have attempts been made to amend the constitution to extend the power of the incumbent leader.

After several months of speculation in 2017 and vague statements about thinking about whether to run (a common tactic of many politicians to create suspense and draw more attention), Putin declared his candidacy. He ran as an independent, which could have indicated both a desire to draw wider public support and also diminishing confidence in the electoral strength of United Russia as a political party. Putin ran against seven other candidates and won with 77 percent of the vote.

The results of the 2018 elections showed that Putin and the ruling party had enough resources and bureaucratic power to pull a clear victory. Another lesson was almost as obvious. Russian politics had not produced a strong and charismatic candidate capable of challenging the established system when the incumbent using his power and the uncritical media was free to do almost anything he decided to determine the fate of the Russian presidency.

Case in point: Russian electoral turnout

Unlike in some countries such as Australia, Russian laws do not require their citizens to vote: Russians may choose whether to participate in elections or stay home. Supporters of compulsory voting argue that this requirement is good for democracy and is more representative than volunteer voting, which sometimes results in very low turnout. Opponents argue that compulsory voting is nondemocratic and brings uninformed people to polling stations. Russia's voting turnout resembles some countries in the West. In 1991, Boris Yeltsin was elected president in an election in which 75 percent of the population voted, the largest proportion in Russia's history. During the first round of the 1996 elections, about 70 percent of those eligible to vote came to the polling stations. In the 2012 presidential elections, the turnout was 65 percent. In 2018, the reported turnout was 77 percent. The average turnout during almost two decades of federal elections has been approximately 66–67 percent. The number is higher, around 70 percent, for presidential elections and lower, about 60 percent, for parliamentary elections. The 2003 Duma elections turnout was 55.6 percent. The lowest so far was the 2016 legislative election, with barely 50 percent of all eligible voters showing up. What do you think: if voting were compulsory in Russia, how would it have affected electoral outcomes?

Source: WCIOM-RBK (2008); Central Electoral Commission (http://cikrf.ru/eng/).

CRITICAL THINKING ABOUT ELECTIONS IN RUSSIA

The format and frequency of elections are determined everywhere by historical context and specific circumstances. In the United Kingdom, for example, there are no presidential elections because there is already an unelected, largely ceremonial head of state living in Buckingham Palace. In the United States, the federal authorities do not establish a special agency to monitor federal and state elections. Only in the most difficult cases can the US Supreme Court become involved to adjudicate a case, as happened in 2000. In Lebanon, there is a special electoral system known as confessionalism, designed to ensure that Christians and Muslims both have a share of power.

Russian democratic elections have long roots but a relatively short history. Most comments about elections in Russia refer to their transparency and the ability of the ruling elites to manipulate electoral outcomes.

The electoral process is never perfect

Nobody says that elections in Russia must be perfect (in which country are they?). However, the official Russian government's position is that the elections in the country have always been democratic and free: people are allowed to express their opinions in any way they want; they can cast their votes for any candidate.

It is also argued that Russian parliamentary and presidential elections are not much different from many similar elections taking place in most democratic countries. For example, the Organization for Security and Cooperation in Europe (OSCE) analyzed the Duma elections prior to 2011 and called them for the most part free and fair. Other elections received positive evaluations for their apparent transparency and accuracy. The 2000 and 2004 Russian elections generally met international standards (Shleifer and Treisman, 2004). The 2011 Duma elections caused most controversy, of course, but a few random procedural violations, it is argued, did not represent fraud and could not have altered the results (Hale, 2011b).

Russian pro-government commentators tend to believe that most of the criticism about Russian elections is caused by a negative perception of Russia's leadership. Violations of electoral laws take place in every country. It is argued that, in many elections, including the 2000 presidential races in the United States, the results were challenged in court, which has almost never been the case in Russia. Like everywhere in the world, there are government supporters and opponents, but the Russian government allows all of them to participate in elections if they are officially registered. Some parties dominate in elections. For example, in Japan the Liberal Democratic Party was dominant for decades and faced little opposition until 2009. As in other countries, newspapers and television in Russia have their preferences and freely endorse political candidates.

Overall, these and similar arguments support the view that Russia has a fairly democratic electoral system, as electoral officials maintained (Churov, 2009b). However, other observers disagree with these assessments.

Elections are not free

The critics underline that elections in Russia have been largely undemocratic. A serious problem is that the ruling elites have imposed an electoral system that, in fact, puts serious limitations on a truly competitive and transparent political process. Critics also focus on specific systematic violations taking place in Russia. Such violations are not random mistakes or the inevitable setbacks of an otherwise developing democracy. They represent deliberate attempts to control the elections by authoritarian means to achieve certain strategic goals: to preserve and multiply the wealth and power of those elites (Stent, 2019; McFaul and Stoner-Weiss, 2008: 72). Putin and Russia's ruling elites, according to this view, have been able to establish a political system that is amenable to their interests, and now they are making sure that the electoral system will produce results in favor of the Kremlin and the elites closely associated with Putin each and every time. Several points of criticism are among the most important.

First, it is argued that the Kremlin does everything possible to create a political atmosphere that is favorable to the functioning of pro-establishment political parties. These parties, such as United Russia and A Just Russia to some degree, receive support from powerful government officials and are in a good position to win elections. On the other hand, only a few opposition political parties are allowed to win seats in the Duma. Critics have long claimed that both the Communist Party and Zhirinovsky's LDPR are oppositional Duma forces only in name, because they prefer not to challenge the established majority between the elections (Trenin, 2006). One of the many mechanisms to reduce competition is the process of official party registration. This procedure excludes many parties from elections and political competition, as we saw in Chapter 7. The other mechanism is party lists. This electoral practice can easily prevent small parties from winning representation in the Duma.

However, when the reputation of the ruling party, United Russia, began to fall in 2019, many candidates running for municipal offices in local elections declared their candidacies as independents, thus conveniently abandoning their United Russia affiliation. This was particularly clear in Moscow and St Petersburg, the two largest Russian cities. In Moscow, according to the opposition, such candidates received preferential treatment from local electoral committees while their truly independent competitors could not register as candidates for bogus reasons. These actions caused massive protests in Moscow in August 2019, during which the police used brutal force against peaceful individuals (Nechepurenko, 2019).

Second, it is also suggested that the media in Russia, especially television networks, have long been under the financial and administrative control of the government (McFaul and Stoner-Weiss, 2008: 70). As a result, pro-government parties and candidates receive practically unlimited airtime and very positive coverage during electoral campaigns. In contrast, the political opposition these days has very limited access to television, which remains the most popular medium in Russia in the first two decades of the 21st century, especially among older age cohorts. This practice of favoritism inevitably influences political campaigns and ultimately the results of elections.

Political mechanisms

Other critical assessments of Russian elections are mostly concerned about finding and explaining the ways in which the elites and other interest groups manage elections in Russia in their favor. We illustrate these assessments with two examples.

The 1996, 2000, 2008, 2012, and 2018 presidential elections showed the importance of the incumbency factor in Russian politics. Yeltsin appointed Putin in 1999, and Putin won the election in 2000. Similarly, Putin appointed his successor in 2007, and Medvedev easily won his election several months later. Medvedev yielded his right to run for the second term and recommended Putin. Next, he won decisively in 2012 and 2018. In the United States, in comparison, vice presidents running for the White House are not that successful. Over the past 50 years, four incumbent US vice presidents have run for the presidency but only one has succeeded: George Bush in 1988. Unlike Putin, President Yeltsin in 1999 was very unpopular. Yet Putin, a quickly appointed and virtually unknown Yeltsin successor, won by a landslide several months later. Trust in Putin measured by polls (see Chapter 4) was never below 45 percent during his two decades in power. One possible explanation for this takes us again to the individual personality of political leaders. When an apparent strongman becomes a front runner, most people tend to rally round the leader. In addition, as polls suggested, the most prominent type of response from an average individual about why they voted for Putin was "the absence of an acceptable alternative" (CSR, 2012).

Russian elections generally reflect the balance of power among powerful groups and business interests. For example, Boris Yeltsin in the 1990s represented influential magnates who had amassed their fortunes during the early years of his government. These powerful business interests did everything possible to keep Yeltsin and then Putin in power to help produce favorable (to them) outcomes in elections. In today's Russia, one reason the elections are not necessarily free is that the business and administrative elites around Putin are pursuing the further redistribution of wealth and further consolidation of their resources and are therefore very much interested in preserving their power in the Kremlin and the Federal Assembly. Political power is needed to win business and financial battles, which in turn help to win political offices (Treisman, 2008: 10).

CONCLUSION

Although Russia as a country has a history of elections, very few of them in the past were democratic if we judge them from the viewpoint of Western liberal democracy. On the surface Russian elections of the past 30 years or so have been based on a multiparty system and voters have enjoyed basic political liberties, but many questions remain about the true nature of these elections. Supporters of the Russian model of "sovereign democracy" maintain that elections are free and democratic, and comparable to elections in most other democratic countries. Some commentators go further, claiming that Russia's electoral system today is a "work in progress," as we have seen in previous chapters, as are many other social and political institutions in the country. In this context, Russia should continue to go through a difficult process of reforms before it establishes a viable, democratic electoral system. However, most critical observers within Russia and outside the country tend to disagree. They consider the Russian electoral system to be deliberately tainted by authoritarianism. The ruling elites increasingly often ignore democratic principles and use elections to further consolidate their own power.

There is still hope that one day Russia will have democratic and free elections. Since 2012, several laws have been gradually implemented, as scheduled, to democratize the electoral system. But the changes have been largely superficial. The keys to manage the elections are in the Kremlin, not in the people's hands. More convincing, democratic reforms will be needed. Otherwise, contrary to what the Kremlin leaders plan, more people will turn away from them. Or maybe turn against them.

9 Political Communication and Mobilization

Flipping through Russian cable channels during primetime, you might find a historic documentary, the latest BBC international news updates, episodes of *The Simpsons* with a Russian soundtrack, a Russian gangster thriller, or a recent National Basketball Association game. Browse the web in Russia and you will find most likely almost the same variety of sites that you could find browsing from San Francisco or London. Article 29 of the Constitution of the Russian Federation guarantees every person freedom of "thought and speech." The basic law also guarantees Russian citizens the right to express their opinions and beliefs by lawful means. The Constitution declares the freedom of the press. It explicitly prohibits censorship. How are these important constitutional guarantees implemented in Russia? Where do Russian people get information related to government and politics, and how do they use it? How do they communicate their own ideas and organize their political actions?

This chapter deals with **political communication**: the general ways in which information related to politics and government is distributed in Russia. Attention is given to common means of communication including television, radio, newspapers, and the Internet. The chapter provides a brief overview of the media and their ownership and major political agendas. It also deals with **political mobilization**, or ways to strengthen, preserve, or change the existing political system.

KEY DEVELOPMENTS

Although new technology is constantly increasing people's access to information, authoritarian governments try to limit or control that access, especially if the information relates to political power. Political censorship is still widespread in many countries these days. Some states, such as China, have designed their own Internet system in which the government owns online access routes so that private businesses and individuals can only rent bandwidth and only from the government. In Russia, as many indicators suggest, the government has been eager to fully control the web. One of the reasons for greater control is national security, as is often stated. The same reason was often used in the Soviet Union to justify the necessity to censor newspapers and broadcast media.

The Soviet period

In the Soviet Union, the Communist Party exercised total control of the country's mass media. The central and regional party committees supervised and managed newspapers, radio, and television. The government played a **gatekeeping** role, determining which information was allowed or recommended for publication and which was not. One of the general criteria determining suitability for publication was agreement with party policies and Marxist–Leninist ideology. Gatekeeping is a special form of **political censorship**: the restrictive practice of reviewing and determining what is allowed to be published or broadcast, based on ideological or political considerations. Until the middle of the 1980s, the vast majority of Soviet citizens lived on a strict informational diet: any printed or transmitted information (such as radio or television) that could have undermined the power of the Communist Party and its main ideological doctrines was carefully censored.

Political censorship was part of political mobilization in the Soviet Union. Censorship noticeably affected individual political behavior and mass participation: most ordinary people and media professionals were aware which information was permissible to publish and publicly discuss. They also knew what was prohibited. For example, newspaper editors were not allowed to publish critical information about their country's domestic and foreign policy, the failing policies of friendly communist regimes (such as in East Germany or Cuba), the accomplishments of free-market capitalism, or human rights violations in the Soviet Union. Nor did reporters and editors dare to print information related to the Communist Party leaders' health or their personal lives, including their marital problems, hobbies, and so on.

Gorbachev's policies of glasnost in the mid-1980s (see Chapter 3) first limited and then eliminated political censorship. For the first time in more than 70 years, people received access to uncensored news, reports, and analyses. At least two key fundamental questions about freedom of speech were debated across the country in the late 1980s and early 1990s. The first question was, can freedom of speech be unlimited? The second question was about ownership. Who should have the right to own a newspaper or radio station, and who should determine what information is published or broadcast? These debates in Russia resurfaced again.

Crucial changes

Many people in Russia supported the new political atmosphere of freedom in the country and rejected political restrictions on free speech. However, scores of others believed that, for the sake of social stability, some restrictions on speech might be imposed.

Because the government no longer legally controlled the media, fierce battles began among various individuals and business groups for the ownership of existing and newly emerging media. The process of consolidation of private media ownership heated up under President Yeltsin. Gradually, up to the mid-1990s, the most important newspapers and radio and television stations came into private hands. Putin realized that, after losing control of the media, the government's gatekeeping and communication capacities would be weakened.

In the first decade of the 21st century and after, the government undertook a massive and sustained effort to place the media under federal control. These policies found substantial support in Russia, where public resentment against monopolies and the super-rich has always been strong. Many Russians continued to believe that mass media should to some degree be regulated and controlled by a central authority. In 2001, 57 percent of Russians said that Russian media needed government censorship (Public Opinion Foundation, March 22). In 2014, almost half of Russians believed in the necessity of censoring the Internet (Levada, 2014). In 2019, however, half of Russians were against the law of punishing "disrespectful" online statements against the government while 37 percent were supportive of the law (Gudkov, 2019).

Because the government did not have the legal means to seize newspapers or television and radio stations, one of the most suitable ways to regain control was by buying out their existing owners. The prime target was television. Gradually, the government gained financial control over the most powerful television networks. Over a relatively short period, most broadcast outlets moved from private hands into the control—through a variety of financial and business institutions—of the federal government. In effect this was nationalization, or the process of taking an industry or assets into public ownership (Alekseeva et al., 2008). To critics, the nationalization of the media in Russia was another example of the antidemocratic policies of the Kremlin, a continuation of the consistent effort by the federal government to expand its political, financial, and economic power in the country (Pipes, 2007).

During the process of nationalization of the television networks, two former media tycoons, Boris Berezovsky and Vladimir Gusinsky, emigrated from Russia, fearing criminal prosecution (see also Chapter 13). When President Putin came to power in 1999, the three most powerful television networks were privately owned. Within a few years, the Kremlin controlled all three, plus several others. The federal government either owned or had commanding shares in all major Russian television networks and two national radio networks (Voroshilov, 2009; Lipman, 2008).

THE MEDIA TODAY

In this section of the chapter we look at the major Russian media, including television, newspapers, radio, and the Internet, and their general role in political communication in the country.

Television networks

A television network is a communication enterprise. It consists of a company responsible for producing programs, such as news reports, talk shows, films, or discussions. The company then distributes its programming through airwaves or cable to local stations called affiliates. In return for receiving daily programming, these local stations share with the programming company the revenues collected for commercials or user fees. There are, of course, other business arrangements, but this is the typical setup in Russia.

Table 9.1 lists the most influential television networks in Russia. The viewing figures were provided by the companies themselves.

Financial power gives the Kremlin, both directly and indirectly, the ability to manage the networks' general policies. Although the law specifically prohibits owners from interfering in matters related to news content, it is difficult to believe that such interference does not exist. In Russia, as well as in many other countries in which the government owns the media, control can be exercised in a number of ways without using evident censorship.

The first way is **agenda setting**, the process by which the owner determines what type of information will be seen as news at any time, and what will not. For example, in 2011, Russians received mostly critical views of the airstrikes in Libya by the Arab League and Western powers to topple the regime of Gaddafi. After 2012, Russian television was blasting the antigovernment Syrian opposition. While condemning the actions of ISIS in Syria,

Table 9.1 Leading Russian television networks: viewing figures and ownership

TV network and location	Number of viewers having access	Ownership
Pervyj Kanal (The First Channel)	200 million worldwide	Joint stock company; at least 39 percent belongs to the federal government
Rossyia-1 (Russia-1) Moscow	200 million worldwide	Federal government
Russia-24	100 million worldwide	Federal government
TV Centr (TV Center) Moscow	100 million worldwide	Government of Moscow
NTV Moscow	120 million worldwide	Gazprom-media (partially controlled by the federal government)

Source: viewing figures provided by the companies.

Russian television was very critical of the United States' actions in that region, including Washington's policies toward Iran. Overall, the media in Russia seldom produce success stories resulting from policies of the United States or NATO countries. Russia also has a government-funded news network which seeks to improve Russia's image globally. It is called RT. Most of RT's content, which can easily be seen on cable or satellite in many countries, as well as accessed on the web, is critical of the United States, Western Europe, NATO, Israel, and the free-market global economic order (Dale, Cohen, and Smith, 2012). Spreading fake news to confuse the public on important social and political issues has been a pattern for years (MacFarquhar, 2016).

The second way to exercise control is **framing**. This is deliberate interpretation of events and polices from a particular standpoint or in certain contexts. Covering Iran, Russian television seldom mentions the dangers of the Iranian nuclear program, emphasizes instead the importance of productive economic relations between Moscow and Tehran, and criticizes Western sanctions against this country. After Barack Obama was elected president of the United States in 2008, Obama's electoral victory was framed as a defeat for the policies of the former President Bush, which Russia had criticized relentlessly. When Donald Trump was elected president in 2016, his victory was framed as a repudiation of Obama's foreign policy toward Russia (Shiraev and Khudoley, 2019; Shiraev, 2008).

Table 9.2 offers some examples of how Russian television networks use agenda setting and framing in their coverage of selected international events or developments. It should be clear that these are major trends in the coverage, while exceptions to these trends obviously exist.

In sum, the television networks tend to report and analyze international events in a way that is in agreement with the basic policies of the government. When the government does not have an official position—this relates primarily to sports and entertainment—the coverage is determined largely by the preferences and demands of the market.

Table 9.2 Russian television's coverage of selected international events and topics

Events and policies	Coverage in Russia
Conflicts in Iraq and Afghanistan	Russian government maintains a negative view of US involvement in both countries. Russian networks' coverage is mostly critical of US policies. Emphasis was put on US casualties and the difficulties that people in Iraq and Afghanistan were experiencing.
Iranian nuclear program	The official Russian position was that the Iranian nuclear program did not represent an immediate military threat. Most reports deal with cooperation between Iran and Russia, and also focus on Western countries' critical position toward Iran.
The war in Georgia in 2008	In contrast to most of the world's media, Russian television journalists and commentators took an anti-Georgian position. Almost every report about Georgia was critical and accused this country of genocide. The atrocities committed by the Russian side were neglected.
Events in Syria	Unlike the coverage in Europe and North America, Russian networks provide a pro-government view of Russia's military actions in the country and generally are supportive of the government in Damascus.
The 2016 and 2020 elections in the United States	A general pro-Trump tone of the coverage was noticeable by many independent observers in 2016 but not in 2020.
Sports news and events: NBA and NHL	Russian people can watch (often live) important basketball and hockey games played in North America. European soccer is shown too. American football and baseball are rarely shown on Russian television due to lack of popularity.

Newspapers

There are several types of owners of today's most popular Russian papers. The federal government is one of them. For example, *Rossiyskaya Gazeta* (Russia's Newspaper) is the official Russian government's daily. It provides the publication of all newly adopted laws and official statements. It also provides regular coverage and analysis of news and events. *Krasnaya Zvezda* (Red Star) is the official daily paper of the Defense Ministry. All military bases, military institutions, and installations have to subscribe to this paper. The materials in it are addressed primarily to men and women serving in the armed forces or working for the military in some capacity. The paper is also known for its patriotic tone and a strong pro-government attitude regarding its domestic and foreign policy.

Political parties own newspapers as well. One of the most popular remains *Pravda* (Truth), once the official daily paper of the Central Committee of the Communist Party of the Soviet Union. Today, *Pravda* expresses the views of the Russian left. *Pravda* remains consistently critical of the Kremlin's leadership and its policies. It maintains a clearly anti-Western and anti-American approach in its coverage of international affairs. Another newspaper, *Sovetskaya Rossiya* (Soviet Russia), is similar to *Pravda* in its reporting of domestic and international events. Like *Pravda,* this newspaper has a clear pro-communist orientation. It calls itself "an independent people's paper," and remains very critical of the free market, social inequality, and the policies of most Western countries.

There are also independent newspapers such as *Izvestia* (News). This was once the official paper of the Soviet legislature; now *Izvestia* is under private ownership. Its publications are designed for the political center and are fairly pro-government. The most popular daily newspaper remains *Kommersant*. This publication focuses on domestic and international events and pays special attention to business and finance matters. Among the most popular weekly papers is *Argumenty i Facty* (Arguments and Facts), which claims sales close to 2 million copies per week. It is a private informational, analytical, and entertainment paper lying largely within Russia's political center.

Novaya Gazeta (New Paper), which is printed in Moscow, has been the strongest critic of government policies in Russia to date. This newspaper's orientation is liberal democratic. It is privately owned and operated. One of its owners is former Soviet President Mikhail Gorbachev. The paper criticizes authoritarian trends in Russian government policies. Compared with other newspapers, it is significantly less supportive of Moscow's confrontational foreign policy. It is also more willing than the other papers to interview people who oppose the Kremlin leaders and experts. *Novaya Gazeta* has a circulation of around 120,000, although that number that does not reflect the popularity of this paper online (Photo 9.1).

Most papers in Russia are not under the government's financial control. A law was signed in 2014 to limit foreign ownership stakes in any Russian media assets to only 20 percent. The law resulted in many foreign companies selling their stock and leaving Russia altogether.

Radio

As in other countries, Russian radio is heavily entertainment oriented. Music programs dominate the radio waves, but there are also many information programs and politically oriented talk shows. The federal government owns several radio networks, such as Mayak (Lighthouse) and Radio Rossii (Radio Russia). The Moscow city government owns a leading information-oriented station, Govorit Moskwa (Moscow Is Speaking). Among several noteworthy developments of recent years has been a deliberate attempt to reduce the power of foreign information sources in Russia.

For example, for several years the US federally funded network Radio Svoboda (Radio Freedom) was able to broadcast its material through almost 60 radio stations located in many areas of Russia. Since 2006, Radio Freedom has only been allowed to broadcast from Moscow. In 2012, even more restrictions were put in place. The authorities claim that decision was prompted by the company's violation of business regulations. The company management disagreed, and believed it was an attempt at political censorship, a view that is accepted in the West. The restrictive measures were a response to the station's critical approach to the government and its policies.

Web

Radio Freedom has its own site in Russian http://www.svobodanews.ru/.
See also Voice of America's Russian service in Russian: https://www.golos-ameriki.ru/

Photo 9.1 Plenty of printed materials is available in Russia today: from global and local news to sports and entertainment. Information critical of the government, however, is available almost exclusively on the web.

As you might assume, traditional FM and AM radio stations and newspapers these days are increasingly switching to digital and streaming technologies for Russian-speaking audiences in their country and worldwide.

Digital media

Because of Russia's vast territory, it is important for a radio network to have local stations that can rebroadcast its signals. This need for local affiliates creates an opportunity for the government to impose legal restrictions on broadcasting companies: to obtain a license to broadcast, you have to provide content that the government considers appropriate. However, with the development of satellite radio and the Internet, the authorities have fewer restrictive options. Therefore, some of the new media based on digital and satellite technologies have become not just a real business challenge to traditional media such as newspapers, television, and conventional radio, but also a political challenge to the government's ability to control broadcasting. Digital newspapers, news outlets, social networks, and blogs remained somewhat unregulated in Russia until the 2010s.

On various independent Russian blogs, it is very easy to find information that is both sympathetic to and critical of the Russian government, its policies, and its political leaders. Critics from the left sometimes praise the government for its populist policies but blast it for policies supporting the free market and big business. Oil and gas companies are under constant criticism for high energy prices and the windfall profits of their managers. In contrast, other authors and commentators publish nationalistic and openly racist materials about Russia's immigration policies, and the necessity to beef up national security and conduct a more assertive foreign policy. From their side, liberal critics blast Moscow's authoritarian policies, physical force against the opposition, and criminal cases fabricated against government critics. They ridicule the Kremlin's confrontational approach in relations with other countries, such as the United Kingdom and the United States. To get some sense of this coverage, see the book's website and visit some Russian sites and blogs in English and Russian.

In the early 2000s, Russian authorities seemed to pay little attention to political discussions on the web. These days, with the rapid spread of social media, the balance of informational power is changing. More people, mostly the young, are switching to the web and ignore television, which has been so far the main source of political news in Russia. Lawyer and journalist Alexei Navalny (b. 1976) maintains one of the most popular political blogs in Russia, critical of corruption and power abuses (see the box "Key figure: Alexei Navalny"). Authorities frequently shut it down. Because of the blog's popularity and message, Navalny has become one of the most recognizable representatives of Russia's political opposition. He and others regularly post their reports on YouTube and other social networks.

The experience of other countries such as China suggests that, when the Internet becomes popular and accessible to large numbers of educated citizens, the government might step in to apply censorship. Critics maintain that the first step in this direction has already been taken. In 2012 a new law in Russia gave the government the power to block certain sites carrying inappropriate content. Although the law aims largely at sexual predators and disallows information promoting drug use and suicide, the definition of "inappropriate" has been vague and may expand. In 2019, Putin signed a new law to enable the creation of a national network, which would enable Russia to operate separately from the rest of the world, in case of a crisis. A largely theoretical idea, it was placed on a legal foundation. Internet providers are now obliged to filter traffic, and a federal agency will receive substantial powers, including official "switch off" rights to shut down any provider. Critics within Russia, of course, disagreed, assuming that this law was another step toward Russia's self-isolation (Prokopenko, 2019).

Despite the possibilities open to it, the Kremlin has generally rejected expensive Soviet-style censorship and adopted different strategies of political communication and mobilization. These strategies are inexpensive and apparently efficient; let us now look at them.

Key figure: Alexei Navalny (1976–)

Alexei Navalny is one of the best-known activists in Russia, and focuses on corruption of Russia's top government figures. He has founded or participated in activities of several officially registered nongovernment organizations including the Anti-Corruption Foundation. He considers himself a politician. He maintains a website and posts regularly on YouTube. In most cases, his posts contain Navalny himself sitting in front of the camera with photographs and short clips accompanying his comments. He usually chooses one politician or government official and then displays and critically discusses this person's material possessions, such as luxury apartments, mansions, foreign property, businesses, etc. and compares the value of these assets with the official salary or tax returns of such an individual. The key is to show an overwhelming discrepancy between what the person earns and what their actual assets are.

It is not surprising to learn from these videos that most of the expensive assets belong to the bureaucrat's spouses, grandmothers, and even their teenage children. Although from the legal standpoint, the law is apparently not broken, the viewer can see the hypocrisy and corruption of such a system, which allows government officials to hide their huge assets (and how did they earn them if their official workplace was a government office?). Over the years, the targets of Navalny's well-researched investigations have included people like the head of the National Guard, Moscow city officials, regional mayors, and even former Prime Minister Medvedev. Navalny also makes critical reviews (and uses sharp words including the famous, "crooks and thieves" to refer to the Kremlin officials) of activities of Russian public officials and top politicians including Putin.

As you should expect, Navalny often himself becomes a target of government investigations, searches, and even arrests based on various charges ranging from "disturbing public order" or "inciting riots" to "receiving financial support from foreign organizations."

Do you think that the government of a sovereign country, like Russia in this case, has the right to control political speech on the web, at least to some degree? Do you believe that political censorship is still needed in some countries (Russia, China, or Turkey) to avoid social unrest? What are your arguments for and against "partial" censorship, the practice that allows political speech in some areas yet limits it in others?

Source: https://navalny.com/

STRATEGIES OF POLITICAL COMMUNICATION AND MOBILIZATION

In the former Soviet Union, the Communist Party used the skills of hundreds of thousands of professionals to implement massive censorship of political communications, including the mass media and interpersonal contacts. The government's goal was to limit the average person's access to information that contained materials challenging official communist ideology. For example, until the late 1980s, it severely restricted the ability of Soviet citizens to travel outside the country, especially to capitalist states. The few lucky tourists who visited France, Italy, or Egypt were not allowed to bring back books critical of the Soviet regime or possess foreign magazines such as *Newsweek* or the *Economist*. The government undertook major and expensive efforts to jam or block the signals from foreign radio stations on Soviet territory. Its strategy was to prevent any form of political news and analysis coming from outside the allowed, pro-government outlets. As you should remember from earlier chapters, the Communist Party was in charge of political mobilization and controlled many other political organizations in the country—all parts of a centralized network of institutions.

From the 1990s, the government's role in political communication and mobilization began to change. There were at least two distinct periods in this process. Initially, during the years of Yeltsin's presidency until the early 2000s, the central government in Moscow appeared to pay little attention to political mobilization. Almost no mass political organizations were created during these years on the federal level to aid Yeltsin's policies and support the reform process (Johnson and White, 2012). The situation changed after Putin's ascendance to power. By reacquiring power over television networks and limiting the possibilities for meaningful political dissent, the central government generally regained important tools for political mobilization. The strategies of political mobilization today are quite different from those in the Soviet Union. In summary:

- The Kremlin and its loyal regional executive offices follow the Constitution and allow in principle a wide range of political freedoms, including freedom of the press;
- However, the government pays serious attention to some sensitive political topics, and above all, it attempts to limit information that could be used to strengthen the political opposition;
- Russian authorities work constantly and use the media and legal action to try to dampen down organized political opposition or popular dissent, especially in Moscow, St Petersburg, and big cites;
- The Kremlin has created its own proactive and complex mobilization policy via media promotion of Russian patriotism, loyalty to the state, hard work, and moral values—all associated with major government policies. Although the strength and effectiveness of the ruling party, United Russia, have been in decline since the end of the second decade of this century, the government has had enough bureaucratic and political tools to exercise political mobilization on its terms.

Let us consider these bullet points in some detail.

What the government ignores

In Russia, people can openly criticize the government and even Moscow's top leaders. For example, most newspapers and television networks practice **muckraking**: investigative efforts to expose examples of excessive bureaucracy, negligence, or corruption among business executives or government officials. Journalists and commentators reveal unpleasant facts and offer critical opinions about the work of private enterprises and government institutions. Their criticisms have evidentiary support. However, legal efforts have been made by the government to limit political speech in the media and on the web by using the charges of "slander" or "instigation" of public rioting.

Unlike in the Soviet Union, today's Russian media publish reports about natural disasters, accidents, wrecks, and violent crimes taking place in local communities and across the nation (similar to what people see daily on the television in any country with free media). With the notable exception of information about ethnic conflicts on Russian territory or accidents related to the military, most reports about various events seem to be uncensored and appear without delay. The government allows reporters and commentators to publish any information related to the health and personal life of senior government officials (although most reporters seem not to be eager to do this).

Private companies publish a wide range of fiction and nonfiction books, and Russian bookstores are filled with new items. The spectrum of political views expressed in these books is striking. Some books promote Russian nationalism. Others are packed with anti-immigrant statements. Some paperbacks are very critical of Russia's past. Others glorify it. Others promote religion as a source of stability, prosperity, and national rebirth. Yet others criticize some of Moscow's policies. The government tends not to censor such publications. Otherwise, the reference to the photo makes no sense. Foreign entertainers frequently perform in major Russian cities (Photo 9.2).

Photo 9.2 Western performers appear frequently on the Russian stage: this poster announces among other things a concert by the American heavy metal band Metallica

In contrast, there are issues to which the government pays special attention, where its actions lead to widespread criticism from independent observers.

What the government opposes

Russian citizens have the constitutional right of assembly, which guarantees Russians the right to form a group or take collective action to pursue the interests of its members. They also have the right to petition before the government. In fact, these rights have been increasingly in question over the last decade or so. In practice the government allows these rights to be applied selectively or even violates them (Rainsford, 2019). Officially, public rallies are legal in Russia. However, only pro-government events tend to go smoothly. The organizers of protest actions are not normally given permission to demonstrate in city centers and are directed to places that are generally further away from the public eye. There are tough rules applied against "public order violators," a category that is legally difficult to define.

The regulations adopted by the Duma and signed by the president into law in 2012 give the authorities vast powers to arrest and prosecute demonstrators who, at the police's discretion, disrupt public order or entice violent actions. Although state-controlled television briefly covers mass protests against government policies, such coverage is usually negative. The protesters are often branded as an angry mob of zealots, disturbed and confused, who seek publicity. Foreign influence is often suggested. Only a few streaming services provide comprehensive coverage of these events, although access to these services is limited for most Russians.

These policies aimed at preventing mass protest rallies, and suppressing news coverage when they do take place, were in part influenced by the mass protests in Georgia, Ukraine, and other countries, which led to serious political change in those countries. Such events were known in Russia as "color revolutions" because the protesters displayed a particular color—orange in Ukraine—as a symbol of their movement. The government in Russia was understandably anxious to prevent similar unrest (Johnson and White, 2012). The events in Bolotnaya Square in Moscow in 2012 and August 2019 ended up with a brutal police crackdown, which was carefully recorded by multiple eyewitnesses (Rainsford, 2019).

Other sensitive topics are Russia's armed conflicts in the eastern Ukraine, northern Caucasus, the Georgia region, military operations in Syria, Central Africa, and other places. Official information from these places was carefully filtered for years. One of the most dramatic events associated with the media coverage of the conflict in Chechnya was the murder of Anna Politkovskaya, a reporter from *Novaya Gazeta*. She was famous for her critical views of Russia's policies, and for reporting on human rights violations in the region. Some of her work was published after her death (Politkovskaya, 2008).

Elbowing out and silencing the opposition is not the only strategy in political communication and mobilization. Since the 2010s, the Russian authorities have been deliberately proactive in their attempts to mobilize government supporters and demobilize the opposition without using oppressive techniques.

What the government promotes

One of the early strategies of mobilization was the promotion of pro-government groups, or movements supporting the president and his policies, such as the Youth Army, established in

2015. This government-sponsored group (its official name is the National Military Patriotic Social Movement Association) was designed to promote the values of patriotism, national service, and national and military history, among others. This group can be distinguished by its brown uniform and red berets, and it had more than 240,000 members in 2020.

The government mobilizes people around several key ideas which it hopes will act as national unifiers. Public schools, for example, are encouraged and funded to create patriotic youth organizations, in many ways resembling the ones that existed in the Soviet Union decades ago. At least four basic strategic ideas about Russia are constantly recycled in the public statements of government officials and echoed by the state-owned media. The first is that democracy of the Western type is not necessarily the best fit for Russia (Putin, 2019a). Next, Russia is destined for a special, unique, and progressive role in history. Third, Russia is surrounded by hostile powers that are plotting to undermine its stability and to take away its sovereignty. And fourth, there was a turning point in Russian history associated with the leadership of Vladimir Putin (Surkov, 2019; Isaev and Baranov, 2009: 190–6).

The failure of the free market to secure economic stability, and the inability of the fragile democratic system to produce an efficient government in the 1990s, led many people in Russia to believe that democracy in its liberal–democratic, mostly Western form was not well suited to Russia. An economic upturn in the 2000s (caused primarily by the high cost of energy resources exported from Russia) gave the government some assurance and then conviction that people would not worry too much about the deficiencies of democracy in Russia provided the country enjoyed economic stability, income growth, and security (Medvedev, 2009b). To further strengthen the idea about Russia's sovereign democracy and the country's "special path" in history, a new foreign policy doctrine was introduced (see the chapters on foreign policy). This official set of guidelines was based on an assumption that Russia has to survive in a very unfriendly environment dominated by the United States. From the late 1990s, most international developments were covered by the Russian media through the prism of a confrontation between a virtuous Russia and the powerful West. Russian people were led to believe that their country's economic rebirth was unwelcome to the West, which saw Russia's rising power in a multipolar world as a threat to the old and unjust international order (Laruelle, 2019).

These ideas become sources for the agenda setting and framing of the news reported in the government-controlled media. Many Russians support such coverage. Communists and nationalists, for example, despite their disagreements on social policies, find the national idea appealing and useful for political mobilization purposes (Umland, 2011). In contrast, promotion of liberal democracy and criticism of the authoritarian methods of the government are either marginalized or severely restricted. The managers of the media companies continue to play their gatekeeping role by excluding information that does not conform to Kremlin policies.

CRITICAL THINKING ABOUT POLITICAL COMMUNICATION AND MOBILIZATION

How does political communication in Russia measure vis-à-vis other countries? What is the changing status of basic civil liberties in Russia, including freedom of speech and freedom of the press? What are the relationships between the Russian media and government? How is political mobilization changing in Russia? Two opposing views have emerged.

Russia is like any other country

From this viewpoint, the Russian media are generally free and independent. Although Russia's experiences with political freedoms have not been perfect, the country is gradually improving its system. According to this view, what happens in Russia is similar to other states in similar historical contexts. Many countries typically have strong executive power and very weak social institutions, and there are often conflicts between journalists and the authorities. Bribery and corruption are often difficult to control, and they definitely undermine freedom of speech. But these negative developments should diminish. Russian journalists, it is argued, like their colleagues in the UK or Germany, also work for big companies and often represent the views of a professional establishment. In Russia, this establishment happens to be close to the government. Therefore, the media can serve a very important political mobilization role, which is needed to consolidate the entire society and pull Russia out of economic and social backwardness.

Ideology, as the argument goes, is part of life. As in every country, broadcast networks and printed publications have their own political, ideological, and cultural preferences. In the United States, the major television networks are commonly considered more liberal than conservative; they frequently side with democratic administrations and serve as sources of political mobilization for a relatively liberal part of America's society. Talk radio in the United States, on the other hand, is for the most part a tool for the political mobilization of conservatives. In a similar fashion, Russian television supports Russian political leaders. The Internet, in contrast, as the argument goes, provides many examples of political dissent.

In response to criticism about persecution of Russian journalists, pro-government commentators argue that, in other countries too, journalists are pressured and silenced. In the United States, they argue, broadcasters often lose their jobs or have to resign for saying "inappropriate" or politically incorrect things on the air or for their actions (such as allegations of sexual misconduct) that have little to do with their professional responsibilities.

Finally, the supportive, pro-government argument goes, in every country journalists must follow the law on what may or may not be printed, aired, or posed. Most countries impose limitations on the use of swearing and profane words, and these are not generally considered violations of free speech. Russia is no exception. The law, for example, tries to prevent deliberate slander or libel. The Constitution only allows the publication of information that has been obtained legally. It also prohibits people from publishing state secrets (see the chapter on Russia's security policies). Journalists admittedly face legal restrictions on coverage of the events in Russia's zones of conflict, such as Chechnya and Ossetia, but then virtually all countries impose similar restrictions in the event of war. The fact that Russia earns very low ranks referring to its political freedoms and free press (Freedom House, an international NGO, considers Russian media "not free") is rejected as a deliberate bias against Russia.

The media are not free

Other observers, however, including domestic and international commentators, maintain that the media in Russia are not free, and freedom of speech faces serious problems in a generally undemocratic environment. The problem is that the government decides which freedoms are to be protected and which are not (Shleifer and Treisman, 2004). The general atmosphere of self-imposed censorship contributes to the implementation of these government policies.

Because of government control, only political figures loyal to the Kremlin have access to the major media on a regular basis. During political campaigns, opposition leaders have very limited airtime. Journalists in disagreement with the government may face serious consequences, including harassment, intimidation, and unemployment. Intimidation of reporters is common, especially of foreign journalists who provide critical coverage of Russia's military or security policies.

Its financial control over the media gives the government power over what appears on air. This happens in violation of the Constitution. The annual reports of Freedom House, a non-government organization studying civil liberties globally, have assessed Russia as one of the most dangerous places in the world to be a journalist, behind only a few other countries. Reporters Without Borders places Russia in 149th place out of 180 available on its Press Freedom Index (2019). The 2012 trial and prosecution of the female punk group Pussy Riot for their unauthorized and blasphemous (as Russian officials called it) performance in a church in Moscow received global attention as an illustration of continuing political censorship in Russia (Gessen, 2014). The constant searches, arrests, and harassment of Alexei Navalny and his organizations across Russia for their investigative journalism are another example in a line of too many.

The Bolotnaya Square events and the aftermath

In December 2011 and through the summer of the following year, Moscow and most large cities in Russia witnessed significant but peaceful rallies and demonstrations. Several gatherings in Bolotnaya Square in Moscow from December 2011 to February 2012 were the largest public protests since 1991. Estimates varied, but the number of protesters was between 60,000 and 160,000 (Gazeta.ru, 2011). The participants demanded the repeal of the results of the December Duma elections and an investigation of electoral fraud violations. Many demands included a new electoral law respecting the rights of oppositional parties. Scores of protesters were wearing white ribbons, now widely recognized as a symbol of political opposition to Russia's political regime and Putin in particular.

The official reaction of the government and the government media to the rallies was extremely negative, dismissive, and defensive (Putin himself made derogatory remarks). In response to foreign criticisms of the way the government held the elections, the media in Russia accused foreign countries of meddling in Russia's domestic affairs. Putin accused the United States' officials of "sending signals" to support the opposition in Moscow (Kuchins, 2012a).

The crackdown and violence against the demonstrators, arrests, and jail —all have served as a signal to millions of Russians: do not dare to openly challenge the system on the streets or on the web. Some commentators have suggested that the Bolotnaya Square events led to a pause in the protest movement in Russia that lasted for years (Raspolov, 2019). Indeed, protest activities were tame for several years afterwards. Further, mass arrests and criminal investigations into peaceful protests in Moscow in August 2019 (against the alleged government fraud in Moscow's municipal elections) also served as a warning that the authorities would continue intimidating and isolating the most active members of the opposition.

However, the publicity of these and other protest actions and their actual political impact (20 of 45 members of the Moscow City Council won their seats running for the opposition, not the ruling party) showed the strength of political mobilization coming from the people, not the government.

Creative authoritarianism

Why do some believe that the system is democratic, yet others maintain that it is not? Can both sides be only partially correct? Probably. The government in Russia appears to adopt a policy of selective tolerance of some civil freedoms and restriction of others. This phenomenon has been identified as **creative authoritarianism** (Shlapentokh, 2009). We look below at how some of its basic elements relate to the media, free speech, and public protests.

First, the government allows people to exercise their freedom of speech in the forms and methods most available to them. As mentioned above, critical reports about the government's policies and public officials do appear in the media, especially on the web. In fact, the Internet has become a hub of both positive and critical information about Russian domestic and foreign policies. Caricatures and YouTube videos ridiculing political leaders are frequent. Books critical of the current regime are sold freely (in Soviet times, their authors would have been jailed or expelled from the country, as the writer Solzhenitsyn was). Officials have found a remarkably clever way of dealing with such critical information: they simply ignore it. In the past, during communism, enormous resources were dedicated to suppressing free speech. Today the government believes it is unnecessary. Television—the most powerful medium—is mostly in the government's hands. Because only a proportion of Russian people have regular access to the web, it is less influential than television. These days, however, the spread of the Internet—a medium that is still relatively free of censorship—is rapidly accelerating.

Reporters and media editors themselves try to show loyalty to the established system. This happens because of an atmosphere of **self-censorship**: that is, people tend to censor their own work because of fear, deference, or a pragmatic judgment that toeing the government line will best serve their interests. Building the political and economic conditions for self-censorship is the third element of creative authoritarianism. The economic boom triggered by high oil and gas prices means that economic factors have become a powerful stimulus. Journalists who please the authorities and are well connected can lay claim to good salaries, benefits, and promotions. They feel they are reporting fairly, but they consciously avoid potential problems with the authorities, and become part of the establishment (Voroshilov, 2009; Lipman, 2008). In particular, because there is not a viable opposition, most journalists prefer to support the status quo. Of course, there are still people inside the political and intellectual establishments who publicly challenge the government, but their numbers are insignificant, they are kept in media obscurity, and they fall well short of providing a powerful source of political mobilization.

Are there elements of creative authoritarianism in the United States or the United Kingdom (or any other country that you want to discuss)? Is creative authoritarianism an inevitable stage of transition from authoritarianism to democracy? In Russia, who will ultimately decide how long this stage should last?

CONCLUSION

Analytical articles, columns, interviews, and reports on Russian policies and its political leadership appear daily in the Russian media. An author or commentator can in theory pass any judgment about the government and aim their criticism at specific policies and officials if they choose. The government also allows empirical studies of public opinion and their subsequent publication and discussion.

Yet critics maintain that freedom of speech in Russia is seriously limited. Mass media, and especially television, the most accessible medium in Russia, are under government control. The restrictions on social networks keep growing. Such limitations on diverse information are detrimental to the functioning of a stable and prosperous society, which is what Russian leaders claim to be building.

Because of the political climate and self-censorship, many reporters and media professionals also choose loyalty to the government over confrontation with it. Under these circumstances, the federal government can often mobilize support, demobilize the opposition, and maintain their main gatekeeping role in the political process. This status quo can change when the traditional physical, political, and legal barriers no longer become effective. The clock is ticking.

Part IV
Russian Policies

In the context of government and politics, a policy is a deliberate and often formal system of principles designed to guide decisions in a certain field. Part IV of the book deals with several key Russian policies. It discusses foreign policy first, focusing on strategies and principles, and then, in the following chapter, it moves to a discussion of specific regions. Chapter 12 discusses security and defense policies, while Russia's economy and business policies, as well as the country's social policies, are covered in the last two chapters of this part.

10 Foreign Policy: Background and Strategies

In general terms, the field of **foreign policy** involves a country's relations with other countries and international organizations. International alliances and foreign policies change with time. Any country's foreign policy depends on many factors, both domestic and global. We have to examine them and trace Russia's consistent features as well as changes in its policy over time. In this chapter we first look at Russia's foreign policy from a historic angle. Then we review the institutions responsible for this policy. After that, we critically examine key strategies of Russian foreign policy in today's world.

FOREIGN POLICY: A BRIEF HISTORY

By the 20th century Russia had emerged as the biggest world state, a multiethnic empire, and a major international player. Emperor Nicholas II (as you should remember from Chapter 2) sought the expansion and strengthening of Russian interests in Eurasia. In 1905, however, Russia suffered a painful defeat in the Russo-Japanese war. Both countries were competing for territories, resources, and influence in the Eurasian Far East. Russia lost that war. Not only did it cede significant territories to Japan, it also sustained almost 50,000 casualties and accumulated a huge financial debt. Several European countries, especially France, became Russia's sponsors (MacMillan, 2013).

Meanwhile in Europe, alarmed by the rapid economic and military developments in Germany, Russia joined Great Britain and France to form a military bloc. Germany, in response, gathered its own powerful allies including the Austro-Hungarian and Ottoman Empires. World War I broke out in 1914. However, the October revolt of 1917 (the October Revolution) brought dramatic changes to the country's foreign policy. The new government run by the Communist Party annulled and repudiated all foreign debts and international agreements. The new government signed in 1918 the Brest peace treaty with Germany and its allies. Russia surrendered huge territories and paid war reparations. The treaty was nullified later that year, however, only after Germany exited the war. Meanwhile, Russia itself was plunged into civil war, at the end of which, many former Russian territories became independent states. Among them were Finland, Estonia, Latvia, Lithuania, and Poland. Neighboring countries occupied large portions of Ukraine, Belarus, Moldova, and Armenia.

The key goal of Moscow's foreign policy (remember, the capital moved from Petrograd to Moscow in 1918) was to guarantee the survival of the state. Other goals involved the promotion of the communist ideology. Moscow sponsored **Comintern**, an international communist organization (The Communist International). Designed in 1919, it was supposed to coordinate the activities of communist parties around the world, to facilitate the collapse of capitalist regimes, and to establish socialism as a form of government. In 1920 Comintern called for a global civil war (commonly known as a "world revolution"), but after the defeat of communist revolts in Germany, Bulgaria, Poland (1923), and Estonia (1924), the Soviet leaders backed off. After Lenin's death in 1924, Joseph Stalin in the late 1920s and in the 1930s focused on the consolidation of his own domestic power. These tasks required a cautious foreign policy. Some Western academics believed that Stalin had abandoned the idea of the "world revolution." Others, including prominent Russian scholars, suggest that he continued pursuing this idea but by less obvious, even covert, means (Zubok, 2007; Khudoley, 2017).

After the Nazi party came to power in Germany, Moscow wanted to avoid a major conflict with Berlin and thus keep the existing European order. In 1935, Moscow signed security pacts with France (an opponent of German expansionism) and Czechoslovakia. In 1933, the Soviet Union and the United States established diplomatic relations. The Soviet Union also joined the League of Nations.

The Kremlin's policies were becoming more assertive. Moscow sent military personnel and sanctioned hundreds of Comintern volunteers to fight on the side of the left-wing government in Spain during the Spanish Civil War (1936–39) and in China (1927–36). Moscow was involved in several military confrontations with Japan in 1938–39. While negotiating with France and Great Britain, Stalin secretly consulted with Nazi Germany and in 1939 reached a political agreement known as the Molotov–Ribbentrop Pact (named after the names of the countries' foreign ministers). In the wake of this treaty, Soviet troops attacked Finland in 1939 and seized some of its southern territories. For this action, the Soviet Union was expelled from the League of Nations.

The Soviet Union soon moved its troops to Estonia, Lithuania, Latvia, and portions of western Belarus and Ukraine, which were Polish territories. Using support from loyal communist groups in the Baltic countries, the Soviet Union seized these regions. Supporters of these actions insisted for years that this was an act of "unification" based on mutual agreement between Moscow and the local political leaders. Critics, however, argued that these actions were illegal and immoral. Yet most others maintained that, although Russia's policies toward the Baltic States and Poland were questionable at best, they were necessary at that time to protect the Soviet Union's security. This view is common in official Russian sources today.

In June 1941, Germany attacked the Soviet Union. The ongoing World War II became the major military confrontation of the 20th century, in which Russia lost about 26 million people, including about 11 million military casualties. During the war, Moscow reached strategic agreements with the United States and Great Britain and joined their forces to defeat Germany. In 1945 the Soviet military, aided by the British and American troops of the Second Front in Western Europe, ended the war in Europe in May 1945 by capturing Berlin. Stalin agreed on the postwar structure of Europe and globally.

Foreign policy during the Cold War

In the 1945 summits in Yalta and in Potsdam, Stalin agreed on the world's postwar composition. Yet Stalin treated his Western partners with deep mistrust. He never believed in a lasting cooperation between the communist Soviet Union and the capitalist powers; he wanted to expand Soviet territory, establish communist governments in several countries, and build a security "buffer zone" between the Soviet Union and the West. Although the leaders in

Moscow, Washington, and London had established very productive relations during the war, in 1945 they failed to create the conditions to make this last. The period from the end of the war to the late 1980s is known as the Cold War: the global state of tension (though not outright warfare) between the Soviet Union and its closest allies, on the one hand, and the United States with its allies, on the other (Zubok and Pleshakov, 1996).

There were several causes of this global ideological division that influenced international relations for more than 40 years. The United States and the Soviet Union both claimed that the opposite side was inhumane and dangerous. Soviet ideology maintained a belief in the inevitability of a conflict between communism and capitalism. Anticommunism was the official policy in Washington. By August 1949 the Soviet Union had become the second nuclear power after the United States. The emerging nuclear competition brought fear and distrust to both countries. Personal factors also contributed to the tension. Stalin, for example, believed that a nuclear conflict was inevitable (Zubok, 2007). In his last work, *Economic Problems of Socialism in the USSR* (1952), Stalin wrote that until capitalism (frequently called imperialism by Soviet sources) no longer existed, war would be inescapable.

Although the new Soviet leader Nikita Khrushchev (1894–1971) proclaimed in 1956 that global war was preventable and that Soviet foreign policy would focus on the process of peaceful coexistence between two antagonistic systems—communism and imperialism—the Cold War continued. For almost the entire second half of the 20th century, both countries (and their allies) engaged in an endless global competition. Mutual suspicions and fears drove the defense and security policies of both sides, and the buildup of arms in the "arms race" drained national resources. The Warsaw Treaty Organization, the Moscow-dominated security bloc of Eastern and Central European communist states, emerged in 1955 in response to the Washington-dominated NATO. The Soviet Union became a major international player. It tried to challenge the United States and its allies, in almost every part of the world.

The Soviet Union joined China and North Korea in their fight against troops from South Korea, the United States, and the United Nations (known as the Korean War, 1950–53). Later, Moscow sent instructors, antiaircraft missiles, weapons, food, and money to the Vietnamese forces fighting against the United States during the Vietnam War in the 1960s–1970s. The Soviet government sponsored and supported communist parties in countries in Central Europe. Moscow crushed anticommunist revolts in East Germany (1953) and Hungary (1956), and a reformist movement in Czechoslovakia (1968). Soviet pressure was the key factor in the state of emergency in Poland in December 1981 to suppress the popular grassroots political movement Solidarity.

The Soviets openly supported Fidel Castro in Cuba, and placed nuclear missiles there in 1962, causing one of the most dangerous nuclear crises in history. In 1979 the Soviet military invaded Afghanistan to help a friendly communist government there, and fought there until February 1989. More than 15,000 Soviet soldiers died and more than 50,000 were seriously wounded in this conflict. During this period, Moscow also provided supplies and either openly or covertly participated in local armed conflicts in Nicaragua, Palestine, Angola, Mozambique, Ethiopia, Yemen, and many other countries.

Foreign policy at the end of the Cold War

The arrival of Mikhail Gorbachev in 1985 meant the beginning of a new and final stage of the Soviet Union. He wanted to change the system at home and make it more efficient and humane. This required changes in foreign policy: Gorbachev hoped to reduce international tensions and to build a new system of global cooperation. Gorbachev called these initiatives in foreign policy *new thinking*.

Case in point: the new thinking in foreign policy

Gorbachev, as a new Soviet leader after 1985, questioned and then challenged some of the basic assumptions of international relations in the nuclear age. In particular, Gorbachev raised three important points. First, he argued that the ongoing confrontation between the superpowers should stop immediately and without preconditions. Second, all nuclear countries, particularly the Soviet Union and the United States, should reduce their deadly arsenals to the minimum needed to guarantee mutual security and international stability. Third, the new world of the end of the 20th century should stop ideological competition and turn to what were described as the universal values of peace and cooperation in international relations. This was perhaps Gorbachev's central point: countries should change the way they understood politics and global affairs (Gorbachev, 1985: 1). He was convinced that the world should and could function according to a set of basic and universal values (Sheehy, 1990: 220).

Only a few times in history (US President Woodrow Wilson is an example of this) has the leader of a great power renounced the old rules of foreign policy in favor of a sweeping idealist agenda based on nonviolence, cooperation, and interdependence (Levesque, 1997). Some historians and political scientists believe that, without Gorbachev, the Soviet Union would likely still exist today. Others disagree and suggest that the changes in Soviet foreign policy were inevitable with or without Gorbachev (Zubok, 2009). Yet others accuse Gorbachev of making unilateral concessions. These critical arguments are especially popular today among Russian foreign policy elites.

The "new thinking" foreign policy led to progress in arms limitation talks with the United States. Top-level meetings between Gorbachev and the US President Ronald Reagan in Geneva (1985), Reykjavik (1986), Washington (1987), and Moscow (1988) resulted in the signing of the Intermediate Range Nuclear Forces (INF) treaty (the United States withdrew from this treaty in 2019). Major progress toward the limitation of intercontinental nuclear weapons was also achieved. Reagan and Gorbachev established direct and informal personal communications, which helped to develop mutual trust (Chernyaev, 2000). Both leaders soon began to talk about burying the Cold War for good. The dismantling of the confrontation between the superpowers proceeded apace, in 1989 and later under George H. W. Bush's administration (1988–92).

Gorbachev took unilateral steps to implement his vision of a new world. By 1989, the Soviet Union had withdrawn its troops from Afghanistan. Moscow stopped supporting pro-communist insurgencies around the world. In 1989, communist regimes in Eastern and Central Europe collapsed while Soviet troops remained in their barracks. By 1991 the Warsaw Pact, the Soviet-led military and political coalition in Central Europe, was dissolved. East and West Germany were on the way toward unification (1990). The Kremlin no longer felt that it should deceive the West about the size of its military budget, and in May 1989 it revealed its "real" size. It was about four times larger than had previously been acknowledged (The State, 1989: 11). The majority of people in the Soviet Union supported the ending of the unpopular war in Afghanistan and establishing productive relationships with the West.

In a nutshell, perestroika and glasnost represent a political program aimed at reforming the institutional, economic, and political systems of the Soviet Union. In 1985, the leaders of the reforms wanted to make the economy more efficient, the political system less authoritarian, and foreign policy less confrontational. They did not envision (and were not ready for) the sweeping changes that would later engulf society and would lead to the collapse of the powerful state in 1991. The **Commonwealth of Independent States (CIS)** appeared in place of the defunct USSR. Eleven out of the fifteen former republics of the Soviet Union have joined. (Estonia, Lithuania, and Latvia did not join, and Georgia left in 2008.) The CIS remains mostly a formal association without real political power. We will return to this in Chapter 11.

Russian foreign policy from 1991 to the early 2000s

Russian foreign policy since 1991 has gone through at least three phases: accommodation, reorientation, and consolidation (Shiraev and Khudoley, 2019). During the early period of the young state, Russia played its role in global affairs by trying to be a key and accommodating partner of the United States and major European countries. During the second period of reorientation, from 1996 to 2000, Russia was reconsidering its foreign policy priorities. During this period, Russian policy was mostly a reaction to international events. After 2000, when President Putin took office, Russia began to rearrange its foreign policy. This was a stage of "consolidation," as Russian commentators try to portray it today. They refer to Russia's increasingly consistent behavior: seeing and building itself as a new center of power, actively seeking new useful partners and alliances, strengthening the country's security, and challenging Western policies on issues that Russia believes challenge its own interests.

After 2000, when President Putin took office, Russia was already rearranging its foreign policy. Important changes took place in Russia's defense and security policies as well. The concept that foreign enemies threaten Russia has become a central theme justifying the strengthening of Russia's defense and security, which certainly reflected the country's foreign policy (Morozov, 2004). Essentially similar policies largely continued during the presidency of Dmitry Medvedev (2008–12), despite his unassertive attempts to establish better relations with the West. The increasingly large resources available to the government during the economic boom of the early 2000s and high oil prices at that time gave the Kremlin an opportunity and the money to invest in defense and security. However, the economic crisis of 2008–09, the economic sanctions in the past decade, and the COVID-19 global crisis forced Moscow to make adjustments. Before we turn to these changes, let us briefly review Russia's foreign policy institutions.

FOREIGN POLICY INSTITUTIONS

As mentioned in Chapters 2 and 3, modern Russia's political system and its institutions, the foundations of which were shaped mainly during the turbulent period between 1991 and 1993, are changing. However, the structure and functioning of the key institutions of foreign policy as well as the decision-making process remain, probably, the least transformed and the most stable among all government institutions in Russia. The importance of the legacy and tradition of the diplomacy of the Soviet period (or even of the Russian imperial period) appears obvious. For example, many Russian embassies' buildings today still have the official coat of arms of the Soviet Union on their façades. The management of foreign policy historically has been and still remains highly centralized. Likewise, legislative influence in foreign policy (unlike in many other countries) remains generally inconsequential. Although Russia's foreign policy today is more transparent than in the days of the Soviet Union, it is still far less transparent in comparison with the foreign policies of many other democratic states such as Canada or the United Kingdom. A prominent feature of Russia's policy offices (as well as other state institutions) is that their functioning is largely dependent on the personality of their institutional leader.

The president of the Russian Federation

The 1993 Constitution endowed the Russian president with substantial powers, including those in the domain of foreign policy. These presidential powers can be explained from several viewpoints.

First, the president directs Russia's foreign policy. Specifically, Article 86 of the Constitution states that the president of the Russian Federation

- is responsible for the management of the Russian Federation's foreign policy
- conducts talks and signs international treaties on behalf of the Russian Federation
- signs international treaties and the ratification letters
- accepts letters of credence of diplomatic representatives in Russia (such letters establish the diplomatic status of foreign representatives)

The president also sends his annual memorandums or statements on the directions of the state's domestic and foreign policy to the Federal Assembly (although both chambers only seldom gather for joint meetings).

Next, the president makes key personnel decisions. According to the Constitution (Article 83), the president forms the Presidential Administration. A special department within the Administration is in charge of foreign policy. There is also a special unit responsible for relations with post-Soviet states. The president forms the Security Council. The president also appoints members of key ministries, top commanders of the armed forces, and diplomatic envoys to foreign countries and international organizations. Although consultations with the respective committees of the Federal Assembly regarding the appointment of diplomatic representatives to foreign countries and international organizations are required, they are (unlike in many democratic countries) for the most part purely formalities.

Third, the president holds other powers related to foreign policy. The control over the implementation of international treaties signed by the Russian Federation is one of them.

Thus, in accordance with the Constitution (Article 85), the president may suspend any executive or legislative act of any Russian region (the regions are called subjects of the Federation) if this act conflicts with the Russian Federation's international commitments. The president also controls citizenship and asylum policies (Article 89).

The Presidential Administration plays a key role in affecting foreign policy. The head of the Administration is informally regarded as the third most important person within the executive branch, after the president and the prime minister. The role of the Presidential Administration in shaping the country's foreign policy has varied over the past two decades, but its importance has increased, especially after 2012.

The Ministry of Foreign Affairs

The Ministry of Foreign Affairs is the federal executive institution responsible for Russian foreign policy. The ministry's main tasks are to develop strategy in the field of international relations, suggest policies to the president, and exercise the country's foreign policy. Figure 10.1 shows its organizational structure.

Russia's foreign ministers have vast responsibilities, ranging from signing treaties, negotiating with foreign countries, and coordinating the work of foreign missions, to managing key job appointments within the ministry, reporting to the president, and interacting with the media. Foreign ministers are usually members of Russia's Security Council.

The structure of the Ministry of Foreign Affairs has undergone some alterations over the past twenty years, but no radical changes have been carried out. Most of its departments are organized geographically. The number of departments responsible for the world's regions is more often determined by the ministry's internal considerations rather than by the importance of a particular region. Thus, for example, it has four departments to deal with the Commonwealth of Independent States, which is a regional organization whose participating countries are some former Soviet Republics. Five other departments deal with Europe, and there is just one department for North America. The Ministry of Foreign Affairs also pays attention to economic relations, such as Russia's ascendance and participation in the World Trade Organization (WTO). In addition to its centralized structure, the Ministry of Foreign Affairs maintains offices in different regions of the Russian Federation and assists them in developing their own international ties, mostly in education and trade.

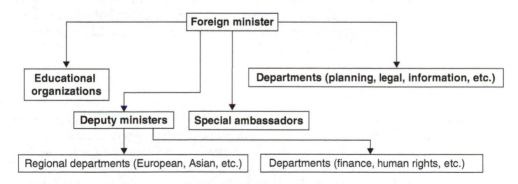

Figure 10.1 Structure of the Ministry of Foreign Affairs (arrows show the Ministry's chain of subordination)

FOREIGN POLICY STRATEGIES

At the beginning of the 21st century, Russian foreign policy strategists generally focused on an independent, often confrontational course with the West. Russia claims that its foreign policy is nonideological. Quite often, however, ideological arguments are used to justify Russia's behavior in global affairs. Several factors, both domestic and international, have shaped this policy and continue to influence it.

The first group of factors is related to the foreign policy of other states. Russia chose to overlook many positive developments in its relations with the West during the 1990s (Rivera and Rivera, 2009) and focused on problems instead. For example, the continuing NATO expansion has been an issue. The civil war in Bosnia in the early 1990s and the conflict in Kosovo were seen differently in Moscow from how they were perceived in Paris, London, and Washington. Moscow presented the conflict in the former Yugoslavia as for the most part a coordinated Western aggression against Serbia. When US-led coalition forces invaded Iraq in 2003, Russian–American relations worsened. The Western support of Georgia in 2008 (during Georgia's war with Russia) and Ukraine in 2014 (during Russia's annexation of Crimea), and other serious points of tension including accusations of Russia's meddling in Western elections, convinced Russian diplomats that Moscow's foreign policy was simply unwelcome in the West.

The second group of factors is related to Russia's domestic situation. Russia has learned that it could act independently and authoritatively against threats such as separatism in Chechnya or instability in Syria. In the wake of terrorist attacks on Russian soil early in this century, such as suicide bombings in Moscow and other cities, airplane crashes caused by terrorism, and the deaths of hundreds of people including children, most Russians showed their support for the federal authorities in their pledge of worldwide unilateral actions against terrorism.

The third factor was cultural–psychological. Washington's crucial error back in the 1990s was, as many critics outside Russia noticed, probably a tendency to treat post-Soviet Russia as a defeated opponent. The United States and the West might have "won" the Cold War, but this did not mean defeat for Russia (Tsygankov, 2016; Simes, 2007: 36). Russia constantly reminded its Western neighbors that it was a formidable power to reckon with (Legvold, 2007). For a decade, Russians have been repeating arguments about the world's multipolarity (or *policentricity*, as they prefer to say it in Russia) with Russia being another power center, like the United States. An increasing number of Russians, including the elites, have come to doubt that American and Western-style economic models and civil liberties could take root in Russia (Surkov, 2019; Trenin, 2017). Was this approach a crucial strategic gain or a big error on the part of Moscow's elites?

Pragmatism and ideology

A new, consolidated view of foreign policy has emerged in Russia, which we call the pragmatic approach (Khudoley, 2017). The term "pragmatic" in the context of foreign policy means acting out of practical rather than ideological considerations. Russian leaders assumed that, to become an equal and capable partner in the international community, Russia must not act from a position of weakness. The flow of petrodollars (mostly the revenues from gas and oil exports), the stabilization of the economy, economic growth, and the improvement of the living standards of the population—these and other encouraging changes should have strengthened, as it was assumed in the early 2000s, Russia's role in world affairs.

The modernization of the armed forces should have indicated Russia's assertiveness and strength, while not posing a threat to other countries. Russia was likely to remain friendly with the West but not dependent on it. While remaining a partner of the United States, especially in the fields of antiterrorism and global security, Russia would most certainly negotiate a new international role for itself in other areas. From the logic of these pragmatic positions, the international order that formed in the 21st century would last for some time. Yet the balance of power could and would change in Russia's favor sometime soon.

Putin's speech at an international security conference in Munich in February 2007 was among the first and most noteworthy affirmations of Russia's strengthening of the pragmatic approach to international relations (Putin, 2007). Not only did he criticize the United States and NATO for their global policies, he also insisted that Russia would no longer follow Western policies uncritically. From now on, he said, Russia would conduct its own, independent foreign policy. Russia would also understand the grievances of other countries dissatisfied with the global status quo and the domination of the West. The speech was an indication that Russia was shifting its foreign policy toward a significantly tougher, less cooperative (from the Western view) approach to the United States and Western Europe. Most Western experts considered the speech by the Russian president as unexpectedly confrontational.

Views of foreign policy evolved again in the second decade of the 2000s. One of Putin's main international projects at that time, especially after 2014, was the formation of the Eurasian Union. This was his strategic idea, which he had already promoted during his 2012 presidential campaign. Russian political and business elites realized that this would be Moscow's top priority, which would give them a chance to create a new global center of power in an emerging multipolar (or polycentric) world. It was expected then that the majority of post-Soviet states, as well as some other countries, would join this pan-Eurasian organization and that the Eurasian Union could succeed economically and politically. As a result of this success, Russia would regain its global leadership role. These perceived possibilities gave a moral boost to those commentators who envisioned Russia's special role in Eurasia. Russia's big business also saw a range of new possibilities in Eurasia, including new markets and, feasibly, a large and relatively cheap labor force.

One should not think that the emerging "Eurasian pivot" in Moscow's policies received unmitigated support in Russia. Many experts, among the left and the right, liberals and conservatives, have expressed their concerns and reservations (Trenin, 2017). Liberals feared the Eurasian orientation would weaken Russia's ties with the United States and the European Union. Conservatives disliked the idea of cultural integration within the envisioned Eurasian confederation: they feared the potential erosion of Russian cultural values. The moderates and pragmatics questioned whether the new proposed union would become Russia's exclusive and thus prohibitively expensive project to carry out. It might, as they feared, drain Russia's financial and economic resources. The nationalists were also divided. Some of them, who believed in a new Russian Empire, generally supported the idea of the Eurasian Union. Others remained skeptical and continued to express their concern about growing legal and illegal immigration to Russia. Their argument was that Russia must have a far less ambitious foreign policy and that Russia's core interests should be mainly confined within its own borders. This populist and anti-immigrant view referring to their own countries has gained strength among many politicians in the West in recent years.

Russia and a multipolar world

By the time of President Putin's return to the Kremlin in May 2012, the ruling elites were warming up to the view that a Eurasian pivot could be one of the first tangible results of Russia's new role: Russia was acting as a key player in a new multipolar world. They believed that President Putin had restored Russian authority by preserving the country's inner stability and sticking it to the West as often as possible (Westad, 2018). Several developments in the second decade of the century provided supporting evidence for Russia's view that the world indeed was becoming multipolar and that Russia should act more assertively in it (see Table 10.1).

In the second decade of the 21st century, it appeared from Moscow's point of view that the Western world was in serious decline. The signs of the decline appeared earlier. The global financial crisis of 2008 and the following economic stagnation that lasted for several years served as evidence that the West was losing its dominant position in the world economy and finances (Putin, 2019b). In official Russian documents, references were made to the "dismal" state of the American and European economies (Concept of the Foreign Policy of the Russian Federation, 2016). Back in 2013 many Russian politicians and experts were making pessimistic forecasts about the anticipated decline and collapse of the US dollar and a gloomy future for the euro. The financial difficulties in Greece and the 2016 referendum in the United Kingdom deciding in favor of Brexit were considered as strong signs of a major crisis in the West. Several Russian experts foresaw the inevitable end of NATO as a military and political organization that, as they claimed, had long lost its sense of a mission.

Furthermore, the non-Western world appeared to be on the rise economically during the first decade of this century. Several positive economic indicators from China, India, Brazil, South Africa, and some other developing countries made a major impression on the Russian elites. It appeared for some time that these countries had weathered the economic problems associated with the global financial crisis and recovered much better than the rest of the world, especially the economically advanced countries. The Chinese economy appeared the strongest and most promising.

Table 10.1 The arguments justifying Russia's view of the world as multipolar

The Western world is in decline.	The global financial crisis of 2008, the following economic crisis that lasted approximately until 2012, and the euro crisis of 2015 served as evidence that the West was losing its dominant position in the world economy and finances.
Non-Western countries are on the rise.	The perceived economic success of non-Western countries, especially the BRICS' development, indicated the rise of a new economic and financial "center."
The West undermines Russia's domestic stability.	It was assumed that the West actively undermined Russia's stability via various outlets of "soft power," thus pushing Russia out of the Western "orbit." Russia had no choice but to form its own power center.

Russia has long seen the BRICS countries (in addition to Russia they include Brazil, India, South Africa, and China, as you should remember) as a future global coalition, as a new political, economic, and financial center of the world. As an international organization, the BRICS appeared as if they could challenge and eventually replace the G7 (the United States, the United Kingdom, France, Germany, Italy, Japan, and Canada) as a global force. When the BRICS rise and the West declines, global changes in the balance of power should follow as well.

However, this major shift did not happen (Nwosu, 2015). The rate of growth declined for India and China. Other BRICS countries have been struggling financially and economically for the most part of the second decade of the century and especially after the 2020 pandemic. At the same time, at home, the government elites' confidence in their own tenure was under serious threat for the first time since the 1990s.

In 2011–12 a series of mass protests swept Moscow and a few other cities. These protests were mostly peaceful, but in Bolotnaya Square in Moscow in May 2012, during a public rally against the presidential inauguration of Putin, violence broke out. Western media and public opinion turned against Putin and his government because of the harsh methods they used to punish the protestors. Criticisms coming from abroad strengthened an already existing opinion (shared by the elites and the state-controlled media in Russia) that Western countries were behind these protests. It was also assumed that Western intelligence, for years, had planned and then deliberately exploited Russian and international journalists, environmental activists, human rights observers, and NGOs to stage a revolt and undermine the government in Moscow.

The government's extremely tough reaction to the protests (the reaction was seen in the West as unjustifiably violent) also involved a series of important legal and administrative actions that had been implemented in Russia in 2012 and later. These actions were designed to limit open displays of public disagreement, to curb the activities of Russian NGOs that used foreign funding, and to constrain the activities of international organizations, advocacy groups, and individuals promoting human rights, civil liberties, transparent elections, and environmental issues. These actions were designed, in part, to curb the influence of the West and to negatively portray its influence on Russian people. In these conditions, Russian officials believed that they had had no choice but to disregard international criticisms. In addition, the country's new geopolitical interests were shifting to other countries, and Asia in particular (Putin, 2019b; Trenin, 2017). With a new geopolitical focus Russia—as many in Moscow believed—should have become a quickly rising global leader.

In addition to these actions, Moscow launched a media campaign to discredit the West and to promote its own conservative values—which were seen as a necessary alternative to Western consumerism, liberalism, and feminism as well as the West's seemingly "excessive" commitment to human rights (Surkov, 2019). The West was portrayed as a key source of immorality, vice, homosexuality, corruption, greed, individualism, and other signs of moral decay—all seen and critically judged, of course, from Moscow's standpoint. The Russian Orthodox Church was often used as a moral backer of true Russian cultural values of collectivism, patriotism, and traditionalism. The government sponsored local historians to promote patriotism, to create a "true" history of Russia's glorious past, and to portray Russia's moral values in a positive light (Nesterova, 2016). Putin has published an article defending Soviet policies of the 1930s in dealing with the Nazi Germany. He essentially justified the Soviet occupation of parts of Poland as well as Estonia, Latvia, and Lithuania in 1940 (Putin, 2020c).

Russia's imperatives in foreign policy

In the context of the two main arguments—about the developing multipolar world in which Russia plays a key role and the necessity to protect the established political system at home—the Kremlin formulated several key goals of its foreign policy (Concept of the Foreign Policy of the Russian Federation, 2013 and 2016).

First, Russia needed to regain its lost status as a world power and reclaim its position as a formidable nuclear, economic, and political force of the 21st century. To achieve this goal, Russia has its own reserves and potentials. Russia has vast oil and gas resources. Russia also produces good-quality competitive products to generate trade, including firearms, aircraft, and military equipment. Russia should further modernize its economy as well as its armed forces. One of the country's advantages is its educated population. Yet Russia's global ascendance needs favorable international conditions.

Second, current tendencies toward multi-polarity require a new system of international relations and a new type of decision making in foreign policy. The existing and failing structures rooted in the power of the United States and the West should be reformed. However, Russia does not need full-scale confrontations. To challenge and diminish the power of the United States and its allies, Russia should use various methods, including international organizations and international law. The United Nations, and its Security Council where Russia has veto power, is considered as one of Russia's venues to conduct foreign policy.

Next, Russia not only needs to resist the unfair world order; Moscow needs to lead and set examples. It should form an alliance of countries—regardless of their political systems—that agree with Russia's foreign policy, accept its strategic goals, and support their implementation. In particular, Russia seeks partnership in Asia, the Middle East, and the Pacific. China has already become a major economic and political partner of Moscow. Moscow should pursue strategic relations with India, Iran, and Turkey.

Fourth, Russia needs to strengthen its currency and make the ruble (Russia's currency) one of the world's key reserve currencies—comparable to the dollar or the euro. In addition, Russia should and will support any financial arrangements that discourage countries from using those traditional (that is, the dollar or the euro) currencies.

Fifth, Russia must promote a new ideology, which is based on conservative social values and common sense in international affairs. These values should gain respect and acceptance around the world. In Moscow's view, emphasizing and responding to the individual's key economic and social interests (such as employment, societal stability, access to healthcare, traditional conservative values, etc.) is more appealing to most people than pushing for some abstract and confusing "human rights." At least three key ideas here will be important for Russia.

- Russia will support liberal political freedoms, but only to a certain degree. Political freedoms, which the West promotes, should come with the citizen's responsibilities, and they can exist only within an orderly political system.
- Russia will support economic freedoms, yet the government should retain significant control over many key industries and fields, including transportation, healthcare, and education.
- Russia will also support personal freedoms; however, the basic rules of morality must be defended against the encroachment of those who promote same-sex marriage,

homosexuality, secularism, pedophilia, and other decadent principles or behavioral "deviances" (which are, according to Moscow, embraced and promoted, by the West).

Finally, Russia as a country will need to create a new image of itself. The country should be seen as generous and caring. Russia should pursue very high standards in business and service. Therefore, among many things, Russia has placed an emphasis on tourism and showed its eagerness to host big international events. Russian leaders treated the Kazan Summer Universiade (2013), the Sochi Winter Olympics (2014), and the World Soccer Cup (2018) as Moscow's top international priorities relevant to Russia's foreign policy. As expected, Russian state and private corporations, such as Gazprom and many others, have sponsored these and other big tournaments. Success in sport, according to Moscow's strategies, should add to Russia's prestige abroad.

Not everything went smoothly in the area of image building and international sports, however. The doping scandal involving Russian athletes had a negative impact on Russia's international prestige. The track and field team was altogether banned from the 2016 games in Brazil, and the entire Russian national team was excluded from the Winter Olympics in South Korea in 2018 (only some athletes were allowed to participate) and the Summer Olympics in Japan (rescheduled due to the 2020 pandemic). Moscow maintained that these sanctions were biased and unfair. This opinion found support among most Russians. According to surveys, 71 percent of Russians did not believe the World Anti-Doping Agency, which had shown that Russian sports authorities attempted to hide and then cover up the doping scandal during the 2014 Sochi Olympics (Levada, 2016). International sports organizations maintained a different view, however, citing the evidence of deliberate cheating and a cover-up by the Russian officials.

CRITICAL THINKING ABOUT FOREIGN POLICY

Russia is a sovereign and powerful country. Russian leaders in the past 20 years have tended to see the world as increasingly multipolar and wanted Russia to play a more assertive role in it. Moscow pursues nuclear nonproliferation, supports antiterrorist policies, and hopes to expand trade and develop other forms of economic cooperation with almost every country (Putin, 2019b). Why did the problems with Russia's international behavior occur? Why, in the early 2020s, did relations between Russia and the West reach their lowest point since the Cold War?

As has already been stated, any country's foreign policy is based on its security concerns and on specific economic and political interests and aspirations. Foreign policy is also based on a country's *ideology*, a predominant set of beliefs about its position in the world, friends and foes, its role in international affairs, and the direction of global developments. We will try to consider all these variables to critically assess Russia's foreign policy.

Does Russia have enemies?

Many in Russia believe in foreign enemies. Russian leaders felt insecure about NATO and the West's economic expansion either through the European Union or by other political and economic means. For a number of years Russia has criticized and confronted most policies conducted by Western countries, especially the United States and the United Kingdom. The view that Russia is surviving in a primarily hostile environment dominated by the United States and its most loyal Western allies was prevalent in Moscow for years (Dubin, 2012). Russia chose to overlook many positive developments in its relations with the West (Rivera and Rivera, 2009) and began to focus on problems instead.

The idea that sworn enemies surround Russia also finds support among many ultranationalists. They see most global developments from either geopolitical or cultural perspectives (Dugin, 2011). Accepting in general the idea about the ongoing "clash of civilizations," they maintain that Russia as a Slavic and Christian Orthodox nation is under siege, promoting the idea that global corporations, Western governments, the Catholic Church, Islamic fundamentalists, and Asian strategists are all trying to diminish Russian influence globally. In 2018, more than half of Russians believed that the main threat against their country came from the West (Levada, 2018d). Why couldn't Russia improve its relations with the West?

Why Russia is choosing a tough line

One answer is that Russia's strategic interests have been different from those of the United States and Western countries (Simes, 2009). For example, Russia needs to sell its oil and gas in large quantities and for a higher price. The West consumes natural resources from Russia but is interested in buying them at a lower price. Russia also has a vital interest in keeping foreign powers away from Central Asia to thwart their attempts to gain access to natural resources there. Moscow also hopes to see a weaker NATO and less influence of the United States among its West European allies. The list of differences can be easily continued.

How is Russia addressing these differences? Neither extreme isolationist nor aggressively hawkish strategies find open support in the Kremlin. The goal of Russia's foreign policy is to win as many strategic battles as possible by peaceful means, including diplomatic pressure or economic incentives (Putin, 2012b, 2019a). For instance, by opposing the expansion of NATO, Russia could compel the West to bargain with Moscow, which could eventually achieve significant economic and political benefits (Clover and Blitz, 2009). Alternatively, by offering economic incentives to China, Russia could secure Beijing's support at the United Nations. It might also use its ties with Iran to elevate its role as a key player in the complex relations between the West and Iran. In effect, this is a *quid pro quo* policy: if foreign countries conduct their policy respecting Russia's interests, then Moscow responds positively (Lavrov, 2011).

At least two problems emerge with this strategic position. First, other states have their interests, and it is erroneous for Russia to believe that other countries should somehow change their interests to accommodate Moscow. Second, independent foreign policies of the United States or the United Kingdom are not necessarily designed to disrespect Russia. Most issues can be solved through negotiation and bargaining. The problem is that Russian officials are convinced that Western powers are not interested in compromise.

Although Russia has been turning to a pragmatic foreign policy, ideology sometimes becomes a serious factor determining Russia's international strategies and moves. Russia is extremely sensitive about its treatment by other states as a junior partner; it is determined to become an equal player in global affairs. Thus, Russia commonly sides with countries that are confrontational toward the United States and the West. Since the beginning of the century, Russia has improved its relations with such countries, such as Iran or Venezuela.

However, since 2014 and the annexation of Crimea, Russia's relations with most other countries have worsened.

One of the reasons for this conviction is psychological. Washington's error back in the 1990s was in the way it treated post-Soviet Russia as an overpowered opponent. The United States and the West might have "won" the Cold War, but not from the Russians' view (Simes, 2007: 36). Russians were particularly sensitive to the perceived loss of their superpower status. As a result, by the mid-2000s, Russian foreign policy had become increasingly self-centered and nationalistic. In numerous statements coming from the Kremlin and other federal offices, Russia constantly reminded its Western neighbors that it was a formidable power to reckon with (Putin, 2019b; Legvold, 2007). For a decade, Russians have been repeating the arguments about their country being one of a few global power centers.

Considering these developments, one may conclude that Moscow is simply not interested in having good relations with Washington or the West (Golz, 2009). Anti-Western policies could actually benefit Russia. First, having an external enemy helps the government to mobilize people around the idea that their nation is in danger. In the past decade, for instance, foreign criticism of Russia's authoritarian push against political freedoms has increased and so has Western support of the Russian political opposition. Putin may actually see the United States' critical attitude toward political freedoms in Russia as a threat to his sovereign rule (Putin, 2019a; Kuchins, 2012a).

Confrontation hurts

The belief in foreign enemies is likely to affect Russia's foreign policy and could hurt it politically. As domestic and international critics assert, after the end of the first decade of this century, Russia's position in the world has worsened. In the westward direction, Russia has an old partner, Belarus, which is unreliable and whose leader is internationally isolated due to his authoritarian policies. Relations with the Baltic states are at a historic low. Russia has not succeeded in drastically improving its relations with the former socialist countries of Central Europe including Poland, the Czech Republic, and Bulgaria. Relations with Slovakia and Hungary have had their ups and downs. Moscow has worsened its relations with the United Kingdom and the United States in most areas. Russia's war against Georgia in 2008 and against Ukraine in 2014 produced overwhelming international condemnation, which Russia dismissed. Moscow continued to support Iran, thus distancing itself from many countries opposing Iran's policies. Russia's support of the authoritarian regime in Syria and military actions there drew significant international criticism. In Latin America, Russia supported left-wing governments in Venezuela and Cuba, thus further damaging its relations with Washington.

Critics maintain that, since Russia's position in the global world has worsened, the only way to reverse the negative trend is to accept a different approach to foreign policy. A change in Russian polices toward more cooperation, openness, and conflict resolution in various regions (we will discuss such policies in Chapter 11) would remove many barriers between Russia and the United States, improve Moscow's relations with Europe, and contribute to substantial changes in global affairs. Accommodation is better than confrontation. This point of view, however, does not now find support in Moscow (Putin, 2019a; Dmitriev, 2012). Furthermore, a more confrontational view has dominated.

However, there are several constructive trends in Russia's foreign policy.

Looking for possibilities

Russia constantly sees itself as an "honest broker" in international affairs (Lavrov, 2011). President Putin hopes to maintain a pragmatic foreign policy aimed at an effective, although somewhat limited, partnership with the West, and the United States in particular. Several issues stand out.

There are voices among supporters of these views that Russia should turn to isolationism. Others insist that Russia needs to pursue its new superpower status and engage its opponents globally. Yet others, like the Liberal Democratic Party, prefer to avoid direct confrontation but pursue pragmatic alliances with China and India to counterbalance the influences of Western Europe and the United States.

The first initiative that brought Russia and the West closer together was the possibility of joint action against international terrorism. An early working coalition between Moscow and Washington, for example, created a convenient and reliable basis for broader cooperation (Goldgeier and McFaul, 2003). In addition, an umbrella of "collective action" allows Moscow and Washington to pursue their national objectives independently: fighting against and eliminating specific violent radical groups.

Second, Russia shares a growing international concern over the proliferation of weapons of mass destruction. After 2000, Russia began to work on international policies and specific programs to secure nuclear, chemical, and biological materials all over the world. The actual record in respect to these policies has been uneven, unfortunately.

Third, Russia shares global concerns about regional security, and in particular the situation in Afghanistan, Iraq, Pakistan, Middle East, and around Iran. Russia supported US actions in Afghanistan in 2001 (Katz, 2009) and continues to believe that a foreign presence is necessary to maintain stability in regions such as Syria. Russia, as a member of the Security Council, did not support the 2003 US-led war in Iraq, but hoped to see a stable regime in Baghdad. Russia intervened in Syria in 2015 on the side of President Assad against rebel groups. Russia also wants to play a key bargaining role in the Middle East and other regions by developing its relations with all the conflicting sides (see Chapter 11).

The fourth shared issue is related to energy resources such as oil and gas. The "energy card" has increasingly played, and will continue to play, a very important role in Russian foreign policy, and this is likely to overlap Russian and Western interests. The growth of alternative sources of energy and the West's diminished dependence on fossil fuel from Russia (or any other region) is critically changing the global situation and may diminish Russia's revenues and thus its role in international affairs.

Finally, today the Russian diaspora is no longer viewed as necessarily hostile to the Kremlin. Moscow has since 2012 turned to the use of public diplomacy, research and educational grants, and the web to woo Russian-speaking communities and individuals, engage them in an international dialogue, and make them aware and supportive of Russia's policies (Concept, 2016; Dale, Cohen, and Smith, 2012).

CONCLUSION

As a sovereign and influential country, Russia conducts an independent foreign policy and pursues its own strategic interests. Moscow pursues nuclear nonproliferation, supports antiterrorist policies, and hopes to expand trade and other forms of economic cooperation.

However, in the geopolitical context, Russia feels insecure about NATO and its possible expansion in the future. Russia has also become a viable competitor for global energy resources. Having its own oil and gas supplies, Russia uses them as bargaining chips in foreign policy. Ideology becomes a serious factor determining Russia's international moves: Russia is extremely sensitive about its treatment as a junior partner; it is determined to become an equal player in global affairs. Yet Russia continues to commit significant errors in foreign policy, and in fact its relations with many countries have worsened over the past few years. Although Russian foreign policy is more pragmatic and predictable than it was 20 years ago, Russia is interested in global stability on Moscow's terms.

Russia certainly agrees that cooperation is better than confrontation. However, confrontation with the West has become a dominant theme in Russia's strategic discussions about its foreign policy. A new "cold war" has emerged in the eyes of many experts since 2014. Conducting its foreign policy, the government in the Kremlin hopes to break away from the Soviet past. Too often it remains shackled to it.

11 Foreign Policy: Countries and Regions

The Foreign Policy Concept of the Russian Federation (2016) pays attention to several regional directions of Russia's foreign policy. It specifies six of these directions associated with their geographic location:

- development of bilateral and multilateral cooperation with the countries from the Commonwealth of Independent States
- development of relations with countries of the Euro–Atlantic region
- reinforcement of Russia's position in the Asia–Pacific region
- substantial contribution to the stabilization of the situation in the Middle East and North Africa
- comprehensive strengthening of relations with the countries of Latin America and the Caribbean
- enhancement of complex cooperation with African states on a bilateral and multilateral basis.

In this chapter, we will discuss all six of these directions. Moscow gave some of them more attention than others. Russia's strategic and geopolitical priorities have changed through history based on global developments as well as the interests of the key decision makers. Some priorities can change rapidly. We shall begin with an analysis of Russia's relations with its closest neighbors. Then we will examine Russia's relations with the United States, the European Union, and other regions (Map 11.1).

RUSSIA'S RELATIONS WITH POST-SOVIET STATES

After the breakup of the Soviet Union, the Russian Federation shared borders with eight of its former republics, including Estonia, Latvia, Lithuania (via the Kaliningrad region), Belarus, Ukraine, Georgia, Azerbaijan, and Kazakhstan. Six other former republics did not share borders with Russia, namely Moldova, Armenia, Turkmenistan, Uzbekistan, Tajikistan, and Kyrgyzstan. All these 14 countries are often called in Russia, "the post-Soviet space" or "the post-Soviet states."

The term **post-Soviet space** refers to Russia as well as several countries that used to be republics of the former Soviet Union. Some of Russia's neighbors see Moscow as an important protector of their security and their core economic interests. Others look at Russia with ambivalence: they appreciate its help yet often question Russia's foreign policy decisions. Yet others consider Russia's policies as a threat to their security.

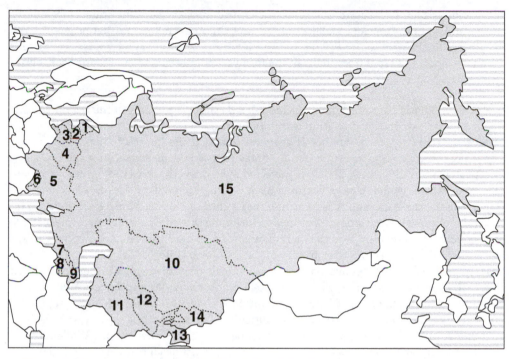

1 – Estonia	6 – Moldova	11 – Turkmenistan
2 – Latvia	7 – Georgia	12 – Uzbekistan
3 – Lithuania	8 – Armenia	13 – Tajikistan
4 – Belarus	9 – Azerbaijan	14 – Kyrgyzstan
5 – Ukraine	10 – Kazakhstan	15 – Russia

Map 11.1 Russia and 14 former republics of the Soviet Union

What else, except geopolitics, motivates Russia and its foreign policies in the post-Soviet space? Consider at least three reasons:

- Historical and cultural ties. Moscow believes that Russia and the former republics of the Soviet Union are closely interlinked due to a shared historical and cultural past within the Soviet Union and the Russian Empire. The Russian language remains common in government and business communications in most countries (although the English language is gaining popularity). Millions of people in the region have mixed ethnic identities, including Russian.
- Security factors. Russia underlines the importance of friendly relations with its neighbors for national security reasons. A stable "near abroad" is a factor that positively contributes to Russia's domestic security and social stability. Russia is interested in maintaining a stable security regime within the region, in which it hopes to play a key role.

- Economic factors. Russian businesses need new markets and investments. Similarly, businesses in the former republics of the Soviet Union need Russia's energy supplies and professional expertise, as well as Russian investors and consumers. Russia too needs cheap labor; migrants from many of the former Soviet republics constantly seek jobs in Russia.

What are Russia's strategic interests and related strategic projects in the region? As one might expect, economic and political integration has been essential to Moscow's plans.

Moscow's strategy for a number of years was creating the Eurasian Union, an international organization as a confederation of states that would resemble, in some ways, the European Union (Clover, 2012). It was projected in Moscow that this new intergovernmental organization would have structures such as the Council of Heads of States and Governments, the Eurasian Parliament, and the Council of Foreign Ministers. Several financial and economic institutions were proposed, including the International Investment Bank, the Economic Commission, and the Commission for Mineral Reserves. A new currency was also proposed (like the euro, the currency of the European Union).

However, such an impressive plan was very difficult to implement. Neither government bureaucracies nor the political or business elites of most countries wanted to surrender their power to Moscow. The task of building a joint parliament was especially daunting (Sadri, 2014). Which country should have most deputies in it? Should that be the one with the largest population? Then how powerful will Russia become in this institution? While Moscow saw this parliament as a source of political integration, most other countries pursued mostly economic cooperation, not necessarily close political ties. At the same time, Russia faced competition from the European Union. The Eastern Partnership program of the European Union was a very attractive opportunity for Ukraine, Moldova, Azerbaijan, Armenia, Georgia, and Belarus to develop closer ties with Europe (Treschenkov, 2014). However, an obvious "pivot" toward the West could have jeopardized these countries' relationships with Moscow.

The **Eurasian Economic Union (EEU)**, a prototype of the Eurasian Union, was finally launched in 2015. This is an economic union that initially consisted of Russia, Belarus, and Kazakhstan. Armenia and Kyrgyzstan also joined. Moscow hoped that the EEU could further consolidate Russia's political and economic influence in the post-Soviet space. The main weakness of the EEU as well as the Kremlin's entire "Eurasian project" is that it remains largely a bureaucratic venture mostly designed by elites. Without serious economic incentives available to all its members and ordinary people, the EEU, at least for some time, is unlikely to be viable.

Estonia, Latvia, and Lithuania, from the early days of their independence from the Soviet Union, did not have any desire for closer collaboration with Russia. On the contrary, they expected to be quickly integrated into the European Union and NATO. Russia was certainly displeased with these developments (seeing them as a threat to Russia's military and economic interests) but could not influence the integration of these countries into the European institutional structures. Central Asian states for years maintained relatively stable relations with Russia. The ruling elites in these countries understood the importance of Moscow's support. Russia has demonstrated that its major concern is stability in Central Asia, regardless of the type of government or political leaders these countries have. As a result, Russia has continuously backed several authoritarian regimes in that region (Shiraev and Khudoley, 2019).

Russia's relationships with Ukraine illustrate both the interest and ambiguity of Moscow's policies toward the former Soviet republics. Russia's strategy of dominating in Ukraine was often overshadowed by Moscow's frustrations over the political battles in Kiev as well as both countries' mutual disagreements. Putin and his advisers hoped that Ukraine would play a very important role in a possible alliance also involving Russia, Belarus, and Kazakhstan. This political alliance, if created, would have been the biggest in Eurasia (Wilson, 2014). Meanwhile, Ukraine's leaders continued their policies of trying to simultaneously please both Russia and the West. In the fall of 2013, Kiev announced its intention to sign an agreement with the European Union on a closer economic association and free trade. Moscow was displeased, and Kiev backed off from the deal with the European Union. This sparked mass protests in Ukraine's major cities including Kiev. Violence erupted and, after the police's pushback, escalated. Dozens of civilians were killed in clashes with the police. The protesters captured several key government buildings. Losing the support of his own law enforcement units, Yanukovych fled the capital. An interim government was formed without him. These 2014 events that toppled the entire government are called in Ukraine the **Revolution of Dignity**.

The events in the capital also sent emotional shock waves across the Ukrainian regions with predominantly Russian-speaking populations. In Crimea, which was a part of Ukraine, pro-Russian nationalists, supported by the majority of the population, seized power. They were encouraged by the presence of Russian troops, which had been quickly and surreptitiously deployed there under the Kremlin's directives. In fact, a sizable Russian contingent, about 25,000 troops, has already been stationed in Crimea after the collapse of the USSR according to an agreement with Ukraine. Russian forces quickly took over most important strategic locations on the Peninsula. A referendum was hastily organized to consider Crimea's independence. A quickly formed new government petitioned Moscow about the incorporation of Crimea into the Russian Federation. This military and political operation, planned in Moscow, resulted in an obvious outcome: Russia accepted the "offer."

The United States, the European Union, and many other countries immediately condemned Russia's actions. They called it an **annexation**, which is the forceful transition of land from the control of one state to another. The annexation was viewed as a flagrant violation of international law. Ukraine protested, and a majority of countries supported the Ukrainian position. The United Nations did not recognize the referendum. Russia rejected the criticisms, arguing that the decision to secede was made by the residents of Crimea (Rosenfielde, 2016). The West ruled out military actions to defend Ukraine's sovereignty and chose a series of economic sanctions against Russia instead.

In the spring of 2014, Russia offered military and political support to ethnic separatists in the eastern part of Ukraine (mostly in the Donbass region) where large numbers of Russian-speaking population lived. The conflict turned into lingering warfare that would last for years. Russia vehemently denied any direct participation in the conflict. Western powers disagreed and condemned Russia's involvement. Ultimately, to penalize Russia's actions in Crimea and in Eastern Ukraine, the United States and its allies continued with a wide range of economic and political sanctions against Russia. Moscow responded with its own countersanctions against the West by drastically limiting the sale of Western products in Russian markets.

During the four years of conflict, more than 13,000 people lost their lives, including more than 3,000 civilians (UN, 2019). One of the deadliest single tragedies caused by the conflict was the downing of Malaysia Airlines flight 17 headed from Amsterdam to Kuala Lumpur.

The plane was shot down on July 17, 2014. Dutch investigators concluded that a rocket that hit the plane was launched from pro-Russian separatist-controlled territory in Ukraine. All 283 passengers and 15 crew on board died. After three years of investigation, the governments of the Netherlands and Australia issued a joint statement in which they laid responsibility on Russia "for its part" in the crash. The statement calls on Russia to accept its responsibility and help establish the truth and achieve justice for the victims (MH17 Statement, 2018). Russia officially denied any involvement in this tragedy (Reuters, 2018). In 2015, more than 40 percent of Russians blamed Ukraine for the downing of the plane, 17 percent accused the United States, and only 5 percent mentioned either Russia or the Ukrainian separatist forces (Levada, 2015).

The Ukrainian events sent alarm signals to the residents of Transnistria, a region in Moldova. Almost 500,000 people living there are predominantly Russian speaking. For years the Russian military remained in the region, and the government of Moldova was increasingly displeased with the Russian military's presence on its territory. Georgia, despite certain positive changes in its relations with Russia after the 2008 military conflict, still sought closer ties with the European Union and, possibly, NATO. Moldova and Georgia also signed association agreements with the European Union and received visa-free status with the countries of the Schengen zone. Armenia was initially willing to sign an agreement with the European Union but later backed off, mostly because of Russian pressure. Yet again, in 2017 Armenia signed a cooperation agreement with the European Union and continued to seek greater ties with the European Union as well as friendly relations with Moscow.

Azerbaijan has notably improved its relations with Russia since 2012 but relies mostly on bilateral agreements instead of joining any intergovernmental organizations controlled by Moscow. Both Armenia and Azerbaijan maintain good relations with Moscow. They both needed Russia's mediating role in settling the conflict in Nagorno-Karabakh, which had been lingering for more than 30 years. Nagorno-Karabakh, on the basis of a referendum, declared itself a sovereign republic and assumed a new name, the Republic of Artsakh. Most countries consider Artsakh to be a part of Azerbaijan.

RUSSIA–US RELATIONS

Over the past two centuries, bilateral relations between Russia and the United States have always played a major, even decisive role in international affairs. During World War II these countries were allies fighting a common enemy. During the Cold War they were adversaries. Great success stories of these countries' cooperation were followed by no less significant setbacks. These days, while Moscow and Washington continue cooperating in some areas, they are competing in far more others. Russia–US trade, for example, has been less than $30 billion a year, which places Russia in only 30th place among US trade partners (US Census Bureau, 2019). Both competition and cooperation continue in the area of nuclear weapons, which we will discuss in Chapter 12 on defense policies.

In the early 1990s, Russia's top elites regarded the United States as a model for successful economic and political development, a standard that Russia could emulate. However, the continuing economic difficulties of the late 1990s convinced most Russian leaders as well as many ordinary Russians that Western—and American in particular—models of economic development did not work out well in Russia. The expansion of NATO and the 1999 Kosovo

Table 11.1 How do you, in general, feel about the United States? (Levada, 2017a, 2018e, 2019c)

	2014	2016	2017	2018	2019
Very good	2	2	2	2	4
Mostly good	41	21	35	29	38
Mostly bad	36	39	40	32	25
Very bad	8	26	16	25	19
Don't know	13	13	16	12	14

crisis also convinced most Russians that the United States was ignoring Russia in international affairs (Tsygankov, 2016).

Both countries found a new ground for cooperation after the terrorist attacks against the United States in 2001. This collaboration continues. Meanwhile, nationalist and hawkish tendencies also grew among the key decision makers in Russia after the early 2000s. President Putin gradually accepted an increasingly tougher policy strategy toward Washington. This hawkish (Russians prefer to call it "assertive") position gained popular support in the country. At the same time, in the United States both Democrat and Republican administrations grew increasingly critical of Russia's domestic and foreign policies.

Thus, relations between the United States and Russia remained lukewarm for years. The bilateral contacts in the fields of science, education, and culture continued, yet remained limited. Attempts at a "reset" of relations initiated by the Obama administration did not bring noteworthy changes. American entrepreneurs were reluctant to invest in Russia's economy, citing bureaucracy, corruption, and lack of transparency there. The United States played an instrumental role in initiating and imposing a wide range of economic and political sanctions against Russia for taking over Crimea and Russia's involvement in the crisis in Ukraine after 2014. Disagreements and tensions between the governments of these two nations intensified on a wide range of issues.

Over the last two decades, most Russians have held mixed views toward the United States. A negative downturn took place early in 2014 after the United States and its allies expressed opposition to Russia's policies in and around Crimea (see Table 11.1). In the past several years, opinion polls have shown that Russians generally disapproved of Washington's handling of international affairs. Only one third of Russians believed in cooperation between Moscow and Washington (Smeltz et al., 2016). The common narrative was that the United States was behind the "color revolutions" across the post-Soviet world (the name for popular uprisings against corrupt governments in post-Soviet states, during which people chose specific colors for their ribbons and flags for self-identification) and in Georgia and Ukraine to change governments there, create friendly regimes, and (most importantly) undermine Putin's hold on power in Moscow (Yaffa, 2016). Russians expressed their insecurity about US strength and power and wanted their country to limit Washington's international influence (Smeltz, Wojtowicz, and Goncharov, 2018). Opinions began to change toward a less negative view of the United States after 2018 (Levada, 2018e, 2019c).

Case in point: the Magnitsky Act and the Snowden incident

Two specific cases of US–Russia relations are particularly revealing. The 2012 **Magnitsky Act** was a bipartisan bill passed by the US Congress and signed by President Obama to penalize Russian officials believed to be responsible for the death of Russian lawyer Sergei Magnitsky in a Moscow prison back in 2009. The case was singled out to make a statement of Washington's disapproval of the ongoing harassment of and discrimination against political opposition, and the individuals who dared to go public and reveal examples of massive government corruption in Russia. The Russian government considered this Act as an interference in Russia's domestic affairs. Almost immediately, at the end of 2012, as an act of retaliation, the State Duma banned the international adoption of Russian children in the United States and imposed a travel ban to Russia on a number of US officials. Later another important bill was passed, forcing nongovernmental organizations with foreign (including US) funding to register in Russia as "foreign agents" and thus make themselves vulnerable to additional and substantial financial scrutiny.

The **Snowden case** has played a very negative role in Russian–US relations. Edward Snowden is an American computer professional, formerly employed by the CIA, who in 2013 illegally copied and leaked classified information from the National Security Agency. By doing this, he revealed massive domestic surveillance and counterterrorism programs managed by the US government. Snowden, who fled the United States, was charged with espionage and theft of government property. He received temporary asylum status in Russia. Although Snowden's actions sparked a major international debate about national security and individual privacy, the United States was very critical of Russia's cozy relations with Snowden and Moscow's portrayal of him as a political refugee. In the wake of this case, the Russian government and the media have stepped up their anti-American campaign, at times reaching Cold War levels in terms of the methods and the scope of the information and arguments used.

Both countries increasingly saw each other as competitors, both accusing each other of aggressive intentions. Russia's television networks continued their relentless attacks on America's policies. President Putin published a critical article in the *New York Times* (Putin, 2013; Murray, 2013). The clearest sign of a crisis in Russian–American relations was the cancellation by Washington of the official presidential visit to Moscow in September 2013.

The most difficult problems between Russia and the United States emerged over the conflict in Ukraine and the incorporation of Crimea into the Russian Federation. Washington as well as European capitals supported the new government in Kiev, which had been installed in place of the defunct administration headed by the fugitive President Yanukovich. The United States, as you know, condemned Russia's actions in Crimea, labeling them as an "annexation," which is the forceful transition of land from the control of one state to another. In March 2014, the United States imposed sanctions against several Russian senior officials and took steps to weaken Russia's positions in international organizations.

As a symbolic yet powerful gesture, the G7 resumed its meetings but without Russia. Moscow replied with defiance and introduced its own countersanctions against Western countries, including the United States. These sanctions included a ban on most agricultural and food products from Western countries. For years, products from Western countries essentially disappeared from Russian supermarket aisles. Substantial problems remained in the area of nuclear arms control. Although both countries were implementing the agreements based on the 2010 treaty, any new initiatives related to disarmament suggestions have been shelved.

In 2016 Russia adopted Law FZ-318 (October 31), which underlined a few conditions for a potentially new stage of cooperation with the United States. Moscow wanted the suspension of the Magnitsky Act (see earlier in this chapter). Russia also hoped for the suspension of the US Ukraine Freedom Support Act of 2014, which was designed, from Washington's view, to assist the government of Ukraine in restoring its sovereignty and territorial integrity. Washington also aimed at deterring the government of the Russian Federation from further destabilizing and invading Ukraine and other independent countries in Eastern Europe and Central Asia (Ukraine Freedom Support, 2014). Moscow wanted a reduction of the United States' military presence in Europe as well as financial compensation from the West for the losses associated with the anti-Russian sanctions. Moscow also signaled that many arms control issues have no longer been its priority, at least for some time.

Russia played an unexpectedly noticeable role in the 2016 and 2020 US presidential elections. American security experts alleged Moscow's deliberate cyber intrusion into the 2016 electoral process and after. US intelligence suggested that President Putin was supportive of Donald Trump and wanted Hillary Clinton to lose (Blake, 2017). The US government also stated that Russia orchestrated the hacking of emails of several political organizations of the Democratic Party. (The hackers allegedly could not or did not break into the Republican Party's online communications.) Those hack attacks resulted in the public release of thousands of stolen emails, many of which included damaging revelations about the Democratic Party and former Secretary of State Hillary Clinton, the party's nominee, who eventually lost the election to Donald Trump (Diamond, 2016).

Moreover, multiple sources revealed that the Russian government directly and indirectly trained numerous online trolls to generate fake accounts in social networks with the purpose of confusing, antagonizing, discouraging, or agitating public opinion in America (Bump, 2018). It is quite possible that this was just a tryout, an experiment to see whether such interference could affect the political process and public opinion in the United States.

The proof of the alleged collusion between Russia and the Trump campaign (involving operating contacts and communications between the sides or coordination of their activities) was eventually dismissed in the 2019 Mueller Report (Mueller, 2019), officially titled *Report on the Investigation into Russian Interference in the 2016 Presidential Election* (Robert Mueller was a specially appointed federal counsel). Nevertheless, the "collusion" and other conspiracy theories have been discussed in the media for years. From anchors on major television networks to comedians on late-night shows, from political experts to casual conversations, the allusions and innuendo about Trump's ties to Russia have been relentless (Shiraev, 2019).

The real extent and political impact of the Kremlin's involvement in hacking Democratic servers and the WikiLeaks disclosures will probably never be accurately measured and assessed (Walker, 2019). The Russian government has continuously denied any involvement in the scandal. The debates related to Russia's involvement in US domestic politics have been for years clearly ideological and distinctly partisan. Trump's domestic critics focused mostly on the president's and his associates' assumed interference with the legal investigation of the alleged collusion. Such interference would be deemed illegal based on American laws.

The election of Donald Trump in 2016 and later developments, despite expectations in some political circles in Moscow, did not generate changes in Russian–American relations. It hardly needs repeating that any serious change of policy course in Russia is largely based on the decision of one person, the president. Most experts in the United States and Russia have expressed little hope for any positive and rapid improvements the US–Russian relationship in coming years (Smeltz et al., 2018). Yet there is always a path toward better relations.

If such relations change, it will be most likely in response to new regional and global challenges, such as the pandemic of 2020. Hopefully, the challenges will not be overwhelming, and relations will then change for the better.

RUSSIA'S RELATIONS WITH THE EU

About one quarter of Russian territory is located in Europe, and more than two thirds of the country's population lives there. Russia has had traditionally robust trade with European states. Russian leaders and ordinary people believe that they belong in Europe geographically and culturally. On the other hand, Moscow often distances itself from the continent and emphasizes deep disagreements between Russia and the West.

According to opinion polls, many Russians right after 2014 maintained a negative view of the European Union. This attitude was caused by—among several other factors—the worsening of official relations between Russia and the European Union after Russia's annexation of Crimea and its actions in Ukraine (TASS, 2016b). These attitudes, from a historical perspective, appeared as an anomaly. Historically, most Russians had had a favorable view of Europe and the European Union and considered Russia a part of Europe (see Table 11.2). Opinions began to improve in 2019, which was not indicative that this positive trend would definitely continue. As you should remember, public opinion related to foreign policy tends to be volatile and, in most cases, rooted in the media's coverage of international events.

Russia and the European Union remain very much interdependent. Europe's dependency on energy, Russia's dependency on modern European technologies, and meaningful

Table 11.2 Russian people's views of the European Union

	2015	2016	2017	2018	2019
Very good	2	1	2	3	5
Mostly good	18	26	37	29	45
Mostly bad	43	39	38	33	23
Very bad	28	19	9	13	11
Don't know	9	14	14	22	17

Source: Levada, 2018f, 2019c.

interactions in the fields of culture, education, tourism, and science explain their interconnectedness. There are large Russian-speaking communities in Germany, the United Kingdom, Spain, and other countries. Nevertheless, in the second half of the 1990s, most political leaders and experts in Western Europe shared an opinion that Russia was not ready for broader integration into Europe.

Russia in the course of 30 years witnessed the signing of the Maastricht Treaty in 1992 to create the European Union; the issuing of the single European currency—the euro in 1999; the signing of the Schengen Agreement allowing easy border crossings among EU countries; more coordinated actions in foreign and security policies; and the enlargement of the European Union to include most European countries except a few from the former Soviet Union and the former Yugoslavia. Russia found itself in an ambiguous position. On the one hand, Moscow formally maintained a positive view of closer ties with Europe, including institutional cooperation and economic partnership. On the other hand, a weaker European Union suffering from policy rifts seemed a desirable development.

Two broad categories of opinion had emerged in Russia by the end of the second decade of the century. **Euro-optimists**, in general terms, tend to believe that increasing European integration and the emerging common border should bring Russia benefits. Some hope for serious economic benefits. Others believe that political changes will follow: the integration eventually should encourage Moscow to reform and accept European political values and business practices. **Euro-pessimists**, on the other hand, tend to believe that Russia's integration into Europe did not and does not serve the country's core interests. Euro-pessimists feel that the European Union is using Russia to its own advantage and that Russia's economic and social success should take place outside the European Union's structure. Some pessimists, including leaders in Moscow, criticize liberal values as decadent (Putin, 2019a; Surkov, 2019). Others reject European models of free-market capitalism and endorse authoritarian forms of state capitalism. Some of them go further and speak about a "post-European Russia" (Lukyanov, 2016).

Ideology has also played a big role in the growing problems between Moscow and Brussels. Russia's poor domestic human rights record is under constant criticism from the European Union. Over recent years the European Parliament passed several resolutions criticizing the Russian authorities for restricting the activities of NGOs, limiting public rallies and peaceful demonstrations, and restraining political freedoms such as freedom of speech and assembly.

Moscow usually dismissed such statements. Some political scientists and journalists turned to discussing a fundamental value gap between the citizens of Russia and the European Union. The logic was that, while Europeans have become unreasonably focused on specific liberal rights related to race, religion, and gender, Russia was the country that preserved the "traditional" values very much related to morality, decency, economic stability, and security for all. President Putin himself outlined the importance of Russian conservative values without mentioning liberal ideas (Putin, 2014; Popova, 2004).

A difficult test of EU–Russian relations was the August 2008 conflict in the Caucasus. We have already discussed it earlier. Unlike NATO, the European Union did not suspend its relations with Moscow. Yet after the 2008 crisis, the competition between Russia and the European Union for influence in the post-Soviet space became tougher (Gretskiy, Treshchenkov, and Golubev, 2014).

The aftermath of the 2014 Ukrainian crisis brought relations between Moscow and Brussels to their lowest point in three decades. The European Union condemned Russia's actions in the Crimea and in eastern Ukraine. Despite Russia's predictable objections, the European Union signed association and free-trade-zone agreements with Ukraine, Georgia, and Moldova. Ukraine received substantial financial aid between 2014 and 2020. The scope and frequency of political contacts between Russia and EU were drastically curtailed. Regular Russian–EU summits, which used to be held twice a year, were canceled. The negotiations on a new visa-free travel between Russia and the European countries of the Schengen Area were suspended. For the first time in the history of Russian–EU relations, severe sanctions were imposed against a large number of Russian political figures, entrepreneurs, and companies. As a countermeasure, Moscow approved its own list of European politicians who were forbidden from visiting Russia.

There is little chance that Russian–EU relations will seriously improve in the early 2020s (Khudoley, 2016). The socioeconomic and political models of the European Union and Russia remain very different. On the whole, the United States, Russia, and the European Union are drifting along opposite vectors, and the existing political gap between them has been not shrinking but, in fact, widening during the past decade.

RUSSIA'S RELATIONS WITH NATO

Until its disintegration at the end of 1991, the Soviet Union had had no official relations with NATO except a few contacts occurring during the negotiations on arms limitation. However, already in the fall of 1991, the new Russian leaders were discussing the possibility of joining NATO. They signaled their willingness through public statements and interviews and by means of diplomatic channels. In 1991 the newly created North Atlantic Cooperation Council had brought NATO members together with the former members of the Warsaw Pact and some other participants.

Yet no major breakthrough related to Russia–NATO integration took place. From the beginning, the Western partners were not rushing to admit Russia. The reasons for such reluctance were somewhat obvious. In the early 1990s, when discussing NATO's enlargement with the members of his administration, US President Bill Clinton remarked that Russia's joining NATO was "blue-sky stuff" which would require a different Russia, different NATO, and different Europe (Talbott, 2003: 132).

Certain positive developments, of course, emerged in the 1990s. Russian and NATO soldiers now participated in an international peacekeeping force in Bosnia. In 1997, Russia and NATO signed the Founding Act, proclaiming that the two organizations no longer considered each other adversaries, and proposed the creation of several formal institutions of cooperation. The main role was assigned to the Permanent Joint Council (PJC), with all the NATO countries and Russia participating in it. Regular security-related consultations between the Ministers for Foreign Affairs, Defense Ministers, and top military officials began.

However, a serious crisis in relations between Russia and NATO broke out in the spring of 1999. It was triggered during the events in Kosovo described earlier in this book. The international community in general blamed the Serbian government for the violence against ethnic Albanians (mostly Sunni Muslims) in Kosovo. Russia disagreed and supported Serbia. After failed attempts by international mediators to manage the conflict, NATO bombed Serbia and forced it to withdraw its troops from Kosovo, which eventually declared independence in 2008. Russia objected to NATO's actions and condemned the forceful partition (as Moscow called it) of Serbia, but to no avail.

A new chance to improve relations came with the election of Russia's new president. During the March 2000 campaign not only did Putin avoid using anti-Western rhetoric, but, on the contrary, he cautiously reexamined the possibility of Russia's future partnership with NATO. In the aftermath of the 9/11 tragedy in New York and Washington, DC, Russia joined the antiterrorist coalition, urged countries in Central Asia to provide assistance to the United States including the opening of US military bases there, and aided the NATO military operation in Afghanistan. Russia and its Western partners again discussed the possibility of Russia's joining NATO. In 2002 in Rome the top leaders of Russia and NATO agreed to create the NATO–Russia Council. They wanted to boost their military cooperation in areas such as counterterrorism, nonproliferation of nuclear weapons, and coordination of search and rescue operations at sea and during natural disasters. Relations, however, were worsening again after the 2003 US invasion of Iraq. The most serious crisis between Russia and NATO occurred in August 2008 when the war in the Caucasus broke out involving Russia, Georgia, and the self-proclaimed states of Abkhazia and South Ossetia.

Since the 2014 crisis in Ukraine, NATO has essentially frozen its relations with Russia, except several meetings of the Russia–NATO Council. Although Russia expressed disappointment about the diminished contacts, it started increasing its military presence in areas close to NATO countries' borders, including the Baltic Sea and the Black Sea. After 2015, Russian and then NATO officials started to publicly call the other side an "adversary" or a "threat" (thus challenging the Founding Act of 1997 when both sides declared that they were no longer enemies).

Russian political elites have always recognized the real military potential of NATO. Moscow maintains that it does not want a return to Cold War hostilities. Yet NATO is under constant criticism from Russia's government and the media. The reasons are ideological, political, and pragmatic (many refer to the legacy of the Cold War). A very negative attitude toward NATO reflects Russia's general perception of the West and Russia's view of its own position in the world. NATO is a convenient target for Russian nationalists regardless of their political affiliation (some of them are conservative, others communists). The Communist Party and the Liberal Democratic Party, since the 1990s, have also been harsh critics of NATO and especially of its eastward enlargement. Attacks on NATO also allow the Kremlin to consolidate the country's public opinion and rally people behind the government, especially during difficult economic periods. The Russian military elites also need to have a "foe" to justify large spending on defense and national security.

RUSSIA'S RELATIONS WITH EUROPEAN COUNTRIES

Germany. By 1994 Russia had finally withdrawn all its troops from Germany. They had been stationed there (in East Germany) since the end of World War II. Putin, when he became president, pursued a special relationship with Berlin. His knowledge of Germany and the German language and personal relations with Chancellor Schroeder facilitated diplomacy. In September 2001, Putin made a speech at the Bundestag in German (Putin, as a KGB officer, had lived for many years in Germany in the late 1980s). Both countries in the early 2000s established a range of intergovernmental institutions responsible for dialogue in the areas of economy, science, and education. German investments in the Russian economy were also growing. Some legal groundwork was drafted in the European Commission for the construction of the "Nord Stream"—a gas pipeline from Russia to Germany across the Baltic Sea. Nevertheless, relations have begun to worsen during the two last decades.

The first reason was Russia's domestic policies, which were turning authoritarian under President Putin. German political parties, NGOs, and the media were increasingly critical of the direction of Russian politics. Chancellor Angela Merkel was much more critical of Russia than her predecessor Schroeder. The second reason for a worsening trend in relations was Russia's changing view of its role in the world and its foreign policy. Although on the surface both Russia and Germany called for broader international cooperation, respect of other countries' interests, and the necessity to act cautiously in international conflicts (such as the bombing of Libya by an international coalition in 2011), many points of disagreement were emerging. Russian actions in Georgia in 2008 and in Ukraine in 2014 (and later) were the signs—in the eyes of German observers—of Russia's boorishness and disregard for international law. Germany voted in the UN General Assembly as well as in other international organizations for the resolution condemning Russia's actions in Ukraine. At the same time, Germany participated in the Normandy contact group, including Germany, Russia, Ukraine, and France, to resolve the situation in the eastern regions of Ukraine. Both governments had a different view (although they recognized the Islamic State as an enemy) of the conflict in Syria and the need to support the embattled President Assad, whose government Russia defended militarily.

The financial crisis of 2008 and the following economic crisis negatively impacted Russian–German trade, but all in all Germany remained Russia's top trade partner. Germany remained in the top-five ranks for both exports and imports (Global Edge, 2020). Both countries wanted to implement the Nord Stream project—a pipeline across the Baltic Sea to deliver gas directly from Russia to Germany (two pipelines were laid between 2001 and 2012, and additional lines were under construction). At the same time, although Germany still relies on oil and gas exports from Russia, German political leaders see the necessity to decrease their country's energy dependency on Russia. High-level contacts between Russia and Germany continued. Yet a number of disagreements between them remained serious.

France. During the Cold War, France often played a reconciling role, trying to mediate and soothe various conflicts and confrontations between the United States and the Soviet Union. After the collapse of the Soviet Union, France immediately recognized Russia as the successor state. A major deterioration of Russian–French relations happened during the 1999 Kosovo crisis and the second (1999) Chechen campaign. The active participation of France in the bombing of Yugoslavia (the second largest participating air force after the United States) caused frustration in Russia (Sobel and Shiraev, 2003).

France stressed that security on the continent not only required a balance of power but also demanded strengthening democracy and human rights, as well as maintaining the priority of the existing institutions, especially the European Union and NATO. During the 2008 conflict in Georgia, the French president acted as a mediator between Russia and Georgia. He was able to implement a ceasefire agreement. However, France did not approve of Russia's recognition of the independence of Abkhazia and South Ossetia: Paris supported Georgia's position in this conflict. France for years, together with the United States and other European nations, supported sanctions against Iran to curb its nuclear ambitions, a policy that Russia continuously criticized as unfair to Iran and unjust (Russia insisted that such measures must be approved only by the UN Security Council). Russia and France supported the nuclear deal with Iran and opposed President's Trump's decision to leave the agreement.

Russia and France also had different views on the necessity and scope of the military action against Libya in 2011. The two countries had different views on the status of Syrian President Assad and his government. Russian policies have for many years received the support of some French political groups, especially the National Front, which is a socially conservative, nationalist political party. Its leaders were very critical of the sanctions against Russia during the conflict in Ukraine. The National Front's anti-NATO, anti-American, and anti-immigrant positions all find sympathy and positive reactions in Moscow (National Front, 2018).

In the second decade of the 21st century France became the fourth largest foreign investor in the Russian economy. France occupied the fifth place in imports to Russia, behind China, Germany, the United States, and Belarus (Global Edge, 2020). However, Russian investments in France remain relatively small. As in Germany (and other countries), French media, both liberal and conservative, tend to be very critical of Russia's domestic and foreign policy, which are perceived as anti-Western and boorish. France also backed the EU sanctions against Russia for its actions in Ukraine. One illustration of the scope of these sanctions stands out. Earlier in 2009 France had agreed to sell Russia two amphibious assault ships of the Mistral class. These helicopter carriers were supposed to be delivered to the Russian navy sometime in 2015. However, in 2014 the French president decided to cancel the deal because of Russia's actions in Ukraine. Principled politics trumped a massive business deal. France agreed to return almost $1.5 billion to Russia for the failed contract (AFP, 2015).

During the 2017 French presidential elections, some French officials accused Russian media of interference on the side of the French right-wing parties. Russia denied the accusations. Yet high-level contacts between the two countries, including summits, continued.

The United Kingdom. Throughout history, relations between Russia and the United Kingdom have constantly swayed from tense to friendly, from openness to mutual isolation—depending on particular events, leaders, and policies. In the early 1960s, London was the main political and trade partner of the USSR in Western Europe. Yet as a nuclear power and a member of NATO, the United Kingdom was also a key strategic foe of the Soviet Union during the Cold War. Relations began changing for the better during perestroika in the late 1980s. Personal contacts between Mikhail Gorbachev and Prime Minister Margaret Thatcher played a very important role in both countries' improving relations.

After the end of the Cold War, both sides formally agreed to cooperate in many areas, including disarmament, science, technology, energy, agriculture, banking, and environmental protection. However, London, like Berlin and Paris, was critical of Russia's slow transition to democratic institutions and governance during the 1990s, the lack of civil liberties, and Moscow's military actions in Chechnya. Moscow was increasingly frustrated by what it saw as a deliberate effort by the West to keep Russia "out."

After 2000, President Putin took steps to improve relations with London. Alas, several events contributed to the worsening of these countries' bilateral affairs. In 2003 Moscow requested the **extradition**—the official transfer of a suspected or convicted criminal to another country—of several influential Russian citizens who had already been under criminal investigation in Russia. One was Boris Berezovsky, a prominent billionaire and a close ally of former President Boris Yeltsin. Berezovsky received political asylum in the United Kingdom. In Russia he faced multiple charges including embezzlement and fraud. London refused the extradition request, believing that the Berezovsky case was politically motivated and thus that he would not receive fair treatment in Russia.

This decision displeased Moscow. In 2007 it was London's turn to ask for an extradition. This time the case was related to the poisoning with a radioactive substance of a former Russian security officer and spy, Alexander Litvinenko, who died in London under suspicious circumstances. What has become known as the **Litvinenko case** involved evidence of the use of radioactive polonium-210 against the former Russian spy. Suspicion for the assassination fell on the Kremlin.

The British government wanted to extradite from Russia a key suspect in this case. The Kremlin refused, citing a law prohibiting the extradition of Russian citizens to foreign countries. The Russian government and the media were very energetic in promoting the position of the Kremlin in this case. Probably as a result of this pro-government media campaign, a substantial proportion of Russians, about 36 percent, believed that the Litvinenko murder was an anti-Russian provocation (WCIOM, 2009h). The fallout of the Litvinenko case was the mutual expulsion of diplomats in 2007 and the cutting of British ties with Russian security agencies. Other disagreements included the judgments of the infamous **poisoning scandal** of 2018. The scandal was about the poisoning in the United Kingdom of Sergei Skripal, a former Russian security agent, and his daughter. According to the British investigation, the Skripals were poisoned by an extremely potent chemical agent traceable to Russia. These and other serious issues have seriously disrupted business as well as diplomatic and cultural ties between Britain and Russia. The poisoning scandal in Britain caused Washington's additional economic sanctions against Russia in 2018.

Russia and Britain had a similar view on the importance of the 2015 nuclear deal with Iran. Yet Russia did not support the unilateral sanctions against Iran imposed by the West, Britain included. Differences also appeared about the war in Syria, where Russia and Britain supported opposite sides in the armed conflict. Obviously, the Ukraine crisis triggered a drastic worsening of already poor relations. From the floor of the UN General Assembly and in many other international organizations, Britain voted for resolutions criticizing Russia's actions. London supported the initiative to hold the 2014 G7 Summit without Russia. Britain recognized Crimea as Ukrainian territory, condemning the actions of separatists in eastern Ukraine. All military cooperation between the two countries was put on hold. When Putin was elected to his next term in 2018, there were no signs of a quick improvement of the countries' bilateral relations. Moscow and London continue to have very different perceptions of history and the present international relations.

Central Europe. After the breakup of the communist bloc and the Soviet Union, most former communist countries of Central Europe (including the Czech Republic, Hungary, Slovakia, Slovenia, and Croatia) no longer shared borders with Russia, except Poland. For convenience, we will include Romania and Bulgaria (both countries that were members of the communist bloc) in Central Europe, although some scholars consider them geographically and geopolitically a part of Eastern Europe.

While Russia hoped for a new type of friendly relationship, for the former socialist countries the priority of the time was to prepare for an early accession to NATO and the European Union. The legacy of communism and Moscow's dominance in the past were among the reasons why Central European countries wanted to distance themselves from Moscow. Another reason was the speed and direction of Russia's own political reforms after 1991. Initially, Russia did not object to the NATO enlargement. President Yeltsin stated this opinion to Polish President Lech Wałęsa (b. 1943) in 1993. Later, Russia's position on the expansion changed. The development of relations with states in Central Europe and the Baltic States was being linked directly to whether they were going to join the North Atlantic Alliance or not. Moscow objected particularly intensely to the NATO inclusion of the Baltic countries, arguing that the boundaries of the former Soviet Union were the "red line" that NATO should not cross.

The legacies of the Cold War continued to influence Russia's policies. Russia has repeatedly accused Estonia and Latvia of violating the rights of their Russian-speaking residents. Moscow disagreed with the Baltic countries' policies regarding the Russian language as well as their policies toward reassessing some events that took place during World War II (Lanko, 2013). For example, how should one judge the local resistance in Latvia, Estonia, and Lithuania that fought against the Soviet occupation? As you remember, Russia rejects the very idea that an "occupation" took place. The official view of Moscow has always been that the Soviet Union played a crucial role in liberating Europe from the Nazi occupation. On the other hand, there is a common view in the Baltic states as well as in the countries of Central Europe that the Soviets used the war against Germany to their own advantage and that it led to the establishment of communist regimes across Europe.

Moscow was taking important steps toward improving its relations with Poland. Unfortunately, there have been many ideological and political disagreements between these two countries. A tragic event in 2010 made things worse. A plane crash near the Russian city of Smolensk is likely to remain a source of disagreement for years to come: President Kaczynski, together with his wife and other politicians and senior military officers, heading by airplane to ceremonies at the site of the 1940 Katyn massacre (see Chapter 1), were killed in the crash. In the aftermath of this tragedy many conspiracy theories emerged. Russia took measures to calm public opinion in Poland and dismiss many unfounded allegations. Following the tragedy political contacts between Russia and Poland continued. Poland, however, continued its commitment to NATO, which was articulated during President Obama's 2014 and Trump's 2017 visits to Warsaw.

During the 2014 events in Ukraine, virtually all the Central and Eastern European countries demonstrated their support for the new government there and condemned Russia's actions by voting for the relevant resolutions in the UN General Assembly as well as in some other international organizations. Most Central European countries spoke for the toughest sanctions against Russia. Poland and the Baltic countries aligned themselves more strongly with the United States than with France and Germany on that issue. The Baltic Sea region remains a strategically tense place due to the presence of Russian and NATO armed forces there essentially a few miles away from each other (Khudoley, 2016). On the other hand, Hungary, Slovakia, and Slovenia continued a dialogue with Russia. Time will tell whether these dynamics remain or change.

RUSSIA–CHINA RELATIONS

In the 21st century, while Moscow's relations with Washington and Western European countries have been worsening, the relatively robust relations between China and Russia have drawn substantial attention from politicians, scholars, and journalists. Since the beginning of this century, the two countries have held regular annual meetings between their heads of states, prime ministers, top legislators, and foreign ministers.

China and Russia tend to share many similar views on international affairs. Moscow supported Beijing's antiseparatist policies in Tibet and the Xinjiang Province and received support from Chinese leaders for Russia's own military actions in Chechnya years ago. Russia also supports the "one China" policy and agrees that Taiwan is an inseparable part of China. Both countries have also been concerned with North Korea's dangerous behavior and have endorsed policies aiming at reducing tensions on and around the Korean Peninsula.

Moscow and Beijing for many years did not publicly clash on a single international issue. There are some differences in their positions, however. China, for example, emphasized that Russia must act with caution in Ukraine. Yet, China has not openly censured Russia's actions and did not join the West in imposing sanctions on Russia (Ying, 2016). Russia has always maintained a positive attitude toward creating a strategic alliance among India, China, and Russia. China, however, prefers a more cautious approach, understanding that such an international alliance might cause an alarmed reaction from the Arab countries, Pakistan, the United States, and possibly many other states. Therefore, China tends to be guarded and even restrained about creating and joining new alliances and has little interest in a formal military alliance with Russia. Beijing certainly cares about its relations with Washington and does not envision building any anti-US or anti-Western blocs including Russia or any other country (Kozyrev, 2018).

According to Moscow and Beijing, Sino-Russian relations are a "priority" for both sides. These relations are not linked to fluctuations in the international situation. Chinese President Xi in 2018 called Putin a "good and old friend of the Chinese people" and "the leader of a great country who is influential around the world" (Withnall, 2018). By the beginning of the third decade of the 21st century, China and Russia were seemingly sharing a strategic interest in being parallel strategic competitors to the European Union and the United States in particular (Kozyrev, 2018).

China needs Russia's natural resources, including gas and oil; Russia needs Chinese manufactured products. From an economic standpoint their collaboration is mutually beneficial. Both countries are interested in maintaining stability in Asia, and both oppose ethnic separatism, including Islamic fundamentalism. A common unifying goal for Moscow and Beijing is to create a global center of power to counterbalance the United States and Western Europe. However, this is a very delicate issue: Russia does not want to see a dominant China at its borders; China does not want to be used as a wildcard in Russia's geopolitical calculations.

In 1996 Russia and China, together with Kazakhstan, Kyrgyzstan, and Tajikistan, formed a group that became in 2001 the **Shanghai Cooperation Organization**. Uzbekistan joined the group later that year. India and Pakistan also joined in 2017. Turkey has also expressed its interest in joining the "six." The initial purpose of the group was to eliminate border disputes, reduce the presence of the countries' military forces near state borders, and coordinate efforts related to the countries' security. Mutual activities of the group also include joint military antiterrorism training and cooperation in antidrug policies. The countries coordinate their efforts in economic, investment, and trade areas. China prioritizes economic cooperation. Russia, however, gives top priority to international security.

In the past decade, one of the most important pieces of China's foreign and economic policies has been the design and implementation of a high-capacity transport infrastructure, linking East Asia to Europe. These massive plans or development strategy received the name the **Belt and Road Initiative (BRI)**. China is working on inviting and including many Asian and European countries (the number is around 60) as well as regional organizations to implement this project. The project proposes several land corridors, and the maritime transport route.

These Chinese plans generally correspond with Russian strategic projects for tighter cooperation in Eurasia. Russia is aware that the BRI draws funding primarily from government sources. The plans include building high-speed railways in Russia, which would require cooperation with the Chinese government and many Chinese companies. The future of Russian–Chinese relations will certainly depend, among many other factors, on how deep and effective Russia's involvement in the BRI will be and how successful and attractive this project becomes in the eyes of other countries and alliances.

How long will these good relations last? Will China and Russia form a new strategic alliance, or is this just a convenient partnership in trade, as some suggest (Ying, 2016)? Opinions have differed. Some believe in a long-term strategic political and military partnership rooted in security concerns. Others maintain that this is just a temporary business of convenience: both countries have less in common in terms of their fundamental interests than people might think. Yet others see in this relationship a new trend of the 21st century by which the political elites in a growing number of countries have decided to trade the promise of economic and social stability to its citizens for a share of these citizens' fundamental political and personal freedoms.

RUSSIA'S REGIONAL POLICIES

Since the 1990s, Russia's strategic goals in the Middle East have been focused on gaining or regaining influence over most Arab countries. Several tasks and priorities associated with this effort emerged after the early 2000s (Shiraev and Khudoley, 2019).

First, Russia needs political and social stability in the Middle East. The revolutionary turmoil after 2011 in Tunisia and Egypt, the civil war in Syria and the rise and fall of ISIS, the ongoing conflict in Iraq, and other conflicts have emerged as substantial challenges to both regional and broader international stability. Moscow saw the events of the Arab Spring (and similar popular revolts in other countries, as we have discussed elsewhere) as mostly harmful to regional stability and potentially dangerous for Russia.

Second, Russia actively pursues a more effective role for itself in this region's politics. This often involves the task of dropping ideological considerations and developing bilateral and multilateral ties with the countries of the region and taking advantage of the West's inaction or mistakes there, such as in Syria. By taking action in Syria in 2015 Russia hoped to restore its status as a major international player (Lukyanov, 2016).

Third, Russia seeks every opportunity to reduce the political domination of the United States. Not only does Moscow support its traditional allies, such as Syria, contrary to Washington's and most other countries' wishes; Russia also actively engages Egypt, Sudan, and several Gulf states in political dialogues and consultations. By maintaining a nonideological and pragmatic policy, as it claims, Russia hopes to become an important and influential force capable of solutions that neither the United States nor other Western countries could implement. For example, Russia maintains relations with both Israel and the Palestinian organizations (including Hamas, which is officially recognized as a terrorist organization by the United States). Moscow abandoned its open anti-Israeli policies in the 1990s, and now pursues dynamic relations with Israel. Large numbers of Soviet and Russian

Jews have moved to Israel permanently over the past 30 years, and the size of the Russian-speaking population in Israel is around 1 million people. Moscow supports a two-state solution for Israel and Palestine and condemns violence between the two sides regardless of which side is seen as responsible for it.

The Russian language is now the third most widely spoken language in Israel (after Hebrew and Arabic). Israel also has the third largest number of Russian speakers outside of the former Soviet republics; Russian-born is the biggest group among the total immigrant population in Israel. Moscow wants to see Israel as a strategic partner in the Middle East. Both countries see Islamic extremism as a major threat. In the trade area, relations are robust. Israel sells agricultural products to Russia, which one can easily find on almost every store's shelf in Russian cities. Still, during confrontations between Israel and its opponents, Moscow avoids taking sides (Khoury, 2018; Naumkin, 2014).

The Arab–Israeli conflict remains an important issue on the region's political agenda, but its significance as a defining issue in Russia's strategies has declined in the second decade of this century. Most Arab states are primarily concerned with the Iranian and jihadi challenges, and several Sunni states have been collaborating with Israel against these challenges (Rabinovich, 2016). Russia understands these strategic changes and conducts regular dialogue with Israel and other Arab states.

After 2017, Washington reengaged with many Arab and Muslim states and took a tough position against Iran's domestic and foreign policies by reinstating sanctions against Teheran in 2018. These and other international developments should impact Russia's actions in North Africa and South Asia both now and in the future. Russia may choose to retain and strengthen its ties with Iran, which could leave Moscow in relative isolation in the region and globally. Russia also could reach out to the United States and its allies, thus adding to the legitimacy of its presence and policies in the region.

Russia cannot push the United States out of the Middle East—it could not do so even after Washington somewhat disengaged from the region after 2008. America's influence still remains strong and lasting. Russia, on the other hand, has no real allies in the region, just business partners. Russia, despite its military abilities and its sophisticated diplomatic efforts, does not really have the means to project power across the region. Egypt, Turkey, and a few other countries can use Russia to make business deals, yet they do not really want to irritate Washington: their strategic relationship with America is vital (Trofimov, 2008).

Russia tries to maintain balanced relations with India and Pakistan. Russia remains a key partner of India in the fields of energy security, nuclear energy, and hydrocarbons (Mukherjee, 2015). Another key area of trade is weapons. In the first 15 years of the 21st century, arms exports from Russia to India exceeded $20 billion (Pulipaka, 2016). Russia accounted for almost 70 percent of India's arms purchases from foreign countries. Among big purchases are Russian jet fighters and helicopters. In 2012, both states signed a new weapons deal worth $2.9 billion (BBC News, 2016). Both countries have reduced some trade regulations and tariffs. Russia has also agreed to build more than 20 nuclear reactors in India over the next two decades. Russia's biggest gas company, Gazprom, has continued its natural gas shipments to India of approximately 2.5 million tons a year for 20 years. India and Russia agreed to cooperate in the field of computer-related technology (Sharma, 2012).

Substantial improvements in Russia's relations with Pakistan came in the wake of the 2001 terrorist attacks against the United States. The decision of Pakistani leaders to join the international action against terrorism has led to an improvement in Russia–Pakistan relations in the economic, trade, and political fields. Pakistanis search for stable partners. Russia is one of them. Russia endorsed Pakistan's full membership of the Shanghai Cooperation Organization (Pakistan and India joined in 2017). Moscow has offered its assistance in developing Pakistan's power plants and also sells military jets and combat helicopters to Pakistan. The Pakistan Army, together with other countries, has participated in Russian military exercises (Jamal, 2016). Russia, of course, is aware of India's attention to the ways relations between Moscow and Islamabad are developing. Moscow sends its assurances that it treats both India and Pakistan even-handedly and that India–Russia ties should remain strong.

Russia's policy in the Asia–Pacific region, to a certain degree, is a continuation of the Soviet policy in the second half of the 1980s and early 1990s. At the same time, it has several unique features.

First, Russia's vast Asian regions—Siberia and the Far East—have opened up to the outside world. Cross-border travel has been simplified, which stimulates trade and tourism with the adjacent regions. Yet Siberia and the Far East are lagging behind the rest of Russia economically. Not surprisingly, Moscow uses its foreign policy to bring more economic and social benefits to these regions. Second, Russia is striving for different, deeper, and more efficient forms of integration in the Asia–Pacific region, emphasizing economic and military ties based on bilateral and multilateral agreements.

Third, the Kremlin maintains the position that the balance of power is changing from the West to the Asia–Pacific region. Moscow is busy creating and formalizing various forms of cooperation including a Moscow–Delhi–Beijing "triangle" as well as the more successful BRICS and the Shanghai Cooperation Organization (see earlier in this chapter). The latter has become the first large post–Cold War international organization without the presence of the United States. Fourth, Russia declares that it is building nonideological, pragmatic relations with all countries in the Asia–Pacific region. Officially Russia does not divide the countries into more or less important in its policies. Yet China occupies, as we have seen earlier, the most prominent place among Russia's partners.

Although Russia has a lingering territorial dispute with Japan, bilateral contacts between these countries are robust in nonpolitical areas including trade, educational exchanges, and tourism. The importance of developing relations with Vietnam is regularly underlined in Moscow. Russia and South Korea have introduced visa-free travel between the two countries. Although Seoul did not support Moscow's actions in Ukraine and in Syria, South Korea did not join Western sanctions against Russia.

After the 1990s, Russia continued an active foreign policy strategy in Latin America. This strategy is based on several strategic goals. Overall, Russia is trying to challenge the US-led international order and Washington's authority in Latin America; enhance Putin's domestic legitimacy in the eyes of Latin American governments; and promote specific Russian commercial, military, and energy interests. Russia has approached its relations with Latin America from at least three key positions (Gurganus, 2018; Yakovlev, 2013).

First, to repeat, Russia for years now has been trying to act in the international arena as a global power, not just a regional actor. Therefore, even the physical remoteness of Latin America does not prevent Moscow from actively developing relations with most countries there. Russia sees them primarily as partners. The second position is economic. Russia focuses on mutual trade and investments. Since the late 1990s, several Latin American countries, such as Brazil and Argentina, have experienced a period of rapid economic growth, which made them very attractive economic partners. After the West imposed its sanctions in 2014, Russia considered its trade relations with Latin America as very important, especially in the fields of power generation and the arms trade.

The third position is political. Russian policy in Latin America, as Moscow states, tends to be nonideological. The Kremlin does not openly support left-wing parties yet tends to agree with their anti-Western and anti-American leanings. Russia, in general terms, distinguishes a cluster of countries in Latin America based on their own foreign policy. This cluster includes the states that are most critical of the United States and its role in international affairs, such as Cuba, Bolivia, Nicaragua, and Venezuela.

On one hand, Putin was the first Russian or Soviet leader to pay an official visit to a number of African countries. On the other hand, Africa is placed last among the list of regional directions in the Foreign Policy Concepts of Russia (2013, 2016). In Africa, Russia first seeks to demonstrate its global position and status in a multipolar world. Moscow pays particular attention to the Republic of South Africa—a country belonging to both the G20 and BRICS. Russia maintains contacts with the African Union and some other pan-African organizations. Russia maintains good relations with Angola, Mozambique, and some other former allies of the USSR. Second, Russia pays attention to Africa in the context of international security. Unlike many other regions, confrontation with the West and competition with China are almost absent here. Russia hopes to see peaceful settlements of military conflicts and takes part in UN peacekeeping missions. Third, Russia moved its economic relations with African countries from an ideological to a mostly market basis in the 1990s. In the 21st century, such relations are developing mainly in the same direction as those with Latin American countries (i.e., energy, mining, and arms).

CRITICAL THINKING ABOUT FOREIGN POLICY

In the 21st century most democratic countries have maintained a very critical view of Russian domestic and foreign policy. The policies at home were seen as increasingly authoritarian and antidemocratic; Russia's foreign policy was criticized as aggressive and expansionist. Moscow entirely dismissed these criticisms. It seemed like there were two types of reality: one was constructed in Moscow; the other was designed in Western capitals. What has been Moscow's argument so far?

Russia's grievances

Russian leaders attribute the worsening of their relations with the United States and Western Europe almost exclusively to Western policies: if Western powers had chosen a different foreign policy in the past, then the relations between the countries would have been different. In particular:

America and Europe should not have supported Bosnian Muslims in the ethnic conflict in the former Yugoslavia in 1992–96. Washington and NATO should not have bombed Serbia, which had fought for its own territorial integrity in 1999. The West should not have granted independence to Kosovo by annexing a part of Serbia's sovereign territory.

NATO should have halted its eastward expansion that began in 1996 and continued for more than two decades.

Next, the United States should not have invaded Iraq in 2003. Other Western countries, including the United Kingdom, should not have supported Washington in this aggressive and unjust war.

The United States and the European Union should not have sponsored antigovernment protests and meddled in the elections in Ukraine in 2004–5. (The West rejected these accusations as totally groundless.) Washington and its European allies should not have supported Georgia in its military conflict with Russia in 2008 over South Ossetia and Abkhazia.

The West should not have been recklessly one-sided and extremely forceful in supporting the rebels in Libya in 2011, who killed Gaddafi, Libya's leader. This created instability in the entire region. Similarly, the West should not have attempted to remove the legitimate Syrian President Assad from power and should not have supported the armed opposition to his government.

The United States and its allies should not have imposed sanctions against Russia for its attempt to restore the "historical justice" (how Moscow labeled this) in Ukraine in 2014 and later (the West sees this as a de facto annexation of Crimea). The West should not have interfered in Russia's domestic affairs by passing anti-Russian laws, imposing sanctions on its business and political leaders, recruiting and directing the activities of anti-Russian nongovernment organizations, and toying with Russian political opposition.

What should be done, in Russia's view, to design a new type of international relations? The most important steps, both strategic and specific, from Russia's standpoint, should include (Shiraev and Khudoley, 2019):

- American and European leaders should accept the reality of the new and rising multipolar (polycentric, in Russia's vocabulary) world; not only should such recognition materialize in their declarations or scholarly papers (there are plenty of such); new practical steps and specific policies must follow; the result of these policies should be an increased role for international institutions such as the United Nations.
- Washington must stop using violence in its foreign policy and turn to peaceful, multilateral solutions to international conflicts.
- NATO must halt its eastward expansion; in particular, Ukraine and Georgia must never become NATO members.
- All political and economic sanctions against Russia should be lifted, and a fair compensation to Russia granted.
- The West should accept Crimea as a part of Russia and diplomatically assist Russia and other conflicting sides in resolving the crisis in the eastern part of Ukraine.
- The West should discontinue the activities of nongovernmental organizations working in Russia and halt their attempts to influence political institutions and public opinion in Russia.
- The West must unconditionally accept that Russia is a sovereign state with its own political institutions, traditions, and political culture.

Implications for Western policies

Any country's foreign policy depends on the specific contexts in which these policies take place. There are domestic (such as frequency of elections, public opinion, or political institutions) and international contexts (such as global developments, regional tensions, conflicts, and their resolutions). Personal factors—such as the individual in the office, or the country elites' views of the world and the way they define their country's national interest—play a big role, too. As we have learned in this book, Russian political leaders and foreign policy experts often see their country and world differently compared with the view from London, Paris, Tallinn, Tokyo, or Washington. How can we incorporate these contexts into different strategies dealing with Russia's foreign policy? Those who study Russia are not unified in their views.

First. Some experts and decision makers outside Russia look at this country as a foe, as a hostile and unpredictable power, which should be treated with extreme cautions and vigilance. They say that Russia cannot be trusted so long as the current government is in place there. Moscow should be resisted.

Second. Others, who are in the majority, see Russia as a predictable competitor, yet not a foe; thus Moscow, in this view, can be and should be engaged bilaterally as well as globally, albeit in selected areas. Russia, according to this assessment, cannot be trusted; yet it can be respected and contained.

Third. Yet others, although they are few, have a completely different view; they downplay the disagreements with Moscow and accept its grievances. They accuse the West and its allies of making serious policy blunders vis-à-vis Russia. They accentuate the immediate and potential benefits of engaging with Russia; they tend to see Russia mostly as a key global actor and a valuable partner.

In light of these arguments, the policy options for most Western countries are likely to lie between the first and second options.

CONCLUSION

As a sovereign and powerful country, Russia pursues its own strategic interests. In the geopolitical context, Russia feels insecure about NATO and its possible expansion in the future. Having its own oil and gas supplies, Russia uses them as bargaining chips in foreign policy. Russia is also becoming a viable competitor for global energy resources. Ideology sometimes becomes a serious factor determining Russia's international moves. For example, Russia is extremely sensitive about its treatment as a junior partner; it is determined to become an equal player in global affairs. Yet Russia continues to commit errors in foreign policy. One of the indicators is that Moscow's relations with many countries have worsened over the past few years. However, Russian foreign policy is more pragmatic and predictable than it was 20 years ago. Russia is interested in global stability. Moscow pursues nuclear nonproliferation, supports antiterrorist policies, and hopes to expand trade and other forms of economic cooperation. The main problem, as always, lies in the details.

12 Defense and Security Policies

Defense and security are two major and interrelated areas of concerns for every state. Defense policies typically involve the use of a country's armed forces, while security policies commonly include a broader set of actions including military and nonmilitary responses within and outside the country. In this chapter, we will examine the government agencies responsible for these policies and their organization and functioning. Then we examine Russia's defense and security policies. As usual, in the critical thinking section we look at different views reflecting some past and present developments. Certainly, several historical developments have influenced the current state of Russia's defense and security policies.

KEY DEVELOPMENTS

Many people for years believed that Russia was surrounded by enemies attempting to harm their country, steal its secrets, bribe the country's domestic political opposition, lie about the Kremlin leaders, weaken the military, and even reduce Russia's birth rates (Dubin, 2012). For many years now, the Russian government has conducted a campaign of boosting national security and creating an impression that Russia was under constant threat from the outside and domestically.

Soviet policies

Defense and security were key policies of the former Soviet Union, heavily influenced by the imperatives of the communist ideology. Constant justification of the existence of foreign threats was part of Soviet defense and security policies. The Military–Industrial Commission, a powerful division of the central apparatus of the Communist Party of the Soviet Union, gained substantial power in the country, especially in the 1970s. The officials of this Commission were allied with the Soviet military establishment, and supervised thousands of plants, factories, and scientific laboratories working on defense projects. By arguing that the Soviet armed forces were inferior to the US forces, they effectively manipulated the fears of powerful Communist Party leaders. As a result, the military–industrial lobbyists in the USSR could obtain huge resources from the government.

Security policies in the Soviet Union were directed and coordinated by a central agency, which has been known since 1954 as the Committee of State Security. This organization is better known as the KGB, according to its Russian abbreviation. The Constitution of the Soviet Union contained no mention of this agency, yet the KGB acquired substantial political power, becoming virtually a secret establishment under the direct control of the secretary general of the Communist Party (Petrov and Kokurin, 2003). The KGB is also known in history for its domestic activities against political opposition, independent thought, and free speech. Vladimir Putin, the future president and prime minister, served in a similar KGB position at Leningrad State University.

Policy transitions

The last Soviet leader, Mikhail Gorbachev, as we have learned in previous chapters, came to believe that the security of his country could be achieved only within a broader context of international cooperation and disarmament. The policies of glasnost also diminished the importance of the KGB and domestic spying. The new Russian leaders after 1991 inherited an incredibly large military infrastructure and the world's greatest nuclear arsenal. On the other hand, Russia did not have enough resources and capabilities to maintain the military at full operational capability. Furthermore, when there was no pressing external enemy and there were mounting domestic problems, defense and security did not seem to be the most important policy issues. Most believed that the country needed smaller, less expensive, but more efficient defense forces as it entered the 21st century.

Putin brought back the concept that foreign enemies threaten Russia—a central theme justifying the buildup of Russia's defense and security. The increasingly large resources available to the government during the economic boom of the early 2000s and the high oil prices gave the Kremlin an opportunity to invest in defense and security. However, the subsequent economic slowdown forced the government to make adjustments and corrections.

Russian leaders assume that today's world is witnessing the strengthening of global competition, tensions between geographical regions, rivalry between different models of development, and overall instability. During this period of complicated international relations, Russia faces many security threats. First, these are NATO global policies and NATO's proximity to Russia's borders. Next, instability in certain parts of the world, such as in the Middle East, also becomes a source of threats. Other countries' military presence near Russia's borders, such as in Afghanistan or in South Korea, is a problem for Russia too.

KEY INSTITUTIONS: THE PRESIDENT AND THE DEFENSE MINISTRY

Russia has a vast government structure in charge of planning and implementing its defense policies. Historically in Russia, the head of the state was also its commander in chief. During peacetime, he would exercise general management of the armed forces.

The commander in chief

Federal law contains provisions explaining the role and responsibilities of Russia's president as the country's top commander. First, the president is responsible for the country's military doctrine, or a principal description of foreign threats against Russia and the general direction of Russia's defense policies. Thirty years ago, the Soviet Union's military doctrine was based on the strategic assumption of imminent threats coming from the United States, its allies, and some other countries (such as China). Later the old Cold War problems diminished (Orlov, 2009). These days, Russia's strategies have grown more global and ambitious. Moscow outlines four conditions under which the president can use Russia's armed forces abroad: for the protection of Russians living abroad, and against acts of piracy, actions against Russia's foreign bases, or actions against friendly states.

Second, the president is also responsible for outlining general military policies based on the country's military doctrine. The president, for instance, approves strategic plans for development and modernization of the armed forces, approves plans for civil defense in the event of war, and outlines general principles of interaction between the military and the economy. Russian men are still obliged to serve in the military, thus the president is also responsible for the national draft. Third, the president also signs international agreements related to military cooperation with other countries, and coordinates both military and foreign policies.

The president has the exclusive right to declare martial law in emergency situations, including severe natural disasters, massive public unrest, war, or other extraordinary conditions. Russian law prescribes that the president must inform the United Nations and the European Council should Russia temporarily suspend any international agreements because of the establishment of martial law. This presidential power is limited, however, in theory: the Federation Council has the constitutional right to reject such decisions (see Chapter 4). This has never happened to date.

The Defense Ministry of the Russian Federation

The legal foundation for the Ministry of Defense's operation is provided in a 2004 presidential decree, amended later several times. The decree names three major tasks of the ministry: institutional, military, and social.

The institutional tasks involve drafting and exercising military policies, coordinating the activities of various federal institutions in terms of defense policy, and coordinating the work of the subjects of the Federation related to the defense of the country. The Ministry also cooperates with its counterparts in other countries. The military tasks are related to maintaining appropriate military capabilities according to the country's military doctrine. In short, the Ministry must guarantee that the country has enough technical and human resources for self-defense. The social tasks are complex. For instance, the ministry is responsible for exercising draft policies. Every young man must serve in the military at 18 years of age (see later in the chapter). The Ministry must coordinate its efforts with federal, regional, and local authorities in order to achieve this. The social tasks also include social protection (benefits, pensions, and health plans) for members of the armed forces and their families. Finally, the ministry is responsible for civil defense policies. It is in charge of protecting the civil population and economic infrastructure during war, and in some cases of natural disaster (see Table 12.1).

Structure of the Defense Ministry

The Defense Ministry in major countries such as Russia, China, and the United States is typically large and extremely complex. According to the Constitution, the president is in charge of the Ministry. The president appoints the minister of defense based on a recommendation from the prime minister. The defense minister prepares strategic plans, controls the daily operations of the Ministry, and reports to the president, and in some cases to the prime minister (see Figure 12.1).

Table 12.1 Basic policies of the Defense Ministry of the Russian Federation

Policy field	Description of policies
Institutional	Drafting and exercising military policies, coordinating the activities of various federal institutions in terms of defense policy, and coordinating the work of the subjects of the Federation
Military	Maintaining appropriate military capabilities according to the country's military doctrine
Draft	Exercising draft policies: planning, drafting, and releasing individuals from mandatory military service
Social	Social protection of the members of the armed forces during service and retirement
Civil defense	Civil defense policies or preparations related to protection of the civil population and economic infrastructure during war or in some cases of natural disaster
International	Developing international contacts and cooperation with other countries in the fields of defense policies

Source: Presidential decree of August 16, 2004.

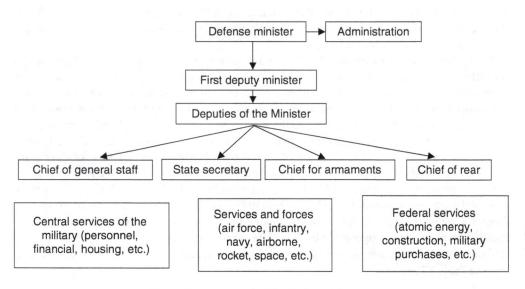

Figure 12.1 Structure of the Defense Ministry

The minister of defense and their deputies together coordinate the activities of Russia's armed forces. The state secretary coordinates policies related to personnel and their selection and training, as well as interaction with other federal ministries and services. The executive body of the Defense Ministry is the General Staff of the Armed Forces of the Russian

Federation. The chief of general staff, who is also appointed directly by the president, is in charge of it. The Defense Ministry, like other ministries in Russia, has adopted principles of collective management. There is, for instance, a Ministry Council, which consists of the minister, the deputies, and several defense officials.

MILITARY POLICIES

Russia increasingly tends to define its strategic defense interests not only within the limits of its geographic location on the Eurasian continent but also globally. Russia also responds to apparent security threats and makes adjustments to its military strategies. Among these are Russia's responses to important geopolitical developments, domestic capabilities for military mobilization, nuclear weapons, and its increasing aspirations in international relations.

Geopolitical strategies

From the geopolitical standpoint, Russia's defense policies are based on constant attempts at the containment of emerging threats from different directions. West of Russia, defense strategists perceive a growing threat from NATO and the possibility that several new countries, including Ukraine, Georgia, and Moldova, might join that military and political organization.

South of Russia, one of the major concerns is the possibility of a violent attempt from foreign countries to spark ethnic conflicts in the Caucasus region. Russia is interested in maintaining stability in this region and opposes any military buildup near its border. In particular, Russia is interested in a peaceful solution to the conflict between Armenia and Azerbaijan. At the same time for many years Russia has not perceived Iran's nuclear programs as a security threat. The desire to have a reliable partner overrides other strategic concerns (see Chapter 11).

In the southeastern and eastern directions, one of the major concerns is the prevention of foreign countries' attempts to establish a military presence in the former republics of the Soviet Union or create instability there. Russia intends to maintain its potentially superior military capabilities in this region, which has tremendous strategic importance for the Kremlin.

How would Russia fight a war? In theory, Russia's military doctrine assumes that the country could fight a war only over a limited period and within a limited territory. Under these conditions, Russia would use its standing army, air force, and navy. The strategic anticipation is that very soon Russia will develop fully professional, well-equipped, and efficient armed forces capable of carrying out various military tasks. At present, however, Moscow still relies on the Soviet-era concept of mass mobilization of men to cope with any circumstances that exceed the full-time forces' capabilities. The draft policies ensure that many (in theory, most) men serve in the military for at least a short time, so the assumption is that during wartime the country would have a sufficient number of trained and experienced men to call on, both rank and file and officers, in addition to the full-time professionals. The military establishment continues to consider it necessary to maintain this large reserve of men capable of bearing arms.

The military draft

For many years, Russia has had a **military draft**, or a legal and mandatory requirement for men to perform military service. This policy is common in many countries including Iran, Israel, and South Korea. Several federal legislative acts provided the legal ground for similar policies in Russia. To implement them, the Defense Ministry maintains specialized military commissariats, or draft offices, in cities and towns across Russia. Each draft office has a list of the male population residing in the district under the office's jurisdiction. Every male in Russia must register at a local commissariat when he is 17 years old. Citizens are eligible for the draft when they are between 18 and 27 years of age. The draft is administered twice a year: first between April and June, and second between October and December.

A limit of service has been established at one year (Presidential Decree, March 8, 2007). Since 2008, as a result of a decision of the government of Russia (March 6, 2008, N275), a number of Russian universities and colleges have established "military departments," or educational and training facilities to substitute for military service. All students eligible for military service who are enrolled in these colleges and universities must undergo training at these departments. As a result, they do not have to serve full-time in the military, but should participate in infrequent, short-term training exercises after graduation. A number of institutions of higher education have military educational centers (the Russian version of ROTC in US schools). Those who attend these centers receive a special grant (four times the average student stipend provided by the government) and then serve in the military for three years as an officer.

The law allows individuals to apply for a deferral (a postponement) or a permanent release from military service. Among the criteria for granting such a release are being a college student, having poor health, having difficult family circumstances (being a single father, a father of two or more, or taking care of a disabled family member), or having a prior conviction for a serious crime (such as murder or rape). In addition, teachers and doctors working in rural areas receive deferrals. Doctors and teachers are in short supply in Russia's rural areas, and the law ensures their services are retained.

Religious beliefs or moral opposition to war do not qualify as legitimate factors for release from military service in Russia. Overall, about 50 percent of males receive official deferrals or waivers so that only about 270,000 individuals can be drafted every year (Latuhina, 2019). For three decades, the Defense Ministry has had to adjust to the country's worsening demographic situation and the declining numbers of the military draft.

The military reform (2008–20)

Russia has attempted to reform its military according to the changing conditions of the 21st century. It needs manageable and efficient armed forces. The size of the military by the end of the second decade of the century was close to 1 million enlisted people not including the additional 900,000 employed by the armed forces (RG, 2017).

Russia should have at least two substructures within its armed forces. One will be formed from trained professionals serving in the military on a fixed-term basis, with individual legal contracts. The other structure should be based on hundreds of thousands of draftees who serve a one-year term and are then sent back home. The differences between these two structures are profound. The people in the first group are trained, older, and motivated to serve. The second group are an inexperienced, generally unmotivated, and uneducated crowd of 18-year-olds.

Another area of reform is drastic increases in compensation and benefits for military officers. President Putin promised to transform the pay structure of the military so that officers would see a significant wage increase. For instance, he promised that junior officers would earn approximately 50,000 rubles a month (roughly US$10,000 a year). Pay increases would be based on merit. Senior officers would be paid three or four times that amount. This task had been generally achieved by the end of the second decade of the century. The government also guaranteed every officer a free apartment. At the same time, the government was planning to discharge almost 250,000 officers, expand the role of nonmilitary professionals, and reform the system of military education (RNS, 2009). With significant budgetary difficulties in recent years, all these tasks seemed extremely difficult to achieve.

Nuclear defense

Russia's top concern remains nuclear security. Back in the 1970s, both the United States and the Soviet Union had already accumulated nuclear arsenals capable of destroying the entire planet (Wohlstetter, 1979). Russia and the United States between them possessed around 90 percent of the world's nuclear arsenal (Legvold, 2009: 78). Both countries were motivated to keep nuclear weapons for two reasons: first, to deter aggression against themselves (the argument is that those who might be aggressors in other circumstances would hesitate to attack a nuclear state, because its retaliation using its nuclear weapons would be so terrible); and second, should an attack take place regardless of this, to punish the aggressor by the use of nuclear weapons.

Initially, in the 1960s, military strategists in both Moscow and Washington wanted to achieve nuclear superiority over their opponent. There were at least two potential ways of achieving this. The first possibility was to mobilize scientific and technological resources and build as many warheads as possible so that the opponent would fall behind, and one country would eventually reach nuclear superiority over the other. The second possibility was to create a nuclear defense system that could destroy the enemy's airplanes and missiles in midair and involved improving the quality and destruction capability of missiles.

These two strategies were ineffective and even dangerous. First, the nuclear race to achieve quantitative superiority was getting too costly. The second strategy, to create missile defense systems, though superficially attractive, presented a problem too: if one country developed a missile defense shield that would make its opponent less secure, then the opponent would try to create new weapons to penetrate those defenses (Leffler, 2007). Gradually, both countries realized that the only way to solve the nuclear problem was arms control and subsequent arms reduction.

Since the 1970s, most diplomatic efforts have been aimed at the reduction and limitation of nuclear weapons and antimissile systems. An agreement against antimissile systems was signed between the two countries in 1972 (the Anti-Ballistic Missile Treaty, or ABM Treaty). The Strategic Arms Reduction Treaty of 1991 (START) between Washington and Moscow effectively cut both countries' nuclear arsenals by up to 80 percent. In 1993 presidents George W. Bush and Boris Yeltsin signed a new agreement prohibiting the use of multiple warheads on nuclear missiles (START II).

Both Washington and Moscow pursue a strategy to maintain parity between their nuclear capabilities. In 2010, a new treaty called Measures for the Further Reduction and Limitation of Strategic Offensive Arms was signed between Russia and the United States. President Putin praised the treaty and promised in his statements to continue missile defense negotiations (Putin, 2012b). The treaty, informally called New START, directed both countries to halve the number of their strategic nuclear missile launchers. Moscow and Washington had to design and implement a new system of inspection procedures. The agreement also limited the number of stockpiled nuclear weapons that are inactive. By the end of the 2010s, each country should have kept 1,550 nuclear warheads, 700 missiles, submarines and bombers capable of delivering these warheads, and 800 other launchers.

Russia criticized Washington's decision in 2001 to walk away from the Anti-Ballistic Missile Treaty (the treaty restricted the ability to develop and deploy defensive systems). In April 2010, Russia and the United States reached a new agreement called Measures for the Further Reduction and Limitation of Strategic Offensive Arms, projected to last until 2021. However, many old Cold War concerns and much old rhetoric reemerged (Shiraev and Khudoley, 2019). These concerns in Russia were caused in part by US plans to build early warning antimissile defense systems in Europe. Washington insisted such systems would protect against a possible attack from Iran or other rogue states. Moscow believed the United States was seeking unilateral advantage at the expense of Russia. Moscow believed it would be forced to match them by escalating the arms race or by other measures.

Since 2010, almost all new US–Russian nuclear arms negotiations have stalled. In 2018 Russian President Vladimir Putin claimed that Moscow had developed or was developing new types of nuclear weapons and means to deliver them, such as supersonic missiles, that could defeat any country's missile defense system (Putin, 2018). The Kremlin insisted that this was a defensive measure. The West considered this announcement as an escalation of international tensions: a new generation of hypersonic missiles brought pressure on many countries to change their military strategies. Supersonic missiles travel at five times the speed of sound (or close to 1 mile per second). Although intercontinental ballistic missiles (ICBMs) reenter the atmosphere at a higher speed, they can be intercepted by antimissile systems. The new types of supersonic missiles are much more maneuverable and very difficult to intercept with existing technologies. A new spiral of arms race was underway.

Would it be more reasonable for Russia to pursue complete nuclear disarmament? In fact, Russia opposed it for years. Two arguments are used to justify this position. The first is that, if the major nuclear powers disarmed, smaller countries might develop nuclear weapons secretly and thus gain a significant advantage over other countries. The second reason is that, in a world without nuclear weapons, the United States would remain the most powerful country because of the sheer size and quality of its conventional weapons. Still, Russia supports nuclear nonproliferation for several reasons. One is that the acquisition of nuclear weapons by new states would increase international tension. Another is the threat of international terrorist groups getting access to weapons of mass destruction and using them against Russia to achieve their political goals. Russia cooperates with other nuclear powers including the United States to ensure that nuclear arsenals are kept secure.

Arms sales

The Federal Service for Military–Technical Cooperation in the Defense Ministry coordinates the sale of weapons to foreign countries. It issues licenses to private and state companies to sell (and purchase) weapons and military-related materials. Most industries producing arms and equipment, including military aircraft, are under state control. The Russian government itself is a major customer too.

The military industries are almost entirely under the state's control. Among the biggest purchasers of Russian weapons are China, Iran, and India. India and China combined make up almost 80 percent of all Russian sales. According to different sources, Russia's arms sales were around US$ 6–8 billion a year at the end of the second decade of the century, which was about two thirds of US arms sales during that period (Army Technology, 2019). Most of Russia's sales are aircraft, followed by air defense systems, infantry weapons, and naval purchases. Russia began to expand its weapons sales, and it now sells to Latin American countries including Venezuela, Mexico, Peru, Colombia, and Brazil. In Asia, Vietnam, Indonesia, and Malaysia remain steady buyers as well. Russia also sells weapons to the Middle East and Algeria. However, the sanctions against Russia (see Chapters 10 and 11) have negatively affected its global trade in weapons.

THE FEDERAL SECURITY SERVICE

The Federal Security Service (FSS) of the Russian Federation is the centralized system of federal services performing security-related tasks. Essentially, it is one of several successor organizations of the Soviet Committee of State Security (KGB). It was created in 1995. According to federal law, the president is directly in charge of the FSS (Federal Law, April 3, 1995). Over the years, this institution has undergone several reorganizations designed to improve its efficiency.

The Federal Security Service performs several functions. The first one is counterintelligence. The FSS has to investigate, prevent, or interrupt by legal means any activity by the intelligence services of other countries, as well as individuals who are considered a threat to the security of the Russian Federation. Counterterrorism is the second function. The service carries out investigative and preventive work against terrorist threats within the Russian territory as well as overseas. Russia for years maintained a policy of preventive or retaliatory measures against terrorists regardless of their location (Golz, 2007).

Intelligence gathering is another function of the FSS. Next, the service also fights organized crime, including corruption, and illegal sales of arms and narcotics. It deals with groups conspiring to change Russia's constitutional order. The list of illegal activities that FSS investigates and fights against can be extended or changed by the legal authorities. The FSS monitors the transmission of sensitive or secret information within Russia and overseas. The FSS is also responsible for border protection. In particular, its role is to prevent people from entering or leaving Russia illegally. There is also the Federal Customs Service of Russia (which is independent of the FSS), an institution responsible for collecting tariffs and controlling the flow of goods, including animals, transports, personal, and hazardous items, into and out of Russia.

The structure of the FSS

The central office is located in Moscow. It directs and coordinates the work of regional offices, offices in the armed forces, and the border patrol units. In addition, there are specialized departments including research facilities, training and educational centers, medical, and other investigative institutions necessary for the FSS's functioning. For example, the Economic Security Service within the FSS organizes measures against spying in the fields of science, technology, and economics. The Department of Military Counterintelligence is responsible for antispying activities within the armed forces. The Department of Self Security works on preventive measures against spying and other illegal activities within the FSS itself. Although the information about the number of people employed by the FSS is classified, estimates refer to approximately 300,000 employees.

Security policies

Any national security organization should work in secrecy. However, in a democratic country, government institutions must provide information about nonclassified aspects of their work. Various interviews, press conferences, and analytical papers have provided information about the work of the FSS in recent years (FSS, 2019; Patrushev, 2007). At least three tasks appear central to FSS activities. The first and central task is to prevent all attempts, open or clandestine, to violate Russia's territorial integrity. The second task is to prevent attempts to stir up political instability in Russia. The third task is to prevent any actions that would undermine Russia's pursuit of its national interests at home and globally. Crimes such as corruption of government officials, racketeering, and hate crimes against minorities have been another major issue of concern to the government (Medvedev, 2009; Bortnikov, 2009): (Photo 12.1).

Photo 12.1 Former President Medvedev started a national anticorruption campaign: antibribery billboards appeared in big Russian cities (the sign reads: "Have you encountered corruption? Call 576-77-65")

The FSS maintains that the West tries to undermine Russia's economic and social development. The majority of the blame is commonly laid on NATO countries, including mostly the United States and the United Kingdom, for their attempts to interfere in Russia's domestic affairs. Georgia, the Baltic countries, and Poland are regularly accused of being obedient servants of Washington and London. Other countries such as Saudi Arabia or Pakistan are suspected of being active in gaining influence among Russia's Muslim elites. Therefore, one of Russia's major security concerns is to prevent any radical political changes in the former Soviet republics in Central Asia that could negatively affect Russia's positions in this region. Russia watches carefully any political movements that could oppose the ruling regime in Central Asian states (McGlinchey, 2009, 2016).

A special area of concern is NGOs (especially registered in foreign countries) working in Russia. They are frequently accused of gathering sensitive information about Russia (about the opposition, social problems, or public opinion). NGOs' activities are viewed as a hidden way to penetrate deep within Russia's society and thus influence its policies. Russian officials and large segments of the Russian population believe that foreign services have been behind most of the democratic political movements in Georgia, Ukraine, Moldova, and other countries during the past decade. Many NGOs engaged in anticorruption or prodemocracy activities have been harassed by the authorities by means of searches, detentions, and criminal charges (Walker, 2019). As you should remember, the 2012 law regulates activities of NGOs receiving foreign funding. These groups must declare themselves *foreign agents* and make themselves available for audits and searches (Ponomareva, 2012).

To fulfill these tasks and address these and other emerging concerns, the FSS conducts a wide range of activities (Kashin, 2015). One of its major activities is counterterrorism. Russia has regular contacts with more than 75 countries in the field of counterterrorism. It is engaged in preventive measures against foreign services and individuals gathering information about Russia's armed forces, the ongoing military reform, and Russia's nuclear arsenal (Massicot, 2019; Patrushev, 2007). The FSS is also concerned about economic espionage, and particularly about those trying to gather facts about Russia's natural resources, and their extraction and delivery. Russian citizens attempting to pass state secrets to foreign services can expect to be charged with treason (under Article 275 of the Criminal Code).

Another activity of the FSS is the prevention of foreign organizations' attempts to collect information about Russia's political atmosphere, especially before and during federal elections. This essentially means that researchers from Western countries will have a very difficult time in Russia should they arrive there to learn about electoral behavior or public opinion. To this end the FSS takes measures to control the activities of foreign nongovernment organizations (NGOs) on Russian territory. It is particularly concerned to frustrate foreign services' attempts to recruit Russian citizens to work for them (such activities are likely to be called spying). In addition to these activities, the FSS provides protection for foreign missions in Russia and Russian missions overseas.

To learn more about the activities in which the FSS is engaged see the Case in point below.

Based on a presidential decree (February 15, 2006), Russia has created an Antiterrorist Committee to coordinate polices at the federal level. The president appoints its chair, who works with several federal agencies and other institutions. There are short-term and long-term priorities and goals. The most important short-term priority is to prevent immediate acts of terrorism on Russian territory. Several terrorist acts have taken place in Russia over

Case in point: examples of criminal activities prosecuted by the Federal Security Service of the Russian Federation

- *Prevention of economic crime.* A large number of illegal loggers in the Khabarovsk region, who were not licensed to cut trees or sell timber, were arrested, and 300 cubic meters of timber (oak, lime, and ash) was confiscated. Estimated damage: 20 million rubles (approximately US$600,000).
- *Prevention of illegal gambling.* A coordinated FSS and Department of the Interior operation resulted in the confiscation of more than 100 gambling machines in the Dagestan Republic. Gambling is illegal according to federal and local legislation.
- *Prosecution of crime related to cybersecurity.* A resident was sentenced to two years and six months in jail for obtaining passwords of 61 individuals and using their bank accounts for his personal purposes. The loss was estimated at 6 million rubles (US$200,000).
- *Prosecution of crime related to illegal immigration.* A citizen of Turkey was sentenced to three years in jail for organizing illegal smuggling operations in the Krasnodar Region.
- *Prosecution of crime related to revealing state secrets.* An Air Force officer was fined 30,000 rubles (US$1,000) for using an assistant who did not have security clearance.
- *Prosecution of an act of espionage.* A citizen of Poland was sentenced to 14 years in prison for spying on behalf of the government of Poland.
- *Prevention of terrorist activities in Russia.* Two Russian citizens were arrested for using the Internet to sponsor activities of illegal jihadist organizations in the territory of Russia.

Source: FSS.

the past two decades, and they have caused a significant loss of human life. Both public opinion and political elites demand strong measures to prevent future attacks and punish their perpetrators. This task is also connected with immediate actions to prevent the escalation of tensions in certain Russian regions, in particular in the southern regions of Russia. Several agencies conduct policies to secure nuclear installations and radioactive materials. It is Russia's prime concern that these materials should not get into the hands of foreign governments aspiring to possess nuclear weapons, or extremist groups.

The Antiterrorist Committee does not have special structures or troops to enforce its decisions. Counterterrorist actions can he undertaken by any federal unit designated for that purpose. There is a special term in Russia, *speznaz* (loose translation: a unit serving a special purpose), to refer to any type of special forces trained and permitted to use force in extraordinary situations such as hostage-taking. These can be any specially trained elite units under the direction of the FSS, internal troops of the Russian Ministry of Internal Affairs (before 2016), or units controlled by the military intelligence service.

As discussed in Chapter 6, a new federal agency has been established with many of its functions related to law enforcement: the **Federal National Guard Troops Service of the Russian Federation** (*Rosgvardia* for short in Russian). This agency reports directly to the

Russian president. The National Guard is separate from the Ministry for Internal Affairs and from the Russian Armed Forces. Rosgvardia's key responsibilities are to secure national borders, take charge of gun control, combat terrorism, fight organized crime, protect public order, and guard important state facilities. The National Guard employs more than 300,000 people, but the number can change, as you can imagine (Rosgvardia, 2020).

The long-term priorities emerge out of the necessity of preventing the growth of Islamic fundamentalism as a potentially potent source of terrorism in the region, in particular in the former republics of the Soviet Union. Pursuing this goal, Russia tends to support authoritarian regimes for its southern neighbors, which provide protection against violent extremism and religious fundamentalism. Russia is also interested in ensuring stability in other countries in the region, such as Afghanistan and Iraq.

These and other developments, according to the Russian government, give it no choice but to expand and improve the country's security operations, both inside the country and elsewhere. The function of gathering intelligence, however, is given to another federal service called the External Intelligence Service.

THE EXTERNAL INTELLIGENCE SERVICE

A 1996 federal law designated the External Intelligence Service (EIS) as a federal agency (Federal Law, January 10, 1996). The president appoints the EIS director. This service is part of a complex federal security system, one of several agencies that often play similar functions. Two major functions of the EIS have been established. The first one is analytical. It involves gathering and analyzing information about the opportunities, actions, or intentions of foreign states, organizations, or individuals related to the vital interests of Russia. The second task is operational. It is about assisting with and conducting practical measures to enhance the security of the Russian Federation. The necessity for intelligence is determined by the president and the Federal Assembly within their jurisdiction.

The law allows the EIS to use various methods to obtain intelligence information, including help from volunteers or undercover agents. Intelligence may be conducted by open methods as well as surreptitiously. The agency must not harm the environment while conducting its operations and should take care over the human beings involved. Intelligence information is received by the president, the Federal Assembly, or by other federal institutions and organizations designated by the president.

State secrets

Russia designates certain information as secret based on the law (Federal Law, July 21, 1993). This information is related to the military, foreign policy, economic intelligence, counterintelligence, or investigative activities. The EIS, the FSS, and other agencies are also involved in the protection of Russia's state secrets. The prosecutor general of Russia and other prosecutors supervise the execution of the law related to state secrets. There is an intra-institutional commission that coordinates federal policies in this area. According to the law, revelation of a state secret may threaten Russia's security. Table 12.2 provides an overview of information that is considered secret if it affects Russia's security.

Table 12.2 Information considered and not considered secret in Russia

Information considered secret	Information not considered secret
About scientific or technical discoveries and technologies related to the military	About environmental problems
	About Russia's healthcare, sanitary conditions, demography, education, culture, agriculture, and criminal statistics
About reserves, extraction, transportation, and use of platinum and natural diamonds. There are also other natural resources about which the government of the Russian Federation can classify information	About the gold reserves of the Russian Federation
About Russia's operations with foreign states (except general assessments of debts)	About natural disasters, catastrophic events, accidents, and other events threatening the life and health of citizens (this information was largely classified in the Soviet Union)
About border security operations or activities to protect the economic zone, and continental shelf of the country	About financial and other types of compensation to government institutions and their employees
About federal budget appropriations for defense, security, and law enforcement	About violation of human rights and liberties and information about the health of top Russian leaders

CRITICAL THINKING ABOUT DEFENSE AND SECURITY POLICIES

An accurate assessment of any country's capabilities involves the evaluation of that country's defense and security policies. Such evaluations vary. These, in turn, often reflect various perceptions of national and international security. Politics plays a role too.

Politics and security threats

We also learned in this chapter that Russia pays unceasing attention to its nuclear security by supporting policies of nonproliferation of weapons of mass destruction. Moscow for years has been actively engaged in nuclear negotiations with Washington. Unfortunately, this seemingly has not been a priority in the late 2010s. For an opportunity to gain strategic superiority in offensive weapons, Russia has dared to challenge the United States and NATO. As history shows, there have been no clear winners in this type of challenge. A new arms race could be extremely expensive and counterproductive.

Russia for years tended to neglect a big threat coming from Iran's nuclear programs. Unlike Western countries, Russia preferred to trust Iran's assurances about the peaceful purpose of its nuclear aspirations. This is uncharacteristic of Russia, which has always tried to choose vigilance over negligence. Here, Moscow inserted politics into security policies: its strategic calculations and the regional politics of pleasing Iran overshadowed for many years its global security concerns.

The next big and serious threat to Russia's security comes from the Caucasus region. These days, violent jihadists commit most of the terrorist acts against the police and security forces in the region. The attackers' ultimate aim is secession from Russia. The Kremlin attempts to improve the socioeconomic situation in the area by allocating significant monetary funds. However Moscow has for years neglected the violation of civil liberties and basic human rights in many areas of the region (OSCE, 2019).

Another security-related issue is Russia's domestic political opposition (Umland, 2009). Insignificant and disorganized in the past, it has become more assertive and powerful. Public protests in 2011–12, in the summer of 2019, and later showed that the opposition had grown into a strong force. The authorities chose violence to shut down the opposition (Dokshin and Limansky, 2019). Russian authorities put forward three assumptions about the opposition. First, mass public protests are impossible to organize without substantial financial backing. If the money comes from abroad (which is not the case), this should be treated as a national security matter. Second, foreign human rights organizations working in Russia are acting on behalf of the intelligence of their countries. Therefore, restrictive administrative measures against these organizations should be implemented. And third, to deal with political opposition, the government should use tough methods. A few people should be punished early to avoid a bigger problem in the future. In short, political dissent is frequently treated as a national security issue.

Security policies' priorities

In any country, evaluating security risks and seeking adequate responses involves complicated analyses of multiple factors. If defense and security officials find out that the country is facing an external threat, they have several options to pursue. These options fall into four categories:

- unilateral options: rapid strengthening of the military and security forces or actual forceful responses without taking into consideration other countries' policies; likewise, withdrawing from military engagement without consulting other countries;
- multilateral options: attempting to seek alliances with other states and groups to address the existing threat;
- accommodationist options: negotiating and possibly granting concessions to an adversary—all of them designed to reduce the existing threat;
- isolationist options: withdraw from the conflict unilaterally hoping to avoid the threat.

In the early 1990s, Russia on many occasions chose primarily isolationist and accommodationist polices. One of the reasons for choosing these policies was the weak state of Russia's economy and the poor condition of its military. Furthermore, the official policy was that Russia no longer had foreign enemies. From the late 1990s, Russia has been switching toward more active unilateral and multilateral options. For instance, it is actively involved in international security operations in Africa and the Middle East. Another priority in this area is friendly relations with the former republics of the Soviet Union south of Russia's border, and other neighboring states including China and India.

Russia's official position is that the country is surrounded by a growing number of enemies, both foreign and domestic, and therefore must secure and defend itself by all means available (Putin, 2012c, 2019a). A strategic policy of restoring Russia as a great power on the world stage has been an important part of the Kremlin's plans.

Russian militarism

Militarism is attitudes and policies that revolve around the persistent aspiration to use military force in response to most foreign and domestic threats. Militarism is typically accompanied by the glorification of war, conquest, domination, weapons, and armed forces. **Pacifism**, on the other hand, as a combination of attitudes and policies, posits that international disputes should be settled by arbitration and other nonviolent means. Pacifism prioritizes nonviolence in international affairs, and glorifies restraint, mutual concessions, respect, and peace (Zinn, 2002). Both militarism and pacifism reflect the never-ending arguments between so-called "hawks" (supporters of military action) and "doves" (supporters of nonviolent policies) in the foreign policy of most countries. Russia is no exception. Has Russia turned to militarism with the ascendance of President Putin, especially in the past ten years?

The militarist tradition has always been part of Russia's policies. During the more than 70 years of existence of the Soviet Union, the country was managed as if it were a giant military camp. From the beginning of their lives, people were told that their duty was to defend the country against imminent foreign aggression. In Russians' daily lives, in folklore, in songs, novels, and poetry learned in elementary, middle, and high school, the soldier, the defender, and the martyr were always glorified (Shlykov, 2002). This tradition has not disappeared. It is quite alive.

The Kremlin-cultivated strategy that the country must restore its Soviet-style might and imperial glory is inseparable from so-called civil militarism, the strategic policy of adopting military goals, priorities, and values in domestic policies, and glorifying the military role in domestic defense (Golz, 2007). Moreover, many military and political experts affiliated with the government in Russia suggest that there is nothing wrong with an increasing competition between Russia and the West (Surkov, 2019). Foreign observers feel that Russia is sending the wrong message to the world: the Kremlin might not want to appear as a warmonger, but almost everything it does supports this image. The profound absence of pacifist or conciliatory arguments in the political discourse of the Kremlin is a clear sign of Russia's defense and security priorities these days.

It is possible that this hawkish approach to national security is another excuse for Russia's authoritarian strategy, based on a simple logic: to resist foreign threats and guarantee the success of social reforms, the country has no other alternative but a strong system of government that will ensure public order, discipline, and national security (Surkov, 2019; Golz, 2007). The critics of the official course are in the minority in Russia. Over the past few years, government officials, political commentators, and policy analysts from the mainstream media in Russia have generally accepted the "hostile environment" context to explain and justify Russia's security policies.

Skeptics maintain that the threat of civil militarism in Russia is exaggerated. A fine illustration of the futility of militarism is the difficulties that Russia is experiencing with the lack of revenue due to decreased oil prices and challenges that the world faces from global health threats.

CONCLUSION

Every country has the right to enhance its security and improve its defense policies. After all, this is a major responsibility of the government of that country. President Putin promised back in 2012 to invest an equivalent of about $800 billion over ten years for national defense (Putin, 2012c). The key question is always about the scope and effectiveness of such policies. A large group of Russian elites supported by nationalist voices maintains that the government is not doing enough to protect the country. They demand a more hawkish, almost militarist, approach to defense and security. Their critics uphold a completely different position, offering two major arguments. First, Russia cannot afford another massive military and security buildup. Second, this type of buildup is absolutely unnecessary because Russia does not have foreign enemies. The main reason, the critics argue, that the government accepts the nationalists' view of defense and security is that it allows the Kremlin to maintain its authoritative grip on society and its resources. The Kremlin disagrees with these assessments. In fact, the "hawkish" approach to Russian security and defense has gained strength in the past decade. Unfortunately, in politics it is always easy to stir up rows based on old grievances, emotions, and fears. It is far harder to calm them down. The future should bring us a more promising tale.

13 Economic and Business Policies

In 1992 Russia was free, independent, and ... broke. The country's economy was in disarray. It retained almost all the characteristics of the old Soviet economy. Major industries were under state control. Although they were then free from obligations to fulfill government plans (such plans no longer existed), they had serious problems in finding resources and customers. The major task for the government was to put aside the legacy of the Soviet-style economy and implement reforms. But what kind of reforms did Russia need? The discussions about the most appropriate economic policies for Russia in the post-communist era were heating up. In fact, they continue today. Russia, like every country on the planet, is constantly searching for the optimal way to manage its economy, finances, natural resources, and employment. Yet economic policies are always linked to politics.

KEY DEVELOPMENTS

Several key developments over the past 20 years have had a decisive impact on Russia's economy and economic policies. There are four overlapping periods in this process. The first one began in the early 1990s. This was a time of rapid privatization of government assets, the introduction of radical market principles of economy and commerce, and deregulation of many branches of the Russian economy. The second period, lasting until the end of the 20th century, involved the rapid consolidation, with the government's blessing, of economic and financial assets in the hands of several large companies and individuals. The third period was marked by the government's attempts to redistribute resources, modernize the economy, and create an efficient economic and financial system under the Kremlin's control.

The start of the third period was also associated with high oil prices and Russia's increasing global integration, which contributed to the country's relative financial stability but created other unexpected problems associated with its greater vulnerability to international financial crises. The global crisis of 2008–11 was a serious test of the survivability of the Russian financial and economic system and its economic policies.

The fourth period, which began approximately in 2014, is characterized by an increased centralization of big businesses and an increased government control of Russia's financial system in the context of falling oil prices, weakening of the ruble, the consequences of the global pandemic, and international sanctions against Russia.

Now we will consider some key economic policies and political developments that gradually shaped the Russian economy.

The reforms of the 1990s

Yeltsin and a close group of his advisers chose a strategy of economic liberalism with the goal of reforming Russia's economy. Their strategy was based on three key policies. First, the government encouraged people to privatize property previously owned by the state. Second, the federal government was no longer responsible for establishing and controlling prices. Third, the government gave up its obligation to ensure full employment, which had been legally guaranteed in the Soviet Union. The main assumption of the reformers was that, after a few painful months of these unprecedented changes, informally called **shock therapy**, the privatized industries and businesses would start to produce and trade. Next, production would stimulate commerce, which would stimulate the banking system. Finally, the growing tax revenues would allow the government to invest in business and assist the most disadvantaged groups of the Russian population, including retirees and children.

Unfortunately, the reality did not meet even the modest expectations of the economic reforms' architects (Gaidar, 2002, 2007). In the economic sphere, the effects of shock therapy were severe. The privatization program became bogged down in bureaucracy and fraud. Inflation soared, and the gross domestic product (GDP) fell by more than 40 percent in the period between 1991 and 1993. Hyperinflation especially hit people on fixed incomes. By 1993, some 31 percent of the Russian population was below the poverty line (Shlapentokh and Shiraev, 2002).

To stimulate private investment and generate confidence among the population, the government introduced state vouchers. This new policy stated that every citizen was about to own a share of the property of the Russian Federation. In an ideal scenario, people were supposed to invest their vouchers in industries and commerce. They would become instant shareholders and owners, ready to receive benefits from their investments. However, the public was largely unfamiliar with how to invest their vouchers. Meanwhile, well-placed figures obtained large blocks of stocks in the most potentially profitable industries. The reforms helped the new elites to consolidate their resources and strengthen their power in the country. Yet the reforms did not improve the overall economic situation (Åslund, 2007). Public frustrations grew. Polls taken in the early 1990s showed that a majority of people were equally afraid of greedy government bureaucrats and criminal groups involved in extortion and racketeering (Shiraev, 1999b).

Economic turmoil

The Russian government turned to bonds and foreign borrowing to rescue its budget. This policy worked until global oil prices began to collapse in 1997. This had a devastating impact on Russia's financial system. In August 1998 the government, being effectively bankrupt, drastically devalued the ruble (the Russian currency) to reduce its domestic obligations, then announced it would not pay billions of dollars in outstanding loans to Russian and international lenders (McFaul and Stoner-Weiss, 2008: 79).

The global financial crisis of the late 1990s was especially felt in South East Asia, in countries such as Korea, Singapore, and Japan. However, the crisis in Russia was different. The principal difference was that most Russians did not have sizable monetary savings. Therefore, the consequences of the crisis were extreme because they immediately affected people's wages, on which they relied to buy daily essentials. Virtually everyone lost approximately three quarters of their monthly salary.

The economic and financial collapse resulted in the inability of the government to sustain social policies. Government support for education, culture and the arts, science, pensions, housing, youth programs, and healthcare dwindled. At the same time, the profits of most oil, gas, and aluminum corporations (now in private hands) grew between 5 and 36 times (Shleifer and Treisman, 2004).

An economic upturn

Several factors contributed to the upward economic development in Russia early in the 21st century.

First, Russia's currency devaluation reduced imports and spurred Russian exports, which together with the fiscal austerity that the government practiced in this period, pushed economic growth in the late 1990s (McFaul and Stoner-Weiss, 2008).

Second, the country had a new president, Vladimir Putin, who was deeply involved in economic policymaking. He supported a policy based on free-market principles but with significant government regulation of key industries (Putin, 2012d). Capital gains and personal income taxes remained low in order to attract new investments and stimulate business.

Third, under Putin, social polices became more predictable. In turn, these policies became possible because of the changing financial situation in the Russian markets. Most importantly, Russia had achieved financial stability. Inflation remained modest, and the Russian economy began to grow in the 2000s at a steady pace of around 6–7 percent annually. This was a major signal to the world that Russia was back as an economic partner.

The improvements also took place partly because of an increased cash flow to the state budget as a result of high prices for crude oil and natural gas. Prices first began to go up in 1998, and have continued to increase since 2002, approaching US$100 a barrel (McFaul and Stoner-Weiss, 2008: 80). The government was able to balance the budget, create a budget surplus, and establish a special reserve fund based on the surplus.

Yet the global financial crisis of 2008 has affected Russia in many ways, and its long-term effects were painful in people's views (Levada, 2009h). Although the Russian stock market crashed in 2008, various government stimulus packages sustained it in 2009 and shortly after. Although several government programs had to be eliminated because there was a significant shortage of tax revenues, the government continued to pay salaries, pensions, and stipends to tens of millions of state employees, students, and retirees. Rather high oil prices in 2011, and increasing sales revenues, helped to patch several budget holes and bring back, at least for some time, a sense of optimism to Russian economy-watchers. Globally, in terms of per capita GDP, Russia moved from 67th to 51st place between 2000 and 2011. Wages on average went up 350 percent (Strategy 2020).

A new, even more serious crisis affected Russia's economy in 2014 and after. Several interconnected factors played a role. First, there was a global decline in oil prices, which fell in 2014 from $100 per barrel to $60 and lower. Russia has been a major exporter of oil, and this sharp decline in oil prices has certainly affected the country's cash revenue. Second, this decline in oil prices coincided with a decline in investors' confidence in the Russian economy, which in turn sparked fears of a Russian financial crisis and led to a decline in the value of the Russian ruble. Third, the initial impact of the Western sanctions on Russian economy was noticeable yet limited. However, Russian countersactions against Western food products contributed to inflation and rising food prices. As a result, the average salary in Russia decreased (Ostroukh, 2016). Overall, from 2008 to 2019, the economy grew overall by only 8.8 percent, which was twice as slow compared with the US economy (Prokofiev, 2019). The global pandemic of 2020 has further slowed the economy.

GOVERNMENT REGULATION OF THE ECONOMY

Several government agencies are directly involved in Russia's economy. There are ministries under the direct control of the government of the Russian Federation, as well as federal committees and federal services. Table 13.1 lists the ministries and their main functions. Ministries are typically in charge of several industrial branches or services such as agriculture, transport, or energy sectors. There are also ministries in charge of direct investments in Russia's regions and the management of natural resources.

Table 13.1 A sample list of ministries of the Russian Federation involved in regulation of the economy and resources

Ministry	Policy and regulatory decisions in the areas of
Finance	Unified financial policy and organization of finances in the territory of the Russian Federation
Natural Resources and Environmental Protection	Study, use, reproduction, and protection of Russia's natural resources
Industry and Trade	The civil and defense industries, as well as aviation technology development, technical standardization and metrology, and foreign trade activities
Construction Industry, Housing, and Utility Sector	Country's housing construction and utilities sectors
Energy	The fuel and energy industries including electric energy, oil, gas, coal, and renewable sources
Agriculture	The agrarian–industrial complex, sustainable development of agricultural territories, as well as study, protection, reproduction, and use of animals designated for hunting
Transport	Civil aviation, the use of airspace, aerial search and rescue, rivers, railroads, automobiles, city electric (subway) systems, industrial transportation, and road services
Economic Development	Analysis and forecasting of socioeconomic and business development
Labor and Social Protection	Management and legal regulation of federal policies in the areas of employment and social protection
Far East Affairs	Coordination of federal policies and federal programs in the Far East Region
North Caucasus Affairs	Coordination of federal policies and federal programs in the North Caucasus Region

Federal services are involved in specific areas of regulation. They exercise and primarily control the execution of specific policies (see Chapter 4). For example, the Federal Service for Labor and Employment "controls and supervises," according to the law, policies in the areas of employment and labor. It also provides federal assistance in cases of unemployment, labor migration, and certain labor disputes. Federal agencies provide specific federal services. For example, the Federal Atomic Agency directs the atomic industry of the Russian Federation, including research, production, and protection of nuclear products. The Federal Space Agency provides federal services to manage federal property related to space exploration. It also coordinates research and exploration of space for peaceful purposes. In addition, Roscosmos (this is what the agency is commonly called in Russia) is in charge of projects in the rocket industry in both the military and civilian spheres. There are special agencies in charge of state border customs, tariffs (taxes on foreign products), antitrust activities, and so forth.

The Finance Ministry

One of the most important ministries involved in the regulation of the economy and business is the Finance Ministry. It has about two dozen types of major functions, including policy and regulatory decisions in the fields of the federal budget, federal taxes, insurance and banking industries, federal debt, precious metals, customs fees, and antiterrorist financial operations. The Finance Ministry manages the collection of federal taxes and is in charge of special stabilizing funds.

The Stabilization Fund was created back in 2004 out of a portion of the federal budget to stabilize the economy in the event of economic or financial problems. If global prices for oil are above a "base price" of US$27 per barrel, the government transfers the surplus money into the fund. The size of the fund is also set as a proportion of GDP, which ranges between approximately 4 and 7 percent every year. If the price falls below the base, no money is transferred into the fund. The fund may be used to stabilize the budget in the event of lower tax revenues in the future, as well as to finance additional social programs.

The executive branch, not the Duma, manages the Stabilization Fund. Typically, the assets of the fund are secured in foreign reserves (US dollars, euros, pounds sterling, and other currencies) or in foreign securities (for example, US Treasury bonds). The Finance Ministry also manages the National Wealth Fund to support the pension system of the Russian Federation, to cofinance voluntary pension savings of Russian citizens, and to balance the budget of the Pension Fund of the Russian Federation (Ministry of Finance, 2019).

Web

The Ministry of Finance of the Russian Federation regularly publishes (in English) reports on the size of the National Wealth Fund as well as on Russia's international financial operations, and the size of the public external debt of the country: https://www.minfin.ru/en/key/

Taxation and tax policies

Taxes are collected in Russia based on the Tax Code and other laws. Russia has a policy of an annual flat rate for individual income tax. With some exceptions, it is 13 percent, which is significantly lower than in most developed countries including the United States and the United Kingdom. Nonresidents pay income tax at a 30 percent rate. In some cases, foreign residents can avoid double taxation or lower their taxes if there is a dual taxation agreement between Russia and their home country. Like many states, Russian tax laws grant tax deductions based on the size of a family (the more children a family has, the less tax it pays), charitable contributions, and other conditions. The corporate tax rate in Russia is 20 percent. There are also capital gains taxes and other payments, tolls, and duties paid by businesses. Oil companies, for example, in Russia pay federal taxes for every barrel of oil sold on the market (Nemtsov, 2008).

There are three types of taxes: federal, regional, and municipal. Overall, the government maintains a predominantly liberal approach to taxation, based on the assumption that lower taxation should stimulate economic production and trade, and thus bring more revenue to the federal budget. The high oil and gas prices of the early 2000s provided confidence to the supporters of this approach. However, the global financial problems of 2008–12 and the global economic slowdown might affect Russia's tax revenues, and the tax system might change in the near future to compensate for the losses. Among the proposed changes are possible eliminations of several exemptions, increased taxation of alcohol and tobacco products, and different versions of progressive income and property taxes (Strategy 2020).

ECONOMIC STRATEGIES

Economic stability is a very strong factor of political and social stability in any country. Some international developments helped Russia to build such stability early. These factors included high oil prices and the willingness of international business to invest in Russia. However, the global downturn in oil prices, serious weakening of the Russian currency, and a range of economic sanctions against Russia, especially after the events in Ukraine and Crimea mean that, between 2014 and 2020, the Russian economy has been nearly stagnant with annual GDP growth near or below 1 percent.

Russia's economic policy is a product of a long and serious political battle among various groups and interests. As you should remember, after the rapid denationalization of property, big portions of the national wealth were already in private possession, including factories, banks, and media networks. Considerable chunks of the country's natural resources, such as coal mines and oil fields, were also privatized. Using legal and illegal means, in a very short period, a few individuals (commonly called *oligarchs* in Russia because of their access to wealth and power) became owners of these vast resources. They all supported the political system that had allowed them to become rich (Gatman-Golutvina, 2000). They needed a bigger share of political power for themselves. This did not happen.

After Putin became president in 2000, most key government positions in Moscow went to President Putin's associates who had worked with him during his tenure in the office as mayor of St Petersburg in the 1990s. Many strategic government jobs also went to former security officials. This personnel shift was noticeable, and its significance for Russian political life was obvious: Russia's top echelons of political power were designed according to

Putin's strategic concept of the "power vertical" (see Chapters 1 and 4). The probability of a viable political opposition in the top echelons of power had been diminished (Shiraev and Khudoley, 2019). Supporters of Putin's policies maintained that such a shift was inevitable and even wanted by the people of Russia: after the decade of instability, a "strong hand" in the government had finally emerged (Shlapentokh, 2014). This meant the subordination of Russia's top business elites and the weakening of their political power.

The Kremlin's policy was clear: Russia's big business must be loyal to the government or face serious consequences. If business elites showed their loyalty, *then* the government would guarantee that the results of privatization would not be reversed. Putin shifted the focus of his policies from supporting the private sector (this policy was pursued still) to building large state companies. They, according to the Kremlin's vision, should be the backbone of the Russian economy. These companies' top managers, such as Alexey Miller of Gazprom, Igor Sechin of Rosneft, German Gref of Sberbank, Nikolay Tokarev of Transneft, Sergei Chemisov of Rostech, Vladimir Yakunin of Russian Railways (they, of course, may come and go, as Yakunin did), and a few others became the most influential people in Russia (Shiraev and Khudoley, 2019) .

Yet the Kremlin's policy toward wealthy industrial magnates and financiers was contradictory. On the one hand, all three Russian presidents, Yeltsin, Medvedev, and Putin, acknowledged the importance of big corporations to the Russian economy and underlined the necessity of developing Russia's global competitiveness. On the other hand, the government showed favoritism toward some of the magnates but not others. Several of the most prominent and most powerful business leaders of the 1990s, including Boris Berezovsky (1946–2013), Vladimir Gusinsky, and Mikhail Khodorkovsky, have been accused of various illegalities. Two of these three have escaped prosecution and had to seek legal protection abroad (they denied the charges against them). Khodorkovsky was the first Russian billionaire to be given a lengthy prison sentence on multiple charges including business and financial violations. He spent more than a decade behind bars before his release in 2013. Overall, the power consolidation triggered heavier state interference in economic affairs and international business. After some time, nearly all the large corporations found themselves under state control to a certain degree. These developments have scared away a number of large international investors. In the second decade of the 2000s, restrictions on the activities of foreign investors grew tougher. State bureaucracy has prevailed over big business.

Key figure: Mikhail Khodorkovsky (1963–)

Mikhail Khodorkovsky (b. 1963), one of the most successful Russian businessmen in the 1990s and early 2000s, is a representative of a new wave of Russian entrepreneurs not associated with the most powerful government elites in the Soviet Union. He started his business activities in the late 1980s and turned to finance in 1990. A year's successful career in business propelled him to the status of an adviser to the prime minister. He also served as a deputy minister of fuel and energy in the Russian Federation. In 1995 he financed the purchase of 45 percent of shares of the Yukos oil company. He became its vice president in 1996 after expanding his ownership of the company. His business and profits grew. By 2000, Khodorkovsky had become one of the richest entrepreneurs in Russia. Although he did not criticize Putin personally and publicly, he was openly critical of corruption in Russia. Khodorkovsky stated his position during an infamous televised meeting between Putin and leading businesspeople. Khodorkovsky was critical of corruption in Russia—an offense that Putin probably took personally. He also supported the opposition financially. Not for long.

On October 23, 2003, Khodorkovsky was arrested and led away from his private plane after landing in the city of Novosibirsk. He was immediately brought to Moscow for investigation and trial. The formal charges were illegal operations with the company's stock, embezzlement, and fraud. Khodorkovsky and his business partner were sentenced to seven years in prison (Rodionov, 2007). In 2007, the General Prosecutor's Office brought new charges against Khodorkovsky: this time they involved theft and money laundering. In 2010, he was tried again and sentenced for 14 years (excluding the years already served). The Russian government expropriated Yukos' assets and paid no compensation to American shareholders, including pension funds, which suffered around $8 billion in losses (Cohen, 2012, 06/22). Amnesty International, a global human rights organization, later recognized Khodorkovsky as a political prisoner.

Opinions about Khodorkovsky vary. One group of official commentators supports the government's position and maintains that Khodorkovsky was a felon who has received a sentence for his economic crimes. Others believe that Khodorkovsky was a threat to Putin's political power and therefore his prison term was a political travesty. Yet others believed that this businessman had been chosen to send a message to Russian citizens to think twice before challenging the regime in the Kremlin. Khodorkovsky's biggest mistake was that he dared to challenge the system and the president (Panyushkin, 2006; Levada, 2009i). In 2013, right before the Winter Olympics in Russia, Khodorkovsky was released from prison. He now lives and works in exile.

Modernization and Western sanctions

Putin began to use the term "modernization" in 2008 when discussing government economic strategies for the forthcoming decade. President Medvedev reiterated this argument and emphasized the importance of modernization and the urgent need for technological improvements (Pain, 2012). For both Putin and Medvedev, massive and rapid high-tech innovations should have boosted the global competitiveness of the Russian economy. Many experts hoped to reverse Russia's technological and scientific backwardness compared with leading European and North American countries (Johnson and White, 2012).

A key goal of modernization was the development of a postindustrial economy with an emphasis on education, medicine, information technology, and social networks (Strategy 2020). To make this modernization policy successful, the government hoped to make big investments in computer, engineering, and science academic programs to create new jobs in high-tech branches and invite private investments. One of the most widely advertised projects was the creation of Skolkovo—a large educational, technology, and business center near Moscow. It was often called a "second Silicon Valley." Yet, such ambitions plans have not been fulfilled due to a host of domestic and international circumstances.

Russia was hit by a chain of sanctions, which are coercive economic measures taken against a country to force a change in policies, or at least to demonstrate a country's opinion about the other's policies (Congressional Research Service, 2019). The sanctions imposed after 2014 have been a reaction to Russia's policies including the country's poor human rights record at home, Moscow's annexation of Crimea, and the use of a chemical weapon in the United Kingdom by Russian security agents. In addition, the United States has imposed sanctions on Russia in response to election interference and cyberattacks, weapons proliferation, illicit trade with North Korea, and support of Syria (see Chapter 11). No other country as large as Russia has been subject to major international sanctions in recent times. Only the restrictions by the League of Nations on Italy, and by the United States on Japan, before World War II bear some comparison (Gould-Davies, 2018).

Critics of Western sanctions argued that the sanctions have been ineffective. Russia's economy did not collapse, and political institutions have continued to function. Supporters of sanctions argued back that, the longer the sanctions are applied against Russia, the more effective they will be (Gould-Davies, 2018). It is difficult to give an exact number, but estimates suggest that the sanctions probably knocked 6 percent off Russia's GDP after 2014, and reduced Russia's energy sector by up to 10 percent (Harper, 2018). Most importantly, the sanctions have created a climate of opinion regarding Russia that most investment and business companies find unfavorable for making investments in Russia's economy and finances (Chatsky, 2019).

There is little doubt that Russia needs to modernize its economy, develop manufacturing, and make itself less dependent on exports of its natural resources. Yet exports have continued to bring significant revenues over the past several years. Oil and gas production account for 30 percent of Russia's gross domestic product (GDP) and half of its government budget (Chatsky, 2019). This makes Russia highly dependent on its oil and gas revenues. This reliance on its natural resources controls Russia's policy choices. In crude terms, Russia is interested in keeping global oil and gas prices high and prolonging the world's dependency on imported fossil fuels. But what will happen if the world reduces its appetite for oil or the prices go down, as they did in 2020? This could be a very unwelcome development for the Russian economy.

One of Russia's priorities for the second decade of the century is to invest in alternative sources of energy including renewables. Russia anticipates a global decline in demand for oil and gas as a result of growing environmental concerns and the increasing use of new sources of energy. Persistent calls for Russia to seek more opportunities in renewables began some time ago (Shakkum, 2006). Nevertheless, relying on high prices for fossil fuels, Russia had not demonstrated an urgent need to invest in solar, wind, biofuel, and other alternative energy sources. This may be a careless, but not uncommon, attitude.

Agricultural policies

If you drive as little as 50 miles from the flashy streets of Moscow or St Petersburg, you will see a different Russia. For many years, Soviet and then Russian officials tried to boost the country's agriculture and improve the living conditions in Russian villages. However, the social and political experiments of the past 100 years have devastated the land and most of the people living there. Although political freedom and social changes after 1991 have transformed Russian villages, the state of Russia's agriculture is one of the main and most challenging problems in the country. Among the biggest obstacles is demographics: the aging population and migration out of the countryside have depleted the rural population. Russia has almost 9.5 percent of the global agricultural land but lacks farmers to work on it. The second problem is the need for massive investments to change the countryside's infrastructure and make the work of the farmer rewarding and attractive. Substantial and speedy improvements in the agricultural sector have been among the highest priorities of the ruling establishment for years (United Russia, 2012).

A big change took place in the early 2000s when a major land reform was implemented. The new Russian Land Codex (2001) allowed private ownership of land for the first time since 1917, when all land was confiscated from its owners. Russian citizens could now buy, sell, rent, or lease land based on market prices. There are limits: no one can own more than 10 percent of the land within one municipal jurisdiction. The priority to purchase was given to the people who already lived on agricultural lands, which had previously been the property of the government. Approximately 46 million acres of agricultural land was allocated to almost 13 million people.

The problems continue, however. Between 20 to 40 percent of agricultural land is not in use, although it has been in the past. The land tax, a main source of revenue for the municipal governments, did not generate the expected revenue. Many peasants are incapable of developing it. The process of buying and selling is complicated, long (it can take up to a year), and requires a great deal of documentation, all of which stimulated fraud and corruption (Chetverikov, 2009).

To revive the agricultural sector, the government launched a massive stimulus program under the umbrella of the National Priority Projects (see Chapter 14). The ambitious National Agrarian–Industrial Complex Project pursued three major goals: development of stock farms, financial and other support for small farms, and assistance in housing construction in the countryside. Specifically, the government assisted farmers by providing credits, assisting with leasing programs, and eliminating or reducing tariffs on foreign-made machinery and equipment necessary in agriculture (Skrynnik, 2012).

The financial difficulties and sanctions established against Russia after 2014 have slowed down these and other ambitious projects (Congressional Research Service, 2019). However, as shown by the immediate impact of international sanctions in the past, any country can adapt to the imposed restrictions and invest in domestic product and services. With the sliding of the Russian currency and the ban on most European food products after 2014, Russian agricultural products produced domestically became increasingly available to the population. Government subsidies to the agricultural sector and the absence of foreign competition in many agricultural areas have generally pointed toward higher profits for Russia's farming community. Although for years Russians could not buy French Roquefort or Wisconsin or Dutch cheeses in their stores, Russians have settled for cheaper domestic brands. Time will tell how patient consumers will be (Photo 13.1).

Russian billionaires

The financial crisis of 1998 destroyed some private financial corporations in Russia but cleared the way for others, especially those with the government's backing. They consolidated and expanded their resources and assets. A period of economic stability followed.

Photo 13.1 Despite the sanctions, most western fast-food chains remained in Russia. Some of them turned to local agricultural products, like McDonalds that began using local potatoes for its fries

During that period, the first Russian billionaires "emerged" and were recognized in international publications. In 2000, no Russian citizen could claim that they were worth US$1 billion. Since 2001, that situation has changed, and Russian industrial and financial magnates began to appear on "Top 100," "Top 400," and other financial lists and reports. However, the number of billionaires in Russia fell from 101 to 49 during the financial crises of 2008 and 2011. Their number went up again to 95 in 2012 and reached 96 in 2019 (see Table 13.2).

The Kremlin's policy toward super-rich magnates has resulted in the formation of a powerful group of individuals whose wealth and power are closely connected to the high offices in Moscow.

Table 13.2 Estimated numbers of billionaires in Russia, after 2000

2000	2002	2004	2006	2008	2009	2012	2019
0	7	24	50	101	49	95	96

Sources: http://www.finansmag.ru; *Forbes Magazine*.

CRITICAL THINKING ABOUT RUSSIA'S ECONOMIC POLICIES

Corruption

Russian political leaders of the early 1990s were economic liberals, believing in the power of the free market to unleash healthy competition and generate prosperity. It was widely believed that private ownership coupled with individual initiative and discipline could transform Russia. However, the country lacked three basic conditions necessary for the successful development of free-market policies. From the economic standpoint, the country had a very weak economic infrastructure. From the legal standpoint, Russia had very few laws capable of regulating the new type of business relations. From the psychological standpoint, the vast majority of people had almost no positive experience of free entrepreneurship. Corruption and extortion have risen. The young Russian capitalism could not produce a miracle overnight. To the contrary, the free-market transition pushed the country to the edge.

In the middle of the 1990s, the government in Moscow faced serious budget shortages. The Kremlin needed money urgently and in large quantities. One of the ways to solve this problem was to cut social programs and increase taxes. However, this could have had serious consequences and affected social and political stability. Yeltsin would definitely have lost the 1996 elections. The government chose a different path. To earn cash, the Kremlin initiated a massive sell-off of government shares in key companies across Russia. Yeltsin's advisers also believed that, in order to avoid the communists' return to power in 1996, the Kremlin should create a large and powerful group of big property owners.

These new business elites would become a backbone, a social base of the government, and would prevent all attempts by the communists to regain power (Gaidar, 2002). These policies were illiberal, because they represented a mixture of authoritarian methods of government coupled with the acceptance of free-market principles—but only when convenient. Under this system, Russian big business promises to support the government and sponsor its policies; in exchange, the government supports the free market, but only when such support is beneficial to the government (Levinson, 2008a). Unfortunately, these practices created the conditions for corruption. According to international surveys, Russia has been one of the most corrupt countries in the world for years (Transparency International, 2019). Such negative assessments certainly affect international investments in Russia. As a result, foreign direct investment in Russia has continued to decline since 2014. In 2019, international investments fell threefold to their lowest level according to the Central Bank of Russia (Aris, 2019).

State capitalism

State capitalism is a way of organizing the economy in which federal government controls a large proportion of the economy and plays an important managing role, as a kind of chief executive officer. In other words, the government becomes the biggest shareholder in key businesses. There are different assessments of state capitalism in Russia. For example, Mikhail Kasyanov, a former prime minister and now in opposition, claimed that since the early 2000s Russia has been moving to restore a Soviet-style economy and many important elements of state capitalism (Kasyanov, 2017). Table 13.3 lists ten of the most successful

Table 13.3 Several top Russian companies, their functions and ownership

Company	Main function	Ownership
Gazprom	Extraction and delivery of natural gas	Joint stock company. Government has a controlling share.
Lukoil	Extraction and delivery of oil and oil products	Joint stock company. Multiple owners including foreigners.
Gazpromneft	Extraction and delivery of oil, gas, and oil products	Joint stock company. Gazprom owns a controlling share.
Norilsk Nickel	Mining and smelting operations; production of nickel, cobalt, copper, platinum, gold, and other metals	Joint stock company. Multiple owners including foreigners.
Basic Element	Aluminum production, management, military production, insurance, construction, etc.	Single owner (Oleg Deripaska).
AFK Sistema	Telecommunications, banking, tourism, retail, advertisement.	Joint stock company. Multiple owners including foreigners.
Aeroflot	Largest airline of the Russian Federation	Joint stock company. Government has a controlling share.
Avtovaz	Car manufacturing	Joint stock company. Multiple owners including foreigners.
Mosenergo	Energy supplier; the largest Russian power-generating company operating on fossil fuels	Joint stock company. Multiple stock ownership. Largest shareholders are Gazprom and the Moscow Government.
OZhD Russian Railways	Railroad transport services	Federal Government.

Sources: *Expert Weekly*; information provided by the companies.

and powerful Russian companies, leaders in their sphere of business: they include oil, gas, metals, communications, and transportation companies. Most of these are joint stock companies. They trade publicly and accept foreign ownership of portions of their stock. Five of them are under either complete or partial government control (the size of the government's share varies).

Supporters of state capitalism refer to the positive economic experiences in countries such as China and Singapore: if capitalism works there within authoritarian political climates, it can work in Russia as well. Besides, Russia in the 1990s was overly reliant on free-market free-market principles. Instead of supporting manufacturing, the government saw capital move into the banking system because of seemingly lucrative possibilities in that sphere. Consequently, Russia entered the 21st century with an underdeveloped manufacturing sector (Shakkum, 2006). A massive federal intervention was needed, or so supporters of state capitalism believed, without which the economy would have suffered.

Supporters of state capitalism models argued from several positions. First, for the sake of economic stability, more government involvement in economic distribution and the economy in general is necessary (Surkov, 2019; CSR, 2012). This allows the government to better control social security benefits, including pension plans, unemployment benefits, medical care, and public education. A second argument relates to technology, especially to those areas that are unlikely to produce a profit within five to seven years, such as green energy. State capitalism can provide certain guarantees in this area by directing investments in several areas that do not seem profitable today. Industries responsible for military and defense production require huge subsidies too. Without government support, these industries would not survive. Fighting corruption is another problem that cannot be solved or even addressed, some experts argue, without the government's intervention (Greenberg, 2008).

Illiberal models

President Putin has asserted publicly and on many occasions that state capitalism was not his choice (Putin, 2009a). The ruling party has maintained a similar position for some time (United Russia, 2012). Does this mean that the Kremlin's choice has always been free-market capitalism? Not necessarily. It looks like Russia has embraced an illiberal, state-managed economic policy for a long period. It involves a mixture of two strategies: the government relies on free-market principles, yet making, whenever necessary, personal and frequent interventions. In simple terms, this is a "carrot and stick" economic policy. The government rewards businesses loyal to the authorities, or at least manageable ones. In contrast, the government punishes those entrepreneurs who appear to threaten some key interests of the Kremlin.

One of the major government methods of control is the legal system. Critics argue that, using the obedient courts and law enforcement agencies, the Kremlin and local government can reward, threaten, bargain with, or punish any business. The evolving case of Russia's richest tycoons provides a powerful lesson: if you remain loyal to the Kremlin, your business is supported; if not, the consequences may be dire (see again the Khodorkovsky case). Of the five most powerful Russian entrepreneurs who emerged back in the 1990s, two, Abramovich and Potanin, remain on relatively good terms with the Kremlin. Three others, Gusinsky, Berezovsky, and Khodorkovsky, have had and continue to have problems. As a result, the first two had to leave the country to avoid charges against them; the Khodorkovsky case was discussed earlier.

One of the problems of illiberal economic strategy is that the government micromanages business. The authorities may redistribute wealth in many ways, but the actual economic management may be grossly inefficient. The critics' point is that the government's intrusive control tended to cause more corruption (Gusev, 2003). Moreover, for many years, Russia's economy has relied heavily on oil, gas, and other natural resources. For years the government needed to keep the revenues coming from the sale of its natural resources because they pay the government's bills (Gaddy and Ickes, 2009). Changing a country's economic course can effectively be pursued in the presence of transparent political competition (Djankov, 2015). The political landscape in Russia over the past 20 years did not allow for such competition to flourish.

Plans for the future

Russian authorities have always been optimistic about their country's economic future (Putin, 2012a). According to Russia 2020, an ambitious federal economic plan, Russia was supposed to join the ranks of the top five global economies by 2020 or even earlier. This would have required an average growth in labor productivity of more than 9 percent per year annually up to 2020. This must be the fastest rate of economic growth ever registered. No wonder that independent observers tended to be skeptical of these grandiose plans from the start (Eberstadt, 2011). In fact, by 2020, Russia was only number 12 in terms of the size of its economy, far behind India, the United Kingdom, and France, which occupy positions 5 to 7 in the list of countries with highest GDP.

Over the past 300 years, Russia has always tried to catch up with the most developed countries in Europe and North America. Russian leaders frequently mobilized the elites and masses to undertake large-scale projects. Some projects were relatively successful. Others were not. Yet others produced massive economic and social disasters (Johnson and White, 2012). An optimistic forecast suggests that continued economic growth and the rise of the middle class may provide the foundation for an effective democratic system to take root (Dmitriev, 2012). Government experts predict that Russia will need 5 percent yearly economic growth to sustain its social programs (Strategy 2020). Yet what if the economy does not grow and the population's living standards go down?

CONCLUSION

Early in the 21st century, Russia, led by Vladimir Putin, has overcome major economic difficulties and moved into a new period of steady economic growth. Several factors, including energy prices, relatively low taxes, and general stability in the country, have contributed to an economic upturn. However, serious problems followed. Russia continues to look for its own unique method of economic development, and sways between two choices: the free market and government regulation. Russia's big advantage is its well-educated workforce. The size of its domestic market is expanding. Russia has natural resources. Yet the obstacles may be more serious than they appeared a few years ago. Sanctions come and go, but the country's population is decreasing due to low birth rates. Its national labor force is becoming more expensive and thus less competitive. It is almost never clear how economies will develop over time, but it looks as if a regulated free market supported by illiberal policies appears the most attractive choice to the Kremlin for now. Will Russian people support this choice in 2024? That remains to be seen.

14 Social Policies: Health, Education, and Housing

What kind of education or healthcare policies should a country have? **Social policies** refer to government's actions related to human welfare including people's quality of life. Although many current priorities and specific problems can evolve rapidly, certain tendencies and trends in Russia's social policies have already been established and can certainly be discussed.

In this chapter, we will look at the very short history of some basic Russian policies related to healthcare, education, housing, and social security. There is a paradox. On the one hand, the government proclaims the principle of individual responsibility: every citizen must be accountable for their future, and the quality of social services that a person has access to depends on a person's individual circumstances and their contribution to society. On the other hand, there is a very strong and deep-seated belief in Russia that the government must play a major role in the distribution of wealth and resources and in providing social services, such as healthcare, in particular.

Several key developments in the past 30 years will help us better understand this paradox and politics surrounding Russia's social policies.

KEY DEVELOPMENTS

The Soviet legacy

The legacy of the Soviet Union has played an important role in the way Russia handles its social policies today. Under the old Soviet system, until the early 1990s, in theory, every citizen had equal access to healthcare, education, housing, and a range of social services such as cheap public transport—all run by the government. The Soviet Union was a welfare state: the federal and local governments were in charge of virtually every social service in every area of life, from an individual's birth to their very last days. At the basic level, the vast majority of Soviet citizens lived under a system that guaranteed some minimum social protection and minimally decent living standards: there was almost no homelessness, unemployment, or chronic starvation in the country after the 1950s. In simple terms, the government guaranteed a roof over everyone's head, a job (employment was required by law), secondary education, and the right to get basic medical help (Shlapentokh and Woods, 2007). It must be mentioned, however, that in most cases many services had limited availability and were of very low quality.

One of the major developments of the 1990s after the elimination of the Soviet welfare system was the rapid worsening of already limited social services. The old institutions, such as clinics and schools, remained formally in place. Yet the economic crisis had nearly emptied the federal budget. The government simply did not have enough resources to maintain comprehensive social programs. Therefore, one of the policy priorities in the early 2000s was to revive social policies and improve social conditions for most Russians. However, the country had inherited a difficult legacy.

Health and population issues

The health and demographic situation in Russia remains difficult. The mortality rates from heart-related problems are three times as high as in North America and Western Europe. In terms of health indicators, Russia was ranked only 95th out of 169 countries in the world according to Bloomberg's 2019 index, as also acknowledged by Russia's Health Ministry (Moscow Times, 2019). Substance abuse, chronic stress, and smoking were among the major contributors to serious physical and mental problems. About 1 million people in Russia were diagnosed with HIV or AIDS earlier in the century (Feshbach, 2008). By 2019, the number of people diagnosed with HIV reached close to 1.4 million, the worse per capita statistic among European countries (Krivova, 2019). Russia still has one of the highest suicide rates in the world: 27.1 suicides per 100,000 people, although the numbers have been declining for several years (WHO, 2019). One of the most serious problems is alcohol abuse and resulting alcoholism. As a medical and social issue, this is a major contributor to many health problems in Russia. Some public officials, including the chair of the Federation Council at one point, considered alcoholism a problem related to national security, and have called for government control of the manufacturing and distribution of alcoholic beverages (Mironov, 2009a). In the past several years, the Duma has passed several pieces of anti-smoking legislations limiting the sales and consumption of cigarettes and other tobacco products. The implementation of such policies remains a difficult issue.

Life expectancy rates in Russia have risen during the two decades of this century. Russian men, on average, are expected to live to 68 years, compared with 77 for women. These numbers remain lower than in most developed countries, such as the United States, the European Union, or Japan. Globally, Russia's life expectancy rates are below those of more than 140 countries (World Factbook, 2019). Russia's yearly birth rates are about the same as the death rates (14 per 1,000 people) (Rosstat, 2019). On average, every year in Russia about 1.7 million children are born, which means that on average a Russian family has only 1.4 children. To sustain its population (not counting migrants who arrive there to stay permanently), a country should have a minimum of 2.1 children per family. As you can see from Table 14.1, Russia is far below that level. The birth rates have declined significantly since the 1950s, with only a small increase in the past few years.

Health and economic problems are likely to have contributed to Russia's steady population decline. According to government assessments, during the early 2020s, the population

Table 14.1 Number of children per family in the Soviet Union and Russia

1959	1970	1980	1990	2000	2012	2019
2.6	2.0	1.9	1.9	1.2	1.5	1.75

Source: Rosstat (2019).

will be declining on average by 400,000 people a year. In 2004, Russia had approximately 144 million people. By 2008 the number had declined to 142 million. However, the rate of decline was slowing, and in 2012, Russia's population was increasing slightly, reaching 143 million and then 146 million by the end of the second decade of this century. Even though the natural growth rates are declining, immigration is a major source of population growth. Russia has a relatively large influx of immigrants: approximately 300,000 migrants move to Russia each year to work and stay there permanently (Rosstat, 2019). Experts recommend a comprehensive immigration reform to establish different categories of legal residency, thus reducing immigration barriers (Strategy 2020).

More than 20 percent of all people living in Russia are above retirement age, and the number is increasing due to increasing life expectancy. The dwindling population and serious health problems affect the economy and the country's budget. The rural population keeps declining too: many young people move into cities to study, seek higher wages, or pursue other opportunities such as marriage. This trend is not unique: globally, more people in developing countries who are searching for jobs and opportunities move from the countryside to big cities.

GOVERNMENT INSTITUTIONS

One of the most substantial innovations in social policies is that the government is giving up its role as the sole distributor of benefits and entitlements. Although the government allocates money, the distribution role is increasingly being assigned to independent institutions, such as funding bodies and local authorities.

Many federal ministries and agencies in the executive branch of the Russian government are responsible for the implementation of social policies. For example, the Ministry of Healthcare conducts federal policies and exercises regulatory functions in the fields of healthcare and disease prevention. The Ministry's departments are responsible for federal strategies in areas such as new medical technologies, population health forecasts, and health insurance. The ministry is also in charge of several institutions responsible for mandatory medical insurance, medical supervision, and others.

The Ministry of Science and Higher Education carries out federal policy in the fields of secondary education and research. The Ministry is charged with directing all elementary and secondary education in Russia, including professional schools. Research is coordinated through various federal programs, grants, exhibitions, and investigative centers. The Ministry is also in charge of federal property used for research-related purposes.

The Ministry of Sport has to coordinate federal programs related to sports, both competitive and recreational. Together with local authorities, this ministry directs the activities of specialized sports schools and other sport-related facilities. Many children with potential athletic skills attend special sport schools for free and compete in sports leagues and tournaments run by local leagues, state, or federal organizations. The Ministry is also in charge of Russia's participation in the Summer and Winter Olympics, including the Special Olympics and Paralympics. Russia hosted the 2014 Winter Olympics and the 2018 World Soccer Cup, so that the role of the Ministry has increased. In 2008, the Kremlin also created a special position of deputy prime minister in charge of the Olympics.

SOCIAL POLICIES

How has the government addressed these and other social issues and problems? What are its plans for the immediate and distant future? The Russian government's emphasis on improvements in social policies was implemented in the **National Priority Projects** (NPP) program, launched in 2005. NPP is a range of massive federal investments and new policies in the fields of healthcare, education, housing, and agriculture. The ultimate goal of these policies is to dramatically improve the living standards of Russian people in many spheres of their lives and make a major change to the country's declining demographic situation. Russia chose to launch this project back in 2005 for several reasons.

First, Russia had accumulated enough resources to finance these massive social programs. Very high gas and oil prices had generated extra profits for the Russian budget, so the government could make investments without running the risk of inflation. In simple terms, the Kremlin had enough money to sponsor an ambitious social plan. The second reason was organizational. Because by 2005, the "power vertical" had been established and most leaders of the subjects of the Russian Federation had to be approved by the Kremlin, the government in Moscow had to strengthen its ability to manage big social programs on a national level. In short, the Kremlin had accumulated substantial power. Third, in the context of political and financial stability, the government was able to move to a three-year cycle of planning, in contrast to the year-by-year system of planning in the 1990s. NPP required long-term planning, and this seemed possible: the price of oil was relatively stable (essentially near or over US$100 per barrel), and most economists did not foresee the global financial crisis and economic crisis that began in 2008. Finally, this massive social program appeared to be the right thing to do: there was a growing consensus in society that one of the government's policy priorities at that time must be the social sphere. The difficulties of the following years have affected these massive social plans.

Healthcare

The Soviet health care system was federally sponsored but community based. A resident of a city or town was legally assigned to a local "polyclinic," an outpatient facility that would employ several health specialists under one roof. Scores of community doctors would visit patients in their homes and apartments when people became sick. Local hospitals took care of inpatient services. Regional government-run health departments reported to local Communist Party offices and to the Health Ministry in Moscow. Generally, the government was capable of monitoring the health of most citizens, fighting infectious diseases, training doctors, dentists, and nurses, and providing most basic diagnostic, treatment, and other medical procedures.

Life expectancy in the Soviet Union had reached 70 years by the 1970s. One of the many reasons was Soviet medicine. The relative effectiveness of the Soviet healthcare system in the first half of the 20th century was due in part to its low cost and a relatively high-quality medical education system. However, after the 1970s, when national healthcare required massive investments in research, new diagnostic technologies, and treatment methods—which were rapidly changing in developed countries—the disadvantages of the Soviet social and economic system became obvious. Although the services were free, the waits were long, and many procedures or medications were simply not available. As a result, corruption in the medical sphere was rampant (Yakobson, 2009).

After the dissolution of the Soviet Union, 1991 and 1993 federal laws reintroduced a government-sponsored health care system but allowed private options. Most doctors, nurses, and medical technicians remained government employees, with only some joining private clinics and hospitals (some combine these two jobs). Russia overall spends almost four times less on healthcare than EU countries. Almost 30 percent of people, even though they are supposed to receive free diagnosis and treatment, pay partially or in full for their procedures. Doctors' salaries have been just 10 percent above the national average, which is less than US $12,000 per year (Strategy 2020).

The most serious problem in the Russian healthcare system has remained consistent over time: shortages. According to Russian official statistics, over the last 20 years more than 15,000 local clinics in the countryside have been closed as a response to the decreasing population there (Nikolaeva, 2019). In the past ten years, there have been shortages of medical professionals in all regions. Doctors in remote areas could not receive mandatory training required for certification. Scores of motor vehicles used in healthcare (including ambulances) had problems because of age or overuse. There has been a serious discrepancy in the way a person's professional skills are compensated: in the West, doctors historically have received salaries that ranked among the highest of all professions. In Russia, doctors' salaries are only slightly above the national average.

Not surprisingly, the government makes attempts to substantially improve healthcare policies on all levels. The Russian government builds its healthcare policy on several principles. The most important one is that healthcare should be free for every Russian citizen, and the government pledges its support for this constitutional guarantee. However, this does not mean that every citizen can receive any kind of medical help at any time. The government guarantees only basic medical care for existing conditions. Access to this basic care is equally available to everyone. Russians have to contribute to this basic type of healthcare through mandatory insurance (a form of taxation). A specialized federal institution manages the insurance-related funds. However, every individual has the right to pay for additional private insurance plans, which can provide more medical services of a higher quality.

For the foreseeable future, one of the main priorities will be to guarantee the accessibility of healthcare. In other words, every individual should have easy access to healthcare outside major hospitals and emergency rooms. To achieve this goal, Russia is working to place more doctors and nurses directly in local communities. For example, the government planned several years ago to have almost 25,000 additional doctors, fully trained and certified to work in communities, including those working full-time on house calls. In addition, it is making substantial investment in purchasing modern equipment for diagnostic and treatment purposes. The wages of doctors and nurses are to be increased so that most of them will not need to seek additional part-time jobs but will focus instead on their full-time obligations. The government also aims to reduce the patient waiting periods for diagnostic procedures to one week.

Russian leaders have promised new and significant investments in healthcare including the creation of many special and accessible centers to diagnose and treat specific health problems (Putin, 2012a). However, the serious economic slowdown after 2008 and overwhelming financial difficulties that Russia faced after 2014 have negatively affected the institutional plans.

Support for families with children

The text of the 2007 Federal Law on Additional Measures of Federal Support for Families with Children is long and filled with numerous and complicated legal details. However, the essence of the legislation is simple: a family with two children is to receive financial support from the government. Initially, this "mother's capital" or "family capital" sum was 250,000 rubles, which is slightly more than US$7,000 per family. The sum was later increased to more than 460,000 rubles due to inflation (reaching approximately US$7,200 by 2020).

Families eligible for the stimulus money can spend it in three areas: education of their children in Russia, improving living conditions, or investing in the family members' pension plans. (In other words, there are safeguards to ensure they spend it on core goods, and not on luxuries such as fancy clothes, flat-screen TVs, or jewelry.) There was originally a waiting period of three years after the birth of a second child before a family could spend or invest the money. However, amendments to the law in 2008 and later allowed people to use the money toward their mortgages without a waiting period. This Federal Law has been extended until 2021. Most likely, it will be extended again.

Pensions

In the Soviet Union, for many years there was a federal retirement policy according to which every individual was entitled to a federal pension based on their employment history. The minimum retirement age was 55 for women and 60 for men. Local pension offices distributed cash to retired citizens on a monthly basis. In Russia after 1991, the government continued to guarantee pensions. However, the decision was made to create a more effective financial system that would allow better management of payments to Russia's senior citizens. In the late 1990s, the Pension Fund of the Russian Federation was established. After a series of reforms over the past 20 years, senior citizens' monthly pensions are now funded from three major sources: mandatory taxes, insured assets, and special savings. Both individuals and their employers should have contributed to the fund (National Projects, 2009).

For a Russian citizen, a portion of his or her pension is guaranteed by the government and calculated based on the length of their employment. Russians can also invest some funds into special accounts to be managed by state or private banks. This system is complicated and has changed several times. The minimum yearly pension a Russian citizen can receive is approximately 120,000 rubles, which is less than US$2,000. The yearly average pension is 180,000 (RIA Novosti, 2000).

Case in point: the Pension Reform

Major changes in pension policies took place in 2019, which were associated with the Pension Reform signed into law a year earlier. The reform has been an ongoing process of changes mainly associated with the retirement age and especially when every Russian citizen must receive a guaranteed pension. At the core of the reform is a series of continuing increases of the retirement age from 55 to 60 for women and from 60 to 65 for men (Federal Law, 2018). The government explained the necessity of the new law by reference to the increased life expectancy in Russia (about 72 years; to compare, it is 77 in the USA and 76 in China), experiences of other countries, and a difficult financial situation. Putin in the past had publicly rejected the retirement age increase but later changed his mind and argued about the necessity to save money for the federal budget.

The reform was met with substantial societal disapproval: about 85 percent had a very negative or negative view of the retirement age increases. The negative view of the pension reform coincided with a sharp decrease of Putin's approval ratings by up to 17 percent, according to polls (Levada, 2019d). Although the majority still supported Putin as president, such a decline in support was likely linked to the very unpopular reform, which is supposed to be fully implemented by 2029.

Housing

In the Soviet Union, local governments were responsible for housing people. According to the law, every person was entitled to a place to live, but the government did not guarantee its quality. Despite this formal entitlement, there was a significant housing problem, which the Communist Party openly acknowledged for years. About one third of the population at that time lived in substandard accommodation (for example, it was common for working adults, their young children, and their parents to live together in a one-bedroom apartment). Very few options existed for families except to be waitlisted for years and rely on the government's goodwill. The Soviet government did not have enough resources to solve the housing problem. The Yeltsin administration in the 1990s initiated a major change in housing policy: it rapidly denationalized and privatized property. For a small fee, people could purchase the state apartments and houses they were currently living in. By 2004 almost 75 percent of housing facilities in Russia were already in private hands, and their number has grown since. More than 90 percent of all construction companies have become private.

According to surveys, 78 percent of Russians live in apartments, and 22 percent live in their own home (Levada, 2019e). Privatization as a policy did not resolve the housing problem: there are millions of people in Russia living in overcrowded or poor-quality facilities. Although people can buy and sell property on the market, a substantial portion of the Russian population are still not in a position to purchase their own housing. As a matter of social policy, local authorities maintain official waiting lists of families in need of better accommodation: these families are hoping to be allocated a federally subsidized apartment or house. Housing continues to be a serious social problem in Russia today. There are several reasons for this.

First, the volume of residential construction until recently was low. Companies preferred to build more expensive facilities because there was high demand from high-income individuals, especially in big cities. The quality of low-priced apartments remained poor. Second, most people who needed to improve their living conditions could not afford an apartment or house.

Up until 2010, Russia did not have a reliable system of long-term finance (that is, mortgages) for potential buyers. Banks these days can sell mortgages, yet they are very expensive and seldom offered for more than 10 years. Among those who found the situation most difficult were young people, the disabled, and retirees. Third, local authorities did not have effective legal mechanisms for allocating land for the construction of houses and apartments. As a result, according to national surveys in the early 2000s, more than 60 percent of Russians were dissatisfied with their housing.

According to government estimates more than a decade ago, to solve the housing problem, Russia had to build another 1,570 million square meters (one square meter is approximately 11 square feet) of living facilities: in other words, to add one half to the total existing space in all houses and apartments (National Projects, 2009). The Russian government can no longer afford to provide free public housing in the style of the Soviet Union. An ultimate goal of the federal housing project was to create conditions within the market economy that allowed individuals with limited means to purchase their own housing, with or without government assistance. It was anticipated that at least one third of Russians should be financially capable of buying real estate using various savings, loans, and credits. The official policy is that, in a market economy, the government too should use market means. Four steps are being implemented.

First, a range of federal programs will provide the conditions to stimulate banks to issue affordable mortgages. In particular, the interest rates on new mortgages are to drop (with government assistance) to 8 percent. This should boost demand and create an additional supply of apartments and houses. Second, young families will receive special assistance in purchasing their living accommodation. Third, the Kremlin has created incentives for banks and local authorities to stimulate new construction projects. This will provide federal guarantees for some loans, which will reduce costs and risks, and eventually make these loans more affordable. Finally, several special categories of people, including orphans, military veterans, and the handicapped, will continue to receive financial help, including loans and grants.

Education

Like almost every country in the world today, Russia has compulsory elementary and secondary education. Most children go to school at the age of 6 and finish at 17, going through 11 grades in the process. Almost 98 percent of Russians are expected to have finished high school programs (Strategy, 2020). Public education is mostly under the control of local governments, although it is funded from both federal and local budgets. The public school curriculum is generally uniform in Russia: federal institutions are responsible for establishing a standard list of classes and subjects that students must take over the entire course of their education. Students in most schools do not choose most classes they want to take; they simply follow the curriculum that has been set. After finishing ninth grade, students can choose whether to continue their studies in high school or enter a vocational school, which offers secondary education plus training for a particular profession, such as plumbing, cooking, etc. High school students also have the choice of going to college for two years, where they can earn an advanced degree in professions such as nursing, teaching, engineering, or management (this is broadly equivalent to US junior colleges). There are also high schools with a special focus on sports, music, or fine arts. Every kind of public education is free of charge.

There are private schools in Russia. They are usually better equipped than public schools and have fewer students per teacher. Tuition and fees are high and unaffordable for most Russians, ranging from US$3,000 to 8,000 per year (and more for boarding schools). According to official statistics, more than 15 million Russian students are in public schools while about 50,000 attend private schools. About 800,000 enter vocational schools each year (Minpros, 2019).

Practically every public school has access to the Internet. Access to global information is important, but a more basic problem is that many children in Russia, especially in rural areas, simply find it hard to get to their schools, which are often located many miles from their homes. Thus, the government has announced a massive purchase program for school buses. Schools now have special boards run by students' parents to help the school system to become more responsive to parents' requests and societal demands.

Higher education

A student with a high school diploma or a professional school degree has the right to apply to study at an institution of higher education (which in Russia might be called a university, college, academy, or institute). There is normally a competitive admission process, so would-be students submit recommendation letters, scores for the standard federal exams, and other supporting information. As you might expect, some schools in Russia are more diffi-cult to get into than others. Historically, among the most prestigious schools are the Moscow State University and St Petersburg State University (the latter being the alma mater of Vladimir Putin).

In the Soviet Union, all institutions of higher education were under dual federal and local control. Moscow was responsible for budgetary and other strategic decisions; local authori-ties often took charge of hiring staff, directing research, and other issues. Nevertheless, most undergraduate and graduate schools in the Soviet Union had relative autonomy. This tradition continues today: the law guarantees autonomy to universities and other institu-tions of higher education. Schools are free to choose their teaching subjects, research pro-grams, and methods of teaching (Federal Law, 1996). Some schools are under the federal government's authority, while other schools report to local governments. There are also pri-vate schools, which must be properly licensed to issue academic degrees to their graduates.

About 1.2 million people receive undergraduate degrees each year in Russia. Most stu-dents attend state schools, while about 20 percent go to private colleges. Undergraduate and graduate education in public universities is free. This means the government subsidizes edu-cation. However, many public universities are allowed to charge tuition and fees for particu-lar educational programs. College students may also receive small monthly grants (called stipends) from the government, with eligibility being based on good grades. Today, schools in Russia are allowed to establish pay-per-study plans to enroll additional students with exam grades too low for them to enter conventionally.

There are about 230,000 foreign students attending Russian colleges. About a third come from the former Soviet republics (Ukraine, Belarus, and Kazakhstan in particular). Law degrees and economics degrees are most popular these days: about 40 percent of all students pursue them. Among foreign students, medicine and engineering are most popu-lar. Almost a quarter of the population aged between 15 to 34 is engaged in education on either a full-time or part-time basis. An average cost of tuition for a foreign student in Russia is slightly above US$2,000 per year (Statistics of Russian Education, 2020; Study in Russia, 2020).

Despite their efforts, Russia's universities are not necessarily in good shape compared with their foreign counterparts. For many years now, Russia's best schools have scored very low in various global ranking systems. Funding is a major problem. Salaries of scientists remain very low, and the best specialists continue to leave their profession or permanently

move overseas. Although today Russia accounts for about 6 percent of the world's population with a college education, only a few universities can compete internationally. Several
federal programs are underway to retain scientists in Russia and to attract Russian specialists from foreign countries back to universities and laboratories at home.

Two major innovations have been implemented in this area. One is the creation of a new
type of educational institution: federal universities. The second innovation is the development of business schools linked to leading foreign universities and colleges, and issuing
degrees acceptable in foreign countries.

Federal universities are relatively large educational and research institutions consolidated from several existing universities and colleges, which are funded by the federal government. The first two schools of this type, the Southern and the Siberian Federal
Universities, have been in operation since 2006. The government plans to finance a number
of experimental programs there, and create educational centers, research laboratories, and
infrastructure in various fields of science and technology. Each school is supposed to have
about 40,000 students and 8,000 faculty members. If this model is successful, many other
universities with a similar structure should appear. The Kremlin has suggested several sponsors for future federal universities: these include government institutions, the Russian
Academy of Sciences, and private businesses. In 2020, Russia already had ten new federal
universities.

In 2003, Russia entered and later adopted the **Bologna Process**, an international initiative to develop a unified standard for academic degrees across Europe (it involves four-year
undergraduate degrees and two-year master's degrees, similar to the US or British systems).
This has, among other things, made it easier to transfer grades earned by Russian students
in Europe and North America and by international students studying in Russia.

CRITICAL THINKING ABOUT SOCIAL POLICIES

Assessments of Russia's social policies are often influenced by ideology and politics.
Supporters of a more pragmatic assessment tend to look at current Russian social policies
and then evaluate their effectiveness.

Policy dilemmas

An important measure of any society's success lies in its ability to provide effective social
services for the young, the old, and the afflicted. In prosperous countries, education,
healthcare, and welfare services are efficient and affordable. However, the debates in such
countries continue: who should pay for these services, and how much? There are at least two
major views. According to the first one, the government's responsibility is to build and protect favorable conditions for wealth creation. Wealth then translates into a wide range of
social services and protective policies against unemployment, illness, or accidents. In short,
the "wealth creation" model should be the backbone of social policies.

The opposite point of view is based on a different assumption: wealth created under free-
market principles does not necessarily translate into effective social policies but rather creates inequality. Therefore, it should be every government's responsibility to take an active
part in social policies. From this perspective, the "wealth redistribution" model rooted in

taxation followed by robust government action, and not necessarily wealth creation alone, is the most effective way to address both real and potential social problems.

Perhaps both policies—"wealth creation" and "wealth distribution"—are very important. But which is more effective? In economically wealthy countries such as the United States, Canada, France, and the United Kingdom, the debates about these models continue today. In Russia's case, which model do you think will be better and why?

No matter how well the federal institutions functioned, they could not quickly change the challenging situation that Russia was facing in the first decade of the century. Russian authorities had to manage a country with a declining population, low birth rates and modest life expectancy, housing and healthcare problems, and scores of other social issues. There were two fundamental policy options to address this difficult situation. One option was to move forward slowly but steadily, in the hope that an improving business climate would bring new capital investments and the high market prices for oil and gas could bring additional and stable financial resources in the future. Those resources would then be used to address the social problems. The other option was to create a financial stimulus program which would serve as a boost for rapid improvements in the fields of housing, education, healthcare, and many other social services.

The Kremlin, despite promises and declarations, has chosen neither option. As we discussed in other chapters, the business climate has not improved, new foreign investments were difficult to attract, oil prices fell, and Moscow's foreign policy actions have negatively impacted Russia's overall economic situation. Russia's economy has been stagnant in the second decade of this century, and many ambitious projects simply received little funding, especially after the global crisis of 2020. President Putin's remark about what size monthly income would determine that a person belongs to the middle class in Russia is illustrative. The President's answer was: 17,000 rubles, which is about US$250 (Putin, 2020b).

Ideology-driven opinions

Ideologues on the left including communists believe that all the highly publicized projects and improvements in social policies are just a smokescreen for the Kremlin's major policies supporting big business. Critics on the Russian left also say that the Kremlin leaders want the people to believe that the country is in "good hands." In the eyes of the opposition, the shift toward the denationalization and privatization of many industries left millions of people with only formal but unfulfilled guarantees of good healthcare and affordable housing. In reality, only few, the wealthy, have access to resources, services, and power.

Government supporters accuse the left of politicking: the opposition gets more public support when the country's economic and social conditions get worse. In a way, the better off the Russian people are, the less chance the communists and others should have during elections. On the other hand, the more socially insecure people feel, the more opportunity this gives to populist and nationalist leaders as well.

Other commentators believe that the current social policies will inevitably increase people's dependency on the government for many years to come. On paper, people use the free market to achieve at least some of their dreams: they can buy and finance a house, accumulate savings, or achieve some financial security through investments. In reality, these plans would be impossible to realize without constant government supervision and huge financial injections into the economy. Many critics of "big government" suggest that, despite the

Kremlin's claims to be giving people more freedom and incentive, the ultimate goal is to keep all the power in Moscow. Take, for example, the goal of the education reform to stimulate diversity in the methods of education. Private and state schools are, in theory, equal players in the process. However, some experts maintain that the government is not actually that interested in seeing competition from private schools. The Kremlin does not want to lose its control over the university system in general (Lukov, 2009).

Pragmatic assessments

Most critics in Russia have been distrustful of the government's optimistic plans and rosy predictions. It was common to hear sarcastic remarks comparing the ambitious NPPs with the grandiose five-year plans for socioeconomic development in the Soviet Union (see Chapter 2), under which everything in the country's future was carefully planned and predicted. Approved during ostentatious Communist Party congresses, they spelled out how many tons of steel the country would produce, how many apartments it would build, and how many bottles of milk Soviet citizens would drink. Lots of people did not believe in these promises, and with some valid reason: many of the economic targets were simply not met.

Does this old communist tradition of planning continue in the 21st century? The federal government in Russia has promised to double pensions, deliver buses to rural schools, reduce the incidence of cardiovascular diseases, place federal universities among the top ten Russian schools, increase birth rates, and provide new loans to young families. Indeed, these might sound like unrealistic promises of everything to everybody. They could resemble electoral campaigns in North America and Western Europe, in which candidates often promise remarkable handouts and future great benefits to voters. However, in Russia, the announced economic plans, "national projects," have not necessarily been part of any political campaign. True, the government faced some risks: if these promises are not fulfilled, the worsening social situation may become a substantial liability for pro-government candidates in parliamentary or presidential elections. In fact, the dismissal of prime minister Medvedev in 2020 was attributed to the failure of these projects.

Many Russians try to assess social policies from the standpoint of fairness: does the proposed plan benefit everyone equally, or does it bring advantages to one category of people and not to others? As you can anticipate, many elements of social policies can be criticized from this standpoint. For example, take the university system. Who should finance universities? The new reform openly endorses outcome-based financing: an educational institution that achieves good educational and research results will receive better funding.

However, this strategy creates financial inequality and other problems: some schools will become financially secure, while others will struggle, having little resources. Next, the claim that the government will guarantee equal access to colleges will be very difficult to fulfill. People rightly believe that the rich and the privileged have better access today, but not ordinary people across the country.

The future of the pension system generates concerns too. For example, the goal of the ruling political party was to make everyone's pension correlate with their average salary before retirement (United Russia, 2012). In other words, the more money you make during your career, the bigger your pension will be. This logic most probably sounds reasonable to many observers. To many Russians, however, especially those with low-income jobs, it is fundamentally unfair. They argue that they have been working for 10, 20, even 40 years during the time when the state promised relatively similar pensions to everyone. Now most of the pot will go to high-income Russians while their lower-income compatriots will get less. Thus, inequality becomes institutionalized, in their view.

Many people remain uneasy about involving the market in the pension system. As was explained earlier, Russians have to contribute portions of their income to special savings funds that will be used for their future pensions. In theory, these contributions should grow over the years as the financial institutions in which they are invested generate profits. In reality, the pension fund could be losing its value because of high inflation and stock market crashes. Supporters of the market principles of social policies maintain that this is basically a problem of timing: do not judge long-term social policies during an economic and financial downturn. When the market goes up and the economy is booming, social policies become more effective. To Russian critics, however, the current losses are what counts, and even if the market and the economy do go up again, people still have very little patience.

CONCLUSION

It is difficult enough to change any country's social institutions, but it is a truly daunting task to transform and make more efficient a massive welfare system rooted deeply in Russian culture and social beliefs. The Soviet Union provided guarantees for healthcare, education, employment, and different forms of social security. It was only minimal support, yet it was guaranteed.

Today, Russia needs to take decisive steps and implement new policies to bring social policies up to the standards of an advanced European country; or it could abandon any ambitious hopes for improvements and move forward slowly. In reality the Kremlin decided to move fast, but the actual progress in social policies has been slow due to a number of factors, including domestic and global. The core of the government's approach is the pursuit of welfare capitalism, a combination of market models with massive government participation. This fits with Russia's leaders' prime goal of achieving a socially oriented market economy under the government's control.

This policy will probably work somehow and for some time. But almost like in Soviet times, the ambitious plans will be constantly corrected by the country's leaders along the way to make them less ambitious, so they will create an impression of continued success among government supporters. We can only guess how the majority of people will respond.

15 Summary and Conclusion

A BRIEF REVIEW

From a historical viewpoint, the period since the early 1990s is incredibly short. Yet these years were filled with remarkable and dramatic events that have few parallels in Russian or even world history (Kotkin, 2008). These were years of change and confusion, great hopes, and growing worries about the future.

An aftershock that followed the breakup of the Soviet Empire was marked by an economic downturn and hyperinflation, trailed by the violent constitutional crisis of 1993. President Yeltsin used military force to disband the parliament inherited from the Soviet era, yet the populist and left-wing opposition won the legislative elections of 1993 and 1995. The devastating war in Chechnya became a painful thorn in the nation's side. A demoralizing financial crisis in 1998 had a profound and sobering effect on the country.

Yeltsin lost his effectiveness as a leader and had enough courage to transfer power to his handpicked successor, Vladimir Putin. A former KGB officer, Putin was young, busy, resilient, and relentless. He appeared the right choice for the country. The world was seemingly happy with Putin.

During the early years of his presidency, Russia lived through deadly terrorist attacks and tragic accidents, but it was already showing some good signs of economic improvement. High oil prices and a mixture of public-sector and free-market policies were helpful in boosting Russia's economic growth. Russia became more confident, and predictable even in the ways in which it was developing tensions with its close and distant neighbors. By the mid-2000s, one national party—United Russia—had become dominant in the country's multiparty system. As in the case of Vladimir Putin, Russia witnessed another smooth transition of presidential power to Dmitry Medvedev in 2008. While United Russia's strategic position as a party was seriously weakening before and after the 2011 Duma elections, Medvedev offered the presidential chair back to Putin, who accepted and easily won the elections in 2012. He won again in 2018. In 2020, Putin proposed constitutional amendments to stay in power until 2036. Critics in Russia and outside believed that the president's "flip-flopping," "extensions," and other legal maneuverings were antidemocratic and clearly staged by the Kremlin to preserve the ruling elites' grip on power.

What is Russia today, and what has the country achieved in the 21st century? See Table 15.1.

Table 15.1 Russia yesterday and today: issues, problems, policies, consequences, and side effects

Issues, problems, and policies	Then: The USSR	Now: Russia	Actual consequences and side effects
Private property	Outlawed	Legal	Wealth polarization. Illiberal economic management
Economy	Industries; agriculture	Industries; agriculture; services	Heavy emphasis on export of energy resources
Economic policies	Plan-oriented; state-controlled	Free market; private and state-controlled	A hybrid system of increasing illiberal government control of the free market
Party system	One party	Multiparty	Dominance of a pro-government party
Civil liberties	Suppressed	Partially recognized	Selective censorship
Foreign policy	Ideology-driven	Pragmatic and ideology-driven	Mostly confrontational toward the West; focused on boosting self-image
Judiciary and legislature	Not free	Relatively free and independent	Dominated by the executive branch
Freedom to emigrate	Absent	Granted	Visa system is in place for travel to most foreign countries
Birth rates	Relatively low	Low but going up	Threats of depopulation are real

THE ECONOMY AND ECONOMIC POLICIES

On the surface, some economic figures relating to Russia have been encouraging. The average rate of economic growth in the early periods of the 2000s was around 7 percent for several years. The global financial and economic crisis of 2008–12 has slowed growth, but all the signs suggested the global economy should recover and Russia's own recovery would also be sustainable. Russia has almost paid off its foreign debt. Capital gains and personal income taxes have remained lower than in most economically developed countries. Since 2003, the minimum wage has risen, the size of the average salary has gone up, and the number of people below the poverty line has decreased by 50 percent in a decade. The government started backing loans and mortgages for those in need; the government insures personal bank savings up to a certain amount. Russia has repealed its "death tax," so people can inherit money and property without paying a substantial financial penalty.

Yet the last five years of the second decade of this century were difficult for Russia. The falling energy prices, the economic and political sanctions launched in response to Russia's domestic and international politics, the growing disappointment with Russia among international investors, especially from the West, and the global crisis of 2020—all of these events contributed to an economic slowdown and additional financial challenges that the country has been facing. Mismanagement and bureaucracy have added to the problem. The wages of doctors, nurses, teachers, and most other categories did not grow. The prices for goods and services went up.

For years, Russia continued to rely too much on its energy resources at the expense of manufacturing and other areas. It is a free-market economy, but for years it depended on raw material exports and state control over most important economic resources (Åslund, 2007). If energy prices are low, federal revenues will be low too. Russia is still far behind most European countries in the average size of people's wages and pensions. Overall, Russia has embraced illiberal economic policies, a mixture of authoritarian methods of government coupled with the acceptance, when it is convenient, of free-market principles.

SOCIAL POLICIES AND DEPENDENCY

Despite the substantial economic transitions that have taken place in Russia over the past 30 years, the authorities are still very much responsible for practically every element of people's lives—from paying state salaries to distributing subsidized apartments; from hot water rationing, changing bus routes, and building healthcare clinics, to changing the Constitution in a record-breaking short time. Most people remain ultimately dependent on the authorities. This reliance on somebody else's power can develop a sense of psychological dependency. The culture of dependency generates support for the leaders already in power, because most people start to believe, especially in times of crisis, that only powerful authorities can help them, the poor and the hopeless, to overcome difficulties and protect them from new challenges.

FOREIGN POLICY AND SECURITY

With the ending of the Cold War, the world has seemingly buried the mutual fears and threats that had been haunting both Moscow and its opponents for more than 40 years. Russia as an international actor rewrote its old script. In the 1990s, Moscow dropped ideology as a factor of foreign policy and declared a transition to a new, pragmatic approach. This process of transition was anxious, complicated, and somewhat disappointing in the end. Russia began seeking a new place in the global world and pursuing an increasingly assertive foreign policy (Lavrov, 2011; Cohen, 2009). However, the old shadow of a foreign threat is back in the area of public debate and policymaking. Moscow pursues a policy of strengthening its influence over the countries that are former republics of the Soviet Union. Moscow has been very active in the Middle East, such as in Syria, and in Africa. It increases pressure on the states that resist its influence. Russia supports authoritarian regimes that remain friendly to the Kremlin. It also uses its oil and gas as instruments of political pressure on some foreign countries (Kuchins, 2012).

While most democratic countries tend to criticize Russian policies, the Kremlin attributes the worsening of relations to a number of Western policies. The message is simple: if Western powers had chosen a different foreign policy in the past, then the relations between the countries would have been different. Among its grievances are:

- America and Europe should not have supported Bosnian Muslims in the conflict in the former Yugoslavia in 1992–96. Washington and NATO should not have dropped bombs on Serbia, which fought for its own territorial integrity in 1999;

- the West should not have granted independence to Kosovo, thus punishing Serbia and annexing a part of its territory;
- NATO should have halted any further eastward expansion in 1996 and later;
- America should not have attacked Iraq unilaterally in 2003. Other Western countries, including the United Kingdom, should not have supported Washington in this war;
- the United States and the European Union should not have supported the anti-Russian side during the elections in Ukraine in 2004–5 and again in 2014;
- the world should not have supported Georgia in its military conflict with Russia in 2008;
- the West should not have been one-sided and forceful in supporting the rebellions in Libya in 2011 and Syria in 2012–13;
- the West should not have imposed sanctions against Russia and should have recognized Crimea as a legitimate part of the Russian Federation.

There were some domestic ideological and political causes for the increased tensions between Russia and most Western countries (Sestanovich, 2020; Kuchins, 2007; 2012). First, Russian military and security leaders had a hard time coping with the country's status as an ex-superpower, and never planned to give up their gargantuan military goals. Second, the anti-Western sentiment across Russia is not only a response to international developments, but also a reflection of Russia's nationalism and authoritarianism. Third, the Kremlin has a legitimate interest in maintaining the popular belief that enemies continuously surround Russia. Russia's power may grow and carry the country's ambitions with it.

History shows that maintaining a permanent image of a foreign enemy helps the authorities to preserve national unity and rally people around the government.

POLITICS AND PARTICIPATION

History also shows that political transition in any country is a painful process. Over just three decades, Russia had to be reassembled in every sense: recreating a legitimate government, economic and military power, a multiethnic state, and democracy. These challenges were daunting. Privation and lawlessness at the early stages, several economic crises, terrorist attacks, and scores of other obstacles and problems slowed down the development of a new civil society. One of the assumptions of modernization theory is that poor countries, by embracing free-market principles and new technologies, should increase demands by their people to strengthen democracy. Applied to Russia, it can be assumed that, as Russians are getting wealthier, they are beginning to demand and receive more democratic governance, more open political system, and more civil rights (Kuchins, 2012, 04/16). In general, the political restructuring in Russia was a transition to a democracy. Yet the type of political system built in Russia today is rather unique and full of contradictions.

According to the Constitution, Russia has three independent branches of government. However, the executive power is disproportionately strong, and getting even stronger as additional amendments and presidential decrees are passed every year. Russia has an increasingly personal form of political rule.

Russia has a functional multiparty system, but it also has a dominant, government-backed, ruling party, United Russia. Other parties have for years had very little chance of power, or even of becoming a serious opposition. However, there have been many signs that this situation might change, especially after municipal elections in 2019.

Russia has scheduled national elections in the past years. Nevertheless, the rules for the Duma elections constantly change to increase the chances for Kremlin supporters. Since 1996, Russia has not had truly competitive presidential elections: pro-Kremlin candidates have always been expected to win.

From a legal point of view, Russia enjoys a full spectrum of political liberties. From a realistic standpoint, however, the government has developed an effective system of regulating free speech by suppressing the opposition, using violence against peaceful rallies, and selectively prosecuting journalists. Self-censorship has become a necessary habit for reporters.

In politics, some commentators anticipate increasing democratic competition and the emergence, in a few years, of a stronger civil society. Most observers, however, have long predicted that Russia is sliding toward an authoritarian regime managed by security service professionals (Dubin, 2012; Kuchins, 2007; Hale, 2011b). Critics in Russia also outline several possible developments in Russia's political system. They include the demands for new, alternative leaders; the aging of the political establishment and their political rhetoric; the growing divisions among the electorate; the growth of protest intentions; and the rise of the middle class, which needs democracy (Dmitriev, 2012).

Putin four times and Medvedev once won electoral votes as presidents largely based on people's positive perception of the economy, the apparent restoration of order, and the reinstatement of Russia's standing in the world (Johnson and White, 2012; Colton and Hale, 2009). However, polls have also shown that around two thirds of Russians do not trust the establishment institutions, including the courts, political parties, and labor unions. Yet in history, people often disapprove policies but remain supportive of the government (Bourdeaux, 2012). Such a tendency—seen in the 1990s and later—to remain loyally unhappy is another paradox of the Russian political psychology (CSR, 2012; Gudkov, 2008a; Dubin, 2008b).

Another issue is the lack of new, nationally recognized political leaders. Earlier in the book, we introduced the blogger and political activist Alexei Navalny. He remains popular in Moscow but not necessarily outside of the large cities. He is a famous critic of the regime, yet studies show he does not offer a popular alternative plan to solve the real social problems facing the country, including medicine, education, personal security, and housing—the four key problems Russians identify in polls. Electoral fatigue and lack of enthusiasm about already well-known political leaders is part of the problem.

FORECASTS

Predictions abound about who offers at least a few possible developments for Russia. Based on surveys and original focus-group research, the Center for Strategic Research (CSR, 2012) outlined four scenarios for Russia's political development in the coming years (Table 15.2). The least probable scenario is political modernization based on cooperation between the Kremlin and the growing political opposition, especially in Moscow. The antipathy of the government toward the opposition's leaders appears so strong that any cooperation seems unlikely. A somewhat probable scenario is political inertia characterized by the weakening of protests yet deepening antagonisms between the establishment and the opposition. This may drag on for years.

Table 15.2 Four forecasts of Russia's political future

Scenario	Triggers	Consequences	Probability
Political reaction	Violence during street protests	Freezing of the democratic reforms	High
Political modernization	Protests continue The government finds a way to embrace oppositional leaders	Modernization of political life accelerates	Low
Radical transformation	New waves of economic crises hit Russia	Mass protests across Russia Government loses its control over regions	High
Political inertia	Protests burn out	Government continues to receive relative support; crisis deepens	Moderate

Source: Center for Strategic Research, Moscow, 2012.

Two other probable scenarios are worrisome. According to one option, political reaction could take place in the form of massive antidemocratic measures to weaken and destroy the opposition. The other option is a radical transformation, the outcome of which is unpredictable because this scenario forecasts widespread popular defiance and the collapse of today's "vertical of power" (Dmitriev, 2012).

Russia as a country, an energy supplier, a nuclear power, and potentially a big trade partner will remain a major player in global affairs in the 21st century. The main question is which direction of development it will choose. If new Russian political leaders are to make Russia respectable, powerful, democratic, and free, the time is almost nigh. The next few years after 2020 could become the most important in Russia's history.

References

Abalkin, L. (1995) *Ekonomicheskaya reforma: Zigzagi sydby i uroki na budushchee* (Economic Reform: Zigzags of Fate and Lessons for the Future). Moscow: Institute of Economics, RAS.

Adomeit, H. (1998) *Imperial Overstretch: Germany in Soviet Policy from Stalin to Gorbachev.* Baden-Baden: Nomos.

Albertazzi, D. and McDonnell, D. (2008) *Twenty-First Century Populism: The Spectre of Western European Democracy.* New York and London: Palgrave Macmillan.

Alekseeva, M. I., Bolotova, L. D., Vartanova, E. L., Voronova, O. A., and Zasurskij, I. I. (2008) *Sredstva Massovoj Informacii v Rossii* (Russia's Mass Media). Moscow: Aspect Press.

Arendt, H. (1951) *The Origins of Totalitarianism.* London: Secker & Warburg.

Aris, B. (2019) "The trouble with investing into Russia." *The Moscow Times.* https://www.themoscowtimes.com/2019/08/29/the-trouble-with-investing-into-russia-a67068 (accessed March 31, 2020).

Army Technology (2019) The top ten arms exporting countries in 2018. May 8. https://www.army-technology.com/features/arms-exports-by-country/ (accessed March 31, 2020).

Åslund, A. (2007) *Russia's Capitalist Revolution: Why Market Reform Succeeded and Democracy Failed.* Washington, DC: Peterson Institute.

Åslund, A. and Kuchins, A. (2009) *The Russia Balance Sheet.* Washington, DC: Peterson Institute for International Economics.

Avtorkhanov, A. (1990) *Lenin v sudbakh Rossii: Razmyshleniia istorika.* Prometheus-Verlag.

Bahry, D. and Silver, B. D. (1990) "Soviet citizen participation on the eve of democratization." *American Political Science Review*, 84(3), pp. 821–47.

Barner-Barry, C. (1999) "Nation building and the Russian Federation," pp. 95–108 in B. Glad and E. Shiraev (eds), *The Russian Transformation: Political, Sociological, and Psychological Aspects.* New York: St Martin's Press.

Barnes, S. (2011) *Death and Redemption: The Gulag and the Shaping of Soviet Society*, New York: Princeton University Press.

Bastrykin, A. I. (2008) "Interview with the First Deputy of the Prosecutor General of the Russian Federation." March 25. http://www.sledcomproc.ru/smi/543/ (accessed November 11, 2009).

Bastrykin, A. I. and Naumov, A. V. (eds) (2007) *Ugolovnoe Pravo Rossii. Prakticheskij Kurs* (Russian Criminal Law. Practical Course), 3rd edn. Moscow: Wolters Kluwer.

Bauman, Z. (1994) "A revolution in the theory of revolutions." *International Political Science Review*, 15(1), pp. 15–24.

Benderskaya, E. G. (2008) "Zaochnoe Razbiratelstvo Ugolovnyh Del v Stranah SNG" (Processing of criminal cases in absentia in CIS countries). *Vestnik Moskovskogo Universiteta*, 5, pp. 99–112.

Blake, Aaron (2017). "The 11 most important lines from the new intelligence report on Russia's hacking." *Washington Post*, January 6. https://wapo.st/2tGn3F (accessed March 8, 2019).

Boldin, V. (1994) *Ten Years That Shook the World.* New York: Basic Books.

Bortnikov, A. (2009) "President met with Director of FSS." Moscow, December 25, ITAR-TASS.

Bottomore, T. (1993) *Elites and Society.* London: Routledge.

Bourdeaux, R. (2012) "Putin's history lesson." *The Wall Street Journal*, May 4. http://online.wsj.com/article/SB10001424052702304743704577381641570549300.html

Boxer, V. and Hale, H. (2000) "Putin's anti-campaign campaign: Presidential election tactics in today's Russia." *AAASS NewsNet, Newsletter of the American Association for the Advancement of Slavic Studies*, 40(3), May.

Brazhnikov, I. (2008) "Den Ochicheniya Gosudarstva" (The day of the state's purification). http://ei1918.ru/drevnjaja_rus/48.html (accessed November 11, 2009).

Brown, A. (1996) *The Gorbachev Factor*. New York: Oxford University Press.

Brown, A. (2009) *The Rise and Fall of Communism*. New York: HarperCollins.

Brownlee, J. (2007) *Authoritarianism in an Age of Democratization*. New York: Cambridge University Press.

Brumberg, A. (1991) "Russia after perestroika." *New York Times*, Book Review, June 27.

Bruter, V. (1999) "Istoriya Sovremennykh Rossiyskih Vyborov, 1993" (A history of modern Russian elections, 1993). International Institute of Humanitarian-Political Studies. http://www.igpi.ru/info/people/bruter/1085749185.html (accessed November 11, 2009).

Brzezinski, Z. (1966) "The Soviet political system: Transformation or degeneration?." *Problems of Communism*, 15(1), pp. 1–15.

Bump, Philip (2018). "Timeline: How Russian trolls allegedly tried to throw the 2016 election to Trump." *Washington Post*, February 16. https://wapo.st/2vK5ndq (accessed August 14, 2019).

Bunich, I. (1992) *Zoloto Partii* (The Party's Gold). St Petersburg: Shans.

Carnaghan, E. (2008) *Out of Order. Russian Political Values in an Imperfect World*. University Park: Penn State University Press.

CECRF (2020) *Central Electoral Commission of the Russian Federation*. http://www.cikrf.ru/eng/ (accessed March 31, 2020).

Chaisty, P. (2012) "Business representation in the State Duma," in L. Johnson and S. White (eds), *Waiting for Reform Under Putin and Medvedev*. New York: Palgrave Macmillan.

Chatham House (2018) *A Declining Russia with Rising Ambitions? Challenges for Russia and the West*. London: The Royal Institute of International Affairs. King's College.

Chatsky, A. (2019) "Have sanctions on Russia changed Putin's calculus?" *Council of Foreign Relations*, May 2. https://www.cfr.org/in-brief/have-sanctions-russia-changed-putins-calculus (accessed March 31, 2020).

Chernyaev, A. (1993) *Shest lets Gorbachevym* (Six Years With Gorbachev). Moscow: Progress-Kultura.

Chernyaev, A. (2000) *My Six Years With Gorbachev*. University Park: Penn State University Press.

Chetverikov, A. (2009) "O Zemelnom Kodekse" (On the land code). http://www.spravedlivo.ru/news/position/951.php (accessed November 11, 2009).

Chistyakov, O. (ed). (1994) "Manifesto, 17 October 1905," p. 41, in *Rossijskoe Zakonodatelstvo 10-20 Vekov* (Russian Law from the 10th to 20th Centuries). Moscow: Yuridicheskaya Literatura.

Churov, V. (ed). (2009a) *Izbiratelnoe Zakonodatelstvo i Vybory v Sovremennom Mire* (Electoral Law and Elections in a Modern World). Moscow: Central Electoral Commission.

Churov, V. (2009b) "Vybory—Osnova Demokratii" (Elections are a foundation of democracy). *An interview*. VIP (7–8). http://www.cikrf.ru/newsite/news/actual/2009/07/24/int_churov_vip.jsp (accessed November 11, 2009).

CICRF (2019) *Central Election Commission of the Russian Federation*. http://www.cikrf.ru/eng/ (accessed March 31, 2020).

Clover, C. (2012). "Clinton vows to thwart new Soviet Union." Financial Times, December 6. http://www.ft.com/cms/s/a5b15b14-3fcf-11e2-9f71-00144feabdc0.html#axzz4AAgBqLUd (accessed June 3, 2017).

Clover, C. and Blitz, J. (2009) "Icy winds threaten US–Russia thaw." *Financial Times*, May 8. https://on.ft.com/3dNggPY (accessed November 11, 2019).

Cohen, S. F. (2001) *Failed Crusade: America and the Tragedy of Post-Communist Russia*. New York: W.W. Norton.

Cohen, A. (2009) "Russia and Eurasia: A realistic policy agenda for the Obama administration," Paper by the Heritage Foundation, March 27. http://www.heritage.org/Research/RussiaandEurasia/sr0049.cfm (accessed November 11, 2009).

Cohen, A. (2012a, 06/22) "Congressional hearing highlights the need to pass Magnitsky PNTR to Russia." *The Foundry*, June 22. http://blog.heritage.org/2012/06/22/congressional-hearing-highlights-the-need-to-pass-magnitsky-pntr-to-russia/

Cohen, A. (2012b, 07/27) "Russia and the World Trade Organization: Congress should not sacrifice human rights." *The Foundry*, July 27. http://blog.heritage.org/2012/07/27/russia-and-the-world-trade-organization-congress-should-not-sacrifice-human-rights/

Collins, N. (2007) *Through Dark Days and White Nights: Four Decades Observing a Changing Russia*. Washington, DC: Scarith.

Colton, T. and Hale, H. (2009) "The Putin vote: Presidential electorates in a hybrid regime," *Slavic Review*, Fall, pp. 473–503.

Communist Party of the Russian Federation (CPRF) (2012) *The Program of the Communist Party of the Russian Federation*. http://kprf.ru/party/program/ (accessed May 21, 2012).

Congressional Research Service (2019) *US Sanctions on Russia*. https://fas.org/sgp/crs/row/R45415.pdf (accessed March 31, 2020).

Conquest, R. (1986) *Harvest of Sorrow: Soviet Collectivization and the Terror-Famine*. New York: Oxford University Press.

Constitutional Court of the Russian Federation (2009) *Decisions*. http://www.ksrf.ru/ru/Decision/Pages/default.aspx (accessed February 27, 2020).

Constitutional Court of the Russian Federation (2019) *Decisions*. http://www.ksrf.ru/ru/Decision/Pages/default.aspx (accessed August 27, 2019).

Council of Europe, Commissioner on Human Rights (2016) *As Long as the Judicial System of the Russian Federation Does Not Become More Independent, Doubts About Its Effectiveness Remain*. https://bit.ly/2OuykG4 (accessed August 27, 2019).

CPFR (2019) *The Communist Party of the Russian Federation. A Brief Informational Note*. https://kprf.ru/party/ (accessed August 27, 2019).

CPRF Program (2019) *The Program of the Communist Party of the Russian Federation*. https://kprf.ru/party/program (accessed March 31, 2020).

Criminal Code of the Russian Federation (2019) http://docs.cntd.ru/document/9017477 (accessed August 27, 2019).

CSR Report (2012) "Society and authority during a political crisis." (Obshestvo I vlast' v uslovijah politicheskogo krizisa). Report of the Center of Strategic Research. Moscow http://www.csr.ru/2009-04-23-10-40-41/365-2012-05-23-10-54-10

Dale, H., Cohen, A., and Smith, J. (2012) *Challenging America: How Russia, China, and Other Countries Use Public Diplomacy to Compete with the U.S.* http://www.heritage.org/research/reports/2012/06/challenging-america-how-russia-china-and-other-countries-use-public-diplomacy-to-compete-with-the-us

Diamond, Jeremy. (2016). "Russian hacking and the 2016 election: What you need to know." http://www.cnn.com/2016/12/12/politics/russian-hack-donald-trump-2016-election/ (accessed July 14, 2020).

Djankov, S. (2015) "Russia's economy under Putin: From crony capitalism to state capitalism." *Peterson Institute for International Economics*. September. https://www.piie.com/publications/policy-briefs/russias-economy-under-putin-crony-capitalism-state-capitalism (accessed March 31, 2019).

Dmitriev, M. (2012) Interview. *Novaya Gazeta*. May 30. http://www.novayagazeta.ru/politics/52832.html

Dobrynin, A. (1995) *In Confidence: Moscow's Ambassador to America's Six Cold War Presidents (1962–1986)*. New York: Random House.

Dobson, R. (1996) *Russians Choose a President. Results of Focus Group Discussions*. June. Washington, DC: USIA.

Doder, D. and Branson, L. (1990) *Gorbachev: Heretic in the Kremlin*. New York: Viking.

Dokshin, V. and Limansky, G. (2019) "This is a historic hell". *Novaya Gazeta*. https://www.novayagazeta.ru/articles/2019/10/16/82387-eto-istoricheskiy-ad (accessed April 3, 2020).

Dorell, O. (2018) "Putin's Russia: These are the candidates in an election some call a charade." *USA Today*, March 6. https://bit.ly/2UYZoxi (accessed April 5, 2020).

Dubin, B. (2008a) "An interview." *Novaia Gazeta*, 40, June 5, pp. 12, 13.

Dubin, B. (2008b) "An interview." *Novaia Gazeta*, 46, June 30, pp. 6, 7.

Dubin, B. (2012) "The myth of the Russian 'unique path' and public opinion," in L. Johnson and S. White (eds), *Waiting for Reform Under Putin and Medvedev*. New York: Palgrave Macmillan.

Dugin, A. (2011) *Geopolitika* (Geopolitics). Moscow: Academicheskij Proekt.

Dye, T. (2001) *Top Down Policymaking*. Washington, DC: CQ Press.

Eberstadt, N. (2011) "The Dying Bear: Russia's demographic disaster." *Foreign Affairs*, November/December, pp. 95–108.

Erlichman, V. V. (2004) *Poteri Narodonaseleniya v 20 Veke* (Population Loss in the 20th Century). Moscow: Russkaya Panorama.

Ferguson, G. (1996) "Parties and politics in Russia." *The Public Perspective*, 2, p. 44.

Feshbach, M. (2008) "Behind the bluster, Russia is collapsing." *Washington Post*, October 5, p. B03.

Filatov, S. (2008) "Interview," October 6, *Radio Station Ekho Moskvy*. http://www.echo.msk.ru/programs/svoi-glaza/544670-echo (accessed November 11, 2009).

Fillipov, A. (2009) *Noveyshaya Istoriya Rossii, 1945–2006* (A Modern History of Russia, 1945–2006). Moscow: Prosveshenie.

Fish, S. (2005) *Democracy Derailed in Russia: The Failure of Open Politics*. New York: Cambridge University Press.

Fitzpatrick, S. (1986) "New perspectives on Stalinism." *Russian Review*, 45(4), pp. 357–73.

Fortescue, S. (2012) "The policy-making process in Putin's Prime Ministership," in L. Johnson and S. White (eds), *Waiting for Reform Under Putin and Medvedev*. New York: Palgrave Macmillan.

Freedom House (2019) "Democracy in retreat: Freedom in the World 2019". https://freedomhouse.org/report/freedom-world/freedom-world-2019/map (accessed June 11, 2019).

FSIN (2020) *Federal Service for Implementation of Sentencing*. Statistical Information. http://www.fsin.su/statistics/ (accessed April 5, 2020).

FSS (2019) Official Site of the Federal Security Service. http://www.fsb.ru/fsb/npd.htm (accessed April 5, 2020).

Gaddy, C. and Ickes, B. (2009) *Russia's Addiction: The Political Economy of Resource Dependence*. Washington, DC: Brookings Institution.

Gaidar, Y. (2002) *The Economics of the Russian Transition*. Boston: MIT Press.

Gaidar, Y. (2007) *Collapse of an Empire: Lessons of Modern Russia*. Washington, DC: Brookings Institution.

Gallagher, T. (2017) "One fait accompli after another: Mikhail Gorbachev on the new Russia." *Los Angeles Review of Books*. www.lareviewofbooks.org (accessed April 5, 2020).

Garmonenko, D. (2019) "Vlast testituet novye pravila vyborov v Gosdumu-2021" (Authorities test new rules for the Duma-2021 elections). *Nezavisimaya Gazeta Online* http://www.ng.ru/politics/2019-02-06/3_7501_newrules.html (accessed April 5, 2020).

Gatma-Golutvina, O. V. (2000) *Byurokratija ili Oligarkhija?* (Bureaucracy or Oligarchy?), Moscow: Russian Academy of State Service.

Gazeta.ru (2011) http://www.gazeta.ru/politics/elections2011/2011/12/10_a_3922210.shtml

Gelman, V. (2006) *Vozvrawenie Leviafana? Politika recentralizacii v sovremennoj Rossii*, pp. 91–92. Moscow: Polis.

Gessen, M. (2012) *The Man Without a Face*. New York: Riverhead Books.

Gessen, M. (2014) *Words Will Break Cement: The Passion of Pussy Riot*. New York: Riverhead Books.

Gibson, J. L. (1996) "A mile wide but an inch deep: The structure of democratic commitments in the former USSR." *American Journal of Political Science*, 2(May), pp. 396–420.

Glad, B. and Shiraev, E. (eds) (1999) *The Soviet Transformation*. New York: St Martin's Press.

Global Edge (2020) *Global Business Knowledge*. Trade statistics. https://globaledge.msu.edu/ (accessed April 5, 2020).

Goldgeier, J. and McFaul, M. (2003) *Power and Purpose: U.S. Policy Toward Russia After the Cold War*. Washington, DC: Brookings Institution.

Golz, A. (2007) "Rossiyskaya Imperiya i Rossiyski Militarism" (Russian Empire and Russian Militarism), in I. M. Kliamkin (ed.), *Posle imperii*. Moscow: Fond Liberal'naia missiia.

Golz, A. (2009) "Ono im Nado?" (Do they need it?), *Ezhednevnyj Zhurnal*. http://ej.ru/?a=note&id=8846 (accessed November 11, 2009).

Gorbachev, M. (1985) "Interview with Time Magazine," *Pravda*, September, 1–2, p. 1.

Gorbachev, M. (1995) *The Search for New Beginning: Developing a New Civilization*. San Francisco: Harper.

Gorbachev, M. (1996) *Memoirs*, 1st edn. New York: Doubleday.

Gorbachev, M. and Mlynar, Z. (1994) *Conversations with Gorbachev on Perestroika, the Prague Spring, and the Crossroads of Socialism*. New York: Columbia University Press.

Gould-Davies, N. (2018) "Sanctions on Russia are working." *Foreign Affairs*, August 22. https:// www.foreignaffairs.com/articles/russian-federation/2018-08-22/sanctions-russia-are-working (accessed April 5, 2020).

Gozman, L. and Etkind, A. (1992) *The Psychology of Post-Totalitarianism in Russia*. London: Centre for Research into Communist Economies.

Graham, T. (2019) "Let Russia be Russia: The case for a more pragmatic approach to Moscow." *Foreign Affairs*, November/December. https://www.foreignaffairs.com/articles/russia-fsu/2019-10-15/let-russia-be-russia (accessed April 5, 2020).

Green, M. (2015) "Putin speeches before the National Assembly: A quantitative analysis." Paper presented at the Annual Student Research Conference at George Mason University, April 15, 2015.

Greenberg, R. (2008) "Director of the Institute of Economics, Russian Academy of Sciences: An interview." *Ekho Moskvy Radio*, August 3. http://www.echo.msk.ru/programs/albac/531344-echo.phtml (accessed November 11, 2009)

Greenpeace (2012) *The Russian Forests*. http://archive.greenpeace.org/comms/cbio/russia.html (accessed April 5, 2020).

Gretskiy, I., Treshchenkov, E., and Golubev, K. (2014). "Russia's Perceptions and Misperceptions of the EU Eastern Partnership." *Communist and Post-Communist Studies*, 47 (3–4), pp. 145–65.

Grossman, V. (1970) *Vse techet* (Everything Flows). Frankfurt: Posey.

Grunt, V., Kertman, G., Pavlova, T., Patrushev, S., and Khlopin, A. (1996) "Rossiyskaya Povsednevnost I Politicheskaya Kultura: Problemy Obnovleniya" (Russian everyday life and political culture: Problems of renovation). *Polis*, 4, pp. 56–72.

Gudkov, L. (2008a) "An interview." *Novaia Gazeta*, 40, June 5, pp. 12, 13.

Gudkov, L. (2008b) "An interview." *Novaia Gazeta*, 63, August 28, pp. 16, 17.

Gudkov, L. (2012) "The nature and function of 'Putinism'," in L. Johnson and S. White (eds), *Waiting for Reform Under Putin and Medvedev*. New York: Palgrave Macmillan.

Gudkov, L. (2019) "The laws about disrespecting authorities and fake news." *Levada Center*. https:// www.levada.ru/2019/04/08/zakony-o-neuvazhenii-k-vlasti-i-fejknyus/ (accessed April 5, 2020).

Gudkov, L. et al. (2011) "About the disappointed in the United Russia" (O razocharovannyh v Edinoj Rossii). December 12. http://www.levada.ru/09-12-2011/lev-gudkov-o-razocharovannykh-v-edinoi-rossii

Gumilev, L. (2004) *Poiski vymyshlennogo tsarstva*. Moscow: AST.

Gupta, R. (2016) "Understanding the war in Syria and the roles of external players: Way out of the Quagmire?" *The Round Table: The Commonwealth Journal of International Affairs*, 105(1), p. 6.

Gurganus, Julia (2018). "Russia: Playing a Geopolitical Game in Latin America." *Carnegie Endowment*, May 3. https://carnegieendowment.org/2018/05/03/russia-playing-geopolitical-game-in-latin-america-pub-76228 (accessed August 12, 2019).

Gusev, V. (2003) "An interview: Rossiyskaya Federacija Segodnja" (The Russian Federation today). http://www.russia-today.ru/2003/no_06/6_SF_5.htm (accessed November 11, 2009).

Hale, H. (2005a) *Why Not Parties in Russia? Democracy, Federalism, and the State*. New York: Cambridge University Press.

Hale, H. (2005b) "Why not parties? Supply and demand on Russia's electoral market." *Comparative Politics*, 37(2), January, pp. 147–66.

Hale, H. (2011a) "Hybrid regimes: When democracy and autocracy mix," in N. Brown (ed.), *Dynamics of Democratization: Dictatorship, Development, and Diffusion*. Baltimore: Johns Hopkins University Press.

Hale, H. (2011b) "The Putin Machine Sputters: First impressions of the 2011 Duma Election Campaign." *Russian Analytical Digest*, 21 December 2011. http://www.scribd.com/doc/94428007/ Russian-Analytical-Digest-106#outer_page_2 (accessed April 5, 2020).

Hale, H. and Colton, T. (2017) "Who defects? Unpacking a defection cascade from Russia's dominant party, 2008–12." *American Political Science Review*, 111(2), pp. 1–16.

Harper, J. (2018) "Do sanctions against Russia work?" *Deutsche Welle*. https://www.dw.com/en/do-sanctions-against-russia-work/a-46407184 (accessed April 5, 2020).

Haslam, S. A. and Reicher, S. D. (2007) "Beyond the banality of evil: The dynamics of an interactionist social psychology of tyranny." *Personality and Social Psychology Bulletin*, 33(5), pp. 615–22.

Hewett, E. A. (1988) *Reforming the Soviet Economy*. Washington, DC: Brookings Institution.

Hopkirk, P. (1992) *The Great Game: The Struggle for Empire in Central Asia*. New York: Kodansha America.

Hosking, G. A. (1992) *The First Socialist Society: A History of the Soviet Union from Within*, 2nd edn. Boston: Harvard University Press.

Hughes, J. (1996) "Moscow's bilateral treaties add to confusion." *Transition*, September, 19, pp. 39–43.

Hughes, L. (2004) *Peter the Great: A Biography*. New Haven: Yale University Press.

IMF (2020) *IMF Data*. https://www.imf.org/en/Data (accessed April 5, 2020).

Imse, A. (1990) "Soviets' one and only is Gorbachev." *The State*, March 15.

Isaev, B. A. (2008) *Teoriya Partij I P Artijjnykh System*. Moscow: Aspect Press.

Isaev, B. and Baranov, N. (2009) *Politicheskie otnoshenija I politicheskij process v sovermennoj Rossii*. St Petersburg: Piter.

Isaykin, A. (2009) "Russia sold arms in 2008 worth $6.7 billion," April 10. www.newsru.com (accessed November 11, 2009).

Ivanov, V. (2009) *Edinaja Rossiya* (United Russia). Moscow: Evropa.

Jamal, Umair (2016). "Russia wants to de-hyphenate India and Pakistan: Should Delhi worry?" *The Diplomat*, September 27. http://thediplomat.com/2016/09/russia-wants-to-de-hyphenateindia-and-pakistan-should-delhi-worry/ (accessed June 3, 2019).

Johnson, L. and White, S. (2012) "Introduction," in L. Johnson and S. White (eds), *Waiting for Reform Under Putin and Medvedev*. New York: Palgrave Macmillan.

Judicial Department at the Supreme Court of the Russian Federation (2019) Judicial Statistics for 2018. Online at: http://www.cdep.ru/index.php?id=79&item=4894 (accessed April 5, 2020).

Just Russia (2012) Electoral manifesto. http://www.spravedlivo.ru/information/section_11/manifest2011/ (accessed March 21, 2020)

Just Russia (2016) A just Russia's program. http://31.44.80.183/files/pf59/075833.pdf (accessed April 5, 2020).

Karatsuba, I. V., Kurukin, I. V., and Sokolov, N. P. (2006) *Vybiraya Svoyu Istoriyu. Razvilki na Puti Rossii* (Choosing Its Own History: Forks in Russia's Road). Moscow: Colibri.

Kashin, O. (2015) "How the hallucinations of an eccentric KGB psychic influence Russia today." *The Guardian*. https://www.theguardian.com/world/2015/jul/15/russia-kgb-psychic-oleg-kashin (accessed April 5, 2020).

Kasparov, G. (2012) Brown glimmering of the Olympic flame. http://www.kasparov.ru/material.php?id=501AB7755FD7F

Kasyanov, M. (2017) Presentation at the Stockholm School of Economics. https://www.hhs.se/en/about-us/news/site-publications/2017/mikhail-kasyanov-on-the-political-situation-in-russia/ (accessed April 5, 2020).

Katz, M. (1991) *The USSR and Marxist Revolutions in the Third World*. New York: Cambridge University Press.

Katz, M. (2009) "Afghanistan: Russia genuinely concerned that America is losing it." *Eurasianet*, September 24. http://www.eurasianet.org/departments/insightb/articles/eav092409a.shtml (accessed June 11, 2020).

Kenez, P. (2006) *A History of the Soviet Union from the Beginning to the End*. New York: Cambridge University Press.

Khasbulatov, R. I. (2004) *Velikaya Rossiyskaya Tragediya* (The Great Russian Tragedy). Moscow: Al-Kods.

Khasbulatov, R. (2008) "Interview October 6." Radio Station Ekho Moskvy. http://www.echo.msk.ru/programs/svoi-glaza/544670-echo (accessed November 11, 2009).

Khoury, Jack (2018). "In Moscow, Hamas Officials Say Russia Promised to Oppose U.S. Peace Plan." *Haaretz*. https://www.haaretz.com/middle-east-news/palestinians/.premium-hamas-officials-rus-sia-promised-to-oppose-u-s-peace-plan-1.6213186 (accessed August 12, 2019).

Khudoley K. (2016). "The Baltic Sea Region and Increasing International Tension." *Baltic Region*, 8(1), pp. 4–16.

Khudoley, K. (2017) "The evolution of the idea of World Revolution in Soviet politics (The epoch of the Comintern and Socialism in one country)." *Vestnik SPbSU. Political Science. International Relations*, 10(2), pp. 145–65.

Kolesnichenko, A. (2011) "The Twilight of Zhirinovsky." December 2. *Transitions Online*. http://www.tol.org/client/article/22872-zhirinovsky-politics-russia-nationalism.html

Komissarov, V. S. (ed.) (2005) *Rossijskoe Ugolovnoe Pravo* (Russian Criminal Law). St Petersburg: Piter.

Korotich, V. (2000) *Ot Pervogo Litsa* (From the First Person). Kharkov: Folio.

Kort, M. (2006) *The Soviet Colossus: History and Aftermath*. New York: M.E. Sharpe.

Korzhakov, A. (1997) *Boris Yeltsin of Rassveta do Zakata* (Boris Yeltsin from Dawn to Dusk). Moscow: Intebook.

Kotkin, S. (2008) *Armageddon Averted: The Soviet Collapse, 1970–2000*. New York: Oxford University Press.

Kotz, D. (1997) *Revolution from Above: The Demise of the Soviet System*. New York: Routledge.

Kozlova, N. (2009) "Dolgi po nasledstvy" (Inherited debts), *Rossiyskaya Gazeta*. #4884, Federal Issue, April 9. http://www.rg.ru/2009/04/08/precedent.html (accessed November 11, 2009).

Kozyrev, V. (2018) "Looking at the EU from the Russian and Chinese perspectives," in S. Bianchini and A. Fiori (eds), *Shifting Boundaries in a Global World. Russia and China at the Crossroads Between Regional and International Projections*. Leiden: Koninklijke Brill NV.

Krivosheev, G. F. (2001) "Rossiya I SSSR v Voynah 20 Veka" (Russia and the USSR in 20th-century wars). http://www.soldat.ru/doc/casualties/book/ (accessed November 11, 2009).

Krivova, O. (2019) "Neobyavlennaja epidemija: V Rossii rastet chislo nositelej VICh" (An undeclared epidemic: The number of people with HIV grows). *Gazeta.ru*. https://www.gazeta.ru/social/2019/07/03/12473089.shtml (accessed April 5, 2020).

Krylova, N. E. (2000) *Ugolovnoe Pravo* (Criminal Law). Moscow: Vuzlib.

Kuchins, A. (2007) "Alternative futures for Russia to 2017." Report of the Russia and Eurasia Program Center for Strategic and International Studies. http://www.csis.org/files/media/csis/pubs/071210-russia_2017-web.pdf (accessed November 11, 2009).

Kuchins, A. (2012a) "Vladimir Putin's return as Russian President." *CSIS Publications* May 4. http://csis.org/publication/vladimir-putins-return-russian-president

Kuchins, A. (2012b, 04/16) "Russia drifts eastward?" *CSIS Publications*. http://csis.org/publication/russia-drifts-eastward (accessed April 5, 2020).

Kuchins, A. (2012c) "The end of the 'Reset': why Putin's re-election means turbulence ahead." *Foreign Affairs*, March 1. http://www.foreignaffairs.com/print/134566 (accessed April 5, 2020).

Kukushkin, Y. (ed.) (1996) "Highest Manifesto, 29 April 1881," in *Russian State: Power and Society, Selection of Documents*. Moscow: Moscow State University.

Kulikov, V. (2008) "Insurance without a name." *Rossiyskaya Gazeta*, Federal Issue, # 4638, April 15. http://www.supcourt.ru/news_detale.php?id=5281 (accessed November 11, 2009).

Lankina, T. (2004) *Governing the Locals: Local Self-Government and Ethnic Mobilization in Russia*. Lanham: Rowman & Littlefield.

Lanko, Dmitry A. (2013). "The Regional Approach in the Policy of the Russian Federation towards the Republic of Estonia." *Baltic Region*, 5(3, 17), pp. 37–45. doi: 10.5922/2079-8555-2013-3-4.

Latukhina (2019) "A Law is signed to draft 132 thousand." *Rossyjskaja Gazeta*, January 10. https://rg.ru/2019/10/01/podpisan-ukaz-o-prizyve-132-tysiach-chelovek.html (accessed October 11, 2019).

Lavrov, S. (2011) Foreign Minister Answers Questions on Three Radio Stations. October 21. http://echo.msk.ru/programs/beseda/819444-echo/ (accessed April 5, 2020).

Laruelle, M. (2019). *Russian Nationalism: Imaginaries, Doctrines, and Political Battlefields*. New York: Routledge.

LDPR Program (2020) https://ldpr.ru/party (accessed April 5, 2020).

Lebed, A. (1996) Press Conference. Moscow, May 13.

Lebedev, V. (2008) "Chair of the Supreme Court of the Russian Federation: An interview," *Rossiyskaya Gazeta,* 4803, Federal Issue, December 2. http://www.supcourt.ru/news (accessed November 11, 2009).

Ledeneva, A. (2006) *How Russia Really Works: The Informal Practices That Shaped Post-Soviet Politics and Business.* Ithaca: Cornell University Press.

Leffler, M. (2007) *For the Soul of Mankind: The United States, the Soviet Union, and the Cold War.* New York: Hill & Wang.

Legvold, R. (ed.) (2007) *Russian Foreign Policy in the 21st Century and the Shadow of the Past.* New York: Columbia University Press.

Legvold, R. (2009) "The Russia file: How to move toward a strategic partnership." *Foreign Affairs,* July/August, pp. 78–93.

Lenin, V. (1916/1969) *Imperialism, the Highest Stage of Capitalism.* Moscow: International Publishing.

Lenin, V. (1917/2006) *The State and Revolution.* Moscow: Kissinger Publishing.

Lenta (2007a) "Medvedev offered Putin the premiership post." December 11. www.renta.ru (accessed November 11, 2009).

Lenta (2007b) "Kasparov announced the end of his presidential run." December 12. www.renta.ru (accessed November 11, 2009).

Levada (2007a) Poll of 21–27 September. http://www.levada.ru

Levada (2007b) "Survey on Russia's electoral attitudes." http://www.levada.ru/press/2007091305.html

Levada (2008a) Poll of May 5. http://www.levada.ru

Levada (2008b) Poll of August 18. http://www.levada.ru

Levada (2008c) Poll of December 24. http://www.levada.ru

Levada (2008d) Poll of September 8. http://www.levada.ru

Levada (2008e) Poll of November 20. http://www.levada.ru

Levada (2008f) Poll of September 9. http://www.levada.ru

Levada (2008g) "Survey on Russian higher education." http://www.rambler.ru/news/science/statistics/565896127.html

Levada (2008h) Poll of October 20. http://www.levada.ru

Levada (2009a) Poll of March 25. http://www.levada.ru

Levada (2009b) Poll of May 6. http://www.levada.ru

Levada (2009c) Poll of February 27. http://www.levada.ru

Levada (2009d) Poll of June 26. http://www.levada.ru

Levada (2009e) Poll of February 18. http://www.levada.ru

Levada (2009f) Poll of January 27. http://www.levada.ru

Levada (2009g) Poll of July 22. http://www.levada.ru

Levada (2009h) Poll of March 20–23. http://www.levada.ru

Levada (2009i) Poll of April 27–29. http://www.levada.ru

Levada (2009j) Poll of February 11. http://www.levada.ru

Levada (2009k) Poll of February 25. http://www.levada.ru

Levada (2009l) Poll of April 1. http://www.levada.ru

Levada (2009m) Poll of March 5. http://www.levada.ru

Levada (2009n) Poll of January 27. http://www.levada.ru

Levada (2009o) Poll of March 30. http://www.levada.ru

Levada (2009p) Poll of August 11. http://www.levada.ru

Levada (2011a) Annual Report. Public Opinion 2011. http://www.levada.ru/books/obshchestvennoe-mnenie-2011

Levada (2011b) Poll of February 11–14. http://www.levada.ru

Levada (2011c) Poll of March 18–21. http://www.levada.ru

Levada (2011d) Poll of October 3–19. http://www.levada.ru

Levada (2011e) Poll of November 25–28. http://www.levada.ru

Levada (2012a) Poll of January 20–23. http://www.levada.ru

Levada (2012b) Poll of February 24–27. http://www.levada.ru

Levada (2012c) Poll of March 16–19. http://www.levada.ru

Levada (2012d) Poll of April 20–23. http://www.levada.ru

Levada (2012e) Poll of May 25–29. http://www.levada.ru

Levada (2014) Poll of 24–29 September. https://www.levada.ru/2014/10/14/internet-tsenzura/ (accessed April 5, 2020).

Levada (2015) Poll of March 27–30. http://www.levada.ru (accessed March 31, 2018).

Levada (2016) Poll of March 25–28 https://www.levada.ru/2016/04/19/raspad-sssr/ (accessed April 5, 2020).

Levada (2017a) "Views of Lenin." https://www.levada.ru/2017/04/19/vladimir-lenin/ (accessed June 12, 2019).

Levada (2017b) "Views of the Putsch of October 3-4, 1993". https://www.levada.ru/2017/10/03/sobytiya-3-4-oktyabrya-1993-goda-v-moskve/ (accessed April 5, 2020).

Levada (2018a) "Russia's enemies." https://www.levada.ru/2018/01/10/vragi-rossii/ (accessed June 12, 2019).

Levada (2018b) "Everybody has lost: Russian didn't value the putsch." https://www.levada.ru/2018/08/14/proigrali-vse-rossiyane-ne-otsenili-putch/

Levada (2018c) "On United Russia." https://www.levada.ru/2018/12/04/edinaya-rossiya/ (accessed June 12, 2019). (accessed April 5, 2020).

Levada (2018d) Poll of October 18. https://www.levada.ru/2018/01/10/vragi-rossii/ (accessed April 5, 2020).

Levada (2018e). Poll of July 18. https://www.levada.ru/2018/08/02/rossiya-i-zapad-3/ (accessed August 12, 2019).

Levada (2018f). Poll 19–23 January. https://www.levada.ru/2018/02/12/otnoshenie-k-stranam/ (accessed August 15, 2019).

Levada (2019a) "On approval of the institutions of power." https://www.levada.ru/2019/05/31/odo-brenie-institutov-vlasti-13/ (accessed June 12, 2019). (accessed April 5, 2020).

Levada (2019b) "Views of Stalin." https://www.levada.ru/2019/04/16/uroven-odobreniya-stalina-rossiyanami-pobil-istoricheskij-rekord (accessed June 17, 2019). (accessed April 5, 2020).

Levada (2019c) "Hostility toward Ukraine and Russia has sharply gone down." https://www.levada.ru/2019/06/14/vrazhdebnost-rossiyan-k-ukraine-i-ssha-rezko-snizilas/ (accessed April 5, 2020).

Levada (2019d) "On pensions reform." https://www.levada.ru/2018/09/27/pensionnaya-reforma-4/ (accessed April 5, 2020).

Levada (2019e) "On living conditions." https://www.levada.ru/2019/08/19/zhilishhnye-problemy/ (accessed April 5, 2020).

Levchenko, A. (2007) "Vybor protiv vseh" (Elections against everybody). http://gazeta.ru/politics/elections2007/info/s2366166.shtml (accessed November 11, 2009).

Levesque, J. (1997) *The Enigma of 1989: The USSR and the Liberation of Eastern Europe*. Berkeley: University of California Press.

Levinson, A. (2008a) "An interview," *Novaia Gazeta*, 23, April 3, pp. 8, 9.

Levinson, A. (2008b) "An interview," *Novaia Gazeta*, 40, June 5, pp. 12, 13.

Levy, D. (1997) *Tools of Critical Thinking*. Boston: Allyn & Bacon.

Liberal Democratic Party of Russia (LDPR) (2009) Party program. http://www.ldpr.ru/partiya/prog/ (accessed November 11, 2009).

Ligachev, Y. (1996) *Inside Gorbachev's Kremlin*. Boulder: Westview Press.

Lipman, M. (2008) "Putin's puppet press." *Washington Post,* May 20, p. A13.

Lukov, V. (2009) "Russian institutions of higher education through students' eyes." *Zhanie, Poinmanie, Umenie,* 3, http://www.zpu-journal.ru/e-zpu/2009/3/lukov/ (accessed November 11, 2009).

Lukyanov, Fyodor (2016). "Putin's Foreign Policy." *Foreign Affairs,* May/June. https://www.foreignaffairs.com/articles/russia-fsu/2016–04-18/putins-foreign-policy (accessed June 3, 2017).

MacFarquhar, N. (2016) "A powerful Russian weapon: The spread of false stories." *The New York Times*, August 28. https://www.nytimes.com/2016/08/29/world/europe/russia-sweden-disinformation. html (accessed April 5, 2020).

MacMillan, M. (2013) *The War That Ended Peace: The Road to 1914*. New York: Random House.

Manikhin, O. (2003) "Vozniknovenie Yabloka" (Yabloko's Creation). http://www.yablokosu/ Elections/2003/History_Yabloko (accessed November 11, 2009).

Massicot, D. (2019) "Anticipating a new Russian military doctrine in 2020: What it might contain and why it matters." *War on the Rocks*. September 9. https://warontherocks.com/2019/09/anticipating-a-new-russian-military-doctrine-in-2020-what-it-might-contain-and-why-it-matters/ (accessed April 5, 2020).

Materialy Politburo (1990) *Moscow: A Special Publication,* March 12. Moscow: Materialy Politburo.

Matlock, J. (2005) *Reagan and Gorbachev: How the Cold War Ended*. New York: Random House.

McFaul, M. (1997) *Russia's 1996 Presidential Election: The End of Polarized Politics*. Stanford: Hoover Press.

McFaul, M. (2019) *From Cold War to Hot Peace: An American Ambassador in Putin's Russia*. New York: Mariner Books.

McFaul, M. and Stoner-Weiss, K. (2008) "The myth of the authoritarian model: How Putin's crackdown holds Russia back." *Foreign Affairs,* January/February, pp. 68–84.

McGlinchey, E. (2009) "Central Asian Protest Movements," in A. Wooden and C. Stefes (eds), *Tempting Two Fates in Central Asia and the Caucasus? The Political Legacies and Emerging Policy Challenges of Transition*. New York: Routledge.

McGlinchey, E. (2016) *Chaos, Violence and Dynasty: Patronage Politics in Central Asia*. Pittsburgh: University of Pittsburgh Press.

Medvedev, V. (1994) *V Komande Gorbacheva* (In Gorbachev's Team). Moscow: Bylina.

Medvedev, D. (2009a) "An interview with NTV." July 26. www.Interfax.ru http://www.newsru.com/ russia/26jul2009/tv.html (accessed November 11, 2009).

Medvedev, D. (2009b) "An interview with Novaya Gazeta." April 15. http://en.novayagazeta.ru/ data/2009/039/00.html (accessed November 11, 2009).

Medvedev, D. (2012) "A comment on the results of the December elections." http://lenta.ru/ news/2011/12/05/roliki/_Printed.htm

Mikulski, K. I. (ed.) (1995) *Elita Rossii o Nastoyashem I Budushem Strany* (The Russian Elite on the Country's Present and Future). Moscow: Vekhi.

Military Doctrine of the Russian Federation (2014, December 25) "Approved by the President of the Russian Federation No. Pr.-2976." https://rusemb.org.uk/press/2029 (accessed April 5, 2020).

Ministry of Enlightenment of the Russian Federation (2019) Official site. https://edu.gov.ru/

Ministry of Finance of the Russian Federation (2020) Official site. https://www.minfin.ru/en/key/ nationalwealthfund/ (accessed April 5, 2020).

Ministry of Internal Affairs of the Russian Federation (2020) "Official site." https://tj.sputniknews. ru/migration/20200128/1030620871/Russia-kolichestvo-migranty.html (accessed April 5, 2020).

Ministry of the Interior of the Russian Federation (2009) "Structure of the Ministry of the Interior." http://www.mvd.ru/struct/3297/3353/ (accessed November 11, 2009).

Minjust (2020) "Russian Ministry of Justice list of prohibited parties and organizations." https:// minjust.ru/nko/perechen_zapret (accessed April 5, 2020).

Mironov, S. (2009a) "Interview with Interfax." July 26. http://www.newsru.com/russia/26jul2009/ nasel.html (accessed November 11, 2009).

Mironov, S. (2009b) "Speech during the 4th Congress of the Just Russia Party." Moscow, June 25. http://www.mironov.ru/firstface/speeches/333.html (accessed November 11, 2009).

Mitofsky, W. J. (1996) "Exit polling on the Russian elections." *Public Perspective,* August–September, pp. 41–4.

Moon, D. (2002) *The Abolition of Serfdom in Russia*. Harlow/New York: Routledge

Morozov, A. (2004) *Diplomatia Putina* (Putin's Diplomacy). St Petersburg: Izmailovsky Publishing.

Moscow Times (2019) "Life Expectancy in Russia Inches Upward to 73 – Health Ministry Official." https://www.themoscowtimes.com/2019/03/21/life-expectancy-in-russia-inches-upward-to-73-health-ministry-official-a64906 (accessed April 5, 2020).

Mueller, R. (2019) "Report on the investigation into Russian interference in the 2016 Presidential Election." https://www.justice.gov/storage/report.pdf (accessed April 5, 2020).

Murray, Charles (2013). *American Exceptionalism: An Experiment in History (Values and Capitalism)*. Washington, DC: AEI Press.

Mukherjee, Pranab (2015). "Russia is a dependable partner of India." http://www.news18.com/news/india/pranab-mukherjee-3–989368.html (accessed June 3, 2019).

Myers, S. L. (2016) *The New Tsar: The Rise and Reign of Vladimir Putin*. New York: Vintage

National Projects (2009) "Presidents' council on the implementation of priority national projects and demographic policy." http://www.rost.ru/main/what/01/01.shtml (accessed November 11, 2009).

Naumkin, Vitaly (2014). Russia, Egypt draw closer. Al Monitor, August 13. http://www.al-monitor.com/pulse/originals/2014/08/russia-egypt-putin-sisi-visit-ukraine-palestine.html (accessed June 3, 2020).

Nechepurenko, I. (2019) "Moscow police arrest more than 1,300 at election protest." *The New York Times*, July 29. https://nyti.ms/347wYFs (accessed September 2, 2019)

Nemtsov, B. (2008) An interview. *Ekho Moskvy Radio*," August 3, http://www.echo.msk.ru/programs/albac/531344-echo.phtml (accessed November 11, 2009).

Nesterova, Y. (2016) "What does it mean to be conservative in Russia?" *The National Interest*, August 10. https://bit.ly/2wfy2YM (accessed July 10, 2019).

Nikiforov, I. (1995) *The World Factbook of Criminal Justice Systems under Grant No. 90-BJ-CX-0002 from the Bureau of Justice Statistics to the State University of New York at Albany*.

Nikolaeva, A. (2019) "An optimization: Or a step forward? Komsomolskaya Pravda." https://www.kp.ru/daily/26952/4005124/ (accessed April 5, 2020).

Nikonov, V. (2003) *Konstitutsionnyj Dizajn*. Moscow: Sovrem'ennaja Rossijskaja Politika.

Novaya Politika (New Politics) (2009) "V Pensionnoi Sisteme Voznikayut Novye Problemy" (There are new problems appearing in the pension system: a review of the press). *News review*, April 20. http://www.novopol.ru/text66277.html (accessed November 11, 2009).

Nwosu, C. (2015). "What Happened to the BRICS?" *Foreign Policy in Focus*, July 31. https://fpif.org/what-happened-to-the-brics/ (accessed June 30, 2018).

Oates, S. (2017). *Meme Tracking: A New Way of Detecting and Tracking the Influence of Post-Soviet Propaganda*. Discussion paper prepared for the DC Area Postcommunist Politics Social Science Workshop, January 19.

Odelburg, S. S. (1949/1991) *Tsarstvovanie Imperatora Nikolaya II* (The Reign of the Emperor Nicolas II). St Petersburg: Petropol.

Odom, W. E. (1990) "The Soviet Military in transition," *Problems of Communism,* May–June.

Orlov, P. (2009) "The General Staff reports about a new military doctrine." *Rossiyskaya Gazeta,* no. 4971, August 11.

Orlov, A. S., Georgiev, V. A., Georgieva, N. G. and Sivokhina, T. A. (2008) *Istoriya Rossii* (A History of Russia). Moscow: Prospect.

OSCE (2019) *On Ongoing Human Rights Abuses and Violations in Chechnya*. https://osce.usmission.gov/on-ongoing-human-rights-abuses-and-violations-in-chechnya/ (accessed October 22, 2019)

Ostroukh, A. (2016) "Number of Russians living in poverty rises." *The Wall Street Journal*. March 21. https://www.wsj.com/articles/number-of-russians-living-in-poverty-rises-1458581478 (accessed April 5, 2020).

Pain, E. (2012) "Socio-cultural factors and Russian modernization," in L. Johnson and S. White (eds), *Waiting for Reform Under Putin and Medvedev*. New York: Palgrave Macmillan.

Palazhchenko, P. (1997) *My Years with Gorbachev and Shevardnadze: The Memoir of a Soviet Interpreter*. University Park: Pennsylvania State University Press

Panyushkin, V. (2006) *Mikhail Khodorkovksy. Uznik Tishiny* (Mikhail Khodorkovksy: A Prisoner of Silence). Moscow: Secret Firmy.

Parnas (2017) Party's Program https://parnasparty.ru/news/353 (accessed April 5, 2020).

Patrushev, N. (2007) "An interview." *Argumenty i Facty*, 41(1406), October 10. http://www.fsb.ru/fsb/comment/rukov/ (accessed November 11, 2009).

Pearson, D. E. (1987) *KAL 007: The Cover-up*. New York: Summit Books.

Petrov, N. and Kokurin, A. (2003) *Lubyanka: 1917–1991*. Moscow: Democracy International Foundation.

Pipes, R. (1984) *Survival Is Not Enough*. New York: Simon and Schuster.

Pipes, R. (2007) "An interview." *Chayka*, 4(87), February 15. http://www.chayka.org/article.php?id=1451 (accessed November 11, 2009).

Pipiya, K. (2019) "My i geneticheski modificirovannye cennosti" (Us and genetically modified values). https://www.levada.ru/2019/05/27/my-i-geneticheski-modifitsirovannye-tsennosti/ (accessed August 22, 2019)

Platonov, S. F. (1937/2009) *Ocherki po istoruii Smutnogo Vremeni* (Essays on the History of the Time of Troubles). Moscow: AST.

Politkovskaya, A. (2008) *Putin's Russia: Life in a Failing Democracy*. New York: Holt.

Ponomareva, Y. (2012) "Shutting down 'slanderers'." *The Moscow News*, 16 July. http://themoscownews.com/politics/20120716/ (accessed April 5, 2020).

Popova, O. V. (2004). "Conservative Values in Russian People's Stereotypes of Politics, Consciousness and Behavior." http://anthropology.ru/ru/person/popova-ov. (accessed June 23, 2019).

Press Freedom Index (2019) https://rsf.org/en/ranking (accessed April 5, 2020).

Prokhorov, M. (2012) "Electoral program." http://mdp2012.ru/points/ (accessed April 5, 2020).

Prokofiev, D. (2019) "Strana Nizov, Strana Gospod" (The country of lower classes, the country of masters). *Novaya Gazeta*. October 24. https://www.novayagazeta.ru/articles/2019/10/23/82472-strana-nizov-strana-gospod (accessed April 5, 2020).

Prokopenko, A. (2019) "Russia's sovereign internet law will destroy innovation." *The Moscow Times*, April 21. https://www.themoscowtimes.com/2019/04/21/russias-sovereign-internet-law-will-destroy-innovation-a65317 (accessed April 5, 2020).

Pulipaka, Sanjay (2016). "Russia's new approach to Pakistan: All about arms sales." *The Diplomat*. http://thediplomat.com/2016/09/russias-new-approach-to-pakistan-all-about-arms-sales/ (accessed June 3, 2019).

Putin, V. (2009a) "Comments during the meeting with the WHO director." June 26. www.newsru.com (accessed November 11, 2009).

Putin, V. (2009b) "Speech in Davos, Switzerland." January 29. http://www.vesti.ru/doc.html?id=246949 (accessed November 11, 2009).

Putin, V. (2012a) "Speech before the State Duma." April 11. http://www.rg.ru/2012/04/11/putin-otchet.html

Putin, V. (2012b) "Rossiya I Menjayushisja Mir (Russia and a Changing World)." *Moscow News*, February 27. http://mn.ru/politics/20120227/312306749.html

Putin, V. (2012c, February 20) *Byt Silnymi: Garantii nacional'noj bezopasnosti Rissii* (To Be Strong: Guarantees for Russia's National Security). http://www.rg.ru/2012/02/20/putin-armiya.html (accessed April 5, 2020).

Putin, V. (2012d) "A meeting with managers and editors of television, radio, and print media." January 18, 2012. http://premier.gov.ru/events/news/17798/ (accessed April 5, 2020).

Putin, V. (2012e) "Speech before the meeting of Russia's ambassadors." July 9. http://kremlin.ru/transcripts/15902 (accessed April 5, 2020).

Putin, V. (2012f) "Speech on the International Economic Forum." St Petersburg. http://kremlin.ru/news/15709 (accessed April 5, 2020).

Putin, V. (2013) "A Plea for Caution from Russia." *New York Times*, September 11. https://nyti.ms/2OK3yEh (accessed August 15, 2019).

Putin, V. (2014) "Russia Does Not Want to Isolate Itself," *Comments Made to the Discussion Club Valdai*. http://tass.ru/politika/1531106 (accessed July 16, 2020).

Putin, V. (2019a) "An interview to the Financial Times." June 27. http://kremlin.ru/events/president/news/60836 (accessed April 5, 2020).

Putin, V. (2019b) "Vladimir Putin spoke at the final plenary session of the 16th meeting of the Valdai International Discussion Club." *A Transcript*, October 3. http://en.kremlin.ru/events/president/transcripts/61719 (accessed April 5, 2020).

Putin, V. (2020a) "Speech at Duma's Plenary Session." March 10. http://en.kremlin.ru/events/president/news/62964 (accessed April 5, 2020).

Putin, V. (2020b) "Twenty questions with Vladimir Putin." A series of interviews. https://www.youtube.com/playlist?list=PL4EIaB8TYHQUGvqdsHgF5H-wkaSQCWe4p (accessed April 5, 2020).

Putin, V. (2020c) "The Real Lessons of the 75th Anniversary of World War II." *National Interest*. https://bit.ly/2ZgBrnl (accessed June 23, 2020)

Rabinovich, Itmar (2016) "The Russia-US relations in the Middle East: A five-year projection." *Carnegie Endowment for International Peace*. http://carnegieendowment.org/2016/04/05/russian-u.s.-relationship-in-middle-east-five-year-projection-pub-63243 (accessed June 3, 2020).

Raikov, G. (2008) "An interview." *RIA Novosti*, February 19.

Rainsford, S. (2019) "Moscow protests: Students fighting for democracy in Russia." *BBC News*, 30 August. https://www.bbc.com/news/world-europe-49446736 (accessed April 5, 2020).

Raspolov, A. (2019) "A fighter of an invisible front." *Nezavisimaya Gazeta*, September 13. https://www.novayagazeta.ru/articles/2019/09/13/81954-biets-nevidimogo-fronta (accessed April 5, 2020).

Remington, T. (2001) *The Russian Parliament: Institutional Evolution in a Transitional Regime, 1989–1999*. New Haven: Yale University Press.

Reporters Without Borders (2011/2012) Press freedom Index. http://en.rsf.org/press-freedom-index-2011-2012,1043.html (accessed March 31, 2020).

RFE/RL (2020) "Russian scholars, legal experts sign up against 'constitutional coup'." March 16. Radio Liberty, Radio Free Europe. https://www.rferl.org/a/russian-scholars-legal-experts-sign-up-against-constitutional-coup-/30490881.html (accessed April 5, 2020).

RG (2017) "President has increased the personnel of the armed forces." *Rossiyskaja Gazeta*, March 29. https://rg.ru/2017/03/29/prezident-uvelichil-shtatnuiu-chislennost-vooruzhennyh-sil-rf.html (accessed April 5, 2020).

RIA Novosti (2000) Statistics on average pensions in Russia. https://ria.ru/20200304/1568153929.html (accessed April 5, 2020).

Rivera, D. W. and Rivera, S. W. (2009) "Yeltsin, Putin, and Clinton: Presidential leadership and Russian democratization in comparative perspective." *Perspectives on Politics*, 7, 3, September, pp. 591–610.

RNS (Russian news services) (2009) http://bratishka.ru/index.php?id=618 (accessed November 11, 2009).

Rodionov, A. (2007) *Nalogovye Shemy, za Kotorye Posadili Hodorkovskogo* (Tax Scams for which Khodorkovsky was Busted). Moscow: Vershina.

Rosenfielde, Steven (2016) *The Kremlin Strikes Back: Russia and the West after Crimea's Annexation*. New York: Cambridge University Press.

Rosgvardia (2020) Federal National Guard Troops Service of the Russian Federation. Official website: http://www.rosgvard.ru/ (accessed April 5, 2020).

Rosstat (2017) Russian Federation State Statistics Service. http://www.gks.ru/wps/wcm/connect/rosstat_main/rosstat/en/main/ (accessed June 3, 2019). (accessed April 5, 2020).

Rosstat (2019) "Population statistics." https://showdata.gks.ru/report/278928/ (accessed October 22, 2019).

Rostow, W. (1967) *The Dynamics of Soviet Society*. New York: W. W. Norton.

Roxburgh, A. (2012a) *The Strongman*. New York: I. B. Tauris.

Roxburgh, A. (2012b) "How the Anti-Putin Movement missed the point." *Foreign Affairs*, March 14. http://www.foreignaffairs.com/features/letters-from/how-the-anti-putin-movement-missed-the-point

Ruble, B. (1990) *Leningrad: Shaping a Soviet City*. Berkeley: University of California Press.

Sabennikova, I. V. (2002) *Rossiyskaya Emigraciya (1917–1939)* (Russian Emigration, 1917–1939). Tver: Federal Archive Service.

Sadri, Houman A. (2014) "Eurasian Economic Union (Eeu): A Good Idea or a Russian Takeover?" *Rivista di Studi Politici Internazionali*, Vol. 81, No. 4 (324) (OTTOBRE-DICEMBRE), pp. 553–561.

Sakwa, R. (1993) *Russian Politics and Society*. London: Routledge.

Sakwa, R. (1999) *The Rise and Fall of the Soviet Union: 1917–1991*. New York: Routledge.

Sanford, G. (2009) *Katyn and the Soviet Massacre of 1940: Truth, Justice, and Memory*. New York: Routledge.

Sestanovich, S. (2020) "The day after Putin." *Foreign Affairs*, March 4. https://www.foreignaffairs.com/articles/russia-fsu/2020-03-04/day-after-putin (accessed April 5, 2020).

Shakhnazarov, G. (1997) "Transcript of a presentation: 'Piat Let Posle Belovezhia.'" (Five years after the Belovezh Agreement). Moscow: April 85, pp. 10–20.

Shakkum, M. (2006) "Koncepcii Promyshlennoi Politiki u Pravitelstva Net" (The government does have a theory of industrial politics). *RF Today*. http://www.russia-today.ru/2006/no_01/01_topic_1.htm (accessed November 11, 2009).

Shamaev, A. V. (2018) "Syd Prisjazhnyh v Rossii: Osnovnye Napravlenija Razvitija." (Jury trials in Russia: Main directions of development). *Molodoj Uchenyj*, 50, pp. 288–90. https://moluch.ru/archive/236/54875/ (accessed April 5, 2020).

Sharma, Rajeev (2012) "Kudankulam and more: Why Putin's India visit was a hit." *Firstpost*. http://www.firstpost.com/world/kudankulam-and-more-why-putins-india-visit-was-ahit-568504.html (accessed June 3, 2019).

Sheehy, G. (1990) *The Man Who Changed the World*. New York: HarperCollins.

Shevtsova, L. (2005) *Putin's Russia*. Washington, DC: Carnegie Endowment for International Peace.

Shiraev, E. (1999a) "Attitudinal changes during the transition," pp. 155–66, in E. Shiraev and B. Glad (eds), *The Russian Transformation*. New York: St Martin's Press.

Shiraev, E. (1999b) "The new nomenclature and increasing income inequality," pp. 109–18, in E. Shiraev and B. Glad (eds), *The Russian Transformation*. New York: St Martin's Press.

Shiraev, E. (2008) "Sizing up Obama in Russia: The first encounter." *Harvard International Review*, December 19. http://hir.harvard.edu/index.php?page=article&id=1811 (accessed November 11, 2009).

Shiraev, E. (2019) "Looking forward.... Maybe": The 2016 United States' presidential elections from Russia's standpoint," in J. Velasco (ed.), *International Reactions to the 2016 Presidential Elections in the USA*. New York: Routledge.

Shiraev, E. and Bastrykin, A. (1988) *Moda, Kumiry, I Sobstevennoe Ya* (Fashion, Idols, and the Self). Leningrad: Lenizdat.

Shiraev, E. and Khudoley, K. (2019) *Russian Foreign Policy*. London: Macmillan.

Shiraev, E. and Zubok, V. (2000) *Anti-Americanism in Russia: From Stalin to Putin*. New York: Palgrave Macmillan.

Shiraev, E. and Zubok, V. (2020) 3/e. *International Relations*. New York: Oxford University Press.

Shlapentokh, V. (2009) "Putin is smarter than the Soviet leaders." November. http://shlapentokh.wordpress.com/ (accessed November 11, 2009).

Shlapentokh, V. (2014) "Putin's destruction of the common vocabulary with the West hurts the Russian-American relations." https://shlapentokh.wordpress.com/ (accessed March 31, 2018).

Shlapentokh, V. and Shiraev, E. (eds) (2002) *Fears in Post-Communist Societies: A Comparative Perspective*. New York: Palgrave Macmillan.

Shlapentokh, V. and Woods, J. (2007) *Contemporary Russia as a Feudal Society: A New Perspective on the Post-Soviet Era*. New York: Palgrave Macmillan.

Shlapentokh, V., Shiraev, E., and Carroll, E. (2008) *The Soviet Union: Internal and External Perspectives on Soviet Society*. New York: Palgrave Macmillan.

Shleifer, A. and Treisman, D. (2004) "A normal country." *Foreign Affairs*, March/April.

Shleifer, A. and Treisman, D. (2011) "Why Moscow says no." *Foreign Affairs*, January/February, pp. 122–38.

Shlykov, V. (2002) *Chto Pogubilo Sovetskij Soyuz: Generalnyi Shtab i Ekonomika* (What Brought Down the Soviet Union: The General Staff and the Economy). Moscow: MFIT.

Sigelman, L. and Shiraev, E. (2002) "The rational attacker in Russia? Negative campaigning in Russian presidential elections." *Journal of Politics*, 64, pp. 45–62.

Simanov, S. (2009) "Andropov: Seven Tajn Genseka s Lubjanki" (Seven secrets of the General Secretary from Luybyanka). http://libereya.ru/biblus/Andropov/Andropov.htm#t1 (accessed November 11, 2009).

Simes, D. (2007) "Losing Russia: The costs of renewed confrontation." *Foreign Affairs*, November/December, pp. 36–52.

Simes, D. (2009) "Coping with areas of US-Russian disagreement and conflicts of national interest." Paper for Designing U.S. Policy Toward Russia, Library of Congress Conference, March 27.

Skrynnik, E. (2012) Agriculture Minister's Report to the State Duma. February 8. http://bit.ly/SXBfzp

Skrynnikov, R. (2006a) *Russkaya istoriya IX–XVII vekov* (Russia's History from the 9th–17th Centuries). St Petersburg: SPSGU.

Skrynnikov, R. (2006b) *Ivan III*. Moscow: Tranzitkniga AST.

Slatinov, V. (2012) Comments on the first 100 days of president Putin. http://www.newsru.com/russia/13aug2012/putin100days.html

Smeltz, Dina, Daalder, Ivo, Friedhoff, Karl, and Craig Kafura (2016) *America in the Age of Uncertainty*. Chicago, IL: Chicago Council on Global Affairs.

Smeltz, Dina, Wojtowicz, Lily, Volkov, Denis, and Goncharov, Stepan (2018) "US-Russia Experts Paint a Dim Picture of Bilateral Relations before Summit" *Chicago Council on Global Affairs*. 12 July. https://www.thechicagocouncil.org/publication/us-russia-experts-paint-dim-picture-bilateral-relations-summit (accessed August 7, 2018).

Sobchak, A. (1992) *For a New Russia*. New York: Free Press.

Sobel, R., and Shiraev, E. (2003) *International Public Opinion and the Bosnia Crisis*. Lexington, MD: Rowman & Littlefield.

Sokolov, N. (2008) "Vek Surka Ili Kratkaya Istoriya Kolovrashenia Rossijskih Uchebnikov Istorii" (A groundhog century, or a brief history of the tribulations of Russian history textbooks). http://www.polit.ru/analytics/2008/10/15/history.html (accessed November 11, 2009).

Solonevich, I. L. (2005) *Narodnaya Monarkhiya* (People's Monarchy). Moscow: Rimis.

Solzhenitsyn, A. (1976) *Lenin in Zurich*. New York: Penguin.

State, The (1989) "Gorbachev reveals Soviet defense budget." *The State*, May 31.

Statistics of Russian Education (2020) http://stat.edu.ru/stat/vis.shtml

Stavrakis, P. J. (1996) "Russia after the elections: Democracy or parliamentary Byzantium?" *Problems of Post-Communism*, 43(2), pp. 13–20.

Stent, A. (2019) *Putin's World: Russia Against the West and with the Rest*. New York: Twelve.

Stephen, P. B. (1991) "Perestroika and property: The law of ownership in the post-Socialist Soviet Union." *American Journal of Comparative Law*, 39(Winter), pp. 35–65.

Stoner-Weiss, K. (2006a) *Resisting the State: Reform and Retrenchment in Post-Soviet Russia*. New York: Cambridge University Press.

Stoner-Weiss, K. (2006b) "When the wave hits a shoal: The internal and external dimensions of Russia's turn away from democracy." CDDRL Working Papers, May. http://cddrl.stanford.edu (accessed November 11, 2009).

Strategy 2020. A new model of growth—new social policy [Strategiya-2020: Novaya model rosta—novaja social'naja politika] http://2020strategy.ru/documents/32710234.html

Strategy of National Security (2015) [Strategiya Nacional'noj Bezopasnosti]. https://rg.ru/2015/12/31/nac-bezopasnost-site-dok.html (accessed April 5, 2020).

Strayer, R. (1998) *Why Did the Soviet Union Collapse? Understanding Historical Change*. New York: M.E. Sharpe.

Study in Russia (2020) Information of the Ministry of Higher Education. https://studyinrussia.ru/actual/articles/skolko-inostrannykh-studentov-v-rossii/ (accessed April 5, 2020).

Surkov, V. (2006) "Vladislav Surkov Razvel Demokratiju" (Vladislav Surkov compartmentalized democracy). *Kommersant*, June 29, 116(3447). http://www.kommersant.ru/doc.aspx?DocsID=686274 (accessed November 11, 2009).

Surkov, V. (2019) *"Dolgoe gosudarstvo Putina" (The long state of Putin)*. *Nezavisimaya Gazeta, February 11* (accessed April 5, 2020).

Talbott, Strobe (2003) *The Russia Hand*. New York: Random House.

TASS (2016b) *Levada Center: Russians Have Worsened Their Attitudes toward the USA, Turkey, and Ukraine, and No Longer Want to Join the EU*. June 2, http://tass.ru/obschestvo/3333320 (accessed March 31, 2019).

Taubman, P. (1987) "Gorbachev, citing party's failures, demands changes." *New York Times*, January 28.

Taubman, W. (2017) *Gorbachev: His Life and Times*. New York: Simon and Schuster.

Tetlock, P. (1989) "Psyching our Gorbachev; the man remains a mystery." *The Washington Post*, December 17. http://www.highbeam.com/publications/the-washington-post-p5554/dec-17-1989

Tetlock, P., Lebow, R. and Perker, G. (eds) (2006) *Unmaking the West. "What If?" Scenarios That Rewrite History*. Ann Arbor: University of Michigan Press.

Transparency International (2019) *Corruption Perception Index*. https://www.transparency.org/ (accessed April 5, 2020).

Treisman, D. (1996a) "Moscow's struggle to control regions through taxation." *Transition*, 19, September, pp. 45–49.

Treisman, D. (1996b) *How Yeltsin Won*. Unpublished manuscript, University of California, Los Angeles.

Treisman, D. (1996c) "Why Yeltsin won." *Foreign Affairs*, September/October, pp. 64–77.

Treisman, D. (1999–2000) "Russia 2000: After Yeltsin comes ... Yeltsin." *Foreign Policy*, Winter. www.foreignpolicy.com (accessed November 11, 2009).

Treisman, D. (2008) "What keeps the Kremlin up all night." *Moscow Times*, February 18, no. 3844, p. 10.

Trenin, D. (2006) *Vrag Naroda* (An Enemy of the State). Moscow: Algoritm.

Trenin, D. (2017) "Russia's Evolving Grand Eurasia Strategy: Will It Work?" *Carnegie Moscow Center*. July 20. http://carnegie.ru/2017/07/20/russia-s-evolving-grand-eurasia-strategy-will-itwork-pub-71588 (accessed July 9, 2018).

Treschenkov E. (2013) "Ot Vostochnyh Sosedej k Vostochnym Partneram. Respublika Belarus', Respublika Moldova i Ukraina v Fokuse Politiki Sosedstva Evropejskogo Soyuza (2002–2012)" [From Eastern Neighbours to the Eastern Partners. The Republic of Belarus, the Republic of Moldova and Ukraine in Focus of the European Union Neighbourhood Policy (2002–2012). Saint Petersburg.

Trofimova, E. V. (2008) "Zaochnoe sudebnoe razburatel'stvo po ugolovnym delam. Ponjatie I perspektivy primenenija" (Court criminal proceedings in absentia. Meaning and possibilities of use). *Vestnik VGU. Seriya Pravo*, 2, pp. 313–22.

Tsygankov, Andrei (2016). *Russia's Foreign Policy: Change and Continuity in National Identity*. Lanham, MD: Rowman and Littlefield.

Tucker, R. C. (1961) "Toward a comparative politics of movement regimes." *American Political Science Review*, 55(2), pp. 281–93.

Tucker, R. C. (1990) *Stalin in Power: The Revolution from Above, 1928–1941*. New York: W. W. Norton.

Umland, A. (2009) "Will it be the second Crimean War?" *Zerkalo nedeli/Dzerkalotyzhnia*, 15(743), pp. 25–9, April.

Umland, A. (2011) "Could Russia's Ultranationalists Subvert Pro-Democracy Protests?", *World Affairs*, December. http://www.worldaffairsjournal.org/article/could-russia%E2%80%99s-ultranationalists-subvert-pro-democracy-protests

UN (2019). Office of the High Commissioner, Report on the human rights situation in Ukraine. https://www.ohchr.org/Documents/Countries/UA/ReportUkraineFev-May2018_EN.pdf (accessed July 8, 2019).

United Russia (2007) Electoral Program adopted by the 8th Congress, October 1, Moscow. http://edinros.er.ru/er/rubr.shtml?110099 (accessed November 11, 2009).

United Russia (2012) Electoral Program for the Presidential Elections. http://er.ru/party/presidential_election/ (accessed April 5, 2020).

US Census Bureau (2019) Trade in goods with Russia. https://www.census.gov/foreign-trade/balance/c4621.html#2018 (accessed November 1, 2019).

Valenty, L. and Shiraev, E. (2001) "The 1996 Russian presidential candidates: A content analysis of motivational configuration and conceptual/integrative complexity," in O. Feldman and L. Valenty (eds), *Profiling Political Leaders: Cross-Cultural Studies of Personality and Behavior*. Santa Barbara: Greenwood.

Van Herpen, M. (2018) "Will populism come to Russia?" *The National Interest*, September 20. https://nationalinterest.org/feature/will-populism-come-russia-31602 (accessed April 5, 2020).

Vaslilchuk, T., Mineeva, Y., and Torop, A. (2019) *"Transit poshel"* (Transit has started). *Novaya Gazeta*. https://www.novayagazeta.ru/articles/2019/07/30/81430-karusel-arestov (accessed April 5, 2020).

Voroshilov, D. (2009) *Mass Media Are Not Free Yet*. Freedom House. http://www.rian.ru/society/20090501/169782000.html May 1 (accessed November 11, 2009).

Walker, S. (2019) "Russian opposition leader Alexei Navalny condemns mass raids." *The Guardian*. October 15. https://www.theguardian.com/world/2019/oct/15/mass-raids-target-russian-opposition-leader-alexei-navalny (accessed April 5, 2020).

WCIOM (2008a) Poll of November 17. http://wciom.ru

WCIOM (2008b) Poll of January 21. http://wciom.ru

WCIOM (2009a) Survey of Attitudes about corruption cf *Vremya Novostey,* 2009–04–28 12:38. www.newsru.com (accessed November 11, 2009).

WCIOM (2009b) Poll of February 18. http://wciom.ru

WCIOM (2009c) Poll of May 20. http://wciom.ru

WCIOM (2009d) Poll of May 6. http://wciom.ru

WCIOM (2009e) Poll of April 15. http://wciom.ru

WCIOM (2009f) Poll of July 19. http://wciom.ru

WCIOM (2009g) Poll of April 23. http://wciom.ru

WCIOM (2009h) Poll of February 20. http://wciom.ru

WCIOM (2011) Poll September 24–5 http://wciom.ru

WCIOM (2012a) Poll of April 18. http://wciom.ru

WCIOM (2012b) Poll of March 24–5. http://wciom.ru

WCIOM (2012c) Poll of February 25–6. http://wciom.ru

WCIOM (2012d) Poll of February 4. http://wciom.ru

WCIOM (2012e) Poll January 25. http://wciom.ru

WCIOM (2020) Poll of February 23. https://wciom.com/index.php?id=61&uid=1750

WCIOM-RBK (2008) Poll of March 3. http://wciom.ru/novosti/v-centre-vnimanija/publikacija/single/9755.html

Welu, C. and Muchnik, E. (2009) "Corruption: Russia's economic stumbling block." *Business Week*, August 27. http://www.businessweek.com (accessed November 11, 2009).

Westad, O. A. (2018). "Has a New Cold War Really Begun?" Foreign Affairs, March 27.

White, S. (2007) "Russia's client party system," pp. 21–52, in P. Webb and S. White (eds), *Party Politics in New Democracies*. Oxford: Oxford University Press.

White, S. (2008) *Politics and the Ruling Group in Putin's Russia*. New York: Palgrave Macmillan.

White, S., Rose, R. and McAllister, I. (1996) *How Russia Votes*. Chatham: Chatham House.

WHO (2019) "World Health Organizations' Suicide Data." https://www.who.int/mental_health/prevention/suicide/suicideprevent/en/ (accessed April 5, 2020).

Wilson, A. (2014). *Ukraine Crisis: What It Means for the West*. New Haven, CT: Yale University Press.

Withnall, Adam (2018). "China's Xi declares Putin his 'best, most intimate friend' as Russia looks to the East for allies." Independent, 8 June. https://ind.pn/2MOKVyr (accessed August 17, 2018).

Wohlstetter, A. (1979) *Swords from Plowshares: The Military Potential of Civilian Nuclear Energy*. Chicago: University of Chicago Press.

World Factbook (2019) "Library. The Central Intelligence agency." https://www.cia.gov/library/publications/the-world-factbook/rankorder/2102rank.html (accessed October 22, 2019).

Wyman, M. (1997) *Public Opinion in Postcommunist Russia*. London: Macmillan.

Yabloko (2016) Yabloko Electoral Program. https://www.yabloko.ru/program (accessed April 5, 2020).

Yaffa, J. (2012) "Reading Putin. The mind and the state of Russia's president." *Foreign Affairs*, July/August, pp. 126–33.

Yaffa, Joshua (2016). "Russia's View of the Election Hacks: Denials, Amusement, Comeuppance." New Yorker, December 20. http://www.newyorker.com/news/news-desk/russias-view-of-theelection-hacks-denials-amusement-comeuppance (accessed March 31, 2018).

Yakobson, L. (2009) "A Vice-Rector of the Moscow Higher School of Economics interview." *Polit.ru*. http://www.polit.ru/analytics/2005/10/03/med1.html (accessed November 11, 2009).

Yakovlev, Pyotr (2013). "Rossiya i Latinsaya Amerika na traektorii vzaimnogo sblizhenija"[Russia and Latin America on the trajectory of mutual convergence]. *Perspectives*, December 11. http://bit.ly/2rGSijT (accessed March 31, 2018).

Yakunin, V. (2018) *The Treacherous Path: An Insider's Account of Modern Russia*. London: Biteback.

Yanin, V. L. and Aleshkovsky, M. H. (1971) "Proishozhdenie Novgoroda" (The Origin of Novgorod). *USSR History*, 2, pp. 32–61. http://www.russiancity.ru/books/b39.htm (accessed November 11, 2009).

Yeltsin, B. (1994) *Zapiski Presidenta*. Moscow: Ogonjok.

Yeltsin, B. (2000) *Midnight Diaries*. New York: Public Affairs.

Ying, Fu (2016). "How China Sees Russia." *Foreign Affairs*, January/February. https://www.foreignaffairs.com/articles/china/2015–12-14/how-china-sees-russia (accessed March 31, 2020).

Zaslayskaya, T. I. (2004) *Sovremennoe Rossijskoe Obwestvo: Social'nyj Mekhanism Formirovanija*. Moscow.

Zinn, H. (2002) *The Power of Nonviolence: Writings by Advocates of Peace*. Boston: Beacon Press.

Zorkaya, N. (2004) "Dumskie Vybory 1993–2003" (Duma elections in 1993–2003). *Vestnik Obshestvennogo Mnenya*, 4(72), pp. 19–30.

Zubok, V. (2007) *A Failed Empire: The Soviet Union in the Cold War from Stalin to Gorbachev*. Durham: University of North Carolina Press.

Zubok, V. (2009) *Zhivago's Children: The Last Russian Intelligentsia*. Cambridge, MA: Harvard University Press.

Zubok, Vladislav, and Pleshakov, Constantinne. (1996). *Inside the Kremlin's Cold War*. Cambridge, MA: Harvard University Press.

Zygar, M. (2017) *All the Kremlin's Men: Inside the Court of Vladimir Putin*. New York: Public Affairs.

Zyuganov, G. (2009) "Speech at a meeting with young deputies of all levels representing four Parliament factions in the State Duma." *Interfax*, June 17.

LEGISLATION AND OFFICIAL DOCUMENTS

Concept (2000) The Foreign Policy Concept of the Russian Federation. Approved by Vladimir V. Putin, President of the Russian Federation, on June 28, 2000. http://www.fas.org/nuke/guide/russia/doctrine/econcept.htm

Concept (2008) The Foreign Policy Concept of the Russian Federation. Approved by Dmitry A. Medvedev, President of the Russian Federation, on July 12, 2008.

Concept (2010) The Military Doctrine of the Russian Federation. Approved February 10, 2010.

Constitution of the USSR (1936) http://www.hist.msu.ru/ER/Etext/cnst1936.htm

Constitutional Court of the Russian Federation (2009a) Ruling of February 27, 2009. http://www.ksrf.ru

Constitutional Court of the Russian Federation (2009b) Ruling of April 20, 2009. http://www.ksrf.ru

Duma (2007) Rulings on October 9 2007; N 5134-4GD.

Federal Law (1991) *On Medical Insurance of the Russian Federation's Citizens*. N 1499-1, June 28.

Federal Law (1992) *The Prosecution Service of the Russian Federation*. N 2202-1, January 17.

Federal Law (1993a) *Foundations of the Legislation of the Russian Federation on Health Care of Citizens*. N 5487-1, July 22.

Federal Law (1993b) *On State Secrets*. N 5485-1, July 21.

Federal Law (1994) *The Presidium of the Supreme Court*. N 50-FZ, October 28.

Federal Law (1995a) *Continental Shelf of the Russian Federation*. N 187-FZ, November 30.

Federal Law (1995b) *On Federal Security Service of the Russian Federation*. N 40-FZ, April 3.

Federal Law (1995c) *Arbitration Courts of the Russian Federation*. N 1-FKZ, April 28.

Federal Law (1996a) *On External Intelligence*. N 5-FZ, January 10.

Federal Law (1996b) *On Undergraduate and Graduate Professional Education*. N 125-FZ, August 22.

Federal Law (1998a) *On Inner Sea Waters, Territorial Sea, and the Adjacent Zone of the Russian Federation*. N 155-FZ, July 31.

Federal Law (1998b) *On Exclusive Economic Zone of the Russian Federation*. N 191-FZ, December 17.

Federal Law (2003) *On Elections of the President of the Russian Federation*. N 19-FZ, January 10.

Federal Law (2004a) *On Jurors of Federal Courts of General Jurisdiction on the Russian Federation*. N 113-FZ, August 20.

Federal Law (2004b) *On Changes in the Federal Law "On Political Parties."* N 168-FZ O, December 20.

Federal Law (2007) *Additional Measures of Federal Support of Families with Children*. N 256 FZ, January 1.

Federal Law (2018) *On Changes in Several Federal Acts of the Russian Federation Regrading Rewarding and Distribution of Pensions* N 350-FZ, October 3.

Land Codex (2001) *The Land Codex of the Russian Federation*. N 136-FZ, October 25.

Ministry of the Interior of the Russian Federation (2009) Structure of the Ministry of the Interior. http://www.mvd.ru/struct/3297/3353/

Organizational Procedures of the Duma (1998) Adopted on January 22, 1998. N 2134-11 GD.

Presidential Decree (1991) #239. November 25. Source: *Vedomosti Syezda Narodnyh Deputatov RSFSR I Verhovnogo Soveta RSFSR*, 1991, N 48, p 1677. http://lawrussia.ru/texts/legal_689/doc689a672x233.htm

Presidential Decree (1993) "On a gradual constitutional reform in the Russian Federation," No. 1400, October 21.

Presidential Decree (2004a) "Questions of the Ministry of Justice of the Russian Federation," N 1313, October 13.

Presidential Decree (2004b) "Regulations about Ministry of Defense of the Russian Federation," N1082, August 16.

Presidential Decree (2006) "About means of counteraction against terrorism," N116, February 16.

Presidential Decree (2007a) "On changes in the Regulations about Military Service," No. 303, March 8.

Presidential Decree (2007b) "About changes in the bylaws of the Foreign Ministry," N 865, January 26.

Strategy for National Security of the Russian Federation until 2020 (2009, May 12). http://www.scrf.gov.ru/documents/99.html

WEBSITES

Federal Security Service of the Russian Federation (FSS): http://www.fsb.ru

Federal Service of State Statistics (Rosstat): http://www.gks.ru

Legal Acts of the Russian Federation: http://www.interlaw.ru

Ministry of the Interior of the Russian Federation: http://www.mvd.ru

Russian Center for Public Opinion: http://wciom.ru/

Russian Federal Statistical Service (Rosstat): www.gks.ru

Index